Understanding Conversion

Understanding Conversion

Karl F. Morrison

University Press of Virginia
Charlottesville and London

The Page-Barbour Lectures for 1990
The University Press of Virginia
Copyright © 1992 by the Rector and Visitors
of the University of Virginia
First published 1992

Library of Congress Cataloging-in-Publication Data
Morrison, Karl Frederick.
    Understanding conversion / Karl F. Morrison.
       p.   cm.
    "The Page-Barbour lectures for 1990"—T.p. verso.
    Companion vol. to: Conversion and text.
    ISBN 0-8139-1360-8
    1. Conversion.   I. Morrison, Karl Frederick. Conversion and text.   II. Title.
BR110.M67   1991
248.2'4–dc20   91-26971
                                                                                   CIP

Printed in the United States of America

To the Memory of
John Hunter Morrison
and
Elizabeth Amalie Morrison

We heard it, the great throbbing of Earth's heart,
The new song inconceivable, unheard,
Of consummate and perfect sound!
Through it, some thunder-striken angel groans
. . . . .
Some unfulfilled and secret longings weep;
And a fire crackles that will ruin worlds!
Something that passes by, an endless riddle.

Kostes Palamas, "The Palm Tree," in *Life Immovable*, pt. 1, trans. Aristides E. Phoutrides (Cambridge, Mass.: Harvard Univ. Press, 1919), p. 235.

Contents

Preface ix

Acknowledgments: How This Book Came to Be Written xxiii

CHAPTER 1. Posing the Question: Perspectives from a Historian's Desk 1

CHAPTER 2. Posing the Question: Perspectives from a Lector's Ambo 28

CHAPTER 3. Love and Penitence 66

CHAPTER 4. The Ordeal of Conscience: Purity and Doubt 92

CHAPTER 5. A True Myth 122

CHAPTER 6. A Noble Humility 154

Summary 185

Abbreviations 196

Notes 197

Index 235

Figure 1 This sketch of a lost twelfth-century illumination depicts the vocation (but not the conversion) of the persecutor, Saul, on the road to Damascus. (Plate from A. Straub and G. Keller, *Herrade de Landsberg: Hortus Deliciarum*, second supplement [Strasbourg: Schlesier & Scherkhardt, 1901], courtesy of Princeton University Library)

Preface

A picture may be worth ten thousand words, but not always, particularly when it comes from a distant age. Figure 1 is an example of a picture that is by no means self-explanatory. It shows the dramatic moment when Saul, the persecutor of the early Church, while riding toward Damascus, was hurled to the ground and blinded by a vision of Christ. Thus began the sequence of events by which Saul the persecutor was transformed into Paul the Apostle. The scene belonged to an unbound album of texts and illuminations made in Alsace during the late twelfth century and destroyed during the War of 1870 when the city of Strasbourg came under bombardment.[1]

An enterprise of great opulence, learning, and discrimination, the album was commissioned by the Abbess Herrad for the moral instruction of nuns in her convent of Hohenburg. Like the other components of this work, the *Hortus Deliciarum*, the picture of Paul's blinding vision is known from detailed notes, sketches, and tracings made well before the siege of 1870.

Herrad's picture conforms with a stylized tradition, heavily influenced by Byzantine models. From other representations of this scene, we assume that the sketches do not record the whole original. The colors have certainly been lost; convention would also have prescribed that Saul's horse and the city of Damascus, too, be shown. The sketches do indicate, however, that the artist adapted convention by adding the sword that Jesus menacingly holds over the terrified Saul and his two characters, the wolf that he had been, and the lamb into which he was being changed.

Even without interpreting the picture, I have had to say something about its history as a material object, the artistic tradition that gave its artist a vernacular of style and symbol, and the love, in the world where it was made, of understanding indirectly and intricately, through allegory.

There is no need to pursue a thorough analysis of the picture. However, to underscore the point that the picture is like a suitcase, of which only the outside is visible, leaving the message inside to be disclosed, unpacked, and deciphered, I should mention a few obvious choices made by the artist. The inscriptions associated with the picture establish that the artist chose to illustrate the account of Paul's encounter on the way to Damascus that is given in the ninth chapter of the Book of Acts, rather than either of the others, in chapters 22 and 26. Thus, he depicted the version according to which Saul's companions heard a voice but saw no one (Acts 9:7), rather than the one which held that they saw a light but heard no voice (Acts 22:9) or the other which had nothing at all to say about what his companions perceived (Acts 26).

With the sword, the artist gave another clue to a hidden narrative. The sword early became a symbolic attribute of the Paul as preacher, a reference to what was thought to be his letter to the Ephesians (6:17, "the sword of the spirit, which is the word of God"). But in the ambiguous way of symbols, the sword also alludes to persecution, in a striking reversal of roles. From the midst of the blinding light, Saul heard the voice of Christ saying, "Saul, Saul, why persecutest thou me?" (Acts 9:4). Until this moment Saul had been a predator, a wolf. Now, abruptly, the tide turns. With a violence greater than his own, Saul is ambushed and helplessly maimed by his prey. Afterwards, the "servant" and Apostle of his former quarry, he was "sent as a sheep in the midst of wolves" (Matt. 10:16), to be martyred at last by the sword.

Finally, the narrative that the artist wanted to evoke in the viewers' minds is indicated by the insertion of the name "Saul," rather than "Paul." In this regard, another element—the six rays from Christ's mandorla—also comes to bear. The use of "Saul," rather than "Paul," is appropriate because the transformation of the wolf into the lamb is not complete. Blinded, Saul does not yet know what has happened to him. Ananias has yet to find him, unfold the mystery of Christ, and baptize him. Renamed, Paul has yet to go into his long exile in Arabia before assuming his apostolate to the Gentiles, yet to be scourged, put on trial, hated, persecuted, and, in the end, saved (cf. 2 Cor. 11:23–33). He has yet to be configured to the likeness of Christ, the sacrificial Lamb of God. The souls of the predestinate groaned within themselves until the adoption should be accomplished in the redemption of their bodies. Adoption was certainly not completed on the road to Damascus.

The six rays and the name "Saul" spring from the artist's awareness that the conversion of Saul has begun but not yet been put to the test, perfected, and consummated. With expert knowledge and scrupulous honesty, editors can impose modern expectations on premodern texts. Editors of the *Hortus Deliciarum* have consistently referred to this illumination as depicting the "conversion of St. Paul." What is known of the manuscript itself did not provide their reading. And, in fact, the scriptural understanding that directed the artist quite powerfully militated against the idea that the scene represented a "conversion," instead of a vocation. Unbaptized, Paul had not entered into the sacramental communion of Christ's body. Therefore, it was incorrect to represent him receiving the sevenfold gifts of the Holy Spirit. But it was appropriate to depict him receiving the "spirit of adoption," which Paul himself identified as consisting of six divine actions that changed those who were called according to God's purpose and that included conforming them to the image of his Son (Rom. 8:15, 28–30).[2]

Indeed, at one level, the illumination resolves into a visual portrayal of Paul's exultant declaration ending the eighth chapter of his letter to the Romans: "Who shall separate us from the love of Christ? Shall tribulation, or distress, or persecution, or famine, or nakedness, or peril, or sword? As it is written, For thy sake we are killed all the day long: we are accounted as sheep for the slaughter." But those who had received the Spirit and groaned within themselves waiting for adoption to be accomplished would be more than conquerors; none "shall be able to separate us from the love of God, which is in Christ Jesus our Lord" (Rom 8:35–39).

This picture represents an initial moment in a long sequence of events that could be called the "conversion" of Paul. It is also a theatrical portrayal silently incorporating a narrative built not only from one section of the Book of Acts but also from essential passages in two letters attributed to Paul.

This is not the place for a full interpretation of Herrad's picture. I mean only to draw an analogy between pictures and words. It takes much care to recover the understanding packed into a picture from a distant age, something that may deceptively appear to be plain for all to see. Perhaps it takes at least as much to unpack understanding from the deep and twisting crevices in a word—say, of *conversion*. What is, after all, called "conversion"? Let us hold firmly to the basic distinction between things and their names, not forgetting the habits of thought that link things outside our minds with names inside them, habits that seem quite natural and undeserving of comment until an alien hand lifts this self-disguising mask of social or ethnic conformity.

In fact, discussing Herrad's picture has raised some principles that run straight through the following chapters.

This book is not an account of conversion experiences but of how people made sense of conversion. Materials are primarily drawn from western Europe, in the period of the so-called Twelfth-Century Renaissance, the very age when Herrad commissioned her splendid album. It is striking how little attention was then given to conversion as a single event, a dramatic peripety, shattering and reforming at the same time. Conversion was normally understood as a continuous process, although a highly predicamental one, with a beginning, development, and end. Thus, the idea that the conversion of Paul was a gradual process of adoption, or transformation, ending with the redemption of the body, which the picture exemplifies, was characteristic. In fact, all of life, rightly lived, was conversion. Conversion was thought to change the entire direction of human existence itself from a movement toward the grave into a transit toward endless life. Conversion was part of a strategy of survival; but, as Herrad's illumination indicates, life rightly lived was not open to all. For, by the hidden mysteries of predestination and election, only divine intervention could graft that strategy into a human heart, sometimes by means of disastrous violence.

The distinction between names and things is basic to my proposition that one can legitimately talk about the idea of conversion but not about the experience. In a companion work, *Conversion and Text: The Cases of Augustine of Hippo, Herman-Judah, and Constantine Tsatsos*, I have set forth evidence for my views:

that the experience of conversion is quite different from what is called conversion in texts,

that scholars cannot penetrate to experience through texts,

that what we actually can study is a document, a written composition, and whatever kinds of understanding it may manifest,

that, in its literature, the classical tradition of the West displays not one kind of conversion but an ill-matched repertory of such patterns, each having a distinctive history, and

that the repertory of changes called conversion has kept the call for moral change dominant and relentless in Western culture, and thus one of the most decisive norms according to which the West has thought about and shaped itself.

The three case studies devoted to Augustine of Hippo (354–430), Herman-Judah (c. 1107–1181), and Constantine Tsatsos (1899–1987) are intended to illustrate general methods of understanding applied in this book. They are also meant to address the cognitive affinities and distances between understanding conversion in earlier centuries and understanding it today.

What I am trying to do in the present book is to enter into the minds of people in a distant age and, by a kind of archaeology, to reconstruct their hermeneutics of conversion. In the following chapters I chiefly consider ideas current in western Europe during the eleventh and twelfth centuries, a period that (for reasons to be explained in chapter 1) proved to be crucial in the history of the idea of conversion. These studies (originally prepared as lectures) were intended for a mixed audience. No serene and uniform familiarity with materials from eleventh- and twelfth-century religious history could be taken for granted. Therefore, as the argument moves stage by stage through ideas in the centuries of primary interest, I have indicated landmarks in other regions and epochs that I hoped would be familiar to one segment of the audience or another and that would provide a secure point from which nonmedievalists could enter into the argument. Occasionally, I used such coordinates to elucidate similarities or continuities. At other junctures, perhaps more frequently, I intended to clarify by contrast.

From the beginning, the distinction between the name "conversion" and what was called conversion is plain. In fact, as I noted in discussing Herrad's picture, there are three quite different terms: a phenomenon called "conversion," the name "conversion," and the thinking that made it possible to separate one out of the undifferentiated mass of human experiences by calling it "conversion." To telescope all this: we have something felt (the experience of conversion) and something made (the name "conversion"), and the process by which the feeling was reduced to the name. The subject of this book is that process, between esthetics and poetics.

Fundamentally, during the eleventh and twelfth centuries, conversion was an artist's idea, an understanding of how a work of art—in this case, the soul—was formed in the image of God, and how, after a period of deterioration (through sin), its maker restored it. "Conversion," the name applied to this change, was a metaphor taken into the language of religion from that of arts and crafts. Something of the original, and not the religious (or metaphorical), sense still survives when the word *conversion* is used to describe, for example, chemical or metallurgical change.

Toward the beginning of the tradition with which we have to deal, Athanasius (c. 295–373), the great fourth-century bishop of Alexandria, exposed the metaphorical sense in the word *conversion*. He wrote: "When a figure which has been painted on wood is spoilt by dirt, it is necessary for him whose portrait it is to come again so that the picture can be renewed in the same material. Because his portrait is on the panel, the material on which it is painted is not thrown away, but the portrait is redone on it." Even so, Athanasius continued, when the true likeness of human nature had been begrimed by "the madness of idolatry and impiety," Christ, the Image of God, came among us so that human beings could be redrawn, re-created, according to the original pattern that he set forth.[3] To say this much is to say that conversion was a study in active and passive relations, always in a single transforming movement. It is also to say that those relations demanded that images be compared with their originals, that the process of transformation was one of critical imitation, or mimesis. There was, Bernard of Clairvaux (1090–1153) wrote, a "form of conversion," an exemplar given by God;[4] but the archetype was reproduced in an innovative, not a mechanical, way.

Let me summarize the following chapters. If we want to enter into the minds of others and reconstruct their hermeneutic patterns, our first step has to be recognizing differences between their ways of thinking and ours. I point out in the first chapter that scholars now think about conversion in their own ways and that those ways are, on balance, quite different from ways of thinking about it in the eleventh and twelfth centuries. It is a confusion of categories to use the word *conversion* as though it were an instrument of critical analysis, equally appropriate to any culture or religion. The word has a profound, mystical sense in the West for which some great religions and languages of the world have no equivalent. Even in the history of the West, it has displayed different connotations at different moments. Thus, the word is more properly a subject, rather than a tool, of analysis. Current paradigms cannot be assumed to have been known to earlier generations. The difference is plainest in questions that were, and are, asked. Evidently, some kinds of questions are possible in some places and times but not in others. In the eleventh and twelfth centuries, writers did not generally distinguish between the experience of conversion and a text about it: for example, between Augustine of Hippo's conversion and the account that he wrote about it in the *Confessions*.

However, this distinction is very important in present-day discussions. Nowadays, the argument is set forth, as it is in this book, that the experience of conversion is lost and that all that exists for study is what texts call conversion. Therefore, as we try to understand portrayals of conversions in the twelfth century, we are really studying twelfth-century words and linguistic constructions. Perhaps, as I suggest, we are even trying to understand foreign ways of understanding that produced the texts.

At any rate, by contrast with writers in Bernard of Clairvaux's age, scholars today recognize the degree to which language shapes thought and the forms that written narratives receive, to which a thing can be confused with the name by which it is called. They are concerned to reconstruct the poetic process of making texts and, to be sure, of using metaphors (such as "conversion") for transfers of meaning that link dissimilar things through hidden similarities.

The eleventh and twelfth centuries were pivotal in Western intellectual history because terms of analysis and patterns of change were then developed and taught that became and long remained dominant. Yet, here another parting of the ways intrudes itself between medieval and modern approaches to conversion. Many modern scholars envision the possibility of establishing a general morphology of conversion, applicable to conversion as a universal human experience. This goal becomes highly problematic when those terms and models of change are seen to be creatures of time and place. As a metaphor taken from numerous arts and crafts, "conversion" was easily made into a portmanteau word. When it is unpacked, as a historical artifact, a variety of models of conversion, some quite incompatible, is found all cobbled together into an ensemble, or repertory, that enabled writers of twelfth-century Europe to explore, interpret, and explain transformations in their world and in themselves. It was a repertory that sanctioned discontent and required self-doubt, process rather than peripety. And it was as much an artifact of the age as a Gothic cathedral.

In the second chapter, I attempt to recover a twelfth-century perspective on ways of understanding conversion. Here, a great divide opens between eleventh- and twelfth-century ideas about conversion and modern studies in sociology, anthropology, and history. For Bernard of Clairvaux and his contemporaries quite easily distinguished two levels of conversion. The first, recognized also by modern scholars, was that of affiliation. A person embraced a creed, submitted to the institution that taught the creed, and passed through thick and thin, living out the consequences of his acceptance and submission.

Beyond, and behind, this narrative of an event and its sequel in social context, writers in the eleventh and twelfth centuries assumed another, quite distinct, narrative working itself out. Indeed, for them the second narrative authenticated the first. According to it, conversion was a process of redemption that was initiated, sustained, and completed, if at all, by God's action. With all its refinements, even the science of theology provided only a partial key to conversion in this metaphysical (or, more properly, supernatural) sense, a sense so wide that it stretched the concept of conversion beyond the point where it could be analytically meaningful, to the point, indeed, where the idea of continuous conversion intersected with that of God's continual creation of the world.

Supernatural understanding was by no means confined to reason. Indeed, conversion was a study in empathy. Understanding conversion came through feelings of oneness. Above all, writers held that to be so regarding empathetic participation in Christ; and this, in turn, came about through imitation of

Christ. Through that mimesis, a believer entered into empathetic communion with all others who were conformed to the image of Christ through the renewal of their hearts, and who had thereby become members of his body.

The practice of empathy has to be learned. On the whole, modern historians are disciplined to be suspicious of empathy in research as a form of bias. Moreover, they are liable to discount the priority given emotions over reason, and methods of training the emotions, as set forth in writings of earlier ages. In the eleventh and twelfth centuries, as in many others before and since, empathy was in the warp and weft of all discourse about conversion. It ran like a scarlet thread through every branch of metaphysics and theology.

Metaphysics and the supernatural are not fields much cherished by sociologists, anthropologists, or historians. But to discount this dimension of commitment in an earlier age would simply expand the ranges in which modern scholars are deaf to their informants. It would omit the supernatural risks and goals that, for the believers of that era, comprised the whole nature of conversion. The great divide between modern scholars and writers in the eleventh and twelfth centuries can approximate that between members of a choir of whom some sing the words of Mozart's *Coronation Mass* without believing them and others with all sincerity of heart, in awe.

Not discounting the fact of historical distance between myself and the authors of the texts under review, I contend that the empathetic power in what was called conversion lay in a radical sense of need. On that cornerstone rested an elaborate, poetic structure of ideas. Scripture provided essential elements. But Scripture was far from self-explanatory. The history of scriptural interpretation was also built into the poetic structure of ideas. Like a geological formation, it consisted of all the varied striations of its career in the world, each one, and all collectively, built up as societies alien to those in which the books of Scripture were written digested their messages into other, and sometimes uncongenial, idioms. The history of conversion was wrapped up in the meaning of the word. The argument of the second lecture, then, is that the poetic, or fictional, made sense of the "form of conversion," just as, so often myth gives meaning to the melee of historical events.

The second chapter describes the contours, the outer shell, of the subject. In the third chapter, the inner structure of empathy begins to come to light. There, I analyse the fundamental perception that pain was necessary to break down the old, to efface the deformed likeness, so that the new one could be formed in its place. Such healing, renewing pain could be voluntarily embraced, as it was by penitents and ascetics, or, because it was thought to be the due of brotherly love, it could be imposed by force on unbelievers or wrong-believers. Penance and persecution were twins, often likened to medical or surgical procedures that inflicted terrible pain in order to cure. It is not clear what social behavior many ancient religions demanded. However, like Judaism, Christianity enjoined social effects of belief on every level of existence. Thus, whether pain were imposed in penance or in brotherly love, awareness of how far short one fell of putting faith into practice stirred up predicaments of conscience.

And still, even though they followed the same template (or "forma"), each conversion was proportionate, according to the capacities of the individual and according to the "measure of faith" that, as the Apostle Paul said, "God hath dealt to every man" (Rom. 12:3). The proportionality of faith and its origin in God's inscrutable acts of grace compounded elements of uncertainty and the chance of self-deception.

Education of the mind and body to empathy were therefore essential parts of the life of conversion. Ascetic discipline, particularly in monasticism, provided comprehensive methods of ingraining habits of self-doubting criticism into the fabric of one's being and ritualizing them.

In the fourth chapter, I trace another armature supporting the outer shell called "conversion:" the artistic process of transition, breaking down the old and forming the new. According to the metaphorical form of conversion, destruction in order to rebuild or cutting and cautery in order to heal could create a field of tension for the conscience so acute that it disrupted social order as well as personal senses of identity. Disciplines, customs, and doctrines did not fetter God's hands.

The monastic virtues of aggression and vigilance were ritualized in collective discipline and personal devotion and infused into doctrines of how the conscience was to be trained in empathy. But where did they come from? There was a prior stage of ritualization. For the educational program within the walls of the monastery ritualized myths and institutions that were cherished by society as a whole. Empathy was not egalitarian. It had limits, beyond which lived Jews, heretics, and pagans. Among Christians, it had degrees, which conversion enacted through ritual play in the Church. But that play, in turn, ritualized play among the dominant elites of princes and warriors. The form, or exemplar, of conversion was not an artist's pattern book so much as it was a poetic scenario in search of actors, in search, moreover, of countless improvisations. That scenario, with the limits and degrees of empathy, was provided in the context of myth.

In the fifth chapter, I consider the dynamic ritualization of play that fulfilled the mythic strategy of survival. Myths in the warriors' ethos established the context in which what was called conversion achieved its meaning. Two distinguishing features of play in those myths were, first, the importance that it gave to beauty as a principle of thought and, second, its overwhelming identification of virtue with manliness, particularly with the warrior's valor. But warriors' myths idealized an exquisite ambivalence; for, on the one hand, they inculcated the virtues of aggression and vigilance, and, on the other, they taught the dependence of every warrior on allies, tested under fire, to defend him against his own weakness. The beauty valued in such an ethos did not prize effeminacy. Such were the values absorbed, hallowed, and ritualized into ideas about conversion.

The prominence of beauty as a cognitive norm in twelfth-century European texts is striking. That it occurs in an ascetic culture poses a distinct contradiction, but one that points toward habits of spirit where apparent opposites of artistic riches and mortification of the flesh were reconciled. That space contained feelings and unspoken habits that acted before words could be formed in the mind, much less written on parchment. They determined the circle for whom ideas were convincing and names, appropriate; they were the calling in the call that not all had ears to hear.

The hermeneutic circle within which discourse about conversion moved reflected the ideals of identifiable social circles. The importance of a male esthetic in the writings with which I am concerned leads to a defining aspect of Western culture when they were set down: that is, to the chivalric ethic of nobility. The hierarchic structure of society provided the language used to speak of the proportionality of faith and, thus, of the limits and degrees of empathy. Language and conceptions inherited from another elaborately hierarchic society, that of the later Roman Empire, were melded with those of chivalry. Not all could believe, or believe in the same degree of purity, or even believe according to the same proportional scale. For as in human society, so in heaven and among the called there were greater and lesser lights.

The strategy of survival was described in terminology of chivalric play, with its ceremonial gradations of honor and rank. To imitate Christ meant to imitate both the Crucified and the Lord of Courtesy. Denizens of court society easily imagined his celestial court arranged by rank and precedence and attempted to duplicate its delights in their rituals. But in what proportion were habits of feeling known as nobility and, indeed, conversion open to those other than the representatives of the chivalric ethos who controlled discourse and enacted the ritualized play of conversion? In what proportion was it open to women? The last chapter is devoted to the identity then drawn between sanctification of the heart and ennoblement, with its connotations of empathy calibrated in due proportion, and to the crucial importance that visual imagination had in the hermeneutic project of understanding conversion.

Art added an essential component to the educational program of conversion. Like the other components, it taught ambivalence. The penitential discipline of monasticism taught that salvation was already and not yet within sight; therefore, relentless criticism was needed to avoid failed conversions through apostasy or, more subtly, through hypocritical misreading of one's own conversion. Social myth taught a warrior's ethos idealizing heroic strength and cunning but also warning that the strength and vigilance even of the most valiant eventually failed and that all were dependent on allies, tested and proven in battle. Finally, art proclaimed the opulence and splendor of chivalric society, but by its moral lessons it also taught the duty of the spiritually enlightened to withstand, if necessary, prevailing social orders and their values; it taught the subversive power of conversion.

One argument that gradually unfolds in these chapters as we pass inward from the outer contours to the armatures supporting the idea of a conversion, is that the idea—both in its social and in its supernatural dimensions—belonged to a particular class in society. It was a class comprised of clergy (chiefly monks), and therefore literate males. Its members—and consequently the scales of empathy ritualized in their daily lives—derived from the knightly and aristocratic orders.

I rely in great part on writings by members of the Benedictine, Cistercian, and Augustinian orders. It is appropriate to question whether ideas nurtured by an ascetic, male, literate, and aristocratic class were shared by other orders in society—by peasants and artisans, for example. As I indicate, there is some reason to ask whether they were, or could be, shared by women, even by those who happened to be ascetic, literate, and aristocratic.

It may appear that I have stressed an austere, ascetic current in Western thought, without giving due attention to others. My answer is this. In the period under review, persons committed to the monastic life were, as we might say, specialists in the ideology and techniques of conversion: that is, in its hermeneutics. They wrote by far the majority of texts bearing on the subject and the most detailed considerations of it. However fortuitous the circumstances of authorship and survival, however varied the ideas that may be implied or fragmentarily stated elsewhere, the bulk of evidence actually surviving in such a condition as to allow relatively systematic study puts the educational program of ascetic theology at the center of discussion. Furthermore, if one can demonstrate that, given its permutations, the model of conversion as a penitential way of life expounded by monastic writers as the "apostolic life" did not stand alone even in the West, the case against any universal morphology of conversion set forth here will be strengthened. My own readings of Carolingian texts, from the eighth and ninth centuries, indicates a far more diffuse, or at least manifold, understanding of conversion within a culture that was as powerfully governed by monastic ideals as the one from which came the texts considered in this book.

"What about Luther?" a friend once asked. He had in mind the lightning bolt that propelled Martin Luther (1483–1546) from his studies of scholastic philosophy and law at the University of Erfurt into the Augustinian monastery there (1505). Certainly, the question could also apply to the enlightenment that came to him while, still a monk, he reflected on Romans 1:16–17, with its decisive words, "The just shall live by faith" (1512–13).

The suggestion of an answer to my friend's question lies in the rarity and evasiveness with which Luther preached on the most revered of all spiritual cataclysms: the cataclysm that Saul experienced on the road to Damascus. Like other celebrated converts (including Augustine of Hippo), he abstained from drawing analogies between his own spiritual transformations and Paul's. What is singular is that, when, late in life (1546), he preached on this event, he studiously avoided the word *conversion,* even though he delivered his sermon on the Feast of the Conversion of St. Paul.[5] On that occasion he did not call anything "conversion."

Like the artist who illuminated the same scene in Herrad of Hohenburg's *Hortus Deliciarum,* Luther turned to the consequences of vocation and adoption, rather than to conversion. He stressed that Christ called Paul to the apostolate, ordained him as preacher, and corrected and instructed him in interpreting Scripture. He emphasized that Christ performed these acts directly and that the call, ordination, and teaching came by grace alone and were heard through faith. They did not occur through any works or merits of Saul, a murderer and blasphemer. As a persecutor Saul, Luther said, had crowned all his other sins by withholding mercy. That he received divine mercy as a pardoned sinner raised him up as an example for the world's comfort.

Luther dwelt on external aspects of Paul's mission—call, ordination, and mission—rather than on inward change of heart. But, characteristically, he also portrayed the Apostle isolated and dependent. His companions on the journey to Damascus saw and heard nothing. Paul himself heard the divine words but saw no one. Even those silent words he apprehended "with the spiritual eyes of his heart," without comprehending them. Obediently he stood up and was led into Damascus, where, in tumult and anxiety of mind, he waited until Ananias came, laid hands upon and baptized him, and disclosed what he was to do.

To ask "What about Luther?" is therefore to ask why Luther, who placed supreme emphasis on the inwardness of grace and faith, chose to speak not of a change of heart but of call, ordination, and instruction, concealed for the moment from the world which it was to transform and, indeed, even from Saul himself. The trail leads back, beyond Luther's writings, to his own complex experience of monasticism and, thus, to the ascetic paradigm of gradual conversion that I have just outlined. His long years as an Augustinian, including his decision to join the order, the enlightenment in 1512–13, and his monastic career in the eight years that followed until the irrevocable break with the papacy after the Diet of Worms (1521), are all silently wrapped up in the mockery that he heaped upon monks as fatuous interpreters of Scripture, blasphemers, fools, apes, "great donkeys." By 1521, when he wrote *On the Vows of Monks*, he was prepared to condemn the life into which the lightning bolt of 1505 had hurled him. Monastic vows, he wrote, were an "immense calamity" for souls, part of a pact with demons. His father's question whether the call to monasticism were from God or Satan had taken root.

Luther could not reflect on the two decisive events of 1505 and 1512–13 without seeing that neither was a conclusive peripety. Indeed, the weight of ascetic spirituality prepared him to consider conversion as a continuing process, always in jeopardy, and to sweep aside as blasphemous doctrines that works, rather than Christ's all-sufficient blood, were conducive to salvation. The customs (*consuetudines*) ingrained as habits by monastic discipline were his special target. They were "traditions of men," he wrote in 1521 (quoting Paul in Colossians 2:8), not Christ's truth or the faith that marked out saints.

Thus, even while he denounced monasticism, he held firm to the monastic ideal of life as a continuing process of conversion. In the last lines of his sermon on the Feast of the Conversion of St. Paul, Luther prayed that, by the enlightenment of the Holy Ghost, the Father of all mercies would help him and his hearers to understand the preaching and to receive right faith in Christ, forgiveness of sins, and eternal life. This prayer, too, incorporates the ascetic paradigm of conversion as a way of life, not open to all and fraught with risks of shipwreck. It witnesses to Luther's pervasive doctrine, not only of utter dependence on grace, but also of the radically predicamental ambivalence of life for Christians in this world, both saved and condemned, both hopeful and despairing, both friends of God and enemies of God.

Through Luther, the ascetic paradigm of what was called conversion passed, with many changes, into Kierkegaard's (1813–1855) "gospel of suffering" and its imperative leap of faith, continually, existentially renewed.

Clues given in the language used to portray what was called conversion lead beyond language, to discourse; for discourse gives language its meaning and its frames of reference. Consequently, they point even further, to unspoken habits of the heart inculcated into those who control discourse in a particular place and time. Evidently, events that modern scholars can recognize as conversion have been and are experienced and thought about in cultures and epochs other than medieval Europe. However, one result of the following chapters is to suggest that, no matter how universal those experiences may appear, scholars may be captive to the mythic contexts and vocabularies to which they themselves have been educated. For ways of understanding what was called conversion in a given society were defined by the particular environment in which the experience and the understanding took place, by the mythic context that defined "templates" of credibility in that environment, and by the informal and formal institutions that enforced those definitions. Understanding conversion was a hermeneutic project in the twelfth century, as it is today. But discourse then was governed by quite a different hermeneutic circle from any now prevailing. Still, given the circularity of all hermeneutic projects, confusion of the name "conversion" with the event called conversion is an all-too-human trait.

Throughout, it may be apparent that this book is by way of an archaeological report. The metaphor-word *conversion* is the artifact from which I have tried to extract its hermeneutic past. In the process I have hoped to discover some means by which it was made, as what began in esthetics was reduced to poetics by using, in Dorothy Sayers's phrase, "lost tools of learning."[6] Even in this introduction the little word *call* has indicated as much. I have used it chiefly in a rhetorical or semantic way (what a thing is called; the process of calling it that). I have also applied it prescriptively (a "call for moral change"). But, steeped in Christian theology, Luther found it a sacred word of empathy. For him a call was not a word or a cognitive process but a peremptory summons from God. It need not be expressed in words or visions; but, unsaid in the said and invisible in the seen, it must be obeyed. And this mysterious call came not to all alike but to each according to a measure assigned by God. For documentation beyond what is supplied here, readers may refer to *Conversion and Text*, which, incidentally, contains an English translation of Herman-Judah's *Short Account of His Own Translation*, an important text frequently cited in the following pages.

Acknowledgments:
How This Book Came to Be Written

The honor of being invited to contribute to the series of Page-Barbour Lectures is a considerable one, and for it I am most deeply beholden to the selection committee and to the University of Virginia. My wife and I warmly thank Professor H. C. Erik Midelfort and the committee which he chaired for the invitation to go to Charlottesville and Professor William Miller, who presided over the committee in 1990, Ms. Janice M. Gibbs, and the others who made us at home there.

The committee entrusted the choice of theme and subject entirely to me. Complete discretion is not often given to individual scholars, even in a society and a profession that cherish academic freedom, and I acknowledge this confidence with gratitude. In fact, there was for me no alternative to the theme of understanding conversion. My studies in the art of understanding (hermeneutics) had already brought me to conversion as a central theme in Western culture.

From many sides, too, a vague but richly faceted public consciousness was taking shape that conversion had an essential role in forming personal and collective identities. International politics reawakened elites in purportedly areligious societies to the primal and irresistible force of religious commitments around the world, and thus to demarcations that set one religion against another and to the astonishing reversals of belief by which individuals and societies could cross those lines. Public awareness of the terrible power of conversion to change lives was interlaced with sometimes sharply conflicting emotions, as it was in regard to cults detached from religious groupings sanctioned by tradition. In quite different ways, debates in Israel over the question whether converts to Judaism were entitled to the same legal privileges as native Jews and the consecration of the Basilica of Our Lady of Peace in Yamoussoukro signaled fears of a subversive character in conversion. For some, witness to conversion as a social force was also sharpened by a sequence of commemorations, including the sixteen-hundredth anniversary of Augustine of Hippo's conversion (1986) and the millennial anniversary of the conversion of Russia (1988). By coincidence, my lectures were delivered in the centennial anniversary year of John Henry Newman's death.

And so, after the radiant dawn of the invitation came the long day's labor of writing the lectures. I chose a subject with which I felt able to cope. But, in the heat of day, illusions of familiarity vanished.

The angry dispute over the Carmelite convent at Auschwitz in 1989 convinced me that the subject touched a nerve deep in contemporary feeling, for one objection to the convent was that the nuns were praying for the conversion of the Jews—that, as a colleague noted, they were (in that of all places) seeking another kind of final solution.

But what were the subjects of the lectures to be? What categories could I use to expose the origins of this deep, abiding, and acute feeling? I asked learned and judicious friends: "If you were giving three lectures on conversion, what would your subjects be?" Some suggested a set of case studies—the conversion of A, B, and C. But this evaded the objectives of analysis. Most of the people I asked looked into the middle distance and said, "Yes, that sure is a hard one," and lost sight of the question. One colleague, Professor John Baldwin, gave me an invaluable lead. "Of course," he said, "you will want to talk about the mystery of conversion." One or two spoke of gender. That helped. It was striking that no one at all mentioned conscience, a matter to which I had given some thought. In the end, I found no neighbor who could tell me how to frame my barn. I decided to organize my materials according to common human needs for life, love, purity, and truth.

But something was still missing—the note of joy and greatness of soul. Finally that missing something came to mind. It was nobility, the latest piece to be added to the puzzle. Perhaps it was also the most comprehensive, since *nobility* is a portmanteau word. It encompasses life, love, purity, and truth within the contours of power and also, to be sure, of glory. As I investigated matters of poetics, I was encouraged to know that T. S. Eliot and W. H. Auden had been among earlier Page-Barbour lecturers.

My colleague at Rutgers, Professor Rudolph Bell, advised me to place western European ideas about conversion in a wider context. If conversion answered common human needs, he reasoned, serious attention was owed the theory that conversion was a universal human experience, following the same, or similar, paradigms throughout the world.

By the time the lectures were given, at least one thing was clear: that my materials and the hermeneutic project were yielding unexpected results. Extensive revisions followed. I decided that the lectures given at Charlottesville needed to be supplemented with studies prepared on and for other occasions. In particular, I had applied certain analytic canons which were not self-evident. The compositional form of the lectures (even when revised into chapters) left no room for explaining them. The best course seemed to append three case studies of conversion in which I had developed the canons in question and indicated results that could be gained by applying them to specific texts, rather than—as in the lectures—to general bodies of material. In the event, these essays are to appear as a companion volume entitled *Conversion and Text: The Cases of Augustine of Hippo, Herman-Judah, and Constantine Tsatsos*.

Several colleagues took an intermediate draft of the lectures in hand and subjected it to thorough scrutiny. I was fortunate in their benevolence, fortunate, too, in the thoroughness which drew them from other, quite pressing matters and which enabled me to consider that draft from quite discrepant perspectives. Professors Michael Adas, Jo Ann McNamara, and John Van Engen assisted me in the understanding of understanding that was under way. Professor John Freed asked, "What about Luther?" The queries raised by these colleagues helped me to state my conclusions more fully, even at points of disagreement.

Professor Thomas F. X. Noble gave invaluable help and encouragement from the first glimmerings of the lectures until the last days of revision. In reviewing the manuscript, he observed that the words used in various segments (for example, those on history, theology, and art) differed. Today, each academic specialism tends to have its own private vernacular. But the observation raised the prospect that, in the distant era with which these studies chiefly deal, there were also different vernaculars for various areas of discourse. No historian could resist the argument that each vernacular has its own history. By this route, I was brought to conclude that what was called conversion in the West was actually a repertory of ways in which people experienced and explained change and that since the metaphor-word *conversion* and this repertory were both historical artifacts, the case for a universal paradigm of understanding conversion was defective, whatever, if anything, might be said about the experience of conversion. Thus, Professor Noble's sound philological observation was decisive, but in a way and to a degree that I imagine he did not expect.

xxvi *Acknowledgments*

Without inculpating the sponsors of these lectures or my critically benevolent friends, I thank them all for the favor of being drawn more closely to a worthy subject and of learning to speak of it—to my surprise—afresh.

The chapter on conscience was written during a year when my research was supported by a fellowship from the John Simon Guggenheim Memorial Foundation. I am grateful for this subvention and for assistance received in connection with my appointments as Ahmanson-Murphy Distinguished Professor of Medieval and Renaissance History at the University of Kansas and Lessing Professor of History and Poetics (State of New Jersey Professor) at Rutgers.

It remains to thank the libraries at which I have had the happiness to gather materials for these lectures, now expanded and revised into chapters: Alexander Library at Rutgers University, Sage Library at the New Brunswick Seminary, and the libraries at the Garrett-Evangelical Theological Seminary, Princeton University, the Princeton Theological Seminary, and the University of Notre Dame.

As I concluded revisions of this study, Pope John Paul II issued the eighth encyclical of his pontificate, *Redemptoris Missio*, admonishing Christians to acknowledge and with all ardor to perform their duty to preach the gospel. He urged them to seek converts throughout the world, even in countries where Christian preaching and worship were forbidden. The pope lamented that through inadvertence and privation, great obstacles had arisen to evangelism, even in nominally Christian countries. They signified, he wrote, a profound crisis of faith. Among the chief of them, the pope declared, stood tolerance for other religious traditions that led to religious relativism or indifference. Wrongly persuaded that all religions sprang from the same roots, he continued, many Christians regarded conversion as an irrelevant or incomprehensible venture. The following chapters analyze one of the many historical striations built into *Redemptoris Missio*, with its rejection of a general morphology of religion and its grounding of moral duty in revelation institutionalized as dogma.

Feast of the Conversion of St. Paul, 1991.

CHAPTER 1

Posing the Question:
Perspectives from a Historian's Desk

The language of conversion can be abrupt. In his zeal for spreading Christianity, Olav Tryggvessön (969–1000), king of Norway, sought to marry the queen of Sweden. Marriage negotiations progressed well until the queen refused to abandon the religion that she held, as her kinsmen before her had done. Olav, she said, could, without hindrance or reproach, worship whatever god pleased him. "King Olav was very wroth and answered hastily, 'Why should I wed you, you heathen bitch?' and he struck her in the face with the glove he was holding in his hand." This was no way to win the heart of Queen Sigrid the Strong-minded. Her response was instant: "This may be your death," she said. Turned into Olav's staunchest enemy, she married the king of Denmark, whom she incited to the battle in which Olav died (1000 C.E.).[1]

Snorre Sturlason's (c. 1178–1241) account of the exchange between Olav and Sigrid provides many clues for anyone seeking to understand conversion. We have only the text. Did the event actually happen and, if so, as Snorre described it more than two hundred years later? Before the deadly insult of the slap, what made Christianity compelling to Olav and the reverse to Sigrid? Did it matter that the description of conflict between a Christian man, revered in Snorre's day as a hero, and a pagan woman, who engineered his death, was written for a self-consciously Christian audience? What is said about the relative status of men and women, converted or unconverted, by the language of Olav's words and gesture (the slap) and by Sigrid the Strong-minded's quest for revenge, not by doing battle herself, but by maneuvers opened to her through marriage?

Questions such as these bear on our task. Snorre's story is brief and to the point. But there are difficulties in understanding the language of word and gesture with which he portrayed the event. It is clear that neither Olav nor Sigrid nor, for that matter, Snorre was drawn to speculate on the intellectual or spiritual aspects of conversion. The subject, then, leads elsewhere, to evidence that does witness to the enduring yet ever changing classical tradition. And still, it is good, at the outset, to remember the abruptness in Snorre's account, together with the absence of speculative theology, and, especially, to note that, in his words, we have encountered language, a text, rather than an event.

Such observations are relatively new in studies of conversion, though they draw on familiar—indeed, on ancient—methods of criticism. Certainly, they invite reexaminations of the subject. Much of my research in earlier years has been devoted to the proposition that powerful lines of intellectual and spiritual continuity bind us to the Europe of Mont-St.-Michel and Chartres, lines more powerful, indeed, than those to the classical world. It should not be surprising, then, that, although the general scope of my remarks will range from Antiquity to the twentieth century, I shall deal primarily with materials from the eleventh and twelfth centuries. I hope that the grounds for analyzing conversion in this way will become apparent as the discussion proceeds.[2] My objective is interpretive (or hermeneutical): I wish to see how the pivotal idea of conversion was understood and, indeed, how it was possible to think about conversion in the Latin West.

The first and perhaps the most essential features of conversion, in its religious senses, are that it is a name, not a thing, and that the word is a metaphor. In the arts and crafts, it had literal senses. Rough marble was "converted" into a statue. Various metals were "converted" into bronze. But, once taken up into the vocabularies of religion, it gained the obscurity of all metaphors. "The greatest thing by far," Aristotle (384–322 B.C.E.) wrote of poets, "is to be a master of metaphor. It is the one thing that cannot be learned from others; and it is also a sign of genius, since a good metaphor implies an intuitive perception of the similarity in dissimilars" (*Poetics*, 23. 1159a). The poet's use of metaphor, like the perception of virtue, was limited to the few.

From the outset, then, the history of "conversion" is a history of metaphorical analysis. Certain consequences follow from this perception. In the metaphor-word *conversion* and in the pursuit of goodness, we find a distinction between what was called conversion and the name it was called, connotations of hidden meanings and associations that made the metaphor "work," not spread out for all to see. And it must be said that the challenge and the reward of studying the idea of conversion and its history lie in the obscurity and incommunicability of the experience known metaphorically as "conversion."

> Jesus, the very thought of thee
> With sweetness fills the breast . . .
> No tongue of mortal can express,
> No letters write its blessedness:
> Alone who hath thee in his heart
> Knows, love of Jesus, what thou art.³

These lines come from a twelfth-century poem, *Jesu dulcis memoria*. An answering stanza from the eighteenth century, in William Cowper's (1731–1800) hymn, *God Moves in a Mysterious Way*, establishes that we have to deal with a very long tradition of understanding, one in which the centerpiece is incomprehensible, incommunicable, and vividly real.

> Blind unbelief is sure to err,
> And scan his work in vain,
> God is his own interpreter,
> And he will make it plain.

But there are also other consequences of regarding the history of "conversion" as a venture in metaphorical analysis. Let me recall our fundamental distinction of three terms: a phenomenon called conversion, the name ("conversion") by which it was called, and, between those poles, the process of thinking that went into calling that particular event by that specific name, the process by which what began in esthetics was rendered into poetics. Our subject is not what was called conversion, nor yet the etymology of that name, but understanding packed into the name "conversion." Although the distinction between names and things is one of the oldest in philosophy, historians have but recently taken it into account. It was beyond the historian's purview when Arthur Darby Nock published a celebrated series of lectures on conversion in 1933.⁴ In Nock's view, conversion was largely a change of mind or behavior marked by a single, identifiable event in history. That event was generally one of institutional adhesion. Conversion was concluded when the convert was admitted to a philosophical sect or mystery cult or when, in a different form, these acts converged in Christian baptism. Conversion, in other words, was a turning point, or peripety.

Since Nock's lectures were published, objections have been raised to what could be called the "peripety paradigm." Nock's discussion of what was called "the conversion experience" and others profoundly influenced by him employed evidence from western Europe, and a call was raised "for more thorough-going studies of the conversion experience among non-Christians, as well as among Christians living in a non-Western environment."⁵

Meanwhile, changes in the methods of literary criticism added other, quite different, doubts concerning the sufficiency of the peripety paradigm. One derived from the ancient philosophical distinction, just mentioned, between words and things. This logical argument held that, detached from the event of conversion, scholars could never know what happened but only what they found in the texts before them, which, however accurate in statement, were always poetic fictions, always works of narrative composed by inclusion, omission, and deployment. Snorre's reconstruction of the interview between Olav Tryggvassön and Sigrid the Strong-minded illustrates the veil, perhaps as impenetrable as a juggler's sleeve, behind which fact is fictionalized into text.

The peripety paradigm also appeared insufficient when it was recognized that readers were not merely consumers of texts, but that they actively constituted the meanings of texts. Reading was integral to the poetic act. Fixed words on the page were only the contours of a text; the other components were ways of understanding, expectations, assumptions, templates of credibility that readers found between the lines because they put them there, voices that readers gave the silent words. Thus, it was possible to think that through this unconscious ventriloquism a given text could have a different meaning at each reading. Stress on "audience response" as constituting the sense of a text has been accentuated by debate about how ethnic context and, especially, gender shape a person's understanding. Do differences of gender make it impossible for men and women, even in the same literate community, to understand a given text in the same way? Distinctions between those who control the terms of discourse and those who do not have indicated that what students find in a text may be quite a different matter from what the author placed, or intended to be found, in the text. Most important, they demonstrate that ways of understanding words, including metaphors, differed at any given time and through the centuries. They mitigate against the anachronistic assumption of any stability of meaning.

The implications of positing a radical instability of meaning for studies of "the conversion experience," peripety or not, are profound. Students cannot determine exactly what happened in the event of conversion or recover the unspoken content that the text held for its author. Does the stress on audience response mean that they can only find their own faces reflected in the surfaces of other authors' works? Not all scholars have given up the object of finding out what happened in the event of conversion, or even of extracting general categories of experiences.[6] But their inquiries, too, are overcast by acknowledgment that a text about conversion and an interpretation of the text are two separate things and that in both cases words are quite different from the events commemorated or poetically "fictionalized" in the text.

I accept these objections to the peripety paradigm. They supply us with some important critical distinctions. What is called conversion is a thing felt, evaporating with its duration. What we have as historical evidence is a text, a thing made. The poetry in what is called conversion is how the text and its narrative (or narratives) were made up—the calling that comes between an event and the name through which it is given meaning.

These distinctions lead further. As I shall argue, they demolish the logic, or even the possibility, of talking about any universal "conversion experience" at all. One result of the revolution of philology in the nineteenth century was the discovery that how a text is transmitted through the ages actually changes the text. This is clearly the case when books are manuscripts and the texts are subject to every sort of scribal error and adaptation. As one scribe after another copies and alters a book, the text and its meaning are changed. The text as received may be very different from the text as originally written.

A very familiar example is the contrast between the first creation account in Genesis, with its glorious portrayal of human life under blessing, and the second, with its portrayal of human life as unfolding through crime and curse. The juxtaposition of these accounts from different sources illustrates how, through transmission, one text may eventually combine elements from various epochs and, indeed, from conflicting factions, classes, or societies. It also illustrates how distinguishing its elements and tracing their separate histories may open up the possibility of an archaeology of ideas.

Therefore, meaning now read into a text—for example, even a text so small as the single word *conversion*—may well be what the history of its transmission has packed into it, not what was there originally or at another time in its transmission. The word *conversion* and the phrase "the conversion experience" thus become not abstract tools of analysis but, more properly, subjects of analysis. What is called "conversion" may be an individual experience, but it is recognizable and has meaning as such only as a historical artifact, produced by many stages of transmission, in the context of particular societies and their traditions.

Although Islam and Christianity were both religions of conversion, conversion was not institutionalized in Islam, which lacked both priesthood and hierarchy. "Medieval Islam produced no missionaries, bishops, baptismal rites, or other indicators of conversion." Proselytism was not uncommonly the work of merchants in their normal pursuit of business.[7] Consequently, conversion is seldom mentioned by historical writers, much less developed as an impelling and dominant current in world history. Furthermore, in the absence of an overarching institutional structure, the distinguishing features of discipline and mystery might characterize sects but not the religion as a whole.[8] I am told, too, that, lacking a word for "conscience" (see chap. 4, n. 1), Arabic has no equivalent for the mysterious inwardness of change connoted by "conversion." To adhere to Islam is "to follow the right way," meaning formal observance. Consequently, nuances of doctrinal understanding, which shaped such narratives of conversion in western Europe as Bede's portrayal of the rivalry between Celtic and Roman practices, were for Muslims not indices of an unfolding apocalyptic conflict between good and evil.

Different as the phenomenon that Muslims called "following the right way" was from the one that Christians called conversion, there is at least one point of similarity. For under the caliphate shifts of religious allegiance led to the impairment of centralized political authority and to factional conflict among believers.[9] Evidently, even in its scriptural origins, the paradigm or morphology of Christian conversion was also subversive. In the centuries of its development at the core of western European tradition, its warrant grew for political as well as for spiritual subversion. Thus, by the twelfth century its call for resistance to unbelievers described areas of conflict other than those against Jews and Muslims. In the Investiture Conflict, papal authority declared the right of subjects to rise against heretical kings; and theologians likewise contended that the community of the faithful were obliged to withstand wicked and unbelieving prelates, indeed, to depose even popes if they betrayed the faith.

Thus, Bernard of Clairvaux and his contemporaries proclaimed a gospel of sedition when they decried rulers of the Church who had been exalted to priesthood and prelacy without conversion of heart. The whole world is Christian, Bernard wrote, but nearly all deny Christ. Their grasping after riches and office, their sexual abominations in the house of God, their wanton dissipation of the Church's goods in shameful self-indulgence revealed them as enemies of the cross of Christ, as minions of Lucifer. The unconverted were within the Church; they governed; even in the see of St. Peter, they performed sacraments of which they partook to their own damnation.[10] This is to say also that the drama of conversion was thought to occur in a supernatural dimension, rather than in the dimension governed by language, customs, institutions, and other contrivances of human nature. However, a fundamental tension came about from the fact that the supernatural phenomenon that was called conversion could only be grasped and expressed through vernaculars provided by nature. It was a case of putting supernatural wine in natural bottles.

For Bernard and his contemporaries, the career of Christ was the supreme "form of conversion" (see preface at n. 4) on which all authentic conversions, with countless variations, were patterned. It was essential that the form or scenario be enacted, that one learn it by doing it. Conflict was also essential to the drama. Thus, the form of conversion was subversive of authority, even of authority in the Church. By erecting loyalties of the heart greater than those of law, it became subversive of civil as well as of ecclesiastical authority. For "we ought to obey God rather than men" (Acts 5:29). Finally, the experience of conversion was subversive of self; for its whole object was to cast off the old and enter into newness of life.

We come, then, to recognize that what was called conversion and "the conversion experience" by Nock and others who have accepted the peripety paradigm was not what twelfth-century Christian writers called conversion, any more than what those earlier writers called conversion had a counterpart in the vernacular of Islam. The view that conversion was concluded by institutional affiliation or by a sacramental initiation, such as baptism, is foreign to twelfth-century texts. The importance of institutional initiation and adhesion to the peripety paradigm leaves the powerful subversive effects of conversion entirely out of account. Inevitably, the inwardness of the supernatural phenomenon that was called conversion made it clear that, according to the archetypal form of conversion, the heart turned, not to an institutional Church, nor even to a formal structure of doctrine called Christianity, but to Christ.[11] As we shall see, this turning was not a matter of a single act but of a lifelong process of reformation.

I have been explaining what kind of venture lies before us. Let me put it in other words. As fairy tales and mundane experience repeat, answers we get depend on the questions we ask. Some questions can be asked only after rich bodies of information have accumulated, only after long, elaborate histories of reflection and debate have opened and unpacked them. Every question is thinkable because the ground has been prepared for it. What lies before us is a venture in finding out how questions are posed (that is, in *Fragestellung*). I maintain that at the present time asking what made it possible to pose the questions about what was known metaphorically as conversion can yield more certain answers than asking how conversion was experienced. My discussion also underscores the essential fact that the *Fragestellung* for us is very different from the *Fragestellung* accessible to twelfth-century writers. Thus, even as we attempt to recover theirs, we must always be conscious that we are applying our own: that we are attempting in our way to understand their understanding. We are applying names to the ways in which they applied names, working within a method that may circle in upon itself rather than advancing beyond itself.

An analogy may be helpful. A mathematics examination states a problem. But the formula in which the problem is stated is very different from the reasoning that made the problem thinkable, very different, too, from the reasoning that selected one among several possible ways to state it. Solving the problem does not always require (or include) understanding the reasoning that lay behind it, nor does a person need to reconstruct that reasoning in order to state the solution.

For us, descriptions of conversion are analogous to the statement of a mathematical problem. Our task is to recover the metaphorical reasoning that prepared the ground for them and that made possible both those descriptions and the idea of conversion as it was known in a distinct culture and epoch. Other writers query this kind of study, since they hold that in history, as in some sciences, phenomena are changed by being observed. In other words, they maintain, rightly, that what we know of other people's understanding is always selected, shaped, and colored by our own.[12]

I am convinced, however, that if we listen carefully, we can hear, albeit imperfectly, the voices of other ages. We must be careful not to edit out what they tell of ambivalences, mixed motives and emotions, and dilemmas, and we must refrain from imposing our canons for the sake of clarity. This self-denial is especially important when we are dealing with texts from societies that cherished the indirect language of metaphor with its obscurity and ambiguity, or when, in fact, we seek to understand ideas about things that could only be expressed indirectly and by allusion and that, consequently, are tissues of incompatibles or logical contradictions—the vague but real category of "ineffables." After all, even if as heirs of the Enlightenment we value plainness and clarity in expository prose, we have not banished logical antipathies from the human condition or expunged metaphorical ways of speaking about them from the writings of earlier centuries or from our own discourse.

What gives the twelfth century a notable place in the poetics of conversion? The answer is important for explaining how social context determines what is to be called conversion and ways in which what is called conversion is to be understood and valued. That answer lies both in politics and in theory. By the twelfth century conversion had been established as a paradigm for individual and collective life. The expansion and consolidation of European society, the development of critical, systematic methods in sacred doctrine (which is also to say, in logic), and the flowering of monastic institutions and ascetic theology demanded that ways of understanding the paradigm set forth in the New Testament be reappraised in the light of Christianity's long and continuing experience of conversion. Missionary enterprises, which had declined after the ninth century, revived and achieved unprecedented vigor in the twelfth and thirteenth centuries, pursued by new monastic orders (such as the Cistercians and the Norbertines), including the military orders, and, eventually, by the Franciscans and Dominicans. Beginning with Pope Alexander III (reigned 1159–81), popes assumed an initiative in proselytism that their predecessors had rarely taken and never consistently sustained. Polemical dialogues between Christians and Jews, always seeking conversion through reproach, multiplied and became a recognizable genre.[13] Reflections on individual conversion proliferated in an outpouring of spiritual writings, which combined religious inwardness with an acute awareness "of belonging to groups and filling roles" in them.[14]

The twelfth century has been characterized as the moment when Western culture first conceived freedom of conscience.[15] Beyond question, there are reasons to find, in aspects of twelfth-century social and cultural practices, evidence of a new and penetrating awareness of human subjectivity— in elaborations of the penitential discipline, with its demand for unflinching self-knowledge, in the emphasis by mystics and troubadours alike on the inwardness of love, and, to be sure, in the establishment of the feudal contract, which derived its force from the freedom of consent.[16] Was not violation of one's conscience a sin against the Holy Ghost, capable of no pardon?[17] But in these assumptions, the proposition of moral autonomy was entwined with many others.

At any rate, twelfth-century writers were the first since Antiquity to have a vocabulary with which to speak about the inner life with great refinement. Linguistic tools for investigating the enigmas of soul and mind were among the casualties of the fall of Rome. Beginning around the middle of the eleventh century, they were recovered and developed. Treatises written in Antiquity and in the era of the Church Fathers were recopied, disseminated, collected, and studied anew, comparatively. Critical methods were invented to test the exactitude of theological language, to make the logical examination of doctrine increasingly meticulous and comprehensive, and, eventually, to digest and assimilate into received traditions the teachings of newly discovered writings by Greek, Arabic, and Hebrew philosophers, including notably Aristotle. These changes were called forth and sharpened by continual dispute; they were developed and spread through recently founded monastic orders and schools, some of which soon became universities. Social tensions created a relentless need to understand both the workings of the mind and the subjects of its inquiry with ever greater refinement. Growing tendencies toward repression and persecution added political urgency. Unprecedented achievements in theology and philosophy, nurtured and given rapid, permanent advancement through new institutions, were among the responses.

Because of the importance esthetics had in the ideas to be considered in this book, I should note one specific achievement in the recovery and reinterpretation of ancient thought. The writings (mistakenly) attributed to Dionysius the Areopagite had been known in the Latin West since the ninth century. However, their rise to general dominance in intellectual and spiritual history began in the twelfth, with Hugh of St. Victor's (1096–1141) commentary on the *Celestial Hierarchy*, "the first philosophy of beauty since Augustine." With this work, indeed, Hugh became "the first author to devote an entire treatise to beauty."[18] Thereafter, the Areopagite's great theme that sensory beauties were contemplative openings to the divine and his elaborate variations on the allegory of light entered into the main currents of esthetics, metaphysics, and mysticism and became normative in architecture and the visual arts.

Thus, writers in the eleventh and, even more, the twelfth centuries were able to investigate the inner life far more completely than had ever been possible since the end of the ancient world. Consequently, they permanently marked ways of understanding that life in Western culture, then taking on an identity that it has kept, with modifications, to the present day.

And yet, the vocabulary that they invented and applied was by no means of one piece, nor, correspondingly, did it employ one variety of understanding. As we burrow through the historical striations in the word *conversion*, past the twelfth-century level, we come eventually to the era of the Church Fathers and, still further, to classical Antiquity.

The crucial fact is that the historical contents built up in the word came about through a constant, relentless, needful testing of beliefs in the crucible of life. Readjustments were made as needed to preserve what were deemed to be essentials. In this way, social context repeatedly made personal experience understandable in ways prescribed and sanctioned by tradition.

Writings from the twelfth century illustrate with special clarity how intricate the poetic process of understanding in transmission may be, and how profound the debt of later transmitters may be to those who went before. This they do in such a way as to suggest that the whole history of the idea of conversion was an elaborate poetic venture, engaging collaborators without number. Incidentally, given the distinctive character of that venture, it also points up difficulties in attempting to define a universal morphology of conversion or to maintain the hypothesis of a universal "conversion experience." Let me explain.

As the circumstances of Christianity changed in the centuries that followed the composition of the New Testament, the nature of what was called conversion also changed. At first expected imminently, the apocalyptic coming of the Kingdom did not occur. Believers realized that loose, personal fellowships could not serve the demands of long anticipation. A myth common to many peoples was assimilated to the idea of conversion in order to explain the delay of the Kingdom and the improvisations that it entailed. That myth was already present in the New Testament, by way of allusions and analogues to the experiences of the Israelites. The narrative sequence of a people's noble origins, catastrophic banishment from its homeland, arduous wanderings and struggles with hostile nations, and eventual entry into (or return to) a land of happy abundance was plain in the Old Testament. It occurred also in Virgil's account of the Trojan conquest of Rome and in variations of the Trojan legend that were current in Europe from the twelfth century onwards.

This mythic narrative of history as the loss and recovery of happiness by a people after long adversities combined with the dramatic scenario of individual conversion as a continuing transition. Banished from Paradise, the human race labored under exile in the Egypt of this world, even as it ventured toward its celestial homeland. The life of the Apostle Paul provided an essential analogue on the level of personal experience. By divine ambush on the road to Damascus, Paul was abruptly removed from his career as persecutor; he became a preacher later, after blindness, baptism, and fourteen years in Arabia. The process of his conversion or sanctification continued until his life's end. Likewise, when Christianity became the dominant religion of the Roman Empire, the world "followed in faith that which it had persecuted in fury."[19] And still, just as Paul's fears and inner warfare—the renewal of his soul—continued by stages, each in jeopardy, so, too, did the struggle for the believing community's spiritual existence include temptations permitted or imposed by God and unremitting dangers from within the community itself. The writings of the Fathers are full of invectives against nominal Christians whose lives conformed with the robust sensualism of the pagan world; and the lament that, while the world professed Christianity, the followers of Christ were few became a constant motif of Western religious literature. The poetics of conversion required both danger and a saving, hidden remnant.

From the second to the fourth century, Rome's attacks caused many baptized Christians to abandon their faith. Even priests and bishops who continued to consider themselves Christians gave over their sacred books to the persecutors or resorted to formal perjuries (for example, by obtaining fraudulent certificates of sacrifice from pagan judges) to avoid actual betrayal of their faith. The questions then arose among Christians who had not acted in such equivocal ways whether the lapsed could be reconciled with the Church and whether clerics among them could be restored to their priestly and episcopal functions. The imitation of Christ entailed temptation. Over the very long run, did it also allow repeated failure and forgiveness?

The dispute over the reconciliation of the lapsed soon widened to include

12 *Understanding Conversion*

Figure 2 In this thirteenth-century illumination, the artist found a way to illustrate the physical blindness with which Saul (later the Apostle Paul) was stricken on the road to Damascus and also, thereby, the incomprehensibility of the event to the eye of his mind until he passed to the next stage of revelation. (MS Garrett 39, f. 266v, published with permission of Princeton University Library)

Figure 3 In this illumination from a twelfth-century Greek codex, the Apostle Paul is shown dictating to Luke, the supposed author of the Book of Acts, which contains the three fullest accounts of Paul's vocation on the road to Damascus. Different degrees of fictive understanding are indicated by Paul, Luke, and the eavesdropper behind the draperies. (MS Add. 720, f. 133v, reproduced by permission of the Syndics of Cambridge University Library)

controversies over whether members of sects condemned as heretical (notably the Arians) could be admitted to communion and, if so, whether they were to be rebaptized. These long and bitter struggles had decisive effects on ideas about conversion in the Church. For believers confronted the experience of apostasy.

Clearly, changes of heart and mind and initiation rituals such as baptism were not safeguards against infidelity. They were only the beginning of a gradual process the outcome of which could not be foretold, one in which there must be frequent, indeed daily, conversions. Authentic baptism could not be repeated. Therefore, rituals and ceremonies of pardon and reconciliation had to be developed; doctrines of the Church's power to judge and correct sins throughout its children's lifetimes had to be framed. The long process of conversion was identified with penitential asceticism, suffering, and martyrdom.[20] The example of Bishop Hosius of Cordova (c. 257–c. 359), who lived through the worst that pagan emperors could contrive, gained a permanent place in the literature of the Church. For nearly a century, he stalwartly withstood persecution and temptations, only to waver in the faith toward the end of his life by accepting a heretical creed proffered by a Christian emperor. He recanted and was reconciled with the orthodox; but his exceptionally long career, blemished only toward the end, illustrated how steadfastness in the faith was never assured until death. Such was the ideal of gradual conversion institutionalized in monasticism and canonized in the *Rule* of St. Benedict (c. 530).

Institutional order and continuity were required; tolerance of personal enthusiasm, including the prophetic spirit, diminished. Conversion, too, was institutionalized. Of course, conversion remained a motive of the Church as it became increasingly an organism of law and hierarchy. But, more decisively for the role that conversion assumed in European society, it was institutionalized in monasticism. Its identification not merely with ascetic traditions but precisely with monastic order was so close that, unless otherwise defined in context, the word *conversio* came to mean entrance into that discipline.[21] (For reasons spelled out later, it is important to say here that the moment in which one entered a monastery was not the full *conversio,* but only its beginning, the *initium conversionis* according to the *Rule* of St. Benedict.)

What came to be a major institution in European society—and for centuries the only one that with its teachings and presence permeated daily life in every region across the continent—was designed and formed for the express purpose of conversion. The power of this institution is evident in the numbers of men and women drawn to it, in the role that monks and their communities played in spreading Church and Christianity throughout Europe, and, by no means least, in the normative effect that monastic discipline imparted to the ethics of secular government as monks educated rulers in their duties as Christian princes.[22] In this way was forged an enduring alliance between the cross and the sword.

The variegations in the word *conversion* are still richer and more dense than I have thus far suggested. For twelfth-century texts on conversion betray an intricate ebb and flow of several, conflicting traditions. When we read those texts, we are aware that the doctrine of conversion set forth is not uniform. It is conspicuously made up of ill-matched ideas of conversion, which do not agree in every detail. Each, we know, has its own history. A text, such as Bernard of Clairvaux's sermon *On Conversion*, can be seen as an archaeological site, at which the antecedents of Christianity are environmental levels. The doctrine of the imitation of Christ consists of numerous striations.

Of course, the authors of twelfth-century texts lacked the tools of historical criticism, developed from the Enlightenment onward. They lacked, especially, the awareness, gained through nineteenth-century philology, that the history of how a text or an idea is transmitted—its experience in the world—shapes its meaning. They read Scripture as though it were a single composition and considered the internal contradictions intruded by its long, complex, and to them unknown history as signs of a hidden, mystic unity. Likewise, by selectively cannibalizing the materials before them, they built the various kinds of conversion that diverse historical traditions delivered to them into what seemed to their eyes a single edifice.

But in analytic moments that structure may appear to us a patchwork or (in three-dimensionality) a bird's nest, rather than a polished sphere.

The importance of these diversities goes beyond what they tell us about a tangled development in the history of ideas. The differences in vocabulary are crucial. In their interplay, language and thought build up patterns of cognition that are distinctive in every tongue and that show themselves most vexingly when we translate from one into another. So marked are the connections between language and cognitive processes that, in the view of some linguists, all translation is impossible; only some indeterminate resemblance or commentary can be achieved. Few would question that translation of some sentiments or genres, above all in poetry, is impossible. The history of "conversion," as a metaphor borrowed from arts and crafts, illustrates what momentous effects the imprecisions and diversities of translation may have.

Thus, when one says that the idea of conversion as the imitation of Christ consisted of numerous striations, what is meant? We mean that a twelfth-century text displays several kinds of events, all called "conversion," drawn from different histories and conveyed in different vocabularies. I hold, furthermore, that thinking about each kind of conversion entailed a distinctive process of cognition. Each was a different application of the same metaphor. Let me give five examples of what was called conversion and therefore also of some historical striations enveloped in the idea of the imitation of Christ.

Perhaps the grandest of all conversions mentioned in twelfth-century writings was the movement of the cosmos. This was imagined as a twofold movement: an egress from, and a return to, God. The conception derived from Greek philosophy, specifically from a tradition that passed from Plato through varied strands of Neoplatonism. It assumed a harmonious ordering of all things, a concord of discordant elements. It brought with it a vocabulary adequate to portraying the universal egress and return, a vocabulary that consisted of balanced pairs of terms, such as the One and the many, form and matter, cause and effect, eternity and time. One essential component in this doctrine of cosmic conversion was the doctrine of the Logos, or Word, through which the emanation of forms from God occurred, a doctrine that Augustine of Hippo specifically mentioned as a stepping stone on his way to Christianity (*Confessions*, 7.9). The paradigm of conversion applied was one of the return to origins: that is, of restoration.[23]

Twelfth-century writers received a second model of conversion from the same antecedents in Greek philosophy. The distinction between mind and body was fundamental in Platonism and Aristotelianism. And this part of their legacy enabled Neoplatonists to conceive of the soul's return to God as a special work, achieved through efforts of the enlightened mind and thus independent of the natural mechanics of the cosmic order. They applied the same paradigm of conversion as a restorative return to origins to the world (or macrocosm) and to the human soul (or microcosm); both were renewed by being purified from the taint of matter, into which they had fallen. Together with their physics and metaphysics, Neoplatonists bequeathed ways of inquiring into the origins, possibilities, and destiny of the soul; and these inquiries, in ethics, esthetics, and epistemology, carried a rich and fully developed vocabulary of introspection. The method by which the soul converted to God was by passing inward and being absorbed in love of the One. The way to virtue was not open to the many or through participation in worldly affairs. The ideal of the converted was the contemplative sage. The motif of the sage's journey inward was taken up into the Christian concept of revelation as "the philosophy of Christ."

Apart from conversion to philosophy, with its subheadings of cosmic and personal conversion, the ancient world knew other kinds of spiritual transformation that were assimilated into twelfth-century writings. For example, a very substantial segment of twelfth-century thinking concerned conversion in the framework of a religious organization, with its vocabulary of sacrament and cult. To be sure, ancient philosophers occasionally applied such terms to their own doctrines. But the experience of conversion through initiation into religious institutions, with priesthoods and liturgies, actually came not through the philosophical schools but through mystery religions.

Appealing to the emotions, rather than to the intellect, these purported to offer a road to virtue through supernatural enlightenment and direct experience of the holy in rituals of baptism and banquet, sacraments of death and rebirth through which believers participated in the divinity, reenacting events in the careers of their gods and, in some rituals, being adored by other worshipers as personifications of those gods. Elaborate doctrines of revelation, miracle, prophecy, and magic were framed to teach how believers could escape from a spiritually alien world. They could find salvation, open only to the initiate, from the aimless, violent turn of fortune or from the icy decrees of irresistible and impersonal fate. They believed that there were ways for them to enlist the arcane and covert powers of their gods to release themselves from dangers and afflictions, to succeed in love, to ruin their rivals, and to avenge themselves on their enemies.

Using the vernaculars of architecture and the visual, verbal, and performing arts, they assured the chosen few of epiphanies of gods in human form in which the worshipers themselves would be transmuted into the divine while remaining human. These private cults were by no means democratic. For even ones open to men and women closed their mysteries to the poor by virtue of the costs of initiation. They were numerous, and a person could be initiated into more than one, combining their separate doctrines and mysteries in a highly idiosyncratic spirituality. Their teachings were hidden; their great sacraments, secret. But enough was known to the uninitiate for the mysteries to introduce into common thinking a pattern of sacramental conversion.

Though numerous, the paradigms of conversion applied in mystery cults are indistinctly known. In general, they seem to have set forth conversion either as redemption or as regeneration into something new. New birth could include doctrines of reincarnation as well as those of divinization. Such were some of their contributions of Christianity as a mystery religion, contributions represented symbolically when writers characterized Christ as Orpheus, Apollo, or Dionysus.

The word *conscience* points to a fourth kind of conversion framed in the ancient world that, although different from those already considered, still combined with them in twelfth-century doctrines. Stoicism was a Greek philosophical school; but before it entered the mainstream of Western thought, it was recast by Romans. In distinctive ways conversion to philosophy and to mystery cults marked a withdrawal from civic religions and, in extremes, from public life, even as, according to Plato, Socrates, near the origins of philosophical tradition, had admonished seekers after wisdom to abstain from politics. Like them and many other strains of ancient thought, Stoicism prized itself as truth accessible to the few and poured contempt on civic religions and other cults, together with the myths that sustained them. All these it condemned as vulgar superstitions. Unlike other philosophies, Stoicism admonished sages to seek wisdom in the midst of public life, discharging obligations to family and state commensurate with the positions which fell to them.

It was also unlike them in suppressing the esthetic and emotional aspects of spiritual venture. Stoicism taught that, as rationality, the divine pervaded all things; in a sense, it was nature. Consequently, union with the divine consisted in the exercise of reason, which was also a return, or conversion, to nature. The great obstacle to living according to nature was the emotions, "perturbations of the soul" which endangered and could even overthrow reason.

Stoic ethics required that each individual mind exercise its reason independently. Teaching a cosmic determinism, both materialist and mechanistic, Stoic physics also insisted that such freedom as existed in the world was exercised by the wise in their assent to its rational order. As they worked out these teachings, Roman philosophers developed the vocabulary of conscience as an autonomous faculty of judgment.[24] Although they believed that virtue was absolute and universal, they also recognized that moral judgments were contingent. Thus, two persons in similar moral predicaments might well have to decide on quite different actions in view of their ages, status, temperaments, mental capacities, and circumstances. What was right for the one could be wrong for the other. The virtue of an act consisted in the intention of the person who performed it.

Even as its vocabulary of conscience made room for psychological contingencies, so, too, did its doctrine of moral transformation portray conversion not as the event of one moment (such as initiation into a cult) but as a long progress toward wholeness full of trial and error, guided by self-control, monitored by self-criticism, and rewarded by self-approbation. And yet, the ethics of Stoicism did not culminate in self-interest and indulgence; emphasis on responsibility for the common good entailed acting in and for the community, even when opposing the dominant will of the community for its good was suicidal for the wise.

Christianity could not assimilate the Stoic pattern of conversion as one of cyclical recurrence: that is, of rounds of senescence and rejuvenation. But Stoic ethics of individual integrity, illuminated by the light of God immanent in the soul, strengthened Christian ideals of adherence to truth under persecution, even at the cost of death, behavior thought to have been exemplified by Christ and the martyrs.

Bernard of Clairvaux and his contemporaries did not consider themselves the intellectual heirs of pagan philosophers. Rather, they insisted that they stood in the spiritual lineage of God's elect, the Israelites of the Old Testament. Consequently, the varieties of conversion that I have mentioned and their respective vocabularies were generally assigned subordinate roles in twelfth-century treatises. Overarching them all was the pattern of conversion set forth in the Old Testament: that from sin to righteousness, cast with the juridical vocabulary of the Law and the Prophets.

The Old Testament offered outlines of various patterns of conversion, including redemption and re-creation into a new creature. But these were subsumed into the inclusive paradigm of conversion as human response to God's vocation or election, a response that brought with it a movement toward the fulfillment of God's promises to his chosen people.

The great virtue was obedience; the central act was atoning sacrifice; the heroic ideal was the prophet. Instead of the discipline of reason, predominant in ancient philosophies, that of prayer, in the legal framework of the Covenant, was most valued. Hebrew writers placed the beginning of conversion in God's choice and action—that is, in grace—instead of in the desires, powers, and intuitions of the sage's mind. Correspondingly, the effect of conversion was not to expand the reason but to sanctify the emotions, chiefly fear and love. Like the Stoics, Hebrew writers understood conversion as a long and variable process. But they found the process not simply a career of self-determination but rather a great historical movement in which individual lives and collective experience moved, according to a providential order, from Creation toward Messianic culmination. Individual conversions to righteousness and Israel's covenantings with God made up one sacred history, drawn out to test the permanence of the chosen people's devotion to righteousness, to see whether, in adversity and temptation, it would remain faithful or betray God with spiritual adultery. Individual conversions had no meaning apart from the experience of the whole people, as it had been, as it was, and as it was to be. Considered prefigurative of Christ's life and teaching, Old Testament events and doctrines such as these were readily assimilated into ideas about the imitation of Christ by individuals and by his mystical body, the Church.

The applications of the metaphor "conversion" then, were extremely diverse. Some of the five paradigms that I have mentioned set forth a return to origins (Neoplatonism) or cyclical recurrence (Stoicism). Others taught that conversion was movement toward new ways or degrees of life (mystery cults, Old Testament). Some promised reformation into a better form of what a believer already was; others, transformation into radically new being. Some came about by the force of a natural homing instinct; others, by the initiative of exceptional minds; others, by divine intervention. For these last—including Christian paradigms—conversion was a work of God.

Slowly, these various patterns of conversion were drawn into an ensemble: the imitation of Christ, especially of his Passion. One of the most decisive antecedent stages in the prehistory of Christian thought came when the Jewish theologian Philo of Alexandria (fl. 40) fused Old Testamental theology with Neoplatonic philosophy. The chief moment of assimilation in the Church itself came during the age of persecution. This change altered how people thought about time and the imitation of Christ. A legacy of apocalyptic thought made the Christian idea of conversion inescapably historical; individual experiences and the history of the world alike moved toward the great eschatological consummation. When persecution began, the eschatological prophecies appeared to have been accomplished. But, as persecutions continued, it became increasingly apparent that the end of all things had been deferred. Christ had not returned in judgment. The millennial kingdom of saints had not been established. Imitation of Christ was not for a brief interlude but for the very long run.

Each age and culture interpreted the idea of conversion as the imitation of Christ according to its own lights. As I shall explain later, the twelfth century added to the traditional repertory an ideal of nobility, drawn from the ethos of chivalric society. Clearly, even in the Age of the Church Fathers, the idea of conversion that became canonical in Western culture was an ensemble work both in the varied and ill-matched paradigms that it brought together and in the vocabularies and cognitive processes packed into those paradigms, to each its own. Different vocabularies signal different ways of construing—perhaps also constructing—realities; but the varied paradigms were, in fact, different realities, with separate, if intersecting, careers.

Combining such discrepant metaphors was itself a virtuoso exercise in metaphorical analysis: the discernment of similarity in dissimilars. It was possible because important, if hidden, similarities did run through all the differences. A few can be mentioned by way of introduction. The force of doubt and discontent is most evident of all. In its inexhaustible varieties, conversion began in rejection of existing circumstances and, even more, in a turning away from one's own established way of life. Happiness was elusive and misery, profound. Predators seemed to flourish, mocking the downtrodden, even as they picked their bones. Great dangers, from which there seemed no escape, threatened mind and body. Previous knowledge was recognized as treacherously flawed or illusory. Devotion to inherited cults and established doctrines brought no rewards commensurate with the abundance of the ungodly. The power of alien gods was proven and imposed by battle. Countless such reasons sparked irresistible doubts demanding that the ways of the gods be vindicated. Even among the committed, they provoked scrutiny of fundamental doctrines and practices. Even there, the basic questions calling for vindication of the ways of God gave no alternative to spiritual movement.

It is worth emphasizing that, while doubt was for some a cause to reject old beliefs, it was also for others a "holy discontent," an impulse to move more deeply, by continual inquiry, into the heart of existing commitments. Pervasive doubt—and, speaking exactly, theodical doubt—was at the origins of what was called conversion, whether from one religion to another or to a fuller exploration of the unexplored within accepted and cherished beliefs.

Another common characteristic is certainly male predominance. There is a subordinate theme in the asexuality of God in Greek philosophies, in the female judges portrayed in the Old Testament, in the initiation of men and women into mystery cults and their priesthoods (not to mention the devotion of some such cults to female divinities), and, finally, in the Stoic argument that, since sexual inequality, like slavery, was a violation of nature, women and men must be regarded as equal in moral obligations and in capacity for moral education. Yet, between Plato's (c.428–c.348 B.C.E.) portrayal of Diotima as the teacher of Socrates in the *Symposium* and the career of Hypatia (c.370–415), a leading teacher of Neoplatonism in Alexandria, few women figure as interpreters and transmitters of the traditions that I have cited, and none was accepted into the canon as an author of texts or an innovator in vocabulary or cognitive process.

A further common strand is a preoccupation with beauty. In this regard, the diversities among the paradigms of conversion are acute. In Platonism and its descendants, beauty was compositional order, a harmonious arrangement of parts. To Stoics, notably Roman Stoics, beauty was in the austerity of moral fitness and in the rationality directing the cosmic sequence of cause and effect, crowned by the cycle in which the world was continually destroyed and renewed. In the Old Testament authentic beauty consists in the glory, majesty, honor, power, and magnificence of the Lord. This, the beauty of holiness, was conveyed by grace to Israel, to those who preached peace, to the meek. And yet, in the face of such considerable differences, Christian writers eager to discover a great underlying coherence were able to detect a common recognition that conversion to truth was esthetic, an essay in beauty that far surpassed physical beauty, which perished as quickly as the grass of the field, and the beauty of human wisdom, which was easily defiled.

Finally, one is struck by the fact that all the paradigms of conversion entail struggle, particularly that of the religious few against the superstitious many. According to them all, virtue was proven in conflict. Each was a rejection of the beliefs of the many, a conflict of religion against superstition. Because of the intimate bond it drew between personal experience and collective history, the Old Testament paradigm of repentance is anomalous. But it, too, consistently set the righteousness of the saving remnant against the wickedness of the many, who killed the prophets and repeatedly fell into idolatry.

The Old Testament was also singular in the repertory that I have defined because it cast the drama of salvation as cosmic warfare between God and Satan, the personification of evil. For ancient philosophers the enemy was within the individual person, whether in the soul's struggle to escape the pollution of matter and, with it, the prison house of the body or in the privation (or finitude) inherent in the makeup of every individual being. The Stoic struggle against the perturbations of soul carried the motif of struggle to the heart itself.

As Christian writers gathered these conceptions of conversion as a war of many fronts, they, too, located the most bitter and treacherous front within the soul, which Satan could deceive by disguising himself as an angel of light and which, most fatally of all, could deceive itself through hypocrisy. Like Old Testamental denunciations of those who honored God with their lips while they had removed their hearts far from him and polluted their hands with blood, these arguments prepared grounds for subversion of established religious authority. Continuity of struggle and, therefore, of process was essential in the imitation of Christ.

At the highest level of abstraction, the paradigms that I have reviewed betray some common needs in their doctrines of conversion as a movement from death to life, from strife to love, from pollution to purity, from ignorance to truth, from human weakness to cosmic power and glory. But these common needs draw us back from poetic metaphors to the proposition that the experience of conversion expressed by them cannot be understood.

In distinguishing between what was called conversion, as a thing felt, and writings about conversion, as things made, and in asserting that the very idea of conversion was a metaphorical thing made by an identifiable historical process, I have simply said that the questions asked about conversion in some past era are by no means those that scholars pose in the present day. The poetics of historians now are not those of theologians in earlier times. I have addressed three conclusions of modern writers that were entirely foreign to the twelfth century. One was the hypothesis that there was a universal pattern, or morphology, of conversion—"the conversion experience."

Another was the insistence that what can be discussed is not conversion but writings about conversion. The experience, whatever it was, in all its power, duration, and immediacy is lost. We have only a text before us; we can investigate not the psychology of converts but ways of understanding with which that text was composed—the calling that made it possible to name a particular event "conversion." And these include rhetorical tricks used to define an audience, to engage its attention, and to captivate its heart.

Finally, I applied the modern critical proposition that an idea is a historical artifact that can be studied as an archaeological site, with numerous striations. From this point of view, the history of an idea's transmission is built into what the idea can mean at any moment in its career. Thus, the twelfth-century idea of conversion was by no means uniform. Rather, it was a repertory of distinctive paradigms of conversion, each bringing into twelfth-century texts its own history of transmission, vocabulary, and cognitive processes.

The idea of conversion as a long, formative process, rather than a sudden, cataclysmic change, gives some indication of why we should be attuned to ambiguities in transmission. The evidence that we have reviewed locates the consolidation of this gradualist view in the experience of the Church under Roman persecution. It discounts the peripety paradigm applied by Nock and many other learned and judicious critics. One of the ablest of literary historians, M. H. Abrams, recognized the pattern of gradual conversion. But he lodged it in the Romantic era as a dominant paradigm in the minds of German philosophers and English poets. He contrasted it with a "Christian paradigm" of "instant and absolute" change exemplified by the Apostle Paul's vocation on the road to Damascus and Augustine of Hippo's illumination in the garden at Milan. To be sure, Abrams recognized that the incandescent moment of conversion could begin long, unfolding changes in thought and behavior; but this he considered a sequel to conversion, which he called the process of redemption.[25]

Some exceptions to this clear-cut position may be apparent from what has already been said. The emphasis on conversion as cataclysmic change, "the Augustinian crisis pattern,"[26] narrows the actual repertory of kinds of conversion to one. Thus, it leaves out of account the diverse paradigms of conversion that were actually used as mutually reflective. Furthermore, it presupposes that conversion was an irreversible peripety and therefore leaves aside the whole range of systemic doubt that made fear of apostasy a great element in the concept of conversion. It also heavily discounts the ascetic ideals, already institutionalized in monasticism during Augustine's lifetime, of conversion as a long, pedagogical process lasting until death, full of pitfalls and reversals, and by no means assured of attaining its goal, no matter what its beginning. Thus, Abrams omits the history already built into the idea of conversion by Augustine's day and, in fact, expressed by him in the *Confessions*.

All this can be summed up briefly: Abrams considered the natural level of conversion (in the context of human practices and institutions), occasionally with reference to metaphysics, but he entirely omitted the supernatural dimension. He did not reckon with the substantial part of theological doctrine that defined conversion as a work of God. Thus also he omitted the ironic mode that preeminently distinguished efforts to imagine and speak of supernatural conversion in ways accessible to human nature.

How much of what is present in theological texts is lost by omitting the supernatural is readily apparent if one examines the texts in which the conversions of Paul and Augustine are described. The peripety of Greek drama, which was Abrams's interpretive analogue for conversion, produced new, if shattering, clarity. By contrast, supernatural conversion produced bewilderment and ambivalence. Paul's temptations and inner struggles continued, together with oppressive fears that even while he was preaching to others, he himself might be reprobate (1 Cor. 9:24–27).[27] Augustine's portrayal of the City of God as a *civitas permixta,* in which the elect and the reprobate coexisted until the Last Judgment, each alike uncertain until then of what the divine verdict would be, and his theology of predestination are shot through with the difficulties of determining whether any conversion, including his own, was irreversible and with the haunting dread that grace, once given, might be removed, just as inspiration was given to, and withdrawn from, prophets. Even the account given in the *Confessions* of the episode in the garden at Milan requires, to say the least, that the "crisis" paradigm be reappraised.

The episode must be taken in the theological context of the *Confessions* as a whole.[28] Augustine wrote the book as an apology, defending himself against enemies who denied the orthodoxy of his teaching and the legitimacy of his title as bishop. They argued that he had not cast off the Manichaeism of his youth and that his entry into the Church was marred by compromise with worldly institutions, as well as infractions of canon law. For tactical reasons Augustine composed a narrative portraying the drama of his slow and twisting religious quest under God's direct guidance until just after his baptism but omitted his entire career as priest and bishop. Thus, he evaded the attacks upon his official credit. His tactic was to construct a self-portrayal of errancy and redemption that buried in silence the public segments of his career, and thus the verifiable events for which his enemies condemned him. To point to the mise-en-scène of the garden as an abrupt and conclusive conversion is to fall into one rhetorical trap laid by Augustine the controversialist. It is also to discount the teachings of gradual conversion that Augustine richly and consistently developed elsewhere and, indeed, in the last four, "theological," books of the *Confessions*, which are now so seldom read as mutually illuminating with the "autobiographical" books but which Augustine himself evidently considered the crown and climax of the work. Above all, in the climactic final book, Augustine identified his own spiritual conversion as a miniature of two other great works of continuing creation, the constant turning of the cosmos toward its Maker and the progressive, historical formation of the Church.[29]

Abrams plainly saw that ways of thinking about the process of redemption enabled many themes in Renaissance and modern literature—including cosmic egress and return, education, pilgrimage, and the chivalric quest—to be assimilated to Christian allegory.[30] All these make sense in the dimension of the natural, even, or especially, when viewed through the lens of metaphysics. However, the manifold repertory of conversion paradigms and the central importance of conversion as a gradual process of testing and education induced by God from outside nature indicate a quite different conclusion: namely, that, in its supernatural dimension, conversion was indistinguishable from Christian life. Consequently, the themes in question did not arise separately, later to be cast in terms of theological allegory. Instead, with all their meanderings, perils, disguised identities, and ironies, the themes of egress and return, education, pilgrimage, and chivalric quest were from their beginnings metaphors of life as supernatural conversion and clothed themselves by birthright in its theological allegories. The metaphysical is a diminished form of this original conception. Moreover, on this diminished scale, the Romantic understanding that conversion deepened the richness of the human predicament did not stand in contrast with the paradigms of Christian theology but rather continued them, as I shall suggest with regard to Herman Melville's *Moby-Dick* and James Joyce's *A Portrait of the Artist as a Young Man*.

The eleventh and twelfth centuries had a conspicuous place in the transmission of the very paradigms that Abrams judged characteristic of the nineteenth century, and consequently in their reconstruction. In this chapter, some effects of redactive criticism on meanings given the text, "conversion," are apparent in the subtext of motifs running through all the paradigms: theodical doubt, male dominance, beauty as a norm of cognition, and virtue proved in conflict. One result was a subtle but decisive change in the portrayal of women that made conversion largely a topos of male discourse.

On balance, scholarly discourse, under the imperative of objectivity, tries to approach conversion from outside the mandorla of religious commitment. Some critical distinctions that I shall draw from earlier centuries may therefore seem unfamiliar. These include underscoring conversion as predicament rather than peripety, as supernatural in essence and natural in manifestation, and as chiefly ironic in conception. The threefold distinction—the phenomenon, the name by which it is called, and the process of naming it—is but gradually working its way into historical research. And, of course, it is double-layered since it defines what historians today are doing as well as what shaped the writings from earlier ages that they are studying. But these terms and even the double-layered transfer were integral to discourse about conversion within the spiritual traditions with which I am concerned. As commonly accepted attitudes of reverence toward the wordless experience of holiness, they were evident in the twelfth-century hymn *Jesu, dulcis memoria*, which I quoted earlier in this chapter. They were also captured illuminatingly in a memoir of John Henry Newman (1801–1890).

Critics, Wilfrid Ward wrote, had ways of discounting Newman, simply passing over "the really profound thought" that he expressed and putting together "an imaginary Newman . . . out of his more superficial gifts. It may be a graceful figure, but it is not the Newman . . . whose power transformed the lives of scores of young men at Oxford, and led hundreds who felt the magic of a genius at once spiritual and intellectual, which they could not explain, to subscribe to the formula, 'Credo in Newmannum.' "[31] Among those who felt this compelling power, long after Newman's Oxford days, was the young Gerard Manley Hopkins (then himself a Baliol student) whom Newman received into the Catholic communion in 1866. Still, Newman's "magic" and "genius" were equally hidden from unsympathetic contemporaries, both Protestant and Catholic, before and after his conversion. Those who took him to their hearts, not least through his writings, were several stages removed from his conversion, as, indeed, was the mask Newman contrived in the *Apologia*. It was very acute of Ward to use the words "magic" and "genius"; for the decisive needfulness of Newman's conversion—let alone what drew others to him—were, like magic and genius (including that required for the detection of metaphor similarities in dissimilars), beyond explanation and therefore, in some sense, beyond understanding.

Need was grounded in empathy, a mode of knowing not much cultivated by modern historians but at the center of earlier ideas about conversion.

> If then our faith we for our guide admit,
> Vain is the farther search of human wit,
> As when the building gains a surer stay,
> We take th'unuseful scaffolding away:
> Reason by sense no more can understand,
> The game is played into another hand.[32]

CHAPTER 2

Posing the Question: Perspectives from a Lector's Ambo

A Basic Tension

In the first chapter I defined conversion as an academic subject. In this chapter I want to try to recapture the thinking of people who were convinced that their lives depended upon conversion. I venture into the region between an event and the name by which it was called—the region of calling, so to speak. By this arrangement of chapters, I want to emphasize one barrier—so deceptive because so obvious—between a modern scholar's professional apparatus and the perspectives of writers in the Romanesque and Gothic ages. It is the barrier of empathy or, more exactly, faith. Thus, if we are to grasp the fundamental values and commitments of that earlier age at all, we must take seriously a dimension of ideas that sociologists, anthropologists, and historians, on balance, happily delegate to other academic disciplines.

They recognize something called conversion as a social phenomenon, an event that alters a person's behavior by bringing about changes in allegiance and submission. However, they lay no claim to the dimension of faith. In that dimension conversion is a subject of theology, rather than of any science of social organization. And yet theology and the supernatural are exactly the context with which writers of the eleventh and twelfth centuries were most preoccupied. For them conversion had effects on human nature and on the social practices and institutions to which it gave rise. Behind, and prior to, those natural symptoms they saw a supernatural cause. For believers, spiritual feelings—in the realm of empathy—were made thinkable and validated by the supernatural; and from its reality followed the crucial disparity between esthetics and poetics. I shall try to recover elements of both dimensions, acknowledging the priority of the supernatural.

What made a poetics of empathy thinkable to those writers? What fundamental needs did they address? For historians, the idea of conversion may be a study in psychology, social dynamics, the tradition of doctrine, or any of a number of other areas of analysis, depending on a scholar's particular interest and competence. For believers, the idea of conversion is, more uniformly, thinkable as a study in good and evil. The need for conversion exists because of sin. The means of conversion, or deliverance from sin, is grace. Thus, for believers the poetics of conversion hinge on God's power, in creation and redemption.

To say this is also to say that conversion is fundamentally an idea vindicating the ways of God: that is, a theodical idea. If there is a God, how can there be evil—how did sin occur in a world created and ordained by providence? If there is no God, how can there be good—how can there be any deliverance?

For believers thought about conversion oscillates between these theodical poles. Writers in the eleventh and twelfth centuries continually stressed the tribulation visited by God upon those in the process of conversion to test and prove their righteous love. But this emphasis was also an indirect way of inquiring into, and testing, the work and love of God. The results could only be uncertain. In fact, believers' entire hermeneutic project of understanding was encapsulated in the Apostle Paul's famous words: "For now we see through a glass darkly, but then face to face. Now I know in part, but then shall I know even as I am known" (1 Cor. 13:12). Paul added what came to be a crucial gloss on this verse when he wrote that believers should think "according to the measure of faith" that "God hath dealt to every man" (Rom. 12:3). Spiritual knowledge was proportionate to the capacities of the individual and to the grace bestowed upon that person by God.

Ideas about conversion as a study in the proportionality of faith plunged writers into an enterprise of learning indirectly through paradox and enigma. Truth, it was thought, was revealed in irony. Truths were considered to be cheapened, and sacred truths profaned, by being spread out in clear, plain language for all to see. The poetics of kerygmatic irony suited cultures and classes that prized knowledge hidden from all and difficult even for the few to attain and that relished tasting "the pleasure that consisteth in hard things."[1] By such poetic means writers passed through the struggle for existence from experiences of what was called conversion, things felt, to texts about conversion, things made.

Reason was considered the faculty that distinguished human beings from animals. In its proportionalities to human capacity and divine grace, faith was a mode of knowledge by no means hostile to reason. A basic assumption of the strategy of faith was that human nature—in individuals and in the great mass of humanity—contained a buried treasure. "O how great are the treasures of good works, how great the riches of pious actions, that lie hidden in the field of the human body," the Cistercian abbot Guerric of Igny (c. 1070/80–1157) wrote in the twelfth century, "and how many more in the cavern of the heart, if only one will arise and dig. . . . [For] human reason and ingenuity, with the help of grace, are the seedbed of all virtues."[2]

What that buried treasure was seemed evident to most writers. It was the image of God in which human nature had been created, an image sadly contorted and befouled by sin and brought to the precipice of death, but capable of being recovered, redeemed, and restored to life. Conversion was the struggle for existence. The survival strategy of faith made it imperative to convert: that is, to recover the treasure, to rehabilitate the divine image latent in the human soul, and to make it productive. The metaphor of the treasure put to use had a counterpart in that other metaphor of fecundity, the seed scattered in good ground, bearing fruit thirty, sixty, and a hundredfold. As Guerric's master, Bernard of Clairvaux, preached: "From Christ's words [Matt. 11:14], we plainly recognize that for us there is no true life except in conversion and no other entrance opening into life, as the Lord likewise says: 'Unless you are converted and become as little children, you shall not enter the Kingdom of Heaven.'"[3] There was an ironic tension between the imperative of conversion and the blindness of the unconverted, not to mention the partial blindness of those still being converted, still seeing through a glass darkly, still walking by faith and not by sight. In the light of this irony between the imperative of conversion and its indeterminacy, how could the command to be converted and to seek the conversion of others be understood?

Remotely, understanding conversion was an extension of the ancient philosophical venture summed up in the command "Know thyself."[4] Although they thought these words were carved on the temple (or pillar) of the god Apollo at Delphi, twelfth-century writers also eclectically followed the pagan satirist Juvenal and Origen, the founder of Christian theology, in teaching that the command duplicated Scripture and, indeed, that it had come down from heaven. Christian doctrine held that the soul knew itself by knowing God, its true origin and exemplar and, vice versa, knew God by knowing itself. However, the soul was a great abyss, hidden even to its own eyes, and God, too, was unknowable, hidden in inaccessible light. Writers characterized the dialogue between the soul and God by quoting the verse "deep calleth unto deep" (Ps. 42:7). For unaided human powers, the command "Know thyself" was as impossible to fulfill as that other command to be perfect, even as the Father in heaven. As to conversion, God, like any human artist, kept the secrets of his creativity to himself. Doing art and talking about art were two different things. The major actors and even the action in the drama of what was called conversion were obscure. Thus, the task for poetics between the event and the name—the poetic process that made it possible to call the event of empathy conversion—was large.

Contours of the Poetics of Conversion

I have said that faith was a strategy followed in the struggle for existence and that it hinged on empathy. Christian writers adamantly taught that this strategy was inaccessible outside the Church—"outside the Church there is no salvation"—even as they acknowledged that it could be, at best, imperfectly understood and, at worst, hypocritically parodied or heretically distorted even among professed Christians. What reasoning lay behind their assumptions about the distinctiveness of conversion? Need, the primal call for empathy, was their point of departure in this poetic task; Scripture gave them templates; the disequilibrium between empathy and poetics warranted their deliberate fictions.

According to their teachings the need for life, primal in the doctrine of conversion, gained compelling power from the need for love. Love, indeed, distinguished the faith that saved from other kinds of belief. It is one thing to believe that God is. This is the faith of knowledge (*fides cognitionis*). It is another to believe God. This is the faith of common meaning (*fides consensus*). It requires yet a third kind of belief to trust in God. This is the faith of assurance (*fides fiduciae*). But any of these can exist without the saving belief in God, which is to move toward and into God through love. Writers were careful to restrict the term *believe in* to God. To "believe in" a human being would be to commit idolatry, rendering to a creature what was due to the Creator.[5] Even the Devil and his minions believe that God is and credit his word; and nominal Christians may, in their hateful errors, mistakenly trust in God. But among them faith is an unformed quality. For only charity, which is God himself, gives belief the form of virtue; only charity in and through faith, and grace in charity, and God through grace justify sinners and enable them "to believe, as it were, into God, entering into him by faith" and love.[6] It is easy to see in these distinctions the other categories: *fides quod* (propositions that are believed), *fides propter quam* (belief that, as a kind of knowledge, warrants action), and *fides qua* (faith by which spiritual transformation is brought about).

Apart from the need for love, the need for life encompassed another great privation: that of truth. The need for truth was urgent. But the entire structure of thought was pervaded by insistence that just as human words did not produce conversion, life-giving faith could not be of human origin. "It is well written in the Prophet Habakkuk: 'The just lives by faith (*ex fide*)' (Habakkuk 2:4). For that faith makes us understand, not only how to believe well, but also how to live well since it is not from us, but from God for us." This, too, was the loving faith that directed the great transitions in sacred history, as the righteousness of God was revealed from faith into faith (*ex fide in fidem*), from the faith veiled in the Old Testament to that revealed in the New, from the faith expressed here in signs and images to the faith accomplished hereafter in the presence of divine reality.[7]

Before this truth could be attained, therefore, a fourth great need had to be addressed: that of purity. For the leprosy of sin passed congenitally from each generation to the next was not only its own death sentence and the cause of hatred but also an insuperable barrier to truth. So long as the body and sensory things were loved, the mind was darkened to spiritual truth. It was necessary that the dross of carnal affections be purged by the refiner's fire, that the soul be cleansed of carnal leprosy, that the heart partake of divine purity before that Truth could be known which was also life and love. Purification could never be complete but only proportional.

There was yet one final need. For life, love, purity, and truth as idealized in these doctrines were studies in ironic proportions. Life was a daily crucifixion, crowned by sacrificial death; God's healing love was harsh, chastening the elect and testing them in the blazing crucible of affliction; purity was relentlessly subject to doubt and shame, measured as it was against the human innocence and divine perfection of Christ; knowledge of truth was always tinged with ignorance. There was, then, a final need for authentication. Given the kerygmatic ironies of proportion built into the ideals of conversion, authentication was sought in such paradoxical symbols as the glorified cross and the martyr's palm.

To be sure, these emblems of shame and defeat, of death swallowed up in victory, betrayed a common human need for power and glory, acknowledged also in the messianic promises of the Old Testament as rewards from God to his faithful people. Twelfth-century writers rebuked Jews for thinking that these promises would be redeemed with material riches, status, and magnificence in this world. Yet they themselves imagined the eternal Jerusalem, where the messianic promises would be spiritually fulfilled, in analogues of indescribable imperial splendor. And they anticipated how their dearest hopes would be fulfilled by creating their monasteries, churches, and liturgies as images of that heavenly court. They lavished upon them the rarest and most costly treasures, worked with exquisite craftsmanship.

Earthly beauty, astonishing in its noble splendor, was one testimony to the power and glory that verified the ideals of conversion. Ennoblement was, above all, a structure of proportions, with greater and lesser degrees. And like the other ideals it was overcast with ironies—first by the ironies of art, which made things appear to be what they were not, and then by the fragility of physical objects. Edifices and treasuries intended as witnesses to abiding greatness sometimes perished quickly, not infrequently at the hands of patrons with more grandiose—or, at least, more up-to-date—dreams than their predecessors or at those of pillagers. The grandeur and perishability of art gave an ambivalent witness corresponding with the ambivalence felt by those who thought that they discerned the glory that was laid up for them, but through a glass darkly.

It is easy to see the beginnings of empathetic conversion in a sense, perhaps a terror, that one's established behavior was destructive of life itself because it nurtured hatred instead of love, ignorance instead of knowledge, guilt instead of innocence, and impotence instead of power. By their very natures the great needs were evidence of the doubts, discontents, and fears that stirred the heart to conversion and, indeed, that made conversion a theodical quest, a quest to vindicate the ways of God, as well as to escape the neediness of the human condition. But escape could never be absolute until the proportionalities of faith and thus also the indeterminacy of conversion were surpassed.

A distinctive feature of these ambivalences was that they employed methods of doubt—provided by ancient philosophers and refined by Christian theologians—to respond to doubt. This was no simple matter of framing an answer to a finite question. Rather, it was one of continual doubt and questioning, in which each destination reached was a new point of departure. Continual doubt was the wellspring of continual conversion.

The poetics of empathy began in faith responding to need. Its critical methods came from many quarters. It was not hard to define conversion. Caesarius of Heisterbach (c. 1170–c. 1240) provided a definition with which no one in his age could disagree. Drawing on well-known early monastic texts, he wrote that conversion was a turning of the heart from bad to good (in contrition), from good to better (in devotion), and from better to best (in contemplation), rising from sinfulness and passing beyond itself to the vision of God.[8] The essential propositions were that conversion was a change of heart, not of mind, and that the turning of the heart was not to Christianity or to the Church but to Christ.[9]

As I have shown, however, there was considerable difficulty in speaking of what was called conversion except in metaphors. It is fundamentally important to recognize that in the eleventh and twelfth centuries, theologians acknowledged that faith had, and could only have, a poetic (or fictive) character (see chapter 5). What poetics made the *Fragestellung* of conversion thinkable? Let me identify some areas of formal thought that were brought into play; for, like most poetics, that of empathy began with propositions about human existence beyond those that explained basic needs.

In constructing their great, deliberate fiction, the idea of conversion, writers turned to their chosen antecedents in the Old Testament. For this reason, the Christian idea of conversion was the Christian idea of history by another name. The entire human race was thought to derive from one act—God's creation— and from the body of one man, Adam. As a whole, it moved toward one destination, consummated at the Last Judgment. Each individual had a role to play in the drama of the world's redemption; the conversion of each person advanced that of the world.

Its historical character set the Christian doctrine of conversion entirely apart from Greek and Roman doctrines and established a major link with the Jewish antecedents of Christianity. But that character was made up of highly dissimilar elements. It can be summarized in a few sentences. First, individual conversion was an organic part of the experience of the entire human race. Both individual and universal experience unfolded continuously through one person's lifetime or through the changing circumstances of all centuries. Further, the sequences of events were not just one thing after another; they made up a history. But the pattern that distinguished history from an unassorted aggregate of events became apparent to human eyes by hindsight. Like the pattern in a woven fabric, it became increasingly obvious as the work advanced toward completion—in this case, as human events moved toward their apocalyptic climax, the end of all time and history, when the whole pattern would be accomplished and all meaning made plain. The drama of history involved bitter, unrelenting conflict. A master of deceit, the ancient enemy, Satan, could intrude illusions of holiness even into pious minds. He could produce counterfeit conversions. Consequently, after conversion began and before it was consummated came an interim, a time of testing and uncertainty, of mingled hope and fear. Finally, the roles assigned to individual persons in the cosmic history of conversion varied according to positions assigned to specific classes of people (e.g., women, men, Jews, pagans) in the great warfare against the world for the conversion of the world.

To say that the Christian idea of conversion was identical with that of history is to conjure up the picture of a wheel. Various spokes converge at the hub of understanding. One spoke is insistence on the uniqueness of each life, and each experience, as a historical phenomenon defined by its own circumstances. Another spoke is the doctrine of sacred history, transcending the limits of time and space, drawing the redeemed into a community that was quasi-historical, both in and not of the world. Furthermore, a third spoke is sacramental and, therefore, antihistorical. Summed up in the phrase "communion [not community] of saints," this doctrine taught the mystic union of all with God in Christ, transformed into blessedness, one life, one love, one fruition. The center of the drama on the sacramental level was not human agents but "Christ in us, moving toward the Father."[10]

My concern is with the hub of the wheel: understanding. How did the identity between the fictions of conversion and history come about? The answer is that they were a variation on the theme of transformation. They rested on the conviction that right knowledge transforms the knower for good. The other side of this proposition, of course, is that ignorance, or partial or wrong knowledge, transformed the knower in harmful ways. Enshrined in the biblical account of the Garden of Eden and in New Testament parables, this doctrine of transformation unified more than ideas about conversion and history.

It cast its shadow even across those traditionally hostile areas, poetry and philosophy. For, insofar as transformative knowing concerned the good, it encompassed branches of moral thought. Insofar as it concerned the true, it included those devoted to the methods, limits, and possibilities of rational discourse. Insofar as it concerned the beautiful, it pertained to all abstract thought about esthetics, as well as to the practice and enjoyment of all the arts.

Consequently, the combination of incompatibles—historical, quasi-historical, and antihistorical elements—in the idea of conversion leads me to a yet more fundamental subject, lodged in the hidden caverns of the human mind. For psychology is another spoke in the wheel. Christian poetics, like others, encompassed ideas about the workings of the mind.

A complete sifting of the subject "understanding conversion" would begin with how people thought about the mind itself, specifically about how we transform the messy disorder of experience into usable knowledge. It would go on to the next step: how knowledge is communicated from one person to another.

I have considered these matters as they appear in Augustine's account of his conversion;[11] they will not figure prominently in this chapter. But, to round out the general *Fragestellung* of conversion, I may say that in general the faculties of mind were thought to be the bodily senses, memory, reason, and will (often, also, desires) and that all were regarded as fallible. Likewise, doctrines about signs explored different areas of interpretation—the relation of signs to things, the relations of signs to knowledge, and the communication of what was known from person to person—and also concluded with a question mark: the indeterminacy of signification. Thus, the general conception of mind and signs produced two important axioms: regarding mind, that misunderstanding is in the essence of understanding; and, regarding signs, that interpretation falsifies. All knowledge—and not only the mode known as faith—was proportional.

The poetics of conversion were built on these foundation stones of psychology, as well as on the incompatibles of historical theory. Hugh of St. Victor stated the interpretive problem. Christ came invisible, hidden, incomprehensible. He came to touch the soul, not to be comprehended by it. He came, Hugh continued, not to fulfill any person's desire, but to draw the heart to himself. And, so that the faithful would advance and the unbelievers fall, never attaining Truth with their depraved understanding, he spoke hiddenly, in parables and enigmas.[12] Embedded in Hugh's comments there is a third hermeneutic principle that needs to be added to the two already identified. For not only was misunderstanding in the essence of understanding, not only did interpretation falsify, but belief entailed unbelief.

Thus far, I have moved by stages from faith to needs that called for faith, and from those needs to areas of formal knowledge that were brought into play to explain faith. But the ultimate authority on the poetics of empathy for writers in the eleventh and twelfth centuries was not any venture recognized as a branch of human knowledge. It was the Word of God.

The conflict-ridden doctrine of proportionality that I have outlined had the sanction of Scripture, most concisely in the parable of the sower. Some of the sower's seeds fell by the wayside, and the birds of the air devoured them: that is, Satan snatched the word from their hearts. Others fell on stony places; these sprang up quickly, but, being rooted in thin soil, they were quickly scorched by the heat of day. These were they who, having no depth of faith in themselves, failed under tribulation and persecution. Still other seed, falling among brambles, represented believers whose faith was choked off by worldly cares, riches, and the lusts and pleasures of this life. There remained, at last, the seed that fell on good ground and that, in its fecundity, brought forth thirty, sixty, or a hundredfold (Matt. 13:3–23; Mark 4:3–25; Luke 8:5–18). "He that hath ears, let him hear," say all the versions. "Take heed what ye hear," Jesus says to the disciples, according to Mark (4:24). "Take heed how ye hear," according to Luke (8:18). Hugh of St. Victor's harsh words about unbelievers echoed those of the parable. For, to those outside the circle of the called, Jesus spoke in parables so that Isaiah's prophecy would be fulfilled: they would see and not perceive, hear and not understand. He spoke to them in parables so that they would not be converted, so that God would not heal them (Matt. 13:10–15).

Thus, the parable of the sower set forth a template for the poetics of empathy. It elaborates the idea that conversions began tenuously; they progressed in the face of deceit, temptation, and suffering. If all went well, they were perfected; they were preserved, and, as a sign of their authenticity, they brought forth much fruit in patience. But they might fail at any of these stages. It was not by accident that the reward of fecundity in the parable was the same promised to Abraham for abiding in fidelity to the Covenant (Gen. 15:4–5). For, in his lifelong faithfulness, Abraham was thought to foreshadow the New Covenant; Christ "took on him the seed of Abraham" (Heb. 2:16). Understanding distinguished the sterile from the fruitful.

But, plainly, understanding of the prophetic word was not linguistic and, therefore, not equivalent with interpretation or explanation. In telling the disciples what the parable of the sower meant, Jesus said (according to Matthew), "It is given unto you to know the mysteries of the kingdom of heaven, but to them [the multitude on the shore] it is not given" (Matt. 13:11). Spiritual discernment came by grace.[13] In the words of a seventeenth-century writer: "You that would get faith first must feel your inability to believe; and fetch not this slip out of thine own garden. It must come down from Heaven to thy soul, if ever thou partakest thereof." The parable of the wise and foolish virgins was a lesson in how the apparently called could misread their own conversions.[14]

The New Testament provides many illustrations of the repertory diagramed in the parable of the sower. The chapter of Matthew's Gospel that begins with the parable of the sower ends with Jesus' failure to perform miracles in his own country because of his neighbors' unbelief (Matt. 13:53–58). "He marvelled," Mark added, "because of their unbelief" (Mark 6:6). Paul failed to win his audience on the Areopagus. There were false conversions (such as that of Simon Magus), abortive conversions (such as that of King Agrippa), secret conversions (such as those of the Jewish rulers who, fearful of being cast out of the synagogue, did not confess their faith), abandoned conversions (such as those of the disciples who "went back and walked no more with him," leaving Jesus with the twelve), and Judas's apostasy. Peter's waverings and penitence illustrated the parable's lesson that conversion was a movement toward perfection through trial and error, sustained, if at all, by grace. "Satan hath desired to have you," Jesus said to Peter, the Apostle whom he had already called and to whom he committed the keys to the Kingdom of Heaven, "that he may sift you as wheat. But I have prayed for thee, that thy faith fail not; and when thou art converted, strengthen thy brethren" (Luke 22:31–32).

Germination, growth, and fecundity are not metaphors of sudden change. With its emphasis on ascetic denial through resistance to worldly cares, deceitful riches, and enticing lusts and with its assertion that spiritual discernment came by grace, the parable of the sower points toward the crucial fact that the fecundity that crowned conversion required, not self-fulfillment, but self-emptying, not a single, incandescent moment of recognition, but slow habits. For dependence on God for the renewal of life demanded humility, sacrifice, and poverty of spirit, "a clear understanding," as Teresa of Avila (1515–1582) put it, "of our worthlessness."[15] For Christian interpreters of Scripture, the prodigal son, like the Magdalene, epitomized the self-emptying of conversion in his "sorrowful journey, tearful repentance, and glorious reception." With abject humility he realized that all his merits were worth no more than the menstrual rag that a woman casts away. By the grace of charity he was incorporated through stages into the body of Christ.[16]

Paul's encounter on the road to Damascus is often invoked as the paradigm of instant conversion. Still, whatever happened in that encounter, Paul realized the consequences of his vocation slowly, not only in the days immediately following it, but also in the fourteen years that he spent in Arabia before he undertook his apostolate and in the tentative beginnings that eventually directed him to the Gentiles. To be sure, he declared that a crown of righteousness was laid up for him (2 Tim. 4:6–8); but these words came when the time of his departure was at hand, when he could look back upon the race that he had finished and the fight that he had won. Earlier, torn by the war with the law of sin in his members (Rom. 7:23), he trained for race and fight: "I do not run aimlessly; I do not box as one beating the air; but I pommel my body and subdue it, lest after preaching to others I myself should be disqualified" (1 Cor. 9:24–27). "Let him who thinks that he stands, take heed lest he fall" (1 Cor. 10:12). The revelation on the road to Damascus was decisive but by no means conclusive. The crown of martyrdom rewarded Paul's endurance, as it did Peter's contrition. As in the parable of the sower, it took time to know whether the seed had fallen into good ground and would bring forth fruit.

Paul's doctrine of conversion from death to life bears the same marks of proportionality that I have identified in the parable of the sower: conversion as a work in progress, subject to many temptations and trials, demanding self-emptying, and promising fecundity. That fecundity was both individual and corporate, for each individual conversion enlarged the body of Christ, each advanced the apocalyptic coming of God's kingdom. At any rate, to return to the paradoxical subject of understanding as misunderstanding, it is enough to remember what different strategies of faith Paul's conversion brought into play for Paul himself, for his companions on the journey to Damascus, for Ananias, for the Jews who sought to kill him, for King Agrippa whom he almost persuaded to believe, and for the devout Athenians who ridiculed him.

The parable of the sower consists of two parts: a fable and the interpretation, the moral, of the tale. It is a self-contained story with a narrative and expository completeness that the anecdotes of actual conversions in the New Testament lack. The latter are, at best, recollections, traces of events. We know nothing about the preconversion and postconversion careers of Mary Magdalene, Nicodemus, the centurion on Calvary, Lydia, or the Ethiopian eunuch. Did the jailer who freed Peter and Silas and submitted to baptism with all his household stand fast in his new faith, despite the consequences? The selective and anecdotal character of conversion accounts in the New Testament and the conformity of those accounts with the template of faith and unbelief set forth in the parable of the sower underscore the fact that the parable and the accounts alike are works of the poetic imagination, that by their sketchy outlines they invite the imaginations of readers to complete the picture. Had not Christ himself implied as much when he said that he spoke in parables to disclose his doctrines to the chosen and to conceal them from the reprobate and, to be sure, when he also spoke in metaphors?

Acknowledgment of the Fiction

Writers were entirely conscious not only that their work was proportionately fictional but that it was necessarily fictional, for the mind, bound to its own nature, had to use the thoughts and words available through nature to speak about supernatural things. There was an inescapable disequilibrium between empathy and poetics. The fact that theologians and poets alike worked with figural language, using *integumenta* to conceal and disclose mysteries, established a point at which their endeavors coincided. The poetic aspect of theology was inescapably in the main learned enterprise of twelfth-century culture: scriptural interpretation. What can be said about how theologians addressed the hermeneutic problems in Scripture can be applied also to their understanding of the difference between the supernatural experience of conversion, a thing felt, and writings about conversion, as things made. And it leads directly to their notions about the point at which the two intersected: that is, where empathy was reduced to form by poetics.

Very early in Christian history, the conviction took root that the supernatural revelation in Scripture was something other than what the words accessible to human nature said. The Apostle Paul himself elucidated his meaning with allegory (Gal. 4:22–31), and scholars after him eagerly invented multiple levels of figural interpretation, each with its rules and objectives. There were other, more blatant, ways to expand the text of Scripture. An extensive library of apocrypha was composed in the early Church to develop the biographies of great apostolic figures. The deeds of Thaddeus, Thomas, and Andrew were composed. So too were the acts of the Apostle Paul and Thecla, his friend. A philosophically minded believer supplied a correspondence between Paul and Seneca. A number of texts describing the later career of Pontius Pilate and letters purportedly by him were composed. Some texts reported that Pilate and his wife converted to Christianity, and even that Pilate was beheaded in the Neronian persecution. On their evidence Pilate came to be revered as a saint in the Abyssinian Church, and his wife, called Claudia Procula, in the Greek. Other stories, however, portrayed the former procurator hounded by divine justice to Gaul, where he committed suicide. Likewise, early writers created a sensational conversion, a name, and various biographies for the centurion who pierced Christ's side. That man, for whom the name Longinus was invented, was reported to have been converted, to have become an evangelist, and, finally, to have been martyred and buried in Mantua, where, indeed, his relics are still venerated in the Church of San Andrea.

The twelfth century, "the golden age of medieval forgery,"[17] continued this tradition. Letters from heaven, from the Virgin Mary, and from Satan were produced.[18] Taking up earlier legends, writers continually embroidered upon the stories of Longinus, preparing materials later taken up in legends of the Holy Grail. Engaged in a vast and magnificent project of rebuilding, the monks of Glastonbury magnified the glory of their house by enlarging the Passion narrative in another way: they discovered that the monastery had been founded by Joseph of Arimathea as a center for the conversion of Britain. In a bid for royal subvention, they also found (or, in the technical term, "invented") the bones of Joseph's descendant, King Arthur, which they solemnly translated from their burial ground to a marble tomb within the church. The literature of conversion and expansion of the Passion history also advanced with additions to scriptural accounts of the holy family of Bethany. Lazarus, Martha, and Mary (now identified as Mary Magdalene) had, under persecution, been put to sea with others in a rudderless boat. They landed in Marseilles and became the apostles of Provence. Lazarus became bishop of Marseilles, where he was martyred and buried. Mary Magdalene spent her last thirty years as a hermit in an Alpine cave, from which angels carried her in her deathwatch to St. Maximin at Aix-en-Provence for the final sacrament and burial. Mary Magdalene's betrothal to St. John the Evangelist had been broken when Christ called him to the apostolate, and to console her Christ had called Mary to a life of penance. Christ himself had also blessed St. Maximin, a companion of the Bethanites on the voyage to Gaul. For he was the man blind from birth, the restoration of whose sight and whose conversion to Christ St. John the Evangelist recorded (John 9:1–38).

The accounts about the Bethanites were invented and elaborated to promote cults of Lazarus (at Autun) and Mary Magdalene (at Vézelay) established in the twelfth century. Like the legends of the conversion of Pontius Pilate and Longinus, and indeed the migration of Joseph of Arimathea to Britain, these stories exemplify the rule that hagiography is a vast literary genre with conversion as its one great theme. They also point to a christological center of piety and cult, the Passion, that made it possible for writers to conclude that events in Scripture or in life were figurative only insofar as they referred to Christ (see chap. 3, n. 7). This figurative, literary cast prevails whether conversion is from other religions to Christianity, from sinfulness to piety, or from secular to monastic life. Apart from illustrating how, by delicate fictions, twelfth-century writers continued the age-old tradition of apocrypha, these hagiographical texts also point toward an even wider means of understanding conversion: that is, by expanding Scripture through writings about holy people. Considered the only infallible rule of holy living, the Bible was a great quarry for writers of saints' lives, acts, miracles, and passions. To demonstrate the holiness of a person, writers had to establish that the putative saint's life conformed in exact and literal detail to the rule of Scripture. A saint's deeds made visible how the precepts of Scripture could be applied in actual life. Consequently, whole sections of some texts are pastiches of quotations from various canonical books of Scripture.

In practical terms, this means that writings about saints were made up of stereotypes drawn from Scripture and that the actual details of a person's life were of little importance. What counted, above all, was that sanctity be verified by conforming to the stereotype. It followed that portions of one saint's biography could be interchangeable with some in another's, since all mirrored the same pattern. In fact, writers did occasionally copy out whole sections of other texts into their own.[19] This practice, condemned as plagiarism in epochs of historical criticism, merely underscores the conviction that the lives of saints and the ideals of conversion that they exemplified were actually glosses on or expansions of the Bible. The thoughts and words of saints brought the mind of Scripture from the realm of the potential into that of the actual.

The reading of Scripture and that of hagiographic writers were cognate enterprises; they were mutually reflective. Both were characterized by indifference to historical details and a zeal for apprehending the meanings hidden beneath the letter of the text. The fabrication of relics and other examples of the forger's art expressed the same impulse to elaborate the poetic fiction of conversion. "Probably," as one scholar has written, "no other area of medieval life was so richly supplied with fictions, deceptions, blatant fraud, and forgeries as that of 'piety'—but also, in no other area did contemporaries thunder against fraud and forgery so powerfully as in this one."[20] Methods were developed for distinguishing forged from genuine legal documents and fraudulent from authentic relics. Yet, while some used these versions of critical doubt to defend the faith from doubt, poetic needs inspired others, even the conspicuously holy. The cult of St. Ursula and her ten thousand maidens rested on visions concocted by St. Elizabeth of Schönau and her brother, Abbot Ekbert.[21]

Something far deeper than indifference to historical details was at work in this task of fictionalizing to reveal and actualize truth, something inherent in the history of conversion itself. A comparable point of reference exists in a much earlier work, one written on a scale far grander than most hagiographical texts and, indeed, a work universally esteemed for its historical acumen and veracity: the Venerable Bede's (c.672–735) account of the conversion of the English people.

Bede's account memorializes the fictional—the poetics—in empathetic conversion. This is manifestly the case in the criteria by which Bede selected, omitted, and deployed his materials, in the malevolence with which he portrayed the beliefs and achievements of Celtic Christians, and in his association of pagans with demonic spirits. Bede's narratives of conversion in the *Ecclesiastical History* and the patterns of understanding that form their invisible framework were, in general and in detail, works of "sophisticated confection."[22] The event of conversion itself was for him a work of poetic fiction: that is, of assimilating the supernatural to the natural, in words.

In this regard Bede expressed a feature essential to the poetics of empathy as a social phenomenon, one testified to in the Book of Acts and by early apologists—the need to give the supernatural revelations in Scripture a place in human nature and in the customs, institutions, and practices that arose from nature. Doctrines were set in a wider social matrix, an environment in which theologians lived, moved, and had their being and to which, since they took it for granted, they gave no notice. Converts built their new religious commitments around earlier patterns of understanding, for they were converted not to an abstract, Platonic form of belief but to what, as members of particular societies and heirs of particular cultures, they thought Christ was. To this day there is a question whether Christianity subdued ancient Hellenism or was appropriated by it. Since their perceptions were built on the collective wisdom that they knew before conversion, conversion paradoxically had a conservative side. In the midst of radical change—in fact, as a condition of transformation—putting the rules of Scripture into effect in daily life entailed a reassertion of the old normalcy. By the patristic age, the poetic or syncretist tactic of transformation that posited a return to normalcy (but not to the old life) had introduced many elements into popular religious practices, liturgical order, and theology that, some considered, had paganized Christianity.

Syncretism—accommodation of the supernatural to human nature—remained a deliberate tactic of reducing empathy to form. It was codified in a letter from Pope Gregory I (c.540–604, reigned 590–604) which Bede incorporated in his *History*. Writing to the abbot Mellitus, Gregory maintained that a successful missionary among the English should not destroy their pagan temples. Certainly, the idols should be destroyed; but the temples themselves should be kept, purified with holy water from infestations of demons, and consecrated to God with the erection of altars and the installation of relics. The feast days of the old cult, too, should be kept, although rededicated to saints and martyrs; and converts could continue to kill oxen at the exorcised holy places and on the familiar days, as long as they realized that they were no longer sacrificing them to the Devil. For, the pope concluded, God himself had achieved the conversion of the Israelites by gradualism of this sort. To be sure, the Roman see knew something about religious variegation itself. A predecessor of Pope Gregory the Great, Leo I (reigned 440–61), complained that curious solar rituals were being performed on the steps of St. Peter's Basilica "partly from the vice of ignorance, partly from the spirit of paganism." And three centuries later Boniface (680–754), the Apostle of the Germans, wrote with evident annoyance that while he was trying to win over ever more heathen and to stamp out the pagan practices that his flock nourished under the thin veneer of their Christianity, they pointed to the pagan riots with which the Romans celebrated the dawn of each new year at St. Peter's and the common use of amulets and charms. The allegation that the Roman clergy allowed such things, he said, embarrassed and frustrated his work. Boniface cannot have been reassured to hear from Pope Zacharias that he and his immediate predecessor had repudiated and condemned them in vain.[23]

In one of his most celebrated vignettes, Bede recounted how a pagan priest, Coifi, decided to convert. Coifi was dissatisfied with the religion over which he presided because, although none had been more zealous than he in serving the gods, many had received greater honors and succeeded more abundantly than he. After an evidently brief but convincing discourse by Bishop Paulinus of York, Coifi determined that Christian doctrine provided more satisfactory knowledge of the origins and goals of life than his cult; in the presence of his people, he immediately desecrated and burned the altars that he himself had dedicated. His people, Bede noted, thought that he had gone mad, and it is unlikely that he or they quickly laid aside the "superstition of emptiness" that until then had constituted their ethnic and personal identities.[24]

King Raedwal of Kent was unusual in erecting adjacent altars, one to Christ on which the Eucharist was offered and the other to the pagan gods on which victims were sacrificed, Bede said, to devils. (In the twelfth century Pomeranians similarly attempted to establish ritual parity between their own deities and the god of the intrusive Germans.)[25] But Bede's accounts of pagan survivals and apostasies in general testify to the consciously fictive character of conversion.[26] This character persists throughout the literature of missions, not least in the career of King Olav I Tryggvessön of Norway, who in the exuberance of his faith, presented a band of chieftains the dilemma of converting to Christianity or being sacrificed to their ancestral gods.[27] Two centuries after the conversion of Scandinavia, Snorre Sturlason mingled pagan with Christian beliefs, happily unaware of any conflict between them.[28] At any rate, exchanges of religious beliefs and practices were natural at a time when Christians and pagans were not only commercial partners but also military allies against common enemies.[29]

The fact of these social variables sometimes has been hard to reconcile with the categorical assertion that true faith was universal—that it was professed always, everywhere, and by all acknowledged teachers. In recent years a band of wizards, bedecked with crosses and golden rings and bearing books purporting to demonstrate the compatibility of occult sciences with Christianity, were barred from a papal audience at Rome.[30] The persistence of polygamy, witchcraft, and ancestor worship among Christians in Africa and the human sacrifice lately attributed to the minister of defense in Liberia, known as a devout Christian,[31] also prepare us to accept the mixing of Christian doctrine with the true or imputed practice of magic and witchcraft by Christians in the age with which I am concerned. The mother of a holy woman sought out old woman, a Jewess whose powers were greater than all the rest, to break her daughter's pious resolves with charms and incantations. An archbishop, charged as a magician, took auspices before setting out on journeys, had special psalms changed against his enemies, and kept "pseudoprophets" in his entourage to encourage him with their prognostications.[32] Some, familar with Church history, recognized that the conversion's paradoxical call to return to normalcy within a new life had brought pagan practices into Christian liturgy even in the Age of the Fathers.[33]

In the centuries after the New Testament era, supernatural conversion became a paradigm not only for change of personal empathy but for the entire course of history. Made permanent by institutionalization, the conversion of the world was also considered to be subject to the same trials and reversals as were individual conversions. Like them, the conversion of the world was a complex poetic fiction of mind and heart, capable of as many varieties of assimilation even among professed Christians as was the dissemination of the word in the parable of the sower. Social context did not provide a uniform base of understanding, an intellectual common denominator. Coifi's conversion was quite a different event for Coifi, for Bishop Paulinus, for the people who thought their priest had become insane, and, to be sure, for Bede, who shaped materials at hand to suit his narrative purpose.

It was clear, and basic to the fictional character of belief, that truths conveyed under the veil of fiction were not accessible to all or with equal force at every time, even to the faithful. A deep and ancient reasoning lay behind this basic assumption, one, indeed, that Tertullian (c. 155–c. 222) captured in his famous sentence, "It is certain because it is impossible."[34] The necessarily fictional character of theology, including ideas about conversion, emphasized that grace alone enabled belief in the first place, to each person according to the proportion of faith bestowed, and afterwards persistence in the faith despite variations among believers, trials, and tribulations. Acknowledgment of the poetics of empathetic conversion derived from and reenforced the doctrine that conversion was entirely dependent on grace: that, in some way, this fiction, too, could only be a work of God.

Writers of the twelfth century recognized that their work was necessarily and proportionately fictional because of the attempt to put supernatural wine in natural bottles. As a consequence, they also believed that whatever power existed in their fictions did not come from themselves but from the measure of faith bestowed upon each by grace. Misunderstanding was incorporated in understanding; and unbelief, in faith. However, some texts appear to glory in certitude and in the power of the individual will to decide its own spiritual commitment. "Who will separate us from the love of God?" Saint Paul asked, with anticipations of martyrdom (Rom 8:35). "No one except himself could separate the Apostle from Christ," Hugh of St. Victor answered. "For, had he wished, he could have denied Christ before Nero instead of confessing him and thereby accomplished himself what neither life nor death could have done."[35] But how could those whose minds had not been impregnated with divine love be won from their depraved and animal understanding to true belief?

The quandry is aggressively set in the tirade of Peter the Venerable (c. 1094– 1156), abbot of Cluny, against the Jews. Etching each line with acid irony, Peter rebuked the Jews for their spiritual blindness. "Take the scandal of stupidity from your heart, O Jew," he wrote. "How long, O Jews, will this bovine understanding dwell in your hearts before you are able, by some effort . . . , to convert to truth?" Tied to the literal interpretation of Scripture, their willful hardness of heart made them blind, deaf, insane. Lacking human reason, were they human beings?[36] Yet Peter also acknowledged that there could be no conversion without grace. No appeal to or exercise of authority, no relaxing pleasure or coercive power, no argument from reason, nor even great miracles could win the heart to faith in Christ.[37]

In worldly love, Chaucer (c. 1340/45–1400) later wrote, "som folk wol ben wonnen for richesse, / And som for strokes, and som for gentillesse."[38] Bribery, coercion, and cajolery were often used in conversion efforts. But Peter the Venerable, and the tradition within which he worked, acknowledged that these devices could not produce authentic change of heart. Theologians recognized that the *Fragestellung* of conversion was unthinkable—that it made no sense—to unbelievers.

What purpose then did Peter the Venerable's bitter diatribe against Jews serve, not to mention his tracts against Muslims and heretics? Why did Bishop Otto of Bamberg (1060/62–1139, reigned 1102–39) pack his bags with luxuries in order to capture for Christ the carnal affections of the unbelieving Pomeranians? Why the Crusades?

Evidently, these efforts did not form parts of a single, well-coordinated program. Rather, they were individual efforts, frequently taken (as in the writing of a treatise or the commencement of a missionary journey) on the initiative of one person. Thus, the motives behind them are to be sought in the aspirations of the instigators. Peter the Venerable did not preach to the deaf with any expectation of being heard. Otto of Bamberg did not distribute his treasures and administer mass baptisms with any illusions of permanence. The Crusades were not proclaimed as instruments of empathetic conversion but rather of vengeance upon the Lord's enemies; and, indeed, in lands that they subjected to Christian government—in the Spanish kingdoms, Sicily, the Holy Land, and, in the thirteenth century, Prussia—the new rulers refused to allow the conversion of their infidel subjects. As unbelievers, they could be held in bondage; as Christians, they would have been freed.

In ninth-century Gaul free Jews had invoked an analogous regulation. They secured an imperial decree forbidding the baptism of a Jewish serf without the master's consent, hitting on this means in order to defend against forced baptism Jews who were most helpless against it. Quite different motives prevailed among Christians two centuries later. As he passed among the Saracen troops of Count Roger of Sicily, Archbishop Anselm of Canterbury (c. 1033–

1109) won the hearts of many by gifts of food and other kindnesses. They went down on their knees in veneration before him (so we are told) and would have accepted Christianity if, under cruel penalties, the count had not forbidden them to become Christian. It is striking that the Cistercian order was among the first great landholders in Spain to refuse the conversion of their Muslim slaves.[39] Even the preaching of the Gospel to the unconverted was a dubious venture, slowly assimilated to the Crusade. For, as Thomas Aquinas (c. 1225–1274) later commented, "the very hiding of truth in figures is useful for the exercise of thoughtful minds and as a defense against the ridicule of the unbelievers, according to the words, 'Give not that which is holy to dogs' " (Matt. 7:6).[40]

Appeals to authority, rational arguments, the use of force, enticements of bribery and pleasure, and the performance of miracles were deployed for what proselytizers thought they said about their own empathies, not about intended converts. The fictions of empathetic conversion were produced for the converted, not for winning others to belief. They expressed the proselytizers' *cultus sui* (their idealized self-image). The vindictive motive behind Peter's treatise against the Jews is indicated in a letter that he wrote at about the same time urging King Louis VII (c. 1121–1180, reigned 1137–79) to impose hardships upon the Jews in France, short of killing them, for their offenses against Christ and his saints. (Louis was the first monarch to enlist in the Second Crusade, on Christmas Day, 1145.) Otto of Bamberg's missions to Pomerania were quests for martyrdom, an essential part of his *cultus sui*. The Crusades were tools of vengeance; and if the would-be avengers were slain, their deaths, like those of other martyrs, would compound the damnation of their slayers. As a frustrated preacher put it in the ninth century, he did not believe that his labors before God had been futile and empty. For, even though an Ethiopian left the bath as black as he went into it, the bathkeeper did not forfeit his wages.[41] In all these instances, gestures toward the unbeliever were tests of the believer's empathies, pursuit of the trials of faith inventoried in the parable of the sower, not least of which was persecution. For faith as a strategy for survival posited a struggle for existence, a struggle of faith against faith. Writers of the twelfth century were not the first to project onto the hostile world dangers of unbelief that they felt within their own hearts.

The fictive sense of danger was essential to the passion with which they embraced poetic truth and the conflicts into which it plummeted them. In believers' minds the fiction made all the dangers and pains of human life a drama in which suffering and death were the keys of deliverance. This was the secret confidence and triumphant promise known to them and hidden from unbelievers. But the drama was not so simple as a conflict between believers and the infidel, nor was faith as a strategy of survival a completely open book for professed Christians. As they interpreted the paradigm of conversion, the turning of the heart to Christ in imitation was followed not only by sorrow but by a sense of abandonment by God, a postenlightenment depression syndrome. Although not present in New Testament portrayals of conversion, the proposition that estrangement from God could come not only through human choice but also through God's withdrawal was present in Old Testament accounts of the careers of prophets and in Gospel accounts of Christ's crucifixion. It soon found a place in the *cultus sui* of asceticism. Himself a zealous controversialist and political agent provocateur, Bishop Athanasius of Alexandria represented St. Anthony (c.250–350) in solitary conflict against a host of torturing demons. Suddenly, a great light descended upon him; the demons fled. "Where were you?" Anthony asked his Lord. "Why were you not here from the beginning to lighten my pains?" "I was here," the Lord answered, "and I held back to watch your fight. Since you prevailed and were not overcome, I shall always be your helper and make your name great throughout the world." Not surprisingly, Anthony is reported elsewhere to have affirmed that "without temptation, no one can be saved."[42]

Twelfth-century writers preserved the conviction that God imposed sufferings on believers and left them to the Tempter to be tried, so as to test their endurance in the refiner's fire and to repudiate them if their faith could be broken.[43] By contrast with this concept of probation, their erotic spirituality also enabled them to understand the trials of conversion as a lover's game. As the soul's spouse, Christ came to his bride, inebriating her with the raptures of consolation, and withdrew from her, teaching her that she derived consolation from dependence upon him, rather than from her own powers. "There is a common saying that too much familiarity breeds contempt. And so He withdraws himself, so that He is not despised for being too attentive, so that when He is absent, He may be desired the more, that being desired He may be sought more eagerly, that having been sought for, He may at last be found with greater thankfulness."

The motif of eroticism did not exclude that of probation. Christ was a jealous spouse as well as an ardent one. He kept his bride under incessantly vigilant and hidden eyes while he was absent. If she played him false with another, incurring blemishes of impurity, he would reject her.[44] Thus, it was essential that a life of sorrow follow conversion, and not simply in helplessness as the soul gauged the immense distance between its own foul and perishing existence and eternal life. To recover the treasures buried in the field of the body and the depths of the heart, the soul, Christ's faithful spouse, must seek fortification in the sorrow of repentance, contemplate its life in bitterness, and implore God to suspend its merited condemnation.[45] For, in the bridegroom's game of hide-and-seek, however sure she might be of repudiation if she failed the test, the bride could never be sure whether she were loved or hated.[46]

Thus far, I have described a field of empathetic needfulness in which conversion served the strategy of survival called faith. I have found that the primordial need of life encompassed other impelling needs: those of love, purity, truth, and power. Above all needs was that for life. All entailed both methods of doubt and struggle against doubt. Again and again, writers repeated that no language could express the sweetness of spiritual understanding, that no one could know it except those to whom it was given to see the invisible and apprehend the inconceivable.[47] Even the letter of Scripture had little appeal unless it were read according to a commentary written in the heart that disclosed its hidden meaning.[48]

Although conversion was a duty imposed by brotherly love, the sermons of preachers were fruitless in themselves, for "the conversion of souls is the work of the divine voice, not the human."[49] In the same way, no one was a prophet, nor were utterances prophecies, nor visions revelations, if the speaker or seer spoke from his own understanding, rather than in God's spirit.[50] The word of the text was a useless husk, food for cattle; and, indeed, all that the human intellect by its natural powers could consume was the "letter that killeth" (2 Cor. 3:6). Spiritual understanding opened to the human mind the kernel, the Spirit that "giveth life," and elevated the soul above its natural, animal nature and above the souls that remained fettered to their own animality. Was it not by an erotic union, the soul held in the embraces of God, that the human heart was impregnated with the incomprehensible, the soul liquefying in joy and love with the heat of the fire that it received?[51] The compelling power in human fictions, even among believers, came from God and was felt by each person according to the measure of faith bestowed by God. Some outlines of the poetics of empathetic conversion have begun to come into view.

Two Examples of the Poetics at Work

Two twelfth-century accounts of conversion will illustrate the fictive character of understanding empathetic conversion in natural terms. They also give examples of how the basic needs at the heart of that understanding provoked conflict both as an instrument of perfection and as a means of moving toward the moment when, free of misunderstanding in the act of understanding, one would no longer see through the enigma of reflected images, and they illustrate different scales in the proportionality of faith.

The first purports to be an autobiographical account by Judah ben David ha-Levi, a Jew of Cologne.[52] As a young man, we are told, he converted to Christianity after a spiritual crisis of several months, abandoned his parents and his new wife, kidnapped his younger brother and deposited him in a monastery for Christianization, and, finally, presented himself for baptism, taking a new name, Herman (1129). His former career as a moneylender was also a thing of the past. He entered the monastic order of Augustinian canons, learned Latin, became a priest (c. 1137), and is thought by some to have held a number of offices in his order. He died after 1181. According to the narrative his conversion aroused great interest; and at some time after his ordination to the priesthood, the "pious exhortation" of others induced him to write his account.

The second text is a biography of Christina of Markyate. Christina was born at Huntingdon, near Cambridge (c. 1096–98?). She was named Theodora at baptism but took the name Christina "out of necessity."[53] Her family belonged to the Anglo-Saxon nobility and more than a generation after the Norman Conquest preserved its social eminence. With a keen sense of dynastic continuity, her parents resisted her early vocation to the ascetic life. They coerced her into a marriage which was never consummated. Through iron persistence Christina escaped her family and her nominal husband, changed her name, took refuge in a hermitage, and began a period of training with ascetic masters (c. 1114–15). In time she began to follow the solitary life at Markyate, near the monastery of St. Albans (c. 1118–22). Her marriage was annulled; she made her monastic profession (c. 1131) and gradually became celebrated as a spiritual adept. She died about 1155–56. Probably within ten years of her death, her biography was written (one supposes) by a monk of St. Albans whose name is not known.

While the characterization of Herman-Judah portrays conversion as a radical change from Judaism to Christianity, that of Christina portrays it as perfection of a commitment that existed in her from her mother's womb. They therefore remind us of the repertory of varieties of conversion that I noted by way of introduction (see chap. 1). By gender distinctions they exemplify the proposition that dramatic conversions were more characteristic of male religious experience than of female, since the order of society enjoined upon women lives of continuity grounded in their physical, and especially their procreative, capacities, while it allowed—and expected—men to bring about "crisis and change" in their lives. Thus, it has been maintained, the spiritual careers of women are generally depicted as continuous lines of development, while those of men tend to be punctuated by abrupt and dramatic change.[54]

The fictive character of these accounts is readily apparent and is not affected by the difference between an (at least purported) autobiography and a memoir composed by a second, and perhaps distant, observer. To say this, however, is not to diminish the fact that the individual judgments of the authors guided the process of selection, omission, and arrangement of materials or, most conspicuously, that the authorial judgments behind Christina's biography were presumably those of a man writing for a predominantly male audience, and by no means those of Christina herself.

Both were works of recollection, rather than reportage of the present; they present exercises in deliberate assembling, sorting, and reconstituting shards of the past. Both support what my comments on hagiography implied: namely, that authors and audiences alike expected hagiographical texts—like scriptural commentaries—to be works of fiction.[55]

The New Testament paradigm of gradualism was for both the point of departure. The characterizations called "Herman-Judah" and "Christina" were drawn from Scripture. Biblical precepts are said to have been fulfilled in their thoughts and works. And, by their accounts of Christ's direct intervention in conversions, both texts witness to the general proposition that the figural content of Scripture, whether manifested in the text of Holy Writ itself or in the lives of the saints, could only refer to Christ.[56]

And yet, once their common Christocentric reading of Scripture is noted, one finds many differences between the two characterizations. The authors applied the New Testament paradigm of gradual conversion in very different ways, for several reasons. Herman-Judah's intellectualism and Christina's emotionalism express distinctions that Christian tradition assigned to gender. Herman-Judah is said to have experienced the corruption of the flesh when Jewish saboteurs of his conversion ensnared him into marriage. A vision confirmed the incorruptibility of Christina's flesh, a sign of the holiness achieved through her chastity. This contrast between fleshly corruption and incorruptibility is a testimony to the Christian stereotype of Jews as sexually incontinent and to the difference between the purpose of Herman-Judah's characterization—to certify that his Christian commitment was irreversible—and that of Christina's—to declare her sanctity.

Thus, the characterization of Herman-Judah as a biblical scholar enabled its author to demonstrate his piety and knowledge of Scripture by describing his debates with other scriptural scholars and by interlarding the text with scriptural passages applied to events in Herman-Judah's life and states of mind. The trials and temptations that were de rigueur in pious literature appear against an assumed background of the historical drama in which God visited divine vengeance upon the Jews for their spiritual blindness, with exile, privation, and contempt. Finally, a rich array of scriptural analogues was brought to bear in order to expand Herman-Judah's slow enlightenment with scriptural associations: with the hostility of his fellow Jews, who sought his death, as Jews had sought that of Christ; with Jacob wrestling with God; with the conversion of the Apostle Paul, changed from persecutor to preacher; with parables of the prodigal son and the pearl of great price; and finally with episodes from the books of Esther and Daniel.

By contrast, Christina's life does not interrogate so much as declare Scripture. The professed ignorance of Scripture attributed by the author to her drew a line of authentication quite different from that appropriate to a scriptural scholar. The objective was to declare that Christina was holy and therefore that, while she lived on earth, her conversation was in heaven. According to her (presumably male) biographer, Christina penetrated the hidden things of God's wisdom by her enduring purity of heart, not by her learning or by any accumulation of crises, and by that means also she determined her actions out of love of Christ according to precepts of the Gospel.[57]

Dramatic analogues were drawn between rejections of her by her intimates and those of Christ by his and between one of Christina's visions and the visit of Christ to Mary and Martha. An implied one ran between her rapture into heaven and that of St. Paul. Scriptural quotations are provided as rules of action; Christina's meditations and prayers are composed in chains of biblical texts. However, the enactment of Scripture in life, according to this characterization, took the form of the immediate presence of Christ, the Blessed Virgin, and other scriptural figures to Christina by way of visions and allocutions. They stepped from the pages of Scripture into her cell; they appeared in the midst of liturgies in her church.

The fictional nature of the accounts goes beyond their diverse use of Scripture for authentication. Both treatises were apologetic, and their quite different strategies of composition reflect the differences between the apologetic purposes that they were meant to serve. Even without independent collateral evidence about Herman-Judah or Christina, the narratives themselves indicate many points at which the authors suppressed pertinent information. The arrangement of materials was calculated to demonstrate that Herman-Judah's conversion was an authentic transit from the carnal-mindedness of the Jews in interpreting Scripture to the charismatic interpretation opened by grace to Christians. The studied deployment of materials in Christina's *Life* likewise catches the reader in a web of narrative whose structure was essential to the argument for Christina's unswerving faithfulness to her divine spouse. Both authors tailored evidence and narrative structure to demonstrate that their subjects had received a divine vocation in early life (before birth in Christina's *Life*) and that conversion was an unfolding of that clear and early call.

The treatise about Herman-Judah addressed a world guided by attitudes that Peter the Venerable set forth in his diatribe against the Jews. The author chose to omit from his narrative the slaughter of Jews perpetrated in Cologne and the surrounding region by warriors enlisted in the First Crusade, stirred up to wreak vengeance on the Jews among them for the death of Christ before they unsheathed the avenging sword against the Muslim desecrators of Jerusalem (1096). Perhaps he wrote amid anxiety that the Second Crusade (proclaimed in 1145) would reenact those massacres.

Despite this silence, deep anxieties are obvious. As expected, fictions drawn from Scripture are woven around a core formed by the great needs. The whole weight of Herman-Judah's conversion turns on the dramatic pathos of his gradual realization that by remaining true to Judaism, he would bring about his own destruction. And yet the treatment of the elemental needs is a study in ambivalence. This is true of the way he reckoned with the needs for life and love. God wills that sinners convert and live, he wrote (chap. 6). He had renounced his property and himself for love of Christ, not only in abandoning his identity as a Jew but also in embracing with poverty, chastity, and obedience a discipline of unceasing mortification and contrition. But was he among those chosen for eternal life or only among the called? Even as he hoped that Christ would perfect the work that he had begun in him, Herman-Judah lived in fear, for he was not sure whether God, the Lord of vengeance, loved or hated him (chap. 21). His frequent comments on the hatred that Christians displayed toward Jews, commonly spitting on them and reviling them (chap. 5), and on the malice of the Jews toward him first as "semi-Christian" and later as convert (chaps. 14, 19) illuminate the environment that sustained such doubts.

When he turned to the need for purity, the author created a new level of ambivalence by weaving together elements of his inherited Jewish doctrines with those of his assimilated Christian ones. This did not concern flat contradictions between Jewish and Christian practices. He recognized that what Jews practiced as legal marriage, Christians decried as corruption of the flesh. The ascetic practices of monasticism that Jews pitied as wanton self-affliction, worthy of scorn as skepticism and unbelief, Christians exalted as ascetic self-denial, requisite for purging the soul of its carnal dross. However, the ambivalence with which his heart turned to Christ is indicated by the remarkable degree to which the author employed Old Testament materials as authentication of the purity of his Christian commitment. He illustrated his quest by an analogy with the strictness with which Mordecai and Daniel had kept the Jewish dietary law even while they lived at the courts of Gentile kings. He interpreted his baptism by analogy with Elisha's purification of Naaman from leprosy. And in the sacerdotal motif with which he portrayed his self-renunciation, there is a reminiscence of the spirit in which Jews menaced by the Crusaders submitted to ritual slaughter in the hope of walking with the righteous in the Garden of Eden, sanctifying the Lord's name, atoning for themselves and their posterity, and bringing God's vengeance on their persecutors.[58]

Ambivalence in portraying the need for truth follows more conventional lines. Words cannot describe the joys of the heavenly banquet prepared for God's elect; only those who experience it can know its delights (chap. 21). The Lord is the author of faith (chap. 5), and conversion is achieved by his direct action. Unenlightened by grace, the Jews remained bound to the literal interpretation of Scriptures, like animals content to feed on the chaff, while Christians, endowed with spiritual understanding, refresh themselves as human beings on the pith (chap. 2). As the narrative progresses, evidence is added to evidence that contrary to the alleged Jewish demand for external proofs, debates and private instruction, miraculous signs (such as trial by ordeal), and the interpretation of dreams contribute nothing to conversion unless a secret visitation of grace opens the heart of the interpreter to spiritual meaning. In the end, conversion was brought about not by long reasoning or by continuing disputations with great clerics but by sudden divine illumination granted in answer to the prayers of two simple, holy women (chap. 12).

The evidence of Herman-Judah's spiritual power is set forth in the many references to his learning and intellectual ability, to the vindication of his spiritual quest with a telling reference to the parable of the prodigal son, and, most strikingly, in the narrative structure of the whole account. It opens with one vision, full of vexing symbols, that sets Herman-Judah off on his pilgrimage of doubt. It ends with another that explains the first vision, ratifies Herman-Judah's conversion, and effectively closes the narrative. By bracketing the narrative between one vision that poses questions and another that answers them, the author portrayed Herman-Judah's entire experience as a series of ventures moving from first to last under God's special providence.

The second conversion account, Christina of Markyate's biography, likewise illustrates the importance of the primary needs at work. Indeed, in its narrative, they are necessary stimuli of conflict as a means of spiritual perfection and a medium of understanding. However, while Herman-Judah's inner strivings engaged him in conflict outside his own religious community, Christina's struggles were intramural.

As I said regarding Scripture, the conflict of faith against faith did not test the authenticity of a learned tradition. Instead, as Christina's biographer located the conflict of faith against faith in her life, it hinged entirely on Christina's resolve, formed in early childhood, to remain a virgin and to enter the monastic community of St. Albans.[59] The biographer displayed the needs of life, love, purity, truth, and power through this prism, entirely without ambivalence. Logic, authority, material rewards, force, and caressing words had been brought to bear to convert Herman-Judah to the faith of Christ. These same enticements were employed to deflect Christina's desires from the one object of her desire. Inviolate virginity, she believed (according to her biographer), was the means by which God would re-form in her the image of Christ. Thus, it followed that when her parents afflicted her because of her resolve to remain a virgin and when her one advocate abandoned her, she recapitulated the experience of Christ when he was rejected by the Jews and denied by Peter.[60]

By contrast with the dilemmas that tormented Herman, only one choice—and that was by no means one that vexed the mind—is acknowledged as confronting Christina: faithfulness to Christ or spiritual fornication.[61] Thus, her biographer wrote, the trials that she experienced came from temptations of the envious Devil, from the weakness of her own lascivious body, from her parents and others who sought to prevent the fulfillment of her vow or vilified her spiritual friendships with men by their slanders, and from the periodic fear that Christ, her spouse, had abandoned her. Among her would-be seducers and malingers were clerics and great prelates, Bishop Ranulf Flambard of Durham, the chief minister of King William Rufus, and, for a time, Abbot Geoffrey of St. Albans. When Christ eventually appeared to her in the form of an infant, she locked him in her arms, clasping him to her virginal breast, and felt him within herself.[62] By such a visitation, however long delayed, the fires of lust were instantly suppressed. She was comforted by the assurance that no temptation could come upon her without Christ's permission and that he would not allow her to be tempted beyond her strength. If he withheld blessings from her, it was only to maintain the vehemence of her spiritual love.[63]

Herman-Judah was only able to hint at the fecundity that he desired, not through his abandoned marriage but through the celibacy of his religious discipline, in those who might read his account. The author of Christina's *Life* exposed a luxuriant array of spiritual reformations, therapeutic miracles, and infusions of the Holy Spirit brought about through her presence, not least of which signs of fecundity was the renown that she brought to St. Albans and the monastic vocations of men and women effected there through her.[64] Such was evidence of the degree to which, by divine grace, the need of power, subsuming those of life, love, purity, and truth, had been satisfied in and through her.

It is worth mentioning also the political aspects of power as ascribed to Herman-Judah and to Christina. Although Herman-Judah may have become provost of an Augustinian house, the account of his conversion attributes no official position to him apart from his priesthood. Intervention by various officers, including the prelates Bishop Egbert of Münster and Abbot Rupert of Deutz, and a casual encounter with Queen Richenza's chaplain give an air of splendor to his conversion. But his own political powers consist in the supernatural powers of the priest to enact and to participate in the Lord's heavenly Eucharist. In this regard, one may see the effect of the author's intent to underscore Herman-Judah's authentic Christian commitment, not his sanctity. But there may also have been a challenge to anti-Jewish inhibitions that Bernard of Clairvaux expressed when a majority of cardinals elected Pietro Pierleoni as pope. Pierleoni's family had been Christian for five generations and a mainstay of the reformed papacy. He himself had served with distinction as a cardinal. But Bernard still was able to thunder that his election was "an insult to Christ," since a Jew had invaded the throne of St. Peter.[65]

It is not surprising that Christina's biographer attributed no political office to her. But the need for power did receive an answer in his portrayal of her as acting upon the institutional Church indirectly, as the adviser, consoler, and denouncer of its officers. The effects of her power were felt in these ways not only by Abbot Geoffrey but also through him by the English royal court, by prelates overseas who wished her to move to their dioceses, and, most remotely of all, by the papal curia itself. The blessing of fecundity had a distinct political counterpart and, in fact, a potentially subversive one in Christina's idealization of the martyrs Cecilia and Valerian, united in a chaste marriage and venerated for martyrdom. It struck her that martyrs were crowned by God and honored in heaven and on earth.

For my purposes, the crucial fact is that their apologetic purposes brought the authors to weave their fictions about conversion around a core of needfulness. The same elemental needs drove both conversions, for both were recognizably improvisations on the same "form of conversion" (see above, preface at n. 4). And in both, conversion, by satisfying those needs, subverted established norms. With all his ambivalence, the lines of conflict for Herman-Judah ran against his community, against the "tradition that [he] suckled from [his] mother's breasts" (chap. 10), which he came to reject as the "errors of my fathers" (chap. 5). And this opposition drove him against his family, the accumulated momentum of an ancient intellectual tradition, and the ruling authorities in his community, which is portrayed as wielding the power of life and death. He is depicted contending as a Jew against hostile Christians both before and after his conversion. Christina was beset by no ambivalence. Her biographer portrayed her need-impelled agonies as the reasons why, though an ignorant woman, she struggled single-mindedly against her family and the signs and prerogatives that distinguished the nobility, against her legal husband, and against corrupt or unenlightened members of the Church hierarchy. Both for Herman-Judah and for Christina, as fictional characters, the inner duel against self was fundamental to these outward and visible battles and, above all, to combat against the Tempter. There, quarter was neither given nor received, but in the heat of battle there were anticipations of triumph and of honors in heaven and on earth.

Inasmuch as action matched belief, conversion, as exemplified in these treatises, motivated strategies of subversion as well as of survival. Of course, the portrayals of Herman-Judah and Christina were credible because they were tailored to conform with traditional and commonly accepted stereotypes, or "templates," of holiness. Stylization was an essential and inevitable result of using tools provided by nature—thought and words—to portray a supernatural phenomenon. If conversions were to be accepted and celebrated as genuine, it was crucial for authors and readers that portrayals be recognizably "in type." And this recognition demanded a high degree of literary stylization. In chapter 5 I shall consider the importance of mythic context in prescribing the contours of such templates.

Taken together with other materials that I have considered, the comparison between the accounts of Herman-Judah and Christina of Markyate suggests a question: For whom were these ideas of conversion convincing? There is no reason to think that they were cogent for the theologically unsophisticated, such as Olav Tryggvessön is represented to have been; to the unlettered, unequipped for the shimmering, elusive delights of metaphor and irony; to those, such as artisans and peasants, whose ideals were not military; or to women. They have the contours of ideals common to an ascetic, literate, aristocratic, male society, pervaded with the ethic of warriors. They also indicate that, in conversion, empathy had its limits and degrees.

Conclusions

I have explored some of the topography between an event and what the event was called: the region of poetics or, as I said, of the calling. It is time, finally, to begin assessing the prospects for a universal morphology of conversion. Writings that survive from eleventh- and twelfth-century Europe are not universally or uniformly familiar. I shall give some landmarks from other eras and lands to provide some general orientation.

I suggested that the answers we get depend on the questions we ask. But what makes a particular question thinkable, and to whom? Certainly, the *Fragestellung* of conversion in Christianity had—and was intended to have—a distinctive cast, whether it were applied to individual or to collective life. The fictions that made the questions of conversion thinkable in Christianity were by no means universally accepted. Nor even among Christians was the flawed understanding that arose from seeing through enigmatic reflections—through a glass darkly—thought out in the same way.

In the twelfth century, Jews readily pointed to the inconsistency between Christian acceptance of the Second Commandment and what they considered Christian idolatry in the devotional use of images and in the worship of Jesus. They found nothing but perverse reasoning behind teachings on the Incarnation and the triune God. They deplored the gross immorality that they judged was concealed by doctrines of the virgin birth. And they had reason to take special note of the ethical disjunction between the Christian ideal of love and the scorn and cruelty heaped upon those outside the Church. The heathen Pomeranians, too, cast the reproach of cruelty in the teeth of Bishop Otto of Bamberg when he scattered the seed of the Gospel among them. They would have nothing to do, they said, with a religion that sanctioned atrocities such as Christian practiced against Christian.[66]

Conversion, with empathetic needs that were unquenchable in this world, was institutionalized in the Church, notably in monastic orders of men. But the ideas that I have reviewed plainly indicate that, with its doctrines of God-given proportionality, personal reform and social reform, not to say revolution against Christianity and the Church, were also institutionalized. The sayings of the Desert Fathers recount that a pagan priest visited Abba Olympios one day. He discovered that the Christian ascetics received no visions from their God, although when he and his colleagues sacrificed to theirs, "he [hid] nothing from [them], but disclos[ed] his mysteries." If Christians' austerities brought no revelations, surely, the pagan went on, it was because they had "impure thoughts in [their] hearts, which separate[d them] from [their] God." Abba Olympios agreed.[67] What distinguished this gentle attitude from the militant ideas that I have discussed?

Although changes of religious and philosophical commitment were common in classical Antiquity, the idea of conversion as I have described it was not part of the classical tradition.[68] The key to the differences is readily apparent if one considers that the Christian form of empathetic conversion was fundamentally the imitation of Christ, the paradigmatic *forma conversionis*. Many basic differences separated the polymorphous nature of ancient religion from the monotheism of Christian cult, the voluntary commitment of Apuleius (c. 123–after 170) from the imperative call of Bernard. Ancient religion demanded no ultimate commitment. Commitments were proportional. "One does not sacrifice everything to Zeus," Aristotle wrote.[69] The gods were not lords of history nor, in their dealings with one another or with human beings, were they notably faithful. Correspondingly, religious obligations were not understood in terms of love, and the prayers of the ancient world represent a bargaining movement from supplication to gratitude, rather than unconditional devotion.[70] Aristotle observed that it would be eccentric for anyone to say that he loved Zeus; neither Greeks nor Romans referred to their gods with the possessive pronouns "my" or "our."[71]

To say even this little is to say that the religious traditions of Greece and Rome knew several kinds of faith that figured in Christian thought but lacked the one kind essential to conversion. All shared the faith of knowledge (believing that gods are, that God is), that of comprehension (believing gods, or God), and that of assurance (believing that gods, or God, will act). But in quite a different key the needful, erotic element of Christianity introduced faith *in* God, the movement of the soul into God through loving imitation and its empathetic participation in God. Christianity added the further proposition of grace: that faith in God came through God's arbitrary gift, to each in a measure assigned, not through a bartering exchange between divinity and worshiper or through exercise of the human reason. Finally, it affirmed, as classical religions did not, that the transit from one generation's faith in God to another's in God, directed according to a divine plan for the redemption of the human race and impelled by conversion, gave all earthly experience its meaning and direction. And just as the career of Christ was considered indispensable to that plan, so, too, the imitation of Christ was thought its enactment or performance. Ancient needs for life, love, purity, and truth found different responses.

True to the traditions of the ancient world, an early Christian in Rome declared, without reference to the trials of faith, that he had escaped pale death and lived in the safety of the Kingdom of Heaven. In words reminiscent of Virgil, his epitaph declared: "I dance ring-dances with the blessed in the beautiful fields of the righteous." The contrast with the idea that I have reviewed is indicated by Herman-Judah's joy in conversion. "Then," he wrote, "I sang with the ineffable victory dance of the Psalmist, 'Our soul has been snatched as a sparrow from the snare of the hunters: the snare is smashed and we are freed'"

(Ps. 123:7).[72] Unlike the Roman, Herman-Judah celebrated a triumph over spiritual evils, not an escape from natural finitude, and the risk-filled means of his liberation as well as the state of freedom. Unlike the Roman, he rejoiced in the arduous discovery of a treasure hitherto concealed even from himself in his body and mind.

One is bound to look further for comparisons.[73] Is it possible that the hidden treasure in the New Testament parable resembles the jewel in the lotus blossom, the radiant light of the Buddha-mind disclosed as the petals of individual consciousness fall open? Does a word equivalent with *conversion* exist in the sacred literatures of Buddhism? The absence of such a word in Arabic encourages me to ask this question, which I cannot answer myself.

I am encouraged, however, to think that there is no equivalent to supernatural conversion as defined in the texts that I have considered. What I find in Buddhist texts, as they are accessible to me in translation, is great emphasis on the exercise of natural powers in order to transcend them all, including empathy. Purification, the quest for truth, and seeking after good and peace are all defined by individual aspiration. There is no place for the intervention of a divine will or grace.

Inward change occurs, but it is brought about by a change of method or master, leading to the eightfold path of enlightenment, perhaps through a series of changes in method as recurrent discontent leads a disciple from master to master. Truth can be discovered or intuitively known. Ecstasy can be cultivated. Still, the entire quest, beginning in discontent and advanced by perception, learning, understanding, attainment of enlightenment, and persevering in the right way, occurs by individual choice and struggle, within the confines of nature.

Thus, while the vocabulary of spiritual change bears some resemblance to the one that I have examined, it appears to lack both the word *conversion* as something other than a change of method or master and the supernatural phenomenon called conversion.

Certainly, there are enough differences between Christianity and some forms of Buddhism to exclude out of hand the idea of a universal "conversion experience" or morphology of conversion. Although the two religions depart from the same point, the pain of existence, they follow quite different paths. For Buddhism is not a struggle for existence but, quite the reverse, a stripping away of independent consciousness and existence in order to enter the state of ultimate reality where existence is identical with nonexistence. Its doctrine of the oneness of all things excludes the concept of a personal god, the object of fear and love, just as that of karma and reincarnation removes the ultimate significance of individual life. The passions are not to be sanctified but caused to cease, together with consciousness. The pain of existence did not begin in a distant historical crime (such as Adam's disobedience); it subsisted in the cycle of procreation and death governed by dharmas, laws or categories of individual being.

Buddhism sets forth no antitheses of righteousness and evil, no juridical program of crime and punishment; it idealizes no reconciling atonement through sacrifice; it anticipates no apocalyptic Last Judgment. In the enduring cycle of procreation and death, lacking prophecy and fulfillment, conversion cannot be a paradigm for historical change, for collective as well as personal redemption. One further remarkable difference is the contrast between Christian teaching that conversion ultimately depends upon grace and Buddhist doctrines that some have achieved enlightenment by their own efforts and that enlightenment can be transmitted from master to disciple.

Yet in some regards the courses of enlightenment set forth by the two religions do resemble each other. In both, mind (or spirit) is the ultimate reality, and enlightenment comes in a process of which faith is the first and indispensable step. Likewise, escape from the world of suffering through the inner powers of mind requires an ascetic struggle of body and mind, a purificatory self-emptying, for which monasteries became the chief institutions. In both religions a striking contrast emerged between the insistence that enlightenment came through ascetic practices, rather than from speculative learning—an exaltation of ignorance—and the cultivation of a vast body of doctrinal literature accompanied by ritual, music, and visual arts laden with scholarly symbols. To say this much is to indicate that Buddhism recognized the slowness with which disciplines of self-emptying took effect, although there were continuing disputes over whether enlightenment, when it came, was sudden or gradual, through an ebb and flow of enlightenments. For some at any rate, there was a question whether those who achieved the Great Enlightenment subsequently needed to persevere in conscious discipline or whether they had become "living enlightenment." Likewise, in their experiences with other religions, Christianity and Buddhism silently assimilated the riches of their neighbors and rivals, even while they distinguished between enlightened and unenlightened, and applied rigorous critical methods to segregate heretics from authentic believers. The obligation to seek the enlightenment of all—the imperative of proselytism—was also common, together with the acknowledgment that enlightenment could not be forced.

But between which schools or sects of either religion are precise comparisons on the matter of empathy to be drawn? Divergences among the major strands of Buddhism are pronounced. My own comments have been drawn from Zen literature. The multiplicity of beliefs make the possibilities of a universal morphology of whatever may be called conversion extremely remote.

In some forms of later Buddhism, the task of striving for the enlightenment of all, even at the cost of their own salvation, fell to the bodhisattvas, who were bound by a fourfold vow: "However innumerable the sentient beings, I vow to save them all. However inexhaustible the passions, I vow to extinguish them all. However immeasurable the dharmas, I vow to master them all. However incomparable the truth of the Buddha, I vow to attain it."[74] I have suggested ways in which these obligations were foreign to twelfth-century Christianity. Concerned as I now am with faith as a strategy in the struggle for existence, I take special note of the vow to save all sentient beings. Doctrines of the universal return of all beings (even of Satan) to God, associated with the name of Origen, provide one point of analogy. So, too, does the consistent teaching that God is the life of all that live. Even so, the Buddhist doctrines of universal oneness and of saving all sentient beings through the extinction of existence, which was not sacrificial, set clear limits to comparison with dominant strands of Christianity until recent times. Even for bodhisattvas, the Christian vision of saints exulting in the Heavenly Jerusalem has little in common with nirvana, for "you cannot be a good Christian and redeem yourself, nor can you be a Buddha and worship God."[75] In subsequent chapters, I shall return to the other bodhisattva vows to indicate other points of similarity and difference.

I have begun to discover some contours of what, by the twelfth century, was implied by Jerome's classic statement, "Christians are made, not born" (*ep. 107*, 1). Bernard of Clairvaux wrote:

> The hope of glory and, indeed, glory itself are contained in tribulation as the hope of fruit and the fruit itself are in the seed. In this way also the kingdom of God is even now within us, a vast treasure in a vessel of clay, in a scrubby field. It is there, I say, but it is hidden. Happy is the person who shall find it there. Who is he? Surely it is he who pays more attention to the harvest than to the sowing . . ., seeing things that are not obvious and divining things that are not seen. . . . Let us count it pure joy when we fall into various tribulations. Let us say from the heart, let us say from conviction: "It is good to go to the house of mourning rather than to the house of feasting."[76]

Even so, when the spiritual pathologists of the twelfth century dissected the penitential life of conversion, they recognized that the subversive force that animated and coordinated all its parts eluded them. Empathy could never be entirely rendered into poetics. No more than John Henry Newman's critics could they explain the "magic" and the "genius" that transformed their own lives or those which they emulated. In the sui generis character of the Christian religion and of the religious texts with which I have dealt, the needful essence of conversion was inconceivable, inexplicable. The indeterminacy and proportionality that called forth the poetics of empathetic conversion could be expressed, if at all, in play that led to the life that was "hid with Christ in God."

There are elements of play—the play that enacted the strategy of faith— everywhere in my account: in the use of a metaphor ("conversion") to denote varieties of change, the dominance of predicament over peripety, the disequilibrium between supernatural experiences and what could be thought and said about them through tools of nature (ideas and words), the deliberate obscurity of parables, the hide-and-seek of allegorical interpretation, analogues of lovers' games and jealous husbands, paradoxes of fecund continence, the fictive art of narrative, and, certainly, the exercise of preaching to the deaf.

In fact, without using the word, it was clear from the beginning that we would end with play. Throughout, the goal of life and history—salvation— demanded knowledge. When, against this imperative, methods of relentless doubt—including especially theodical doubt—are called for, misunderstanding is essential to understanding, interpretation falsifies, and belief entails unbelief, play is more than a metaphor or analogue for proportional understanding. For language, interpretation, and explanation are all tools of memory. By contrast, when this imperative is poised against these impediments, understanding is not recollective. It is enactment. More precisely, empathetic understanding is actual only in the playing of the play.

Play was necessary because of the indeterminacy of conversion, because the plodding routines of moving from known to unknown did not serve the project of seeing through a glass darkly; one could not pass with sure steps through methodical doubt from visible creation to the invisible things of God. Thus, one played. Despite the difference between ancient and Christian paradigms of conversion—the first unhistorical, the second bound up with history—there is much to recall Plato's statement that human beings are puppets "of the gods, either their plaything[s] only or created with a purpose—which of the two we can not certainly know."[77] This would have been one logical conclusion when Bernard of Clairvaux represented God permitting human souls to be the prey of "the most wicked, most callous, and cruelest hunters," Satan and his minions, baiting their hidden snares with surpassing craft.[78] The character of souls as God's playthings is also suggested by the metaphor of God as an architect building the eternal Temple with living stones but in time removing those that proved unsound and burning them into lime to make, from the punishment of the wicked, the cement of love bonding the saved one to another.[79]

In recent times St. Thérèse of Lisieux (1873–1897) employed another figure of speech to express the same surrender to an unknowable and incalculable power. "For some time," she wrote, "I had been accustomed to offer myself as a plaything to the Child Jesus. I told Him not to treat me like an expensive toy which children look at but dare not touch. I was a cheap little ball which He could fling on the ground or kick or pierce or leave neglected in a corner or even press to His heart if it gave Him pleasure. To put it in a nutshell, I longed to amuse the little Jesus and offer myself to His childish whims." Suddenly, he did pierce her. One recalls Sir Thomas More's (1477–1535) more lascivious metaphor. In the Tower awaiting his fate, More said, "Me thinketh God maketh me a wanton, and setteth me on his lap and dandleth me."[80]

Scripture gave little warrant for mirth in this play. If my concordance does not deceive, there are no references to smiles in Scripture, and the relatively few references to laughter are overwhelmingly to scorn or to foolish laughter destined to give way to grief.

Religious observance and discipline are specific kinds of ritualized play, perhaps even rituals of play. As the words both of Thérèse of Lisieux and of Thomas More indicate, the rituals as well as the ritualizations of play were cast in the language of male dominance, dominance, too, that belonged to a class of ascetic, literate, men faithful to an aristocratic, military ethos.

The fictive game subverted and transformed Christianity, Church, civil society, and self. Yet it was not enough for people to be played by the game. The inexplicable element in survival strategies of faith demanded much more than involuntary surrender from the converted. It demanded that in their empathetic needfulness they, too, play the game, enacting the role of Christ, and that with penitent self-emptying they hazard much to find and make fruitful the treasure buried within them. To assimilate the poetics of empathy into the fabric of their being, they had to play out the ritualized form of conversion; the players and the game had to become identical.

Plainly, the struggle for existence about which I have been writing had nothing to do with existence in this world. The survival strategy of faith idealized sacrificial death. The need for life and the belief in sacrificial death as the threshold of true life, glorious and unending, made the game extraordinarily intricate. To unbelievers, the chiaroscuro wager of bodily death against life hereafter could only seem an imprudent gamble. But to those bent on theodicy, the wisdom of God is foolishness to men, and this, too, was built into the fictive rituals of conversion.

"I will apply myself according to your custom at this time of Christmas," Hugh Latimer (c. 1490–1555) preached.

> I will, as I said, declare unto you Christ's rule, but that shall be in Christ's cards. And whereas you are wont to celebrate Christmas in playing at cards, I intend, by God's grace, to deal unto you Christ's cards, wherein you shall perceive Christ's rule. The game that we will play at shall be called the triumph. . . . Whensoever it shall happen the [evil-disposed affections and sensualities in us] rise in our stomachs against our brother or neighbor, either for unkind words, injuries, or wrongs which they have done unto us: straightways let us call unto our remembrance and speak this question unto ourselves, "Who art thou?" The answer is, "I am a Christian man." Now turn up your trump, your heart (hearts is trump, as I said before), and cast your trump, your heart, on this card. . . . If we be the true Magdalenes, we should be as willing to forsake our sin and rise from sin, as we were willing to commit sin and continue in it and we then should know ourselves . . . true Christian men and women. And then, I say, you should understand, and know how you ought to play at this card . . . and so triumph at the last, by winning everlasting life in glory.[81]

Latimer, "our first master of comic prose,"[82] preached this sermon a quarter century before he uttered his famous words at the stake: "Be of good comfort, Master Ridley, and play the man. We shall this day light such a candle by God's grace in England as I trust shall never be put out."

Empathetic conversion was understood as a ritualized game of hazard, a blood sport. I shall explore this theme in the next chapter.

CHAPTER 3

Love and Penitence

Even at the outset it was clear that understanding conversion presupposed doctrines about God's existence and power. Why do the good suffer and the wicked flourish? Conversion was among the experiences that vindicated the ways of God; it was a study in theodicy. In general the supernatural phenomenon that was called conversion occurred when people became convinced that in a world ruled by God, their habitual behavior was destroying them: in other words, that it failed them in the face of basic needs of empathy.

In this chapter I shall consider the need for love. Among all the needs, this is both one of the most encompassing and one of the most complex. For expounding empathetic conversion with reference to love required that assurance of love be present even when the faithful were mocked, afflicted, and laid desolate. As I have noted, writers saw the possibility that in their sufferings God played with them as wives suspected of infidelity or even as toys, that he was, as Augustine of Hippo depicted him, their laughing torturer.[1] Few subjects could illustrate more directly the nature of conversion as predicament, rather than peripety.

The general contours of the idea of conversion described continuing and danger-filled transformation, rather than abrupt and permanent change. What was called conversion was not a single event but a way of life governed by proportionality.

Believers continually hungered and thirsted after righteousness. When would the empathetic neediness of that hunger and thirst and the expedients of trial and education pass away and be replaced with fullness? The pilgrimage ended, Augustine wrote, only when this corruptible put on incorruption and this mortality, immortality, for only then could the soul lay aside its struggles against itself and the fragility of the body and escape its toiling in the weary languor of this world. Only then could its privation be changed into satiety and its striving, into full and perfect peace.[2]

The idea of conversion as a way of life mingling love, uncertainty, and affliction was grounded in the gospel call to repentance. Its institutionalization in monasticism was reaffirmed in the establishment of new monastic orders and congregations during the eleventh and twelfth centuries. Upholding the faith in its apostolic purity was thought necessary to salvation, and that, in turn, was seen to follow most reliably of all from submitting to the communal discipline said by the Book of Acts to have prevailed in the early Church.

Monastic training was a comprehensive form of educating empathy. It might appear that, by depending on rules and customs (*consuetudines*) to inculcate, direct, and enforce the apostolic life (*vita apostolica*), believers routinized conversion and made it a matter of following established customs and internalizing them as habits.

But monastic vigilance was not extolled as a virtue for martinets. It was a virtue for enemies of hypocrisy and other shams of holiness that confused outer (even mechanical) behavior with sanctification of heart. It disclosed the terrible uncertainties of dependence on God's hidden, inscrutable, and incomprehensible judgments. Born children of wrath, Christians became by baptism children of grace. But only the whole course of life and final grace would determine whether they would be children of glory. Visions disclosed that many conversions had not been completed. Although even observant monks kept rules and formed ascetic habits, they were not crucified with Christ by their *consuetudines*. They thought themselves monks, but they were not.[3]

This ardent, fearful doctrine was a fundamental departure from classical doctrines of empathetic education; it reversed the basic proposition that human nature was shaped by habituation to pleasure, which made some patterns of behavior attractive, and to pain, which made others repellent. Thus, it also cast in a way unanticipated by classical philosophies the human need for consolation. While by their educational methods ancient philosophers cultivated serenity of mind, Christian ascetics educated themselves to the wholesome terrors of an accusing conscience and prayed for the grace of tears. *Apatheia* indeed characterized some varieties of Christian spirituality in the West. But even when it appeared in that setting, it was incongruously paired with devotion to the Passion of Christ. For, as in the initiation rites of many societies, pain was recognized and employed as a pedagogical means by which to shake "the foundations of personality and mak[e] it ready to accept new identities."[4] Flogging was a normal part of classroom instruction. The Church Fathers Jerome and Augustine witness to its frequency, to its physical pain, and to the inward terrors that it ingrained in the emotions.

Boethius's (c.480–c.524) *Consolation of Philosophy* preserves the ancient zeal to educate the mind to imperturbability through indifference to circumstances. By contrast, speaking within the tradition with which we are concerned, John Bunyan (1628–1688) sought affliction and gloried in the sharp wounds inflicted upon him by the Devil and his seed, for, Bunyan wrote, "should I not be dealt with thus wickedly by the world, I should want one sign of a saint and a child of God."[5]

Among the perceptions of common human needs driving this tradition, that for life was primary. Yet, as already noted, the need for life subsumed others, including one not far behind it in compelling force: the need for love, which sanctified both joy and agony. I shall have to examine how this paradox was put together before turning to the pattern of empathetic education by which it was taught and sanctioned.

The Pains of Love

Pagans were capable of chastity and, indeed, of blameless virginity. And yet self-denial did not distinguish converted from unconverted any more than did suffering and death; the distinguishing factor was the cause for endurance.[6] To be construed figuratively, a scriptural passage had to witness by a hidden, symbolic likeness to the mission of Christ, such as in his incarnation, in his gift of the Holy Spirit after his ascension, or in his second coming.[7] Hence, for believers, too, pain lacked spiritual meaning unless it referred to Christ. The sufferings of pagans, like their virtues, were meaningless beyond themselves. By contrast, when in faith Christians submitted to the chastening of the Lord, they realized that without chastisement they were bastards and not his true children—"For what child is that whom the father chasteneth not?"—and that he punished them in love for their profit, so that they "might be partakers of his holiness" (Heb. 12:5–11).

When they imitated Christ in taking up the Cross and joining their anguish to his by empathetic participation, their sufferings became sacrifices. When for his sake they resisted inner or outer enemies unto blood, their deaths became martyrdoms. When in passionate ardor they endured either the agony of absence from their divine Spouse or the devouring blaze of his rapture, they were slain to be made alive. Thus, they escaped the meaninglessness of pain, for the sufferings of the converted were punishments merited by sin, tests sent to divide true from counterfeit believer, purgations to burn away the dross from the elect souls, propitiating sacrifices, and means of sanctification. The pains that they suffered were delectable wounds of a cruel yet tender love; to use a phrase of St. John of the Cross (1542–1591), the soul was "wholly dissolved in the wound of love," a wound in which it became one with the burning of the divine fire that cauterized and healed it.[8] Yet, one's mind had to be educated to read this complex network of symbolism; one's emotions had to be educated to take it to heart. Long before John of the Cross, Hildegard of Bingen (1098–1179) captured a similar fusion of love and pain when she wrote that God continually gazed upon the wounds of Christ, wounds still kept open by continual human sinning in the world and displayed to the Father by the Son as propitiation.[9]

Accordingly, the two great rituals of conversion, baptism and the Eucharist, memorialized, enacted, and imparted pain. The singular characteristic of baptism and Eucharist was that actors in them were thought to enact the *forma conversionis* set forth in the life, Passion, and resurrection of Christ. Believers were thought to live and relive those events not by simulation but in actuality. Through baptism they died and were raised again to life in Christ. Through the Eucharist they became the sacrifice that, offered once and for all on the cross, was also daily laid upon the altar.

The pursuit of sacrificial suffering was part of the tradition of ascetic discipline.[10] For many, the crux of zealous vigilance and of zeal to be sacrificed with Christ fell exactly in the distinction between love and lust, and by this route they recognized that erotic suffering could demand other, penitential kinds. Few motifs were more persistent than the identification of purity with chastity and the resulting infliction of pain to stifle lust. The account of Benedict's (480–c. 546) self-laceration with nettles inspired deliberately cruel imitation in a distant age and place.[11] Juan Cirita (d. 1164) fought the fire of lust with a different fire, offering his left arm to the flames until it was burned to the bone.[12]

The intense dread with which sexuality was identified with spiritual pollution is indicated also by dreams. It is most evident in the account of a monk of Clairvaux, driven by temptation to the point of returning to the world and saved from that fate by a nightmare in which he saw himself brutally castrated by a savage and terrifying man. The dream made him spiritually—or, as we might say, psychosomatically—a eunuch. But even accounts of a gentler imparting of the gift of chastity—as in another monk's vision of an angel who came to him and anointed his genitals with balsam, or in Thomas Aquinas's of angels vesting him with the girdle of chastity, or in Christina of Markyates's of herself embracing the infant Christ who entered her—even in such accounts, the inward pain of sexual temptation is intense.[13]

It was paradoxical that even while it answered the need for love, conversion did not end but instead opened the way to suffering. In the Christian tradition the re-creative educational process of conversion was a pathological experience, grounded in the need of love. Characteristically, converts endured great physical and mental pain before and after enlightenment. Their understanding but not their need of pain changed after their minds were "reformed," but in most cases the new understanding brought new dimensions of suffering. One of the few similarities between the religious quest of Teresa of Avila and that of John Bunyan was postenlightenment depression. John Calvin (1509–1564) was true to this tradition when he taught that moral struggle arising through love of righteousness and hatred of sin only began with conversion.[14]

As psychologists of love, mystics and troubadours knew that the course of true love could be full of pitfalls. Just as a suitor's ardor was fanned by denial, the sweetness of fruition was all the rarer, all the more delectable, for the tribulations endured in reaching it, which is also to say, for the countless dangers of losing it. Ever incomplete in this world, empathetic conversion could bring only foretastes of the perfect love of God and neighbor that eternal life would bring. Consequently, one lived with a zealous and vigilant sense of the trials to which lovers were put, the proofs of love demanded of them, and the risks of forfeiting its complete and lasting joy.

Imperfect Conversion

The idea of faith, and hence of conversion, as proportional had profound consequences. As progressive, educational change, conversion entailed vigilant and continual criticism. Suspicions were plainest regarding those who converted from other religions, but they were no less intense regarding those moving from one way of life to another within the Church. This was implied by the Benedictine *Rule*'s precept that to achieve salvation, monks needed to remain under discipline in Christ's "school" until death. The common point of departure, both for those whose education in the faith had just begun and for veterans in the monastery, was fear of apostasy.

Those who knew that conversion from Christianity to paganism was possible had no reason to think that conversions to Christianity were necessarily permanent.[15] To be sure, suspicion of converts is by no means peculiar to one religion.[16] The striking fact is that it conspicuously figured in Christianity, a proselytizing religion dedicated to the conversion of the world.

Indeed, fear and experience of apostasy were pervasive. The entire history of schism and heresy in Christendom and the apocalyptic role assigned to hypocrites ("false brethren" subverting the Church from within) witness to the scope of this intramural suspicion. "There is nothing between us and you," the unconverted Pomeranians are reputed to have said to the missionary Otto of Bamberg. "We are not going to give up the laws of our fathers; we are content with the religion [*religio*] that we have. Among Christians, there are thieves; there are robbers whose feet are cut off and whose eyes, put out. And Christian exercises all manner of crime and punishment against Christian. Far be such a religion [*religio*] from us."[17] (Centuries later, Bertrand Russell [1872–1970] similarly pointed to the mutual cruelties as one reason why he was not a Christian.)[18] Perhaps dimly, the Pomeranians had seen that even within the Church conversion sanctified violence, both personal and collective; without instruction, they could not have known that this resulted from sanctifying fear as the beginning of wisdom. And self-corrosive fear was inescapable if one realized that while some were converted entirely by the vocation of God, others were drawn into the net of faith by the fickleness of their own minds, and still others, by instigation of an evil spirit.[19]

Those who experienced and wrote about conversion from the Apostle Paul onward, and certainly throughout the era with which I am concerned, continually used the word *conversion* metaphorically, as an instrument for criticizing secular values, hierarchic order, and, above all, themselves. The persistence of doubt and other agonizing temptations among Christians is one pronounced difference between the experiences of empathetic conversion that they expected to have and did record and the calmness of soul to which Stoics, Epicureans, and Buddhists aspired, not to mention the calm assurance of status that Apuleius portrayed in the *Golden Ass* at the end of Lucius's conversion to the cults of Isis and Osiris. Attuned to the extremely divided feelings that upward social mobility can inspire, sociologists, using the metaphor of center and periphery, have captured a tension reminiscent of agonies dramatized in medieval texts. Those who feel at a distance from the center, Edward Shils wrote, seek "by becoming school teachers, priests [and] administrators" to approach the center. But they continue "to perceive themselves as 'outsiders,' while continuing to be intensely attracted and influenced by the outlook and style of life at the center." Thus, "those who participate in the central institutional and value systems—who feel sufficiently closer to the center now than their forebears ever did—also feel their positions as outsiders, their remoteness from the center, in a way in which their forebears probably did not feel it."[20]

Shils could have added that such persons may be subject to the doubts of others as well as to their own, suspect as well to their old as to their new communities. The limits of empathy were manifold. For conversion engendered social as well as personal tensions. Augustine of Hippo never lost the scent of "a notorious character," one who was so suspect to Bishop Ambrose of Milan, the very man whose preaching spectacularly prepared for his conversion, that Ambrose deliberately and steadily kept him at arm's length.[21]

One need but recall Benedict of York. Persecuted, wounded, and driven to despair during the ferocious anti-Jewish riots in 1189–90 that marked the accession of Richard I of England, Benedict converted to save his life. Baptized and renamed William, he recanted when the king restored order. He declared himself a Jew and resumed his original name, scorned by Christians as "the Devil's man." "And in a short time," Roger of Hoveden recorded, "he died at Northampton and was a stranger to the common burialgrounds of Jews, because he had been made a Christian, and of Christians, because, as a dog to his vomit, he had returned to his Jewish depravity."[22] The election of Anacletus II (reigned 1130–38), the "Jewish pope," could be cited as an example of assimilation, given Anacletus's previous glittering career in the Curia and the long eminence of his forebears in papal service. But references to his family, the Pierleoni, in the generations between the conversion of his great-grandfather and his election and polemics against him on behalf of his rival and eventual supplanter, Innocent II (reigned 1130–43), illustrate how durable the rhetoric of suspicions could be. Forgetting five generations of Christianity, Bernard of Clairvaux declared it an insult to Christ that the offspring of a Jew should sit in the chair of St. Peter.[23] Those who employed military force to achieve baptisms had reason to know that those whom they had dragged to the font were likely to revert to their old practices as soon as danger was past.[24]

Three centuries later, even the canonist Juan de Torquemada (1388–1468), uncle of the inquisitor who after 1492 hounded the Jews from Spain, was far from extreme in his attitude toward Jewish converts to Christianity. Some contended that the evil seed of infidelity tainted Jewish converts and their descendants to the fourth generation. What implications, Torquemada asked, did the rule about tainted seed have for Christians who converted from the wickedness of idolatry or, indeed, for the descendants of early Christians who distinguished themselves by the most impious acts of blasphemy, sodomy, betrayal, usury, and heresy? Four generations of tainted seed was not long enough to account for the recent lapse of the entire kingdom of Bohemia into heresy or for the intrusion of heresy closer to home, as in the twenty-two persons who, he recalled, had lately burned at the stake. It was no wonder, he concluded, if there were wicked Jews among the converts, but this was not to be explained by tainted seed.²⁵ Bernard of Clairvaux had indicated as much when he denounced Christian moneylenders, asking whether they could be called Christians, and not baptized Jews.²⁶ Evidently, I have touched upon an attitude in Christianity that contributed to anti-Jewish thought and action.²⁷ However, it is essential to recognize that, while it was directed with special ferocity toward Jews, the limits set to empathy derived from a general fear of apostasy. The Jews exemplified apostasy, but they were by no means the only apostates.

Converts were suspect to others. (As long-established English Catholics said in John Henry Newman's day, "All converts are dangerous.")²⁸ Yet my point carries me closer to Shils's observation, for converts were also suspect to and among themselves. Whatever else it implied, Jerome's incisive sentence— "Christians are made, not born"—meant that all Christians were converts. Thus, insofar as converts aroused suspicion, the entire community of believers was shot through with universal and mutual suspicion. At rare moments latent possibilities were brought to the surface. This occurred, for example, with special pathos when Christian majorities subjected Jewish converts to hostile scrutiny. The instance of sixteenth-century Italy is conspicuous. For when the Counter-Reformation Church imposed many severe restrictions, including the regularization of the ghetto, some Jewish converts were driven to spy upon and denounce others to vindicate their own adherence to Christianity. But the suspicion of crypto-belief in former ways was endemic in a society of converts.

Indeed, the indeterminacy of what is called the "conversion experience" is striking. Characteristically, the converted kept their illuminations secret for a time. Othloh of St. Emmeram (c. 1010–c. 1070) had acted in this way when he entered the monastic life without the knowledge of kinsmen or friends. After the die was cast, he was tormented (by Satan, he later discovered) with the thought that he had acted in ill-considered youthful rashness, contrary to Scripture, and allowed himself to be swayed momentarily from his decision by his father's entreaties.²⁹ Similarly, Herman-Judah cast his entire spiritual pilgrimage as a prolonged attempt to understand a vision given to him at the age of thirteen. The moment of enlightenment came to him late in this trail of hesitations; and dreading vengeance from the Jewish community, he practiced a fervent Nicodemism for some time after divine illumination swept his doubts away.³⁰

These cases exemplify a pattern of empathetic conversion frequently called that of the "twice-born," in which a first moment of enlightenment is followed by a period of wavering. And still, the idea of conversion set forth in the parable of the sower makes the term *twice-born* completely inadequate. The pattern described is a continuous and manifold process, a powerful ebb and flow of ecstasy and sadness.

I spoke earlier of a postenlightenment depression syndrome in which the convert's joy gave way to despair at the realization of how impassable a distance lay between human frailty and divine perfection. It was also possible for the call to normalcy which led some converts to Christian syncretism to lead others back to their old equilibrium. In the latter cases converts discounted or poured contempt on previous sufferings. Perhaps yielding to the counsel of others, they returned to former ways until recalled by subsequent illuminations, not infrequently in the form of extreme physical pain. Such, indeed, was the experience of Othloh, who was finally driven to reenter monastic life by a paralytic seizure that left him able to move only his tongue and lips.[31]

Frequent and vehement temptation intruded the possibility of apostasy into daily life, indeed, into the experience even of the greatest saints. The imitation of Christ demanded that his disciples also follow him into the wilderness, that they, too, be tempted as he was. Burdened by their own temptations, believers had before their eyes the examples of Peter and Judas, apostolic models of wavering conversions, as Nicodemus exemplified concealed ones. Both Peter and Judas suffered remorse. Peter denied Christ with his lips, not his heart; his contrition was impelled by love of Christ. God had predestined him in martyrdom to the crown of immortality.

Which example would prevail in the spiritual quest of any Christian soul—that of Peter, who like his Master passed through the ordeal of temptation, or that of Judas, who succumbed to it? Peter's betrayal was pardoned, and in a second calling the risen Christ entrusted his flock to him, as Prince of the Apostles. Judas was called to the crown of apostolate but not predestined to the crown of immortality. His betrayal was impelled by envious hatred; his remorse was not a confession of sin so much as an act of his deluded mind; his death was unsanctified. Thus, despite all his manifold works of justice, the impenitent Judas was condemned for one crime, the betrayal of his Master. Even so, both Peter and Judas had been called by Christ and worked beside him; and Satan entered Judas with the bread that he received from the hand of the same Master who had called him to the apostolate.[32]

Pathology and Mental Disciplines

By stages we have moved deeper, from expressions of the need for an austere, testing, and educating love to the fear of apostasy that lay behind that need. We can go yet further beyond ideas to the teaching methods by which minds were formed to approved limits and degrees of empathy. For the very techniques of education inculcated pain and habits of causing pain.

The key mental function altered in conversion was discernment. The object of discernment was knowledge of God—"the most certain knowledge of [God's] substance," in Othloh of St. Emmeram's words.[33] Discernment penetrated the outer symbol and grasped the inner reality; it transcended the logic of words to the logic of understanding (*intelligentia*), or rather spirit,[34] in which wisdom was identical with *pietas*. Authentic humanity consisted in the exercise of discernment; for those who saw God were re-formed into his image and likeness, the manifold wisdom and spiritual *conditio* in which human nature had originally been made but which had become deformed through sin.

Without authentic knowledge of God, human beings were prisoners of their own carnality; they were animal, rather than spiritual. Such were pagans, Jews, heretics, and false Christians. The chosen, too, but partially converted, were still fettered to their carnality, still subject to fleshly temptations with which God permitted Satan to test them, even after God had given them the grace of understanding.

The pathology of empathetic conversion existed in great measure because the turning of the heart from animality into sanctified humanity did not—and could not—occur by magic. The essence of conversion was that neither God's action nor the human wish to convert (*voluntas conversionsis*)[35] be subject to mechanical or pharmacopoeial manipulation. Magic, like astrology and simony, purported to put the Holy Spirit at the beck and call of sinners. It was commonly agreed that the *voluntas conversionis* engaged a variety of mental acts, which were identified and discussed. And yet the need to revere the unqualified freedom of the Spirit by denying any manipulative control, such as magic or astrology promised, negated the sufficiency of those acts, even as theology demanded them. Such tensions made the pathology of conversion an uncertain "psychomachia," a blind melee of virtues and vices within the soul itself. Let me examine this structure of counterbalancing demands and negations.

The letters and treatises with which I am concerned were written by men subject to monastic discipline, which was itself widely regarded as a paradigm of empathetic conversion resembling more closely than others the exemplar of Christ. Quite naturally, monastic authors considered that the specific experience of enlightenment came about through the same cognitive acts that the general spiritual exercises of their daily lives required. Those cognitive acts were reading, meditation, prayer, and contemplation.

A similar array of disciplines had been employed in ancient philosophies to teach self-mastery and thereby to achieve transformation of the self. There, too, vigilance was required, and relentless scrutiny both of one's way of life and of motives for actions. In some philosophies, as in Christian ideas derived from them, the objective of training in these disciplines was to lead the soul to contemplative knowledge of God.[36] Assimilated to the Church's penitential institutions, each of the disciplines was a ritualized exercise in pain and, more precisely, in the pain of helplessness.

Christ commanded his followers to be perfect, even as the Father in heaven was perfect. How were human beings to keep this commandment? By what stages could they pass toward perfection? Surely reading the evidence of Scripture (*documenta Scripturae*) was the first stage. The liberal arts were tools of conversion, a relay in which literacy was given by God so that the literate could edify others.[37] The converted commonly prided themselves on their rhetorical skills, and not for piety's sake only, as Othloh implied when he wrote that as a youth he always wished to spend his time among studious and learned clerics, rather than among peasants (*villanos*).[38] Professing their own rusticity, they yet cast disdain upon the lamentable styles of earlier writers and demonstrated their literary virtuosity in accounts of conversions, their own or those of others. However, the greater their virtuosity, the greater their sense that "no small miracle" lay at the heart of it.[39]

Miracle diminished human control. Skill in words, even in reading scriptural texts, need contribute nothing to conversion. Satan quoted Scripture. Pagans could read. Among Christians, good and evil alike read Scripture. But, if one matched their conduct against what they read there, it would be hard to conclude that Scripture told anything convincing about God or the observance of his commandments. "The outward letter is profitless to a reader; for reading of the outward letter has little savor unless a gloss on the text be drawn from the literal sense, unless there be the heart to disclose the inward sense."[40] What distinguished reading that formed the *voluntas conversionis* from profitless reading was intention (*intentio mentis*) formed by experience. The mixture of "blandishments with terrors"[41] that enlightened readers found in the text of Scripture came not from the silent words on the page but from their own spiritual imaginations.

Right intention came from meditation as little as it did from reading. Metaphors of food and eating (including rumination) were used to characterize the goal of meditation: inwardly to digest, by absorption and elimination, the hidden truth bitten off by reading.[42] Techniques of rhetoric were exploited to enhance the ruminative sifting of memory by bringing subjects vividly to life as spectacles in the theater of the mind. The dramatic structures of conversion accounts express the wish of the authors to stimulate in their audiences processes of empathetic visualization like those which they themselves practiced as a mode of emotional assimilation.

Yet monastic writers knew useless meditations as well as arid reading. A self-regarding torpor was an ever-present trap. Othloh related that he begged God to visit him with temptation and to flog him, as his schoolmasters had done when he was a boy, in order to evade that danger.[43] Meditation was reason seeking faith (*intellectus quaerens fidem*), not least when it led the meditator to doubt the *essentia* or omnipotence of God and doctrines of catholic belief.[44] In Othloh's meditations a man of threatening countenance who, in a vision, flogged him with more than human cruelty and savagery was understood to be the Good Samaritan, pouring soothing oil and wine, more bitter than any vinegar, into the wounds of sin.[45] Even greater dangers could lie in the way of meditation. For God permitted the Devil to tempt human beings; he knew and allowed suffering in his general plan to test them all, as though in a furnace of affliction. God permitted the Devil to intrude false thoughts, robbing human minds of knowledge of God. Thus, a shadow fell over the whole enterprise of meditation: Was the spectacle played before the eye of the mind a revelation, perhaps a chastisement, from God or a delusion intruded by Satan, with God's permission, that prevented knowledge of God?

Reading provided food; meditation consumed and digested it. Prayer extracted the savor; contemplation was the sweetness itself.[46] But in the specific experience of conversion as in general monastic discipline, the two highest cognitive acts, like the preliminary ones, occurred in an ironic tension between the divine command to be perfect and human incapacity for perfection. As in many hierarchic schemata, the theory of cognition that defined conversion was constructed from the apex down, rather than from the base (e.g., reading and meditation) up. The apex of conversion was not human endeavors but acts of violence by which God seized his chosen ones and, with mighty hand and straining arm, led them along the hard road of conversion out of the Egypt of this world.[47]

The words *conversion* and *penitence* were virtual synonyms, but even prayer, the main cognitive act in the discipline of penitence, was thought to display the irony of the impossible command to be perfect. Certainly, prayer has a central place in accounts of, and prescriptions for, conversion. There are abundant testimonies to the necessity of prayer for oneself and intercessory prayer for others as a means to pass from the *interiora* of meditation higher, to enlightenment. The external apparatus of cult was designed to provide formidable buttresses to mental prayer, in words and in canonical hours, in places set apart by awe of holy presences, in visual arts employed as stimuli to pious imaginations,[48] and, above all, in psalmody. Psalmody was acknowledged as an especially powerful device. Combined with prayer, it aroused the intention of the heart. Thereby, it prepared the way that the Lord would take into the heart so as to open the mysteries of prophecy or to pour out the grace of compunction.[49] With some such idea in mind, Othloh related that in one of his temptations, evil spirits pressed his lips together so that he could not move them in psalmody.[50]

In the inward act of prayer, worshipers confronted the distance between God's majesty, goodness, power, and *pietas* and their own insufficiency, wickedness, weakness, and most grievous sin. For they exalted God when they abased themselves. God had promised to save all who called upon him with contrite and broken hearts. Even so, there was no assurance that self-lacerating prayer, reenforced by other ascetic disciplines such as fasting, vigils, and flagellation, could overcome the deficiencies of reading and meditation. The vigor of prayer was impaired by physical and mental agonies, by temptations (notably including sexual ones), and, indeed, by the beauty of the arts intended as aids to concentration. Thus, some who seemed adept in the rituals of piety actually prayed empty words with their lips, while the intention of the heart was elsewhere, "simulating rather than following the way of truth."[51]

The most inscrutable irony lay in the fact that, despite the literal sense of God's promise, he did reject some who wished to be his disciples.[52] The chosen were fewer than the called. But suffering was even here, at the moment of calling. Recounting their own conversions, Othloh of St. Emmeram and Herman-Judah independently applied to themselves Augustine's description of his contemplative enlightenment in the garden (*Confessions*, 8.12). Suddenly, they wrote, light flooded into their hearts and put the shadows of doubt (and ignorance) to flight.[53] In these two accounts, as in Augustine's, the contemplative moment came late in a series of bitter physical and mental afflictions imposed or allowed by God. Othloh alleged that he was "led to faith" not by contemplative enlightenment but "by the most savage torments."[54] Other conversion accounts agree that the understanding produced by contemplation complemented what was induced by pain, whether in the overpowering terror of signs and portents or in unbearable disease. In this regard, too, the accounts of Othloh and Herman-Judah resemble that of Augustine, who portrayed God, his laughing, pitying torturer, as advancing, and indeed protracting, the long course of conversion with sickness, pain, and grief.[55] Enlightenment changed the perception of suffering. It enabled the converted to seek and to embrace pain as tests that God sent to prove and to purify them and as tokens of his savage love. However, it did not end the suffering. The confidence that enlightenment gave Othloh came with an admonition to prepare for more and greater temptations. For the greater the grace of divine inspiration by which one is taught, he wrote, the more powerful in the same degree will be the onslaught of temptation that one suffers.[56]

The principal acts of cognition that were thought to figure in empathetic conversion demonstrate that a relentless spirit of criticism presided over each mode of thought by which humanity was believed to be reconstituted in the sinful soul. At every stage the soul was subject to reforming violence. The rational acts of cognition were thereby subordinated to affective ones. In the end, the pathology of empathetic conversion was about pity, love, and fear. Later, in chapter 5 (after n. 63), I shall indicate how these ritualizing traits of monastic discipline reinforced patterns of conflict current in society as a whole, especially those of male rivalry and bonding.

Even conversion to the monastic life, with its cognitive disciplines, was an instrument to produce another kind of conversion, "a turning of the heart," Caesarius of Heisterbach wrote, "from bad to good, or from good to better, or from better to best." And this turning began at the heart (*ad cor*) with contrition, progressed in the heart (*in corde*) with devotion, and was consummated as the heart passed beyond itself (*de corde*) to God in contemplation.[57] Caesarius's stages correspond, in the mystical tradition, to the purgative, illuminative, and unitive ways. But the casting of the heart could be illusory to those whose conversions came through the superficialities of their own minds or through the instigation of evil spirits and, to be sure, to some whose vocation was of God.

Widening the Circle of Pain in Love

As an educational program the pathology of conversion taught that suffering should be inflicted as well as endured.[58] This was one consequence of the limits set to empathy. Experiences of enlightenment inevitably were expected to have social consequences, for, at the least, they imposed upon those to whom they were vouchsafed the obligation, in brotherly love, to seek edification of the community. In the Age of the Fathers, Augustine had prepared the classic defense of persecution as a work of love in his protracted struggle against the Donatists (*ep. 185*). Consequently, the theory of cognition entailed a theory of action which projected upon the wide world the pathology of the inner life and its outward ritualizations. Through their private spirituality, converts cultivated attitudes of passivity toward God. Through their work of edification, they reversed the roles. There they claimed the authority of divine inspiration and sought to vindicate their conversions through force by attempting to stamp the seal of their apostolates in the hearts of others. It was not necessary that there actually be conversions.[59]

To be sure, confidence that conversions could be won—and thus the apocalyptic coming of God's kingdom hastened—through human agency provided a spur to proselytism; but awareness that conversion came by the grace of faith, a gift of God, demanded rewards in case of failure. Thus, great prelates were able to exhort princes to advance the work of conversion and to promise them victory in all their undertakings and, at the same time, to add that whatever adversities the princes suffered for the name of Christ would sanctify them. Whether their efforts brought lasting conversions or martyrdom, proselytizers knew that crowns were laid up for them in heaven. Not infrequently, at least for clerics, the quest of martyrdom for oneself beckoned with greater certainty than that of conversion for others.[60] Archbishop Adalbert of Hamburg-Bremen (c. 1000–1072) preached to the heathen, rebuking them for the berserk riots and sexual convulsions with which they passed their drunken nights. It was just the liquor, it was all in play, they said, and heaped derision on Adalbert; but he did not lose his reward.[61]

As missionaries in India, my own forebears encountered similar blank walls. When they preached in the bazaars, they reported, "we are told that if we are good men we ought to imitate the sages who instead of troubling people by their doctrines as we do retire to their groves and lovely places and there spend their time in meditation in secret on the attributes of God. . . . No one [they say] will ever forsake the religion of his fathers to join us . . . and [they have used] many of our books . . . for wrapping paper and making kites."[62]

Always in danger of death, the missionary Bishop Otto of Bamberg moved among the Pomeranians with great power, forbidding them the "profane superstitions and pagan observances" that constituted their ethnic identity, destroying their temples which were also the centers of their social unity,[63] overturning their priesthoods, and disrupting their political orders. He carried with him stores of magnificent raiment and precious works of art to be used in gaining the favor of prospective converts and vestments and liturgical furniture designed to express to their carnal eyes the exalted power personified by him. Yet with all his elegance of bearing and noble affability, he persisted in the austere ritualized discipline of his personal spirituality. His diet was poor and meager; his meditations, full of penitence and contrition; his devotions, marked by flagellations in which the great prelate submitted to be flogged by priests until his sides streamed with blood. The mission, with all its consequences for Pomeranian society, was an extension of Otto's ritualized quest for martyrdom through love of Christ and contempt of self.[64]

An earlier writer had captured the rationale behind this teaching. We are members of Christ, our supreme head, he wrote, and by imitating and cleaving to him we ought to go where he has gone. He passed through humiliation, flogging, mockery, and the most shameful death of the Cross to the glory of the resurrection; and he now sits, crowned with glory and honor, on the right hand of the Father. So, too, if we are sons of the all-high Father, the writer concluded, we ought to be worthy to suffer reproaches for the name of Jesus, abiding with him through worldly sufferings, so that we may rise and reign with him.[65]

Some writers found it impermissible to cast the waters of baptism upon unwilling infidels; others argued that no constraint should be used to produce conversion. Yet the dominant judgment, codified by Pope Innocent III (1160/61–1216, reigned 1198–1216), was that if unbelievers consented to baptism, even so as to escape threatened pain, they must be forced to remain obedient to the teachings and discipline of the Church.[66]

What was at the heart of this violent, dual role in empathetic education? Here I return to the indeterminacy of conversion, to the awareness that where there was conversion, there was also the chance of apostasy, exemplified not only by Judas but also by King Solomon, the paragon of spiritual wisdom and the builder of the Lord's temple. Christian writers cast scorn upon those who converted from other religions only to return to the "vomit" or "dung" of their ancestral cults.[67] And yet their fervor was trained not in rivalries on ethnic frontiers but at home against those who had put their hand to the plow and then turned back, becoming ministers of Satan. Professor John Van Engen has suggested to me that, if there are in the collections of Burchard and Ivo twenty canons about entering a monastery, there are eighty restricting departure from it.

The monk who wished to return to the world became a stock figure in devotional literature, like apostates to paganism a test for the power of saints to overcome. St. Romuald of Camaldoli (c.952–1027) prevented the defection of his own father by confining him in chains and flogging his feet until he came to a better mind.[68] And by his prayers Ailred of Rievaulx erected an invisible barrier "like a wall of iron" to keep one of his brethren from leaving the monastic precincts.[69] Caesarius of Heisterbach morosely recalled how a novice had been enticed to leave the monastery of Hemmenrode and fell ill. By God's just judgment, Caesarius recounted, the man's disease turned into madness, and while his friends desperately called him to confession, he continually screamed out the names of women with whom he had sinned. In anguish, those nearest him sundered puppies and placed their warm flesh on his head; but neither this nor any other fleshly remedy could deliver him from the delirium that punished his apostasy.[70] The experience of divided papal elections, including that of Innocent II and Anacletus II, raised the practical matter of heresy or apostasy in the see of Peter and the legal and coercive measures that could legitimately be taken to repress it.[71] Even in the see of Peter some, like Lot's wife, looked back and perished.

One sharpened one's prophetic sword against the evident apostasies of converts from paganism and against the covert ones of false brethren who labored to subvert the Church, rebuilding Babylon within the walls of Jerusalem, or who, by their "judaizing" interpretation of Scripture, threatened to transform the Church of Christ into the Synagogue of Satan.[72] It was certain, as Caesarius observed, that many who thought they were monks were not, since they had not followed Christ in crucifying themselves to the world.[73] Could one avert scrutiny of potential apostasies within oneself, especially those of the old carnality, to which God allowed the Tempter to entice the called?

What if ascetic discipline brought pain? The Apostle Paul himself required continual affliction, his "thorn in the flesh," to keep him from the catastrophe of pride. What if criticism of others, even of great officers in the Church, brought affliction or martyrdom? After Christ called him to conversion, was it not a sign of his apostolate that Paul was almost never free of danger from enemies and persecutors and that his faith was sealed by martyrdom, just as other great athletes of the faith also found princes of the earth and whole kingdoms arrayed against them?[74] Perhaps the others in their spiritual blindness would not convert and thereby witness to the ardent faith of the evangelists. Even then, the unregenerate could bear witness of another kind, authenticating the evangelists' calling by visiting upon them persecution and martyrdom.

Yet, looking toward the immanent end of things, some writers insisted that the tribulation characteristic of their age was deception by false Christs and false prophets, which could cause even the elect to totter. Those of the elect who held fast to truth could never be completely overthrown. As to the others, God could send them the working of error, as he had done to Adam and Eve, so that they would believe the serpent's lie, or give them over to their own blindness, as he had done the Jews, bitterly punishing their infidelity. Outward conformity and great office were by no means conclusive signs that God had not hardened the heart so that through works of pride and envy, his prophecies might be fulfilled, just as was the case when many disciples abandoned Jesus and twelve remained, one being a devil.[75]

Let me dwell upon one point. There is an irony in the fact that even as Christian exegetes consulted Jewish ones as authorities on scriptural interpretation and assimilated their exegetical methods, "Jewish understanding" remained a phrase of rebuke in their vocabularies. But, for this, there is a prior irony. They argued that the Jews were impenitent for their crimes and still rebelled against and blasphemed Christ, whom their fathers killed. They insisted that the Romans' killing, captivity, and dispersal of the Jews rightly punished those ancient crimes of spiritual blindness and that the residual effects of the Diaspora justly continued the punishment as long as the blindness persisted. And still, no free act of will could have averted these catastrophes. For the Jews' sufferings befell them to fulfill prophecies about the conversion of the Gentiles; no one could convert the Jews, ending their blindness and punishment together, until the divinely appointed moment when, according to the apocalyptic vision of the Last Times, the gospel of Christ had been preached throughout the world.[76]

Understandably, mistrust stalked on each side, especially among those to whom forced conversions, followed by mass apostasies, were recent in memory.[77] It was possible for Herman-Judah to believe, mistakenly as it happened, that the Christian clergy were making him their laughing stock even as he stood in the baptismal font. Converts were received gingerly, as when a bishop of Trier commended his baptized Jewish physician to his vassals, urging them to provide charitably for his material needs, since "that race of human beings [the Jews] is very unstable in the faith and always wishes to abound in the necessities of life."[78]

In what ways did the ideas of ritualized moral education that I have considered express both the universal need for love and an address to that need explored outside Christianity? In the second chapter I referred to the fourfold vow of bodhisattvas, accepted in some late forms of Buddhism (at n. 72). Here the second vow is relevant: "However inexhaustible the passions, I vow to extinguish them all." While both Buddhism and Christianity departed from the same point—the pain of existence—Buddhism prescribed a state of suspended perceptions and sensations in which suffering and painlessness were identical. By contrast, Christianity sanctified the emotions. Among Christians, mental disciplines (the liberal arts, meditation, prayer, and contemplation) schooled believers to hold the Passion of Christ before their mind's eye for imitation in ritualized play. Among Buddhists, they were means to extinguish consciousness and passion together, means, as the Zen master Lin-chi wrote, to slay all that came between the seeker and his goal, to slay parents, kinsmen, and, yes, Buddhas.[79] I know of no Christian writer who combined the love of God with an injunction to recrucify Christ.

To be sure, there are points of similarity, at least among some variations of Zen Buddhism, in the use of physical austerities, including self-mutilation, as educational techniques by ascetics and the relentless application of doubt in the progress toward enlightenment. Like Christianity, Buddhism held up the insufficiency of doctrinal understanding to achieve true purity of mind and the chance that lacking the Great Enlightenment, even bodhisattvas, remarkable in their wisdom, moral purity, and spiritual attainments, could fail to achieve complete self-emptying and consequently freedom from the pain of existence. According to some masters, it was also necessary to impose suffering upon others under discipline. Speaking of the tendency of monks to go to sleep while sitting in meditation, the head of a Zen monastery recalled: "Formerly, I used to hit sleeping monks so hard that my fist just about broke. Now I am old and weak, so I can't hit them hard enough. Therefore it is difficult to produce good monks. In many monasteries today the superiors do not emphasize [the discipline of meditative] sitting strongly enough, and so Buddhism is declining. The more you hit them, the better."[80]

However, even in the overflowing benevolence that required bodhisattvas to save all sentient beings before achieving their own salvation, it was not possible for Buddhists to imagine a personal God, a god who was love, or, finally, a god who inflicted suffering, in ritualized play, as an instrument of charity. By the same token, it was also impossible to portray the deliberate application of physical and mental suffering by ascetics to themselves and to others as a propitiating sacrifice. Likewise, a spirituality of suspended perceptions and sensations could not inspire holy wars.

Later History

The subject of empathetic conversion brought into play a large educational repertory of suffering. Ascetic writers used the rhetoric of pain to describe the erotic longing of the soul for God. They used it also to express the drama of crime and punishment in which Christians cast human history, with metaphors of the jailer's whip, the surgeon's knife, and the refiner's fire. Yet the indeterminacy of conversion, the persistence of temptation after it, the deceptive cunning of antichrists, and the continuing series of apostasies in order that prophecy be fulfilled locate a primary source of pain. Was not God the author both of crime and of punishment? "He wills evil to be," Hugh of St. Victor wrote, "and in this he wills nothing but good, because it is good that there be evil. . . . If we do good, God wills this. . . . If we do evil, he wills that we not do good, and he approves this because it is good."[81]

This premise naturally had a bearing on what it was thought the identity of the convert was changed into, and thus on ways of explaining the educational need to endure and to inflict pain. It was possible to dismiss as "most insane and impious" the thought that God both caused hatred and deceit and then punished the acts to which they led.[82] But it was not possible to dismiss the theodical quandaries of why if there were a God, there was evil in the world, or why, if there were no God, there was good. Thus, it was not possible to extricate theodicy from empathetic conversion.

The goal of conversion was unity with God, an empathetic participation in which the "I" and the "you" became one. Conversion was the turning of the heart, a movement through purgation and enlightenment to that union. Yet, suspicion and a rigorous critical method were ingrained into each step of spiritual ascent and into each educational discipline used to reform discernment from animal to spiritual understanding. Converts were subject to suspicion from the communities they left and from those they entered. But the most arduous criticism came from themselves as they pondered whether their conversion was a call from God, the caprice of fickle self-indulgence, an instigation of the Devil, or an illusion introduced or permitted by God.

The fields of tension created by this relentless criticism long survived the eleventh and twelfth centuries. "The gate is strait," wrote an Englishman in the seventeenth century, "and therefore a man must sweat and strive to enter. Both the entrance is difficult and the progress of salvation too. . . . It is a tough work, a wonderful hard matter to be saved," one requiring humiliation, faith, repentance, and warfare against "devils, the world, and a man's own self."[83]

The dual educational character of pathology represented by Bishop Otto of Bamberg, who, in the play of ritual, deployed the tools of physical mortification and spiritual contrition to humble himself and those of preaching and material coercion to catch unbelievers in the net of faith, recurred throughout the centuries. In the aftermath of the Enlightenment, for example, it marked the life and thought of Prince Demetrius Augustine Gallitzin (1770–1840), whose conversion and improbable career made him the "Apostle of the Alleghenies." Laboring on the Pennsylvanian frontier as Otto had done on the Pomeranian, Gallitzin followed extreme ascetic practices, so extreme, in fact, that his ecclesiastical superiors admonished him; he afflicted himself, partly, we are told, in an effort to atone for his father's sins. "The gift of tears," Gallitzin's biographer wrote, "was characteristically his up to the end; in fact, it became more pronounced as he approached the end of his life. . . . This was all the more surprising as long communion with a corrupt and hard world had produced in him certain rash and harsh mannerisms, and holy anger often impassioned him with flaming eyes and an invective that made the people fear and tremble and the children to start crying in church."[84]

As I have shown in chapter 2 (after n. 35) believers imposed pain on others not to achieve the conversion of unbelievers but to test and train their own empathies: that is, in rituals of play, they were serving the *cultus sui*. A similar willingness to impose on others the pain of one's own cult of self, of one's own self-education, that was represented by Otto of Bamberg's career also characterized the history of Christian missions in later times. One need not pause with the zeal of Virginia's earliest settlers "for the planting of Christianity amongst heathen." While British ambassador to the United States, Lord Bryce (1838–1922) commemorated these effects when he addressed the Laymen's Missionary Convention, meeting at Chattanooga in 1907. Within half a century of Spanish conquest, he said, the entire native populations of Haiti and the Bahamas had perished. The same pattern of conquest and extermination was still in full action throughout the world, not least in South America. "In half a century or less," Bryce said, "that which we call European civilization will have overspread the earth and extinguished the organizations and customs of the savage and semi-civilized tribes or nations." Tribes, kingdoms, ancient beliefs, and established morality—all having "endured from the Stone Age until now"—would irrevocably perish; the desolation, especially that of moral order, would leave those upon whom it had been visited "with nothing, adrift upon a wide and shoreless sea." Bryce was an indefatigable traveler; he had seen the desolation everywhere, at first hand.

He ascribed this profound and universal suffering not to religious motivations but to avarice and lust for power on the part of extortionate merchants and rapacious warriors who followed in the trail of missionaries. In his view the motives of Christian missionaries were benign; those of the civilizers who followed them "too often come as a crushing force in a destroying hand." And still, he recognized the religious contempt for customs that to Western eyes seemed bad and morality that seemed immoral. He did not notice the new secular religion at work in his own mind when he argued that "having taken these weaker races under our control, we cannot evade the responsibility that lies upon us to think and to care for them." "Natives ought to be regarded as children, and have the measure both of care and of tenderness which is given to children, for under the conditions in which their life has been passed, they cannot be expected to rise quickly to the level of civilized man." The task of Christian missionaries was to provide them a "new basis of moral life . . . a sacred bond to make them feel and believe that they and we are all the children of one Father in heaven."[85]

Changes in the world of thought also occurred, with lines of continuity. For example, the conception of Job as a "misbeliever," a righteous rebel against the cruelty of God, was developed by some writers beginning in the nineteenth century. However, this "vindication of Job's rebelliousness" did not drive out the medieval conception of Job as a type of Christ in patient submission.[86] Likewise, the idea of conversion as a loving way of life shaped by pain survived, but as the experiences and writings of Simone Weil (1909–1943) and Edith Stein (Sister Teresa Benedicta of the Cross, 1891–1942) illustrate, the coordinates of thought persisted and yet changed. The religious careers of both women began in Jewish homes, Weil's agnostic and Stein's observant. They progressed through advanced studies in existentialist philosophy. But whereas Weil's further inquiries led her first to socialism and then to a Christian socialist commitment outside the institutional and sacramental limits of the Church, Stein's drew her eventually to become a nun in the austere and contemplative Carmelite order. Stein might therefore appear to have been the more tradition-bound of the two. But, even as she employed the modern conception of Job as a just man crying out against God, Weil invoked the medieval conception of him as an analogue of Christ, a model of self-emptying affliction amid which the sufferer, feeling abandoned by God and yet obedient unto death, never abandoned perfect love of God.[87]

Among the many paradigms of empathetic conversion deployed by twelfth-century writers (see chap. 1, after n. 22), Stein and Weil consistently applied only those bearing on the imitation of Christ. Paradigms of conversion by rehabilitation and restoration through grace predominate, together with an emphasis on the autonomous, enlightened will. However, the subject of conversions in nature, including cosmic egress and return or periodic cycles, was hardly considered. As I shall show in chapter 6 (after n. 61), this was in direct contrast to ideas of conversion taken out of the inherited repertory and applied by Herman Melville and James Joyce.

In their very different ways, Weil and Stein held to the idea that pain was meaningless unless one was taught to refer it to Christ. They turned again and again to Christ's Passion as the central event elucidating human existence and to the imitation of Christ crucified as the means by which human life was raised from its animal finitude to supernatural participation in the life of God. Stein embraced the ritualized playing out of this imitation provided by the Carmelite order. Weil invented and enacted her own rituals. For them both, as for the authors whom I have considered, pain itself was unsignifying; everything hinged on the recognition and desire of pain, through ritual patterning, as obedience to a divine order and thus as a means of entering into the movement of God himself.

The three stages of spiritual ascent toward interpenetration with the loving God—purgative, illuminative, and unitive—recurred in the writings of Weil and Stein. The beginning was in purifying pain and torment: the annihilation of finite sensual affections, desires, and habitual thinking rooted in the senses, imitation of Christ in the agony of feeling abandonment by God with the total surrender to suffering that it entailed, self-emptying even to the point of being detached from detachment, the quest for physical pain, distress of soul, and social degradation all at the same time epitomized in the agony of the Crucifixion, as Weil wrote, "this agony beyond all others, this marvel of love."[88]

These are familiar contours of the pathology of conversion, ritualized in play. Yet, with its concentration on the autonomy of the isolated individual will, existential philosophy excluded some characteristics that I have particularly emphasized. The consequences of ignoring the imperative of conversion, the absence of the idea of suffering as in some sense sacrificial, the vague role of the community (despite the obligation of neighborly love) and with it the even vaguer peril of apostasy all sharply distinguished the teachings of Weil and Stein from those in the eleventh and twelfth centuries. So, too, did the absence (except in comments on theological treatises from earlier centuries) of a doctrine of angelic and demonic presences, enacting with and through human beings the strife of good against evil. The theodical quandary of God's responsibility for evil, particularly in moral choice by the good, is dispelled by reducing the choices before the will to one: whether to desire, or not, "that everything that has happened should have happened, and nothing else."[89]

A striking aspect of the ideas that I have reviewed is the deliberate construction of intellectual disciplines inherited from ancient philosophies—reading, meditation, prayer, and contemplation—as intrinsically a system of education in moral criticism, of initiation into ritual enactment. Weil and Stein also armed themselves with these disciplines as tools of empathetic formation and, with them, the inherent sense of danger in the spiritual venture, in seeking through those artificial disciplines, limited by the finitude of individual mind and soul and circumstances, to apprehend the incomprehensible reality at the heart of all that is.

Thus, through their quite discrete reworkings of tradition, Weil and Stein retained its pervasive sense of play, which is also to say, of risk. The sport of hunter and hunted recurs in Weil's sense that the soul's inherent love of beauty was the trap used by God to capture it and expose it to supernatural love; the beauty of the world was the enticing mouth of a labyrinth in which venturers were "eaten and digested by God."[90] As a student of existentialist philosophy before she embraced Christianity, Stein wrote her doctoral dissertation on empathy. As a Carmelite, she expressed this enduring concern in other ways. Her profound study of writings by St. John of the Cross enabled Stein to grasp the movement of the soul in conversion as "the play of love between the divine Lover and the beloved soul."[91]

The cognitive power of such play moved Weil through her purgative journey in her early engagement in the workers movement, in her experiences as an agricultural laborer and a worker on the Renault assembly line, as a teacher, and as a commando in the Spanish civil war, and, finally, in the privation that, although in England, she voluntarily assumed in solidarity with those in occupied France and that brought her to her death. Differently ritualized, the same play brought Stein to self-emptying first in the Carmelite order and later in the chambers of Auschwitz.

Conclusion

The pathology of conversion centered not so much on the experience of pain as on the understanding of pain. By itself, suffering was meaningless. Referred to an end—namely, Christ—it gained meaning both in regard to the formation of the individual mind and heart and in regard to the unfolding of a broad historical panorama: the divine plan for the redemption of the world. Understanding dictated behavior that induced pain, to be sure, notably in the imitation of Christ's Passion. However, for purposes of understanding understanding, it is more important to recall that the way of thinking that I have explored patterned how behavior was remembered and how memories were narrated: in short, it configured an underlying and comprehensive educational program of empathy.

I return, therefore, to the subject of fiction and to a fascination with pain. Hegel (1770–1831) touched upon a basic need of narrative when he observed that happy and peaceful epochs were empty pages in the book of history. In a similar vein Augustine of Hippo commented on the universal delight in suffering that wholly absorbed spectators in tragedy and that prompted neighbors to run from near and far to gawk at a mutilated corpse, a delight that he himself played upon with great mastery to snare the attention of readers when he framed the narrative of his conversion as episodes of anguish.[92] The authors of the letters and treatises with which I have dealt were perfectly aware of how to deploy the motif of suffering, ritualized in the approved modes of orthodox cult, to engage their readers' empathetic participation. It would be wrong not to mention that the authors created the texts as mirrors in which they themselves could be delighted spectators of their own sufferings in rituals of love.

Stein's skill as a textual critic enabled her to detect another level of play, decisive for these inquiries, between spiritual experience and writings about that experience. St. John of the Cross, she wrote, was unable to describe and explain the "mysterious script" that the Holy Spirit sang to his understanding; he assumed that the same Spirit that infused love in him would open to other souls "access to the mysterious expression of this love," disclosing what was unsaid in the words. The heart of the poet, experiencing the "magic" of spiritual music, could not be fettered by the method of the narrator or commentator; nor could the writer always "confront his poem as an objective datum that is almost alien to him."[93]

"Christians are made, not born"; but the education of a Christian to the ritualized play of love was fraught with risk. How can I summarize the pathology of faith centered on fear of apostasy? It has two aspects: the one submissive, the other coercive. The convert's earthly existence became a continual test. Whether the test would approve or reject the convert remained to be seen at the Last Judgment. The certainty was that the object of the testing, through agonies of penance, was to dissolve the old identity so that the new could be constituted, much as in the conversion brought about by sculptors when they break down corroded bronzes and throw them into a furnace in order to cast new and finer statues.[94]

Yet doctrines of dependence served the need for power and glory. Magic and astrology were forbidden arts. But if mastery of the unseen causes of fear were out of reach, men and women could control how they represented their terrors through the arts of imagination. The arts of government (or discipline) gathered many such into the treasure-laden baggage that Otto of Bamberg carried with less gentle means of persuasion into the mission field. Other imaginative arts were employed in conventions of narrative by which the unruly mess of experience was modeled into story. Endowed with all memory's mythic power to correct the past, the pathology of empathetic conversion resolves into a variant of the tragic scenario. It recapitulates the stages of ancient tragedy: pathos, discovery, peripety (attended by catharsis), and epiphany. The analogy with drama is natural in view of the theatrical character of liturgical enactments of death and rebirth, natural, too, in the association commonly drawn between history and theater. But the ascetic paradigm of conversion drew out the peripety for the whole of life, rendering it a continuous predicament. The ritualizing control of art gave assurance that a pattern was being followed that would issue in an epiphany yet to come. Conversion was a long peripety enacted on the stage of this world, "a spectacle to angels and men" (1 Cor. 4:9), a catharsis, still incomplete and unresolved, of pity, love, and fear. The need for life led to the perception that believers were dead and that their life was "hid in Christ." The need for love has led to a Lover and Savior who hid himself.

What if the discovery were a poetic invention of understanding in search of faith, which is to say, love? What "if," as the Apostle Paul wrote, "Christ be not risen" from the dead (1 Cor. 15:12–14, 20), or if, as in Iseult's fraudulent ordeal, Christ was pliant as a sleeve fitting any arm, or if, as the psalmist suggested to the very different minds of Othloh and Anselm of Bec's opponent, there were no God? Then the ritualized, mimetic turning of the heart in pity and love, catharsis and epiphany, would be a work of the human imagination. In their long peripety converts would fulfill, live out, a myth, and, in fact, only pathos and fear would remain. What made apostasy the keystone of the pathology of conversion was the ironic sense that the whole poetic structure could be, with much of art, a flight from the pain of existence.

In the next chapters, I shall consider how the ritual play in monastic discipline entered into ideas about the moral formation of conscience and how it also embraced elements drawn from the warrior ethos of chivalric society and employed the visual, as well as the verbal, arts: that is, how empathies in the warrior's play were ritualized into the monk's.

CHAPTER 4

The Ordeal of Conscience: Purity and Doubt

Basic Glossary and Some Problems

What made it possible to understand conversion? The task I have set is to find out how some people could think about conversion as they did. What experiences, presuppositions, and motives were prerequisite to the questions that they thought up and asked? I have some traces of answers which suggest an underlying pattern of empathetic education, one that encompassed both devices accessible to and through human nature and supernatural action.

The ideas thus far considered expressed the thinking of a male society, ascetic, literate, and aristocratic. We now know that the subject of education to ritualized play of love points to a deeper level of assumptions about moral choice cherished by that society. How, in the thinking of the world that I am studying, could a conscience enlightened by grace and formed by tried and tested methods of education be so unsure of its conversion as to subject itself, in anguished love, to daily trial by ordeal until life's end? Clearly, the educational program could not produce assured results. To gain some picture of the pedagogical substratum on which the idea of empathetic conversion was built, I must review ways of thinking about conscience, the instrument of moral choice, and about the methods and consequences of its education.

It has been argued that even as they have no word equivalent in meaning to *conversion* (see chap. 1 at n. 8), Muslims speak of conscience without having a word for it. "What does not exist for Muslims is conscience as an autonomous authority, because conscience can only appeal to God or be touched by him. But God is also the originator of those laws that one would refuse to obey for reasons of conscience. Muslims follow not their conscience but the will of God."[1] A definition in search of a word is a loose cannon. Given the distinction just quoted, particularly its association of public law with the will of God, the following discussion will indicate that while Muslims may speak of cognate matters (such as duty and remorse), they do not speak of conscience in any of the major senses developed in the Latin West, which posit conflicts between inward and external laws. Thus, language provides a trace of the unfamiliarity with the duty of resistance imputed to Muslims.

Circumstances in twelfth-century Europe were very different. And still, it might appear that through many meanings the Latin West reached the same definitionless point as Muslims are said to have done. The word *conscience* was in common use, but it also had a multitude of meanings. Frequently the meaning of the word *conscientia* in any text must be clarified by reference to its particular context. Technical terms were invented and conveyed as, with the development of theology, philosophy, and law, reflection became increasingly systematic. However, the basic vocabulary was inherited from the pre-Christian world; the word *conscientia* had at least ten synonyms (including words that denoted simple information, bodies of knowledge, faculties or states of mind, the act or event of recognition, "the inward person," conspiracy, and fraud).[2] Its few occurrences in the New Testament hardly imposed semantic precision.

In fact, the overarching contribution of Scripture to discourse about conscience was to add behavioral ambiguity to semantic, particularly when dictates of the righteous heart conflicted with the laws of rightful authorities. The portrayals of Christ and his Apostles provided examples both of obedience and of defiance toward rulers, whether civil or religious. Was Christ's injunction "He that hath no sword, let him sell his garment and buy one" (Luke 22:36) ironically subsumed in his other command, "Render unto Caesar the things that are Caesar's and unto God the things that are God's" (Matt. 22:21)? Though it was often applied to civil obligations, the sentence "We ought to obey God rather than men" (Acts 5:29) was addressed by Peter to the high priest and his council, who, cut to the heart, laid plans to kill Peter and the other Apostles. Yet had not Christ himself come to fulfill the Law and bowed his head in submission to its established ministers?

The earliest known analytical treatise devoted to the subject was written about 1235 by the celebrated Parisian scholastic Peter the Chancellor. By that time the Stoic doctrine that every soul contained a spark of the divine, enlightening its reason, had been recovered. One result was to make ever more intricate any explanation of how a soul illuminated by this *synderesis* or *scintilla animae* could choose to sin, and whether a soul was bound to obey dictates of a sinful conscience.³ Even thereafter, when increasingly technical discussions moved toward the emergence of casuistry as a science, discussion of conscience retained in many branches of discourse an imprecise, contingent character.

Still, the plenitude of definitions in the Latin West did not reach the definitionless point ascribed to Muslims. For the meanings attributed to the word *conscience* were signs of a deep and complex history and the seedbed of powerful innovations in ethics, politics, and social order. The idea of conscience in the twelfth century illustrates particularly well effects that the historical compounding of ideas can have.

The basis for autonomy of conscience lay in the Stoic ideal of sages, disciplining their minds to follow reason. Roman thinkers adapted this Greek legacy, sharpening the individuality and incommunicability of every moral choice. The rightness of moral intent required each person to calculate an action according to that person's temperament, status, and circumstances.

In the early Church this nucleus was quickly melded with other elements drawn from Scripture. The cool self-approbation of the Stoic sage was fused in an unlikely way with the agony of Christ, tempted by Satan in the wilderness, weighed down with sorrow in Gethsemane, struck to the heart by abandonment on the Cross.

The twelfth-century vocabulary of conscience suggests the intricate history behind the idea. The terms used by Roman revisers of Stoicism (notably Cicero, who was not a Stoic, and Seneca, who was) to diagram the calculation of duty continued, together with the ideal of reason unperturbed by the passions. To be sure, the freedom of the will to determine the rightness of its own moral intent was enveloped in Christian theology. But the trait of moral autonomy in it is still recognizable.[4] It is clear, for example, in Bishop Otto of Freising's (c. 1114–1158) statement that the "books of life" mentioned in prophecies of Daniel and the Apocalypse were human consciences, each to be opened at the Last Trump, each adjudging itself, in the twinkling of an eye, to eternal life or death.[5]

And yet it was decisive that a quite different ancient paradigm of conversion, one drawn from mystery religions, also had powerful effects. By contrast with the calculating self-mastery of Stoic reason, this paradigm taught spiritual rapture. It idealized the spiritual embraces of the soul and Christ, its spouse, "where the voice of the turtle, the voice of exulting and salvation, is heard, where a new song, the song of Sion, is sung, and an endless alleluia, heard, where the heart of man is gladdened with the wine of rejoicing and inebriated with the undiluted wine of conscience."[6]

This idea of an autonomous but divinely possessed conscience set purity, rather than the certainty promised by the Stoic legacy, as a goal. Of course, scriptural authority indicated as much. Because of their readings of Scripture, twelfth-century writers considered *heart* and *conscience* as synonyms, both requiring purity. Consequently, they thought the same issues were in play when Christ declared, "Blessed are the pure in heart; for they shall see God" (Matt. 5:8), and when the Apostle Paul wrote that he had served God with purity of conscience (2 Tim. 1:3). But menacing reasons also lay behind appraising purity over certitude.

The venture of understanding empathetic conversion does not indicate any inherent rightness of the conscience because of its freedom or even because of what it took to be an experience of divine intoxication. Herman-Judah recorded that scruples of conscience about violating the Mosaic Law for a time hindered his conversion to Christianity; they had been, he decided, snares of the Devil.[7]

The difference between certitude and purity called for many forms of criticism, including the cruel love with which God tested his faithful people and the severity that believers visited upon themselves in an effort to purge the defilements of sin, including especially those congenitally imbedded in the very fibers of their being.

It also returns me to the proportionality of faith, inasmuch as certitude, but not purity, can be absolute. In the heavenly vision of God promised to the pure in heart, what was called conversion became permanent. For, theologians argued, we are unlike God and alien to him in the degree to which we do not see him. By seeing him more and more perfectly, so they reasoned, we become proportionately ever more like him. Through that continuing mimesis, we are cleansed of our carnal squalor; we partake of God's purity; we are sanctified. The mission of Christ was essential to this catharsis. For, they continued, without being cleansed, we can never be joined to the eternal. Paradoxically, we can be purified only through the earthly existence by which we are held captive. In Christ's incarnation, divine wisdom condescended to take on our weakness. By contemplating Christ's life in this world and imitating him with love, we move through the humanity that we have in common with him to purity of heart and, after death, to the vision of what is promised to the pure in heart. But, they concluded, "no one has the ability to love God unless it is given by God,"[8] or other than according to the proportion of faith bestowed on that person by grace.

From this vantage the autonomous conscience could by no means be understood as "the voice of God." As long as it was tainted with sin, it was rather "a kind of knowledge" that could attack the soul "like an alien, dark, hostile power."⁹ Its assault could come in the anguish of the penitent redeemed, but also in the self-delusions of the lost. The human conscience was a great abyss, open to God but hidden from the soul itself,¹⁰ an abyss teaming with savage reptiles, envenomed thoughts swiftly coming, swiftly going. "The heart of man is depraved and inscrutable," the Prophet Jeremiah (17:9) said in an often-quoted sentence, "and who may know it?"

Snared in ignorance as often as in knowledge, the mind incurred the pollution of guilt in two ways, for it deceived itself and concealed the deception from itself. The proud thought themselves constant; prodigals called themselves liberal; the avaricious, diligent; the inhumane, merciful. Verbosity paraded as eloquence. To itself, the evil of curiosity pretended to be fired with spiritual zeal; and cruelty, with justice. Without knowing it, hypocrites disguised vice as virtue, masked their failings to themselves. They were spiritual suicides, persecutors of their own consciences, the Devil's martyrs. They had certitude of conscience. And still, however firm their self-assurance, however warmly they defended and commended their own conduct, they lacked the testimony of a pure conscience.¹¹ For selfish purposes they deformed the moral judgments of others, encouraging them to do whatever pleased them when they should have used the scalpel of rebuke to lance the abscesses in their victim's minds and drain the pus from their consciences.¹²

Fruit on the vine of Christ, these false brethren, perverse Christians, contained venom, not wine. They were unwilling to be put through Christ's winepress of mortification and contrition, even though that was the only route to the wine cellar of his delight. They should take care lest they be cast out to be eaten by swine. For otherwise there was laid up for them a surprise such as, according to Rupert of Deutz (c. 1075–1129), the Jews experienced in the destruction of Jerusalem, when even in their savage conscience they had to acknowledge that the Lamb whom they had killed lived again and had come in his mighty wrath against them.¹³ "Nay," said a writer in the age of the English Civil War, "thou . . . mayst pass through the world and die with a deluded comfort that thou shalt go to heaven and be canonized for a saint in thy funeral sermon and never know thou art counterfeit til the Lord brings thee to thy strict and last examination, and so thou receivest that dreadful sentence, 'Go ye cursed.' "¹⁴

The kind of proportional knowledge (or purity) that conscience was and the place that it might have in a history of conversion are indicated by that fact that writers in the twelfth century uniformly decried hypocrisy as the besetting evil of their day and a sign of the advent of Antichrist.

I have only begun to identify the vocabulary used to speak about conscience, although the two contrasting ideas that I have mentioned—the autonomous and the God-intoxicated conscience—give some measure of the subject's intricacy. These two ideas originated in the ancient world. Of course, the historical evolution of ideas about conscience did not end with the fall of Rome. Even as they recovered and assimilated the texts, thoughts, and terminologies of centuries long past, twelfth-century writers added words of their own. They translated ancient ideas into their own frames of reference and, consequently, glossed, embellished, and rendered them intelligible in their own words, significantly drawn from the language of chivalry. The result was not to simplify but rather to elaborate the already ornate heritage that they were taking to heart.

It was a telling fact that the vocabulary used to describe the proportionalities of faith was taken from a culture that was itself organized according to hierarchic degrees. From all the major spiritual and intellectual traditions on which it drew, Christianity received the inward ideal of self-knowledge (*cognitio sui*). From late Roman society, it also inherited another, quite different ideal, a public one, which also pervaded the chivalric world: esteem or, to use the word in a sense that is still current, though archaic, worship. Together self-knowledge and esteem converged in a behavior dominated by rules of decorum, significantly called a "cult" of the self (*cultus sui*); one object of which was to purify the mind.

The degrees of chivalric honor corresponded with the nice distinctions required by those rules and supplied the glossary deemed adequate to express the proportionalities of faith. To be sure, distinctions and glossary were melded with an ample residue, in Scripture and in patristic writings, from the political order, the cosmologies, and the rituals of late Antiquity, all of which had a living survivor and heir in the Christian Church. This legacy in vocabulary and exemplars permanently established that discourse about conscience had a public as well as a private dimension. *Fama* (repute) was the social pendant of *conscientia;* and even though the inward testimony of conscience, a spiritual good, was to be preferred to the outward testimony of repute, a temporal one, still both were needful: conscience, as John of Salisbury wrote, for God, repute for one's neighbor, and both for oneself.[15]

Much later, Thomas Aquinas reduced to formula what tradition had already conveyed to twelfth-century writers, in looser form, about the virtues of *fama*, not only as the element that made possible friendship and all other offices of human association[16] but also as a means for the reparation of conscience,[17] the "good odor" with which works of justice filled the Church, and, both in direct experience and in the long accumulations of collective memory, the means of edifying the brethren by example.[18] The works of Christ's crucifiers, of ancient and contemporary heretics, and of the self-righteous demonstrated to Thomas how fallible a guide conscience could be, ulcerated by fires of anger, hatred, and concupiscence, swollen with pride, or possessed by demons.

It was no sin to disobey conscience and thereby defend its purity when it dictated acts forbidden by God's external law, such as fornication, theft, or preaching heretical doctrine. Thus, to protect their good repute, many abstained from evil acts. Motives counted. To seek *fama* on one's own account pertained to vainglory; but to seek it for the sake of one's neighbor, Thomas wrote, was an act of charity. Those who neglected their *fama* for the sake of their neighbors committed the sin of cruelty.[19] Yet ecclesiastical authority was beyond either conscience or repute. Anyone unjustly excommunicated (in hatred or anger, for example), while knowing that divine grace negated the sentence for its error and remaining secure in his innocence, should still humbly obey or seek formal release from the judgment. If he contumaciously disregarded it, he would commit, despite the clarity of his conscience, a mortal sin.[20]

In moral discourse good repute (*fama*) was related to deference or decorum entailed by status and owed by a person to his or her own status. This duty was called *honor* or *honestas*. And so I complete, for the moment, the basic glossary codified by the new learning in the twelfth century so as to speak about purity of conscience. One could speak rightly of *honor* (or *honestas*) as a cult of one's status and, in that sense, as *cultus sui*. Still using the glossary of the twelfth century, the children of the Renaissance cherished this cult; some followed it spectacularly into the duty of resistance. Martin Luther invoked the correspondences between *conscientia, fama,* and *honor* when he said, "My conscience is a prisoner of God's word. I cannot, I will not, recant, for to act contrary to conscience is neither safe nor honorable." Thus, too, Henry VIII (1491–1547) and Catherine of Aragon (1485–1536) in the long conflict over their divorce appealed repeatedly to honor and conscience.

When he declined an invitation to attend the coronation of Anne Boleyn, Thomas More, a silent dissident from the divorce, spun a fable encompassing both. Coming to the moral of his tale, he wrote to the three bishops who had invited him to accompany them:

> And so, though your Lordships have in the matter of the matrimony hitherto kept yourselves pure virgins, yet take good heed, my Lords, that you keep your virginity still, for some be there that by procuring your Lordships first at the coronation to be present, and next to preach for the setting forth of it, and finally to write books unto all the world in defence thereof, are desirous to deflower you and when they have de-

flowered you then will they not fail soon after to devour you. Now, my Lords, it lieth not in my power but that they may devour me, but God being my good Lord, I will provide that they shall never deflower me.[21]

Still, in the twelfth as in the sixteenth century, kings, the Church, and God had their *honor,* and the first two, their *honestas* as well. (*Conscientia* and *honestas* could not normally be considered attributes of God's understanding, for they denoted imperfection—uncertainty, relative goodness, and change—under the light of self-criticism.) These were by no means conterminous with each other or with the *honor,* or *honestas,* of other degrees; nor was the argument unknown that to preserve the honor of a king, one might be called to fight against what the king himself deemed to be his *honor.*[22] And so we have a little glossary of words: *conscientia, fama,* and *honor* or *honestas.*

It is tempting to distinguish, as Thomas Aquinas did, between *conscientia,* an inward and spiritual good, and *fama,* an outward and temporal one, and to associate *conscientia* with *honestas* (as self-esteem) and *fama* with *honor* (as temporal distinction). Indeed, some texts leave no alternative to this symmetry between private and public aspects of the *cultus sui.*[23]

However, even as it preserved the outward goods of *fama* and *honor,* Christian spirituality rendered their sanctions inward. In the external sense they were conferred by others upon a person. In the inward sense qualities of heart and mind sanctioned the public goods. Evidently, as long as *fama* derived from the praise of others, those who strove for repute labored to satisfy the expectations of those who could bestow it, rather than to exercise the freedom of their own consciences. Their currying of favor could lead them to prodigal expenditures for illicit pleasures, for obscene theatrical performances, to take one example. In their avidity for praise and lust for glory, the pagan Romans had attained a certain moral excellence. Sacrificing all other desires to that for *fama,* they subordinated all merely useful goods to *honestas.* Thus, they repressed vices in their quest, and they achieved not only *fama* but also *honor,* empire (*imperium*), and glory (*gloria*). But canceling the freedom of conscience through pursuit of *fama* at the price of obscene luxuries led to *infamia.* The temporal greatness of the Roman Empire was a towering example of vainglory (*inanis gloria*). Even the association with inward virtue that Roman philosophers drew with glory (or *fama*) and *honestas* was fragmentary. For they failed to recognize that true virtue came not by perfecting human nature through moral discipline but through the miraculous re-creation of human nature so cleansed of sin and re-formed in God's image and likeness as to participate in his purity.[24]

Thus, quite different meanings became attached to the same words. *Fama* and *honor* continued to denote external, temporal goods, which might or might not correspond with the internal goods of *conscientia* and *honestas*. But they also became spiritual goods in the circular relationship by which God took on human nature so that human beings could become God, a circularity between divine archetype and human image exemplified in art when it was thought that a portrait and its subject were mutually present in one another. Thus, they became goods that might be hidden even from the hierarchic Church, a creature of time, though they were manifest to the communion of saints, revealed from faith to faith.

The correspondence in understanding relating all these terms thus lies close to the right of resistance, but as their ambiguities suggest, it is very far both from the range of meanings that pre-Christian writers invested in the word *conscientia* and from the isolated autonomy characteristic of some post-Enlightenment doctrines which deprive conscience of its pendants, *fama* and *honor,* and which replace the ideal of purity with that of certitude.

Roman and Christian Conscience

I propose that this distinctive range of associations with purity informing the phrase *conscientia et fama* existed because for Christian writers discourse about conscience was part of discourse about pollution as death. Another fact was crucial: discourse about holy living and holy dying presupposed extremely elaborate distinctions between the deathless soul and the perishing body. Other related matters, such as obligation, were subordinate to this all-encompassing theme. In order to begin unpacking some of the associations that gave the two terms their meanings, I shall compare portrayals of remorse in two texts: Catullus's (c.84–54 B.C.) poem on Attis (*Carmen* 63: "Super alta vectus") and Peter Damian's (1007–1072) *Liber Gomorrhianus*.

The subject of both works is self-emasculation as religious sacrifice. The Roman voluptuary portrayed Attis, rapturous in his adolescent strength and swept up with frenzied devotion, dedicating himself by emasculation to the goddess Cybele. After a night shot through with manic dance, his blood bespattered on the ground, the "not-quite woman" fell asleep and woke to sorrow. Delivered from wild possession, he saw his loss with a clear mind. He wandered to the seashore and turned toward his distant homeland, lamenting the exile that he had imposed upon himself to be a handmaiden of Cybele, roaming "a sterile man" in the wilds of Phrygia. "Now, now, I sorrow for what I did; now, now, I repent." Seeing him yearn to flee her domain, the angry goddess unchained her lion to drive him back into the untamed forest, where Attis lived out his days as her handmaid. In an epilogue Catullus prayed the goddess to stay far from his house, to incite others, not him, to manic frenzy.

Peter Damian, the ascetic of Ravenna, a principal representative of monastic spirituality in the eleventh century, wrote about a different emasculation: that of men who made themselves eunuchs for the Kingdom of Heaven's sake (Matt. 19:12). "They are eunuchs," Damian wrote, "who repress the arrogant impulses of the flesh and cut off from themselves the performance of their vicious operation." Yet there were men who had not expelled the venom of carnality from their hearts and who, indeed, contrary to law and nature, had left the natural use of women only to give themselves up to vile affections, burning in lust for one another, "men with men, working that which is unseemly" (Rom. 1:26–27). His belief that semen was made of blood agitated in the contraction of male genitals enabled Damian to conclude that the hands of sodomites were full of blood and that they would be polluted, not only by the blood of others, which they willingly shed, but also by their own, which they unwillingly poured forth.[25] Bestiality was better than the crime of incest between spiritual fathers and sons, for intercourse with beasts destroyed only one soul.[26]

The most obvious difference between the two texts is that while Catullus portrayed Attis's remorse for his physical emasculation, Damian rebuked his contemporaries for the lack of sorrow with which they tainted and mocked their spiritual emasculation. Catullus's poem did not go beyond the pain of private grief, sardonically punished by a threatening and jealous goddess. But Peter Damian's treatise represents a much more complex frame of reference.

Damian knew that *fama,* as well as *conscientia,* defended the sodomites. Yet even if such men abounded in honorable conduct, were fervent in psalmody, excelled in love of prayer, and in every regard led devout lives according to the witness of proven repute (*fama*), still, falling under the Old Testamental sentence of death, they could scarcely be allowed to go to pray with others in church, much less to function in holy orders.[27] The evidence was patent, Damian wrote, and yet sodomites did not even know that they had wounded themselves. Blinded in their inner eyes and given "over to a reprobate mind" (Rom. 1:28), they could see no polluting crime. They sought and received the tacit approval of others who were not sodomites themselves, whether out of compassion or self-interest. "Blessed are the clergy who fornicate, if they are judged at the bar of sodomites," Damian wrote; "for they wish judgment to be meted out to them by the same measure as they mete it out to others."[28] But all who failed to condemn their practices consented to them and thus participated in their sin and condemnation.[29]

"For how do I love my brother as myself," he asked, "if I heedlessly allow the wound that I know without doubt is cruelly killing him to widen unchecked in his heart?" Inspired by the verse "Cursed be he who withholds his sword from blood" (Jer. 48:10), Damian unsheathed his double-edged sword of correcting words to advance the salvation of his brethren.[30] But since those most in need of his exhortations turned deaf ears to his words, their consciences gave no favor to his treatise. He admonished Pope Leo IX to wield the iron blade of the Apostolic See, uprooting the sprouts of every error from the field of wavering conscience.[31]

Thus, in addition to the notes of conscience and repute, Damian took account of hierarchic order. Here, too, he encountered predicaments. His enemies, entrenched in the assurance of their own *conscientia* and approved by *fama*, also held their own "honors," and this was not true only of those opponents who held ruling, judging, and teaching offices in the Church. For Damian's experience of heresies, and of ecclesiastical politics generally, had demonstrated that unyielding dissidents were all too willing to ignore or defy established order, "to tear almost everything in pieces, to spit on everything, to laugh with public derision at everything that is said. 'There is,' they say, 'no pope, no king, no archbishop, or priest.'"[32] Damian's argument therefore both identified the norms of *conscientia, fama,* and legal authority and illustrated their lack of cogency.

The penitential fabric of Damian's thought about conscience contained one further element foreign to the grief that Catullus portrayed, and this was perhaps the most problematic of all: namely, love of God and neighbor. Damian's assertion in the *Liber Gomorrhianus* that he wrote under the imperative of brotherly love carried for him connotations of the severe discipline of physical mortification and spiritual contrition that he himself practiced with his monastic brethren.[33] Damian accepted the cruel mercies of flagellation and unsparing rebuke as surgical tools by which fraternal love tried to purge and cure the soul. Holy love was ordered by degrees (*caritas ordinata*); love of God was immeasurable, but love of neighbor, expressed as it must be in chastisement of the fallen, knew its limits.[34]

Just as the nature of fire was always to move from the lower to the higher place, so fraternal love, ablaze in one's inmost being, was never directed to another person alone. It was transferred through that person to the common Maker of lover and beloved. Love of neighbor, Damian wrote, is profitless, arid, and insipid unless by it the lover passes through a secondary love of the seen neighbor to the principal love, that of the unseen God. Love of the world turned to bitterness. But by the transference from love of neighbor to love of God, the mind cast off the chains of carnal affection and in contemplation savored the delights of its spiritual marriage feast. Thus, it followed the example of Christ, who spent his nights on mountaintops in prayer and his days in cities performing wonders. Thereby, he taught that those who hungered to contemplate the supreme mysteries should by compassion be mingled in the needs of the weak. For in a wondrous fashion charity surges up to the heights when in mercy it is drawn to the depths of one's neighbors, and inasmuch as with kindness it comes down below, by that much, with power, it soars again on high.[35]

The purifying love of God needs to be stressed. Like Catullus's, Damian's portrayal of inward sorrow culminated in a vengeful, loving deity. But unlike Cybele, Damian's God punished to restore a deformed justice and loved, not out of death-bearing jealousy, but in order to call forth penitence that led from pollution to cleanliness, from death to life, a vocation at work both in every individual experience and in the vast panorama of history that was the sum of such experiences. As the keystone of Damian's thought about the inner life, his doctrine of love infused his doctrines of conscience with miracle—the miracle of creation, crime, atonement, and judgment at the end of days, judgment that displayed both the vengeance and the mercy of the God that love was. Such was his address, by way of conscience, to the needs of life, love, purity, truth, and power. But, at no turn did he find a way to demonstrate outwardly and compellingly the inward grace of purity.

The Separate Spheres of Conscience and Law

Very occasionally, historical texts record "conscience of sin" as a ground for evil conspiracies or "conscience and a sense of honor" as that for good.[36] Scriptural models required political disobedience, including passive and active forms, when the righteous dictates of the heart collided with unrighteous exercises of religious and civil authority. But, nurtured in penitential spirituality, the doctrine of conscience played no major role in political discourse in Damian's time, nor, soon after his death, did it enter into the first major controversy between empire and papacy, the Investiture Conflict.

Pope Gregory VII (reigned 1073–85) was a comrade-in-arms with Damian in the cause of Church reform; his name eventually was given to their common struggle. Quite naturally, in view of Gregory's penitential spirituality, the word *conscientia* occurs in his papal letters; but its appearances are rare, its meanings generally ambiguous, its applications secondary to objective juridical or hierarchic norms. The bishop of Toul was said to have lain with a woman publicly, by whom he begot a child and with whom he coupled by oath and marriage in the fashion of laymen. Moreover, simoniac as he was said to be, he was also alleged to have commanded military atrocities. Gregory understood that the bishop might be guilty as charged, having acted from hatred of his own conscience, and, in that case, that he ought to be cast out. But for the pope the salient fact was that the allegations must be judged according to procedures defined in canon law.[37] As a pastor Gregory knew that fear of one's own conscience, as well as hatred of it, or depravity, or a desperate conscience could drive one into wickedness.[38]

The pope was sure that God was in his conscience; he appealed to the witness of God, conscience, and the canons.[39] But conscience (even in ambiguous senses of the word) played no role in Gregory's correspondence pertaining to the Investiture Conflict, in imperial rebuttals, or in chroniclers' accounts of the dispute. It follows that the pairing of *conscientia* and *fama* is likewise notably absent from juridical and political discourse.

The reasons why purity of conscience could not serve agents of government as a term explaining or justifying legal action are implied in what has already been said. Peter Abelard's (1079–1142) treatise on *Ethics*, written soon after the end of the Investiture Conflict, provides the materials for a concise summation.

Abelard accepted the norms of *conscientia* and *fama*. To act against conscience was to act in contempt of God, and thus to sin, for it required a deliberate assent to what one knew to be wrong.[40] *Fama* was a bulwark against sin. We avoid wrongful actions, Abelard wrote, because by doing them we would incur punishment and damaged repute. Moreover, contrary to arguments that confession should be made to God alone, public confession made it possible for others to strengthen the penitent with their prayers and for the soul, revealing its wounds to spiritual physicians, to receive the healing medicine of humility.[41]

As his discussion advanced, Abelard demonstrated that these propositions were qualified in such ways as to render them improbable or dangerous to agents of government. Abelard's emphasis that the morality of an act depended on the rightness of intent recalled Stoic antecedents. But his discussion of intent demonstrated how difficult establishing correspondence between objective and subjective judgments was. External prescriptions of law change. "When we see Jews who have converted to Christ freely eating the sort of food that the Law forbade them, how can we defend them as guiltless, unless we assert that God has now granted this to them?" The concession excuses (or voids) the contempt of God that the earlier prohibition imposed.[42] Moreover, sin can be brought about by the work of demons, stirring human weakness to lust or other impulses. It was well to preserve the integrity of the will by arguing that in such cases the soul was under constraint but not under bondage. Such, for example, was the case of a religious bound with chains and compelled to lie between women, brought to an involuntary pleasure by the softness of the bed and the touch of the women, and yet not consenting to the pleasure imposed upon him by nature.[43] Yet even this assertion of personal responsibility was modified by the doctrine that the Devil did nothing except what God permitted.[44]

Finally, the correspondence of guilt and intent was clouded by the limits of human knowledge. Lacking reason, infants and fools were incapable of sin because they were incapable of the contempt of God entailed in rational consent to sin. The wicked, the persecutors of the martyrs, believed that they did well; and they were spurred on by their zeal and ardor for pleasing God through persecution. The crucifiers of Christ acted without fault, and even believers must be on guard against deceiving themselves in judging the goodness of their intent.[45]

Thus far, Abelard's arguments illustrate the inconvenience of conscience for normative discourse on government. The considerations with which he concluded the fragment of the wider treatise on *Ethics* that he intended to write illustrate their danger for agents of government. Insisting on the virtues of public confession over confession to God alone, Abelard yet presented a scathing indictment of hierarchic authorities as spiritual judges. Irreligious and indiscreet, bishops disclosed the sins that had been confessed to them, thereby inflicting new wounds instead of healing the old. Ignorant of the canons, they set inappropriate penalties; avaricious, they relaxed penalties in return for money. They boasted that in his commission to St. Peter, Christ had given them the power to bind and loose sins; but they did not pause to consider that Christ conferred that power not on offices but on persons who imitated Peter in his merits.

Indeed, Abelard continued, the judgment of bishops was invalid if it departed from divine equity. A person unjustly excommunicated could be sure that God himself broke the decree, not excluding from grace those wrongfully separated from the Church. God did not follow iniquitous sentences of excommunication any more than he did other legally correct sentences against the innocent. Abelard barely concealed the dangers to hierarchic order presented by his separation of spiritual truth from legal authority when he concluded that a person unjustly excommunicated should not contumaciously defy his bishop or presume to intrude himself into the Church, thus incurring a guilt that he did not have before.[46] But a long series of schisms, heresies, and controversies, beginning before Damian encountered his hierarchic dissidents in Florence, left no doubt why, in general, agents of government found that conscience and repute served no need in their vocabulary of political discourse. Disputed papal elections which more than once left the very tomb of Peter an arsenal and the loyalties of western Christendom divided between rival popes may also have convinced them of the irrelevance in justifying legal action on grounds of conscience.

Underlying Methods of Association: Thomas Becket

That irrelevance became abundantly manifest when Thomas Becket (1118–1170) and his followers did explain and justify political action with such arguments.

The case was from start to finish a study in remorse issuing in political defiance. It began with the archbishop's assent to the Constitutions of Clarendon (1164). Masquerading these provisions as customs of his grandfather William the Conqueror, King Henry II (1133–1189) intended to restrict the scope of ecclesiastical jurisdiction in England and to enlarge that of the royal court. Though as a courtier Becket at first assented, his retraction followed almost at once. The long controversy which ensued established analogies in his followers' minds with other holy penitents, such as David the King and the Apostles Peter and Paul.[47]

And yet the density of argument from conscience on Becket's side stands in remarkable contrast with the virtual absence of reference to conscience in his enemies' counterarguments.[48] The methods of association that lay behind the application of the basic glossary to this specific case could not stand up in a court of law.

In his vast and meandering, but capital, treatise on political association, the *Policraticus*, John of Salisbury (c. 1115–1180) included nothing that could be called a meditation on conscience. The absence is especially notable in his celebrated chapters justifying tyrannicide not only as licit, right, and just but as a work of charity in freeing a people from bondage.[49] By contrast, in the letters that he wrote concerning Becket's dispute with King Henry II, to whom both he and Becket referred as a tyrant, he proved to be the major theoretician on conscience in the archbishop's faction.

As already mentioned, he taught that conscience and good repute alike were needful for the virtuous life in relation to God, neighbor, and self. He also left no doubt that contrition, aroused by penitential discipline, was the mainstay of conscience. Like his contemporary Gerhoch of Reichersberg (1092/93–1169), he set his face against many innovations of his day in philosophy and theology. Though he himself was excellently trained in Roman and canon law, his mistrust of law's development as a formal discipline also resembled that of Bernard of Clairvaux who, like Gerhoch, denounced the suppression of spirituality at the Church's heart, the see of Peter, by the papacy's mounting preoccupation with the ornate technicalities and opulent profits of legalism.

When John counseled his archbishop and friend, he urged him to lay aside distracting occupations, necessary and advantageous as laws and canons might be, for it was spiritual exercise and purifying interrogation (*discussio*) of conscience that turned aside the lash and obtained God's mercy. "Who," John asked, "ever rises in compunction from reading the [Roman] laws or even the canons? I say more: a scholar's exertions now and then bloat knowledge into pride, but rarely or never inflame it to devotion. I prefer you to ruminate the Psalms and turn over Gregory's moral books [Pope Gregory I's *Moralia in Job*], instead of philosophizing in the scholastic manner. . . . For if you do this, God will so be your helper that there will be no need to fear what man contrives."[50]

According to one of Becket's biographers, the association of this affective, anti-intellectual cast of mind with meditation on death had been given graphic expression at Clarendon. There, in a moment of compromise, Becket agreed to subscribe to constitutions designed to enlarge the king's dominance over the clergy. Becket's crucifer is said to have turned upon him. "What virtue is left to a man," the crucifer demanded, "who destroys both conscience and repute (*fama*)?" Becket, he said, was such a man; "for today you have entirely destroyed conscience and repute by leaving to posterity an example hateful to God and contrary to honor (*honestati*). You stretch forth your hands, consecrated to God, to preserve damnable constitutions and, to the confusion of the Church's freedom, you plight your troth with the impious ministers of Satan." Smitten with grief, Becket imposed penance upon himself, withdrawing from the ministry of the altar until he should be absolved by the pope.[51]

Whether this account is historical or fictional, it nevertheless witnesses to an association that did exist in Becket's mind between conscience and repute, on the one hand, and, on the other, death. As in Peter Damian's thought, so, too, in that of Becket and his followers, the needs for life, love, and truth were of one piece with that for purity of conscience: all demanded the enactment of the "form of conversion." For when, recanting his assent to the Constitutions of Clarendon, he was charged before a royal court at Northampton, he entered the king's presence carrying his processional cross with his own hands. His enemies never forgot this gesture as the work of a man who, despite his swollen pride, was unsure of the merits of his case and armed himself with the banner of the Lord's cross as though he were entering the presence of a tyrant.[52] Becket's companions also saw the militance of the deed but found a deeper significance. He carried the cross, one of them commented, "as though he were the Lord's standard-bearer, raising his banner in battle and fulfilling both spiritually and figuratively that saying of the Lord: 'If any man wishes to be my disciple, let him deny himself, take up his cross, and follow me.' Truly, this mystic deed foretold the cross that was to be his."[53]

Throughout the conflict Becket and his followers continually appealed to the sanctions of conscience and repute, sometimes mentioning the terms together, sometimes separately, but always drawing analogies between their own afflictions and Christ's Passion to sustain their resolute defiance of the king and the bishops loyal to him. With their eyes on fame that outlived affliction and life itself, they also repeatedly associated their actions with those of saints and martyrs in the apostolic and patristic ages of the Church.

If we are to understand what made conscience, "fame," and "honor" thinkable to John, we must look beneath the surface of these justifications of resistance. Undergirding his use of the basic glossary, and so his contention that the consciences of Becket and his supporters were in the right, was a symmetrical method of definition and association. John's method was by no means original with or unique to him. I have undertaken in another place to sketch the history of this method from the Age of the Church Fathers to the twentieth century.[54] Here it will suffice to observe that the method consisted of three defining modes of association: likeness, contiguity (precisely, affective closeness), and, most difficult of all, contrast. These were notes of assimilation as well as of association. They implied their symmetrical opposites, notes of estrangement: unlikeness, distance, and negation.

From the brief discussion thus far, the consequences that John drew by applying these notes can be summarized as follows. Likeness to Christ demonstrated uprightness of conscience. It was formed by penitential disciplines of contrition and mortification, rather than by study of Roman and canon law. In Becket's case it was demonstrated by similarities between his motives, conduct, and experiences and those of Christ and his saints throughout sacred history. Likeness followed from emotional contiguity. John held that charity, imparted by the actual presence of Christ or the Holy Ghost in the archbishop and his followers, established the most intimate affective contiguity. Finally, when he took up the note of contrast, John moved easily into the dazzling paradoxes that the two natures of Christ, his divinity and his humanity, conferred upon Christian theology: paradoxes in which poverty equated riches; weakness, power; foolishness, wisdom; ugliness (as in the wounds of martyrs), beauty; and the self-denial of the cross, victory, exaltation, and everlasting glory. The conclusion that John drew was that Becket's struggles were not merely associated (as parallels or analogies) with Christ's but that in his struggles Becket was affectively assimilated to, and in some sense identical with, Christ.

At the dramatic moment of Becket's murder, John of Salisbury appears to have been hiding ingloriously behind an altar.[55] Yet glory was consistently his aim. Throughout the years of his own exile, John learned to use letters and collections of letters not only as documents of conscience but also as tools by which cases could be argued, favor solicited, *fama* enhanced, and *honor,* the *cultus sui,* vindicated. This pragmatic linkage of *conscientia, fama, honor,* and letters was never more evident than when he resorted to letters in his campaign to achieve the crown of *fama* and move the *cultus sui* to the highest level: that is, to gain papal approval for the cult of Becket as a martyr-saint.

When, in that supreme promotion of cult, he labored to define Becket's death so as to identify it with Christ's, John emphasized the same notes. Likeness was proven by the fact that in the long years of proscription and exile, Becket had by constancy of virtue followed in the royal way, treading in the footsteps of Christ and the Apostles. John drew parallels between dialogue in scriptural accounts of Christ's Passion and Becket's own words. Above all, he maintained, the eucharistic canon itself could be applied to Becket, a living sacrifice, holy, well-pleasing to God, who had long crucified his flesh in disciplines of mortification and who, having offered Christ's body and blood upon the altar, at the last offered his own before the same altar.[56] Contiguity of several other kinds followed from emotional closeness to Christ and figured in John's celebration of his archbishop's death: spatial contiguity to the altar, temporal contiguity to the feasts of Christ's birth and of the Holy Innocents, and spiritual contiguity to martyrs in their defense of justice and the liberty of the Church.[57]

Finally, John carefully inventoried contrasts between the events of Christ's death and Becket's. Christ's death was an execution, carried out by a legitimately established public power after due process of law in which the defendant had the chance to answer his accusers. He was crucified by those who knew not God, outside the city and before the Sabbath so as not to pollute either. By contrast, Becket's death followed from no legal process or conviction. He had no opportunity either to appear before a judge or to answer his accusers. He was killed by men who professed the law of God and the faithfulness of friends, in the city and on a day consecrated by the holiness of Christmas.

But these contrasts and others actually enabled John to underscore the likeness between the two deaths and thus their contiguities. Ministers of Satan had been at work in each. Certainly, they were not permitted to do in the sacrifice of the disciple and servant what had been allowed in the crucifixion of the Master and Lord. Still, Becket's murderers in some regards even exceeded the vehemence of Christ's; and, since unlike the crucifiers they acted outside the law, they committed the greater crime.[58]

The contrary defining notes of unlikeness, distance, and negation served not the goods of *conscientia, fama,* and cultic *honor* but wickedness, *infamia,* and contempt. They are also evident in John's argument as methods of defining right conscience and *fama* by comparison with their opposites. Unlikeness, so plain in the sinful nature that called for contrition in the first place, was served by external offices of law, which themselves were called into being to repress sin.

John of Salisbury assured Becket that the English bishops appealing to Rome against him were striving to use the form of law to evade the force of justice. In the same way, at Rome itself, the thinking of laws and canons was so twisted that the litigant who gave the greater bribe got the more potent right.[59] John flatly contradicted Abelard's argument that technicalities of law might constrain judges to punish those whom they knew to be innocent or to reward those who were patently guilty. He insisted that the contrary was true. Judges, he wrote, must give sentence not according to the prescriptive forms only but also according to their own consciences. Not imperial or canon law but the law of God bound them to hand down judgments according to conscience. It branded them as sinners, to their damnation and shame, if, with false judgments, they harmed the innocent.[60]

Had not Becket himself interfered with the due course of justice for such reasons and been punished? The archbishop of York, Roger of Pont l'Evêque, had first blinded his catamite and then corrupted the king's judges to have him hanged on a gibbet to silence his testimony to the things that he had endured in contempt of nature. "Out of brotherly love, [Becket] had compassion on this criminal, inasmuch as he was a fellow courtier [*concurialis*], and, expecting the fruit of a better life, [Becket] withheld the vengeance that he deserved." But the secret oath of purgation that Becket arranged out of charity and prudence to deflect due retribution was not enough for Roger. "The Caiaphas of our time" took his case to Rome. By extravagant bribery he returned from the papal court juridically cleared of guilt. Turning against Becket, he inspired his death and, despite the miracles at the martyr's tomb, continually defamed his memory.[61]

By the measure of unlikeness, John held purity of conscience against the corrupt and corrupting institutions of law. He believed that with Christ in the very footing of the conscience, Thomas and his friends would have no need to fear the threats of tyrants, the snares of those wise after the flesh, the perfidy of traitors, the craven-heartedness of judges, or the avarice and inconstancy of those who sought what was theirs rather than what was Christ's. Perversion of law, even to the uttermost, could not overturn the *honestas* of the archbishop's faction. Which of the elect, John asked, had passed from delight to delight or flourished and exulted in this world and reigned with Christ? Quite to the contrary, throughout the course of all ages the Lord had made his friends blessed by administering to them with his own hand the saving cup of bitterness.[62]

Just as contiguity was conterminous with charity, so was affective distance with pride. Here, however, the inaccessibility of conscience gave ample evidence of the inconclusiveness of argument from conscience and the depth of estrangement in the controversy over Becket.

Becket and his supporters knew that the witness of conscience arose in a secret place.[63] The ancient maxim "Know thyself" was supreme wisdom. But, John wrote, we cannot presume to unfold the hidden things of another's heart with our vain imaginings. Neither human nor angelic wisdom could go further than imaginative fantasies; only God's could know the counsels and thoughts of the human mind as they were.[64] Even as they held firm to Becket's understanding of what was meant by the commands to obey God rather than man and to render unto Caesar the things that were Caesar's and unto God, God's, even as they asserted that by their sufferings Christ was recrucified in them,[65] they knew that the hearts of their enemies had been hardened to destroy their honor.[66] Even as they admonished their enemies to unfold and reread the books of their own consciences and to pray, in doubtful matters, that the Holy Ghost would teach them the rule of charity, they knew how lightly such foes, employing the same terms—*conscientia, fama,* and *honor*—could dismiss their analogies.[67]

Conscience was incommunicable. John liked to think that the burden of lying tormented the guilty conscience and that the tribulations visited upon Becket and his followers came about because the burning prick of conscience was mercilessly goading the wicked.[68] But this retribution could not be taken for granted. Dumbfounded by the appeal that the English bishops lodged with the papal court against Becket, John could not imagine by what conscience or impudence they had asserted the innocence of the king, a man whom, he continued, the whole world knew to excel in injustice and violence.[69]

On the other side, Becket's enemies said that he had always been proud, wise in his own eyes, a follower of his own will. In his arrogance he had brought great destruction upon the church and, indeed, had shamefully abandoned his own see by clandestine flight into exile.[70] He claimed power not only to rule the church arbitrarily but also to dispose of the royal office, which the king held "from no one except from God alone."[71]

John of Salisbury agreed that Becket's zeal, pressed to extremes, had needlessly aroused the king against him, and at least once he had been prepared to leave the archbishop's camp.[72] Those who wished to seem his friends warned him against the danger that conscience of truth might make him hard; fear, make him desperate; and confidence, overbold. Some, they advised, whose malice accustomed them to divine in another's conscience what they did not know, thought that his acts proceeded from pride, not from the truth of virtue.[73] Indeed, reading what they might in the secret places of his conscience, his enemies condemned him at Northampton as *infamis* for perjury and treason, and they later admonished him to spare his *fama* and his glory and to strive to win over the king with humility and charity.[74]

Considering themselves abandoned by their shepherd, the members of the religious community at Canterbury cheerfully ignored the tribulations that he endured laboring for their freedom, honor, and glory; and while other churches rendered to him what charity demanded, his own profusely squandered money on empty pictures to delight the eyes of the ignorant masses, pretending that that kind of luxurious spectacle was for the public good.[75] In the same way the foolish, including proud prelates, sought repute (*fama*) by lavishing money on "actors, mimes, and other such monstrosities of men," instead of fearing the Lord and calling on his name.[76]

Becket's great enemy, Bishop Gilbert Foliot of London (c. 1110–1187), an accomplished ascetic and legist, wrote forthrightly. Adverting to St. Augustine's condemnation of the sufferings that the schismatic Donatists brought upon themselves in their quest for the martyr's crown, he struck at the root of Becket's analogy with Christ. It is not the punishment, he wrote, that makes a martyr but the cause. Severity endured with holiness is a glory, but endured with perversity and arrogance, a disgrace. Becket's insolence to the king had imperiled the entire church. "By what shameless effrontery, father," Gilbert asked the archbishop, "did you invite us to death, when by signs manifest to the world you showed more clearly than day that you were afraid and fled? Why did charity persuade you to impose upon us the burden that you yourself had cast aside? . . . And, as to the annual revenues [that you demand], are they of such moment to you that you want to recover them by the blood of your brethren? When Judas returned the money, the Jews refused it, because they knew it was the price of blood."[77]

Negation completed the structure of defining association employed by John of Salisbury. Just as there could be no communion between Christ and Satan, what was understood as *conscientia, fama,* and *honor* on the side of Becket demanded the negating presence of his enemies. Profound estrangement was not only present but indispensable, for the terms lost their cultic meaning and goal without negation. The duty of resistance made no sense without the counterweight of the duty of obedience; where there is no conflict, there is no virtue. Persecution was a sign of a saint and a child of God.

Therefore, understanding the invincible blindness of their enemies' consciences could not dissolve the stern charity of Becket and his followers into kindness. Even if Christ were being crucified again, John of Salisbury wrote, he would not be killed. He would have his crucifiers yet more bitterly crucified in vengeance for his dove. Indeed, he was already crucifying them with plague and sword and calling forth his angels to punish yet more gloriously those who monstrously gloried against him. The comforter of those who mourned was at the gates. By his power he would grind into dust those whom he found withstanding his majesty; he would cleave the necks of the insolent with the sword of the dove.[78] Such would be the outcome for those who failed in the quest for life, love, purity, and truth.

Understanding Conscience

It could appear that with all its vagaries conscience has led me away from the hermeneutic project of understanding. One could also be misled by the absence of the word *conscience* as a governing term from the scholarly literature on empathetic conversion. However, it was, if ever, in conscience that understanding shaded into compassion. And understanding conscience was nothing else than understanding the empathics of conversion, which is to say, the re-forming of the heart. In quest of purity of conscience, writers also continually expressed the needs for life, love, and truth that conversion addressed. Despite apparent discrepancies, I have been moving within the familiar hermeneutic circle of need.

The word *gloria*, which at first seemed a shy spectator of the dramas of conscience, was, in fact, a major actor in them. It needed to be added to the basic glossary, and so included in the underlying method of association. Writers praised its purity and innocence as the glory of conscience. They used *gloria* interchangeably with *fama* and *honor*, substituting it in such phrases as *conscientia et fama*. Sometimes, this plainly amounted to nothing more than a common equivalence of *gloria* and *fama* with celebrity in the world. But, as "brightness," the word *gloria* had deep theological resonance. On the level of spiritual association, it alluded to the two ways by which human beings participated in divinity: first, by nature through the Light that lighteth everyone that cometh into the world and, second, by grace through union with Christ, the eternal splendor of the Father. *Gloria* differed from the other words in the glossary because it denoted both an attribute and a process—indeed, the process of conversion from faith to sight, of being sown in dishonor and raised in honor. By that process the soul moved from the foretastes and shadows of this world into the brightness that was God, whiter than thrice-purged wool, a radiance that the human mind on this side of paradise apprehended as the blackness of its own dazzled sight. Many were the called; few, the chosen. And still, even the chosen had sinned and fallen short of the glory of God.

What impelled this transit of conversion, from faith to sight, from darkness into light, and from glory into glory? The pairing of conflict with creation, as well as with conscience, is the key. It is also a clue to the patterns of association that lay behind the doctrines of conscience. One example of such a pattern is the method of assimilation and estrangement that undergirded John of Salisbury's use of the basic glossary. In recent centuries writers, sensing that destruction was the cost of creation, took Prometheus or Faust as the paradigm of Western culture. The first exemplified self-sacrificial altruism; the second, terrifying conflicts of motive within the creative spirit. In either case, the creator paid the penalty of creating. There was a significant narrative difference between these figures and the creator-paradigm in our centuries, Christ. For while the narratives of Prometheus and Faust had the organic unity of beginning, middle, and end, the account of Christ's re-creation—the conversion of the world—was not a single narrative but rather an aggregation of countless fragmentary episodes, variations, and repetitions, beginningless and endless as long as time itself ran. The figure of a fascicle or garland or the concentricity of a sphere came to writers' minds more readily than that of a straight narrative line. Each individual convert was a new branch on the growing vine, a new stone in the unfinished Temple. Each was incorporated as members are in the body of a dove or as the body of a dove is in that of a hawk, "since one bird cannot be incorporated into another bird so long as it keeps its former life."[79]

Thus, the exemplar of Christ—the form of empathetic conversion—being immanent in the world, unlike those of Prometheus and Faust, encompassed the suffering and death of the creation in that of the maker. And it did not place the moment of creation at a distant, historical instant but rather infused it throughout each moment, as an artist is present, though invisible, in every particle of his work. The doctrine that the Creator was transcendent above his creation led to the same conclusion. For, Augustine wrote, all imitated God; the good, rightly, the wicked—even Satan—perversely, and all imperfectly in proportion to his (or her) capacity.[80]

Under the aspect of glory, the doctrine of conscience belonged to a category of doctrines, including that of the just war, that was framed in Western culture to explain, sanction, and perpetuate conflict as part of creation. The Archimedean point was captured in the axiom that there was no virtue without conflict. Certainly, it addressed universal erotic needs, such as those for abasement and reconciliation, dependence and dominance. That it assumed a form and an empathetic complexity foreign alike to pre-Christian antecedents and post-Enlightenment ideas is due partly to monasticism, the ascetic subculture, with its fierce militance, that shaped it; to the supreme power that institutions of revenge, including feud, were acknowledged legitimately to exert as integrating factors in society; and to the pervasive and increasingly well-calibrated cult of honor in the dominant class, a military, landed aristocracy. In idle moments I wonder whether this category of doctrines perpetuating conflict were due to a mentality shaped by the encirclement of Europe over the space of centuries by non-Christian peoples perceived inside Europe as implacably hostile, even demonic, powers.

There was an interplay between created nature and the actors reforming it from faith to sight, from glory into glory, which is also to say purity. In that interplay, conscience was both subject and object. For even as it acted, so also was it formed. It shaped and was shaped by the conflict of conversion. Thus, the blending of discipline and grace lay behind a distinctive feature of conscience: conscientious resistance to external authority sprang from a calculated, savage, and continual warfare within the soul.

The formation of conscience by historical analogies required the pious empathetically to identify their immediate sufferings with the past ones of Christ and his saints, and, indeed, to reexperience in their own persons a secret drama of conflict and suffering that encompassed all the faithful in all ages. In this way they enacted, or "performed," the "form of conversion," using it not as the hypocrites did as an empty form of outward observance but rather applying it as a scenario for the change of heart. Physical and mental struggles, self-induced, endured by empathetic participation or imposed by others, were gates to the secret amphitheater, essential aspects of the *cultus sui*. Thus, a biographer of Becket wrote that the eager and devout reader would find the very image of Christ's athlete and his agony painted in the account that followed and could study himself in it as in a mirror.[81] Devotional life was full of visual aids or, so to speak, stage props, enabling believers through the dramatic imagination, if not in fact, to experience the glory of martyrdom.

Thomas More was true to the old and universal practice of empathetic participation through drama when he advised the penitent to go to "some secret solitary place" and there imagine himself giving an account to God "of his sinfull lyvyng." "Than let hym there before an altare or some pitifull image of Christes bitter passion (the beholdyng whereof may put hym in remembraunce of the thing and move hym to devout compassion) knele downe or fall prostrate at the fete of almighty God, verely belevyng him to be there invisibly present as without eny doubt he is."[82] Secret physical mortification also was essential to the merciless wrestling that formed conscience. The cult of God and the *cultus sui* coincided in such practices, exemplified by the hair shirt swarming with maggots and fleas that Becket's closest companions found, to their astonishment, when they prepared his body for burial and by the punishments that Thomas More visited upon his body with the hair shirt that (as only his daughter Margaret, who washed it, knew) he wore next to his body and with a scourge of knotted cords.

Long traditions of monastic spirituality formed these two lives: Becket's by way of Cistercian discipline and More's by way of Carthusian. But Becket and More also represented a wider world of devotion to which in their different centuries they belonged. In that world the dramatic imagination—visualizing oneself an actor in the drama of salvation—was achieved by purifying the conscience in the mold of secret agony, as well as by public contrition. Nor was this insistence on hidden dramatic performance of cult foreign to Peter Damian. The double self-denial of such good works not shown before men was a powerful stimulus to what was understood to be love of God, neighbor, and self. As I shall maintain in the next chapter, it was also essential to what recent scholars call the reception of Christian myth and to what believers in the age under review considered the movement from faith through practice to knowledge, and from knowledge to wisdom accessible to the pure in heart.

The norms of *conscientia, fama, honor* (as *cultus sui*), and political authority ordained by God created an uneasy stage on which to enact this drama of transition from glory into glory. Beneath those two great lights which God created in the social firmament, ecclesiastical and secular government, actual experience configured many circumstances in which other demands took precedence over the spiritual and private good of conscience. Hardly any writer emphasized more than Peter Abelard that sinfulness was a matter of intent—the will to do evil—rather than a characteristic of various kinds of action. Yet even he insisted that authorities must sometimes punish where there was no guilt. Imagine, he wrote, a destitute mother who, lacking clothes for the crib, takes her newborn babe into bed with her to protect it from the cold. She wraps it in her own rags. Falling asleep, she smothers the child even while she embraces it with all her love.

The mother was innocent, Abelard wrote, but her bishop would be right to impose a heavy punishment upon her. The object of the penalty would be to admonish other women to caution. Likewise, he continued, building an argument that John of Salisbury (who heard him lecture) refuted, judges might be constrained by law to condemn defendants whom they knew to be innocent because they lacked evidence to refute the false testimony. The innocent were often punished, he wrote, and the guilty let free.[83] Evidently, the consciences of the judges and the condemned were equally guiltless in such cases. There was a saying among little children, Joan of Arc (c. 1412–1431) recalled, that people were often hanged for telling the truth.[84]

The soul learned the "duty of resistance" against external authorities— against the king for the honor of the king or against the Church for its honor— in the sleepless war of the self against itself in passing from darkness into glory. Despite long experience of the tragic flaw of freedom, the Church imperfectly provided for the parallelism of an inward testimony (*conscientia*) and an outward one (*fama*). The pope, as a late conciliarist pointed out, was not vicar of Christ in at least one respect, for he could not scrutinize another's conscience. And William of Ockham (1280–1349) devoted particular reflection to the problem of whether, if judgments differed, a pope should follow his own conscience or the advice of experts sitting in council, and what consequences should ensue if the pope, in following his conscience, were found to be heretical or in error.[85]

The case of Joan of Arc illustrates how tardily the methods of association underlying all the terms in my glossary might, if ever, be brought into alignment. During the legal process rehabilitating Joan of Arc, a quarter century after her death, it was determined that in her revelations Joan had received a private law from the Spirit of God which released her from the common law and that she had followed the judgment of the Church (attested by canonistic references) when, despite the ardors of prison, hostile interrogation, and sickness, the threat of torture, and the pains of death, she stood by that private law. For, the argument for rehabilitation continued, the Church does not judge of hidden things. As long as there were doubt as to whether inspiration were from the good or from the evil, something altogether hidden and known only to God, the Church did not judge of these things. Because the Church could be deceived in them, it reserved them to God's judgment and left them to the individual conscience. The judgment of the court against Joan was defective because it intruded into this secret, forbidden precinct.[86]

Under the aspect of glory as purity, the interplay of associative ideas sustaining *conscientia*, *fama*, and the cult of honor sanctioned conflict, both internal and external. It also made it intelligible by giving it a dramatic form that powerfully engaged the empathetic imagination, by drawing the faithful mind into performance of the drama and thereby, through experience, from belief to knowledge. Verbal compositions were by no means the only tools used to reeducate, or reform, the mind. All the visual and performing arts were deployed to the same end, which I have called the reception of myth. I cannot end without some reference, however brief, to the light that this friction produced outside the spheres of theological and political thought, in the effort to create an environment where the passage from glory into glory could be visualized, experienced, and thereby known.

Throughout these chapters, there have been scattered references to imitation (or mimesis), a major device of all the arts, especially of the visual and performing ones. Mimesis entered the account of understanding conversion at the very beginning, in the idea of a "form of conversion" to be followed, with countless improvisations, by all believers. The importance that ritualized play, by enacting dramatic roles, had in the empathetic formation of conscience is evident, notably in Becket's association of himself with Christ. And discussions of ritual role-playing in the spiritual arena are direct reflections of fascination with and experience of the theater, a delight that pervaded society, requiring mimes, actors, and musicians in the entourages of the great and as ornaments in public celebrations. Even the paintings that monks of Canterbury paid for with money that John of Salisbury thought due Becket were monuments to thought about the formation of conscience. The monks plainly had alleged the conventional argument that paintings served the common good by being a form of instruction with visual images that, like verbal ones, could be transcribed into the book of conscience. The conflict, rooted in penitential spirituality, that has preoccupied me here produced a rich and continually innovative harvest in the mimetic, ritual arts of painting, sculpture, liturgy (and liturgical drama), poetry, and music. As I shall show in chapter 5, the devices that these enterprises shared for purging, and thus reforming, the conscience were the ironies of art.

If civilization is play, conscience as the play of darkness and glories certainly falls among the games of hazard. That is so despite the fact that great popes of the nineteenth century condemned freedom of conscience because what seemed at the time radical secular doctrines transformed it from aleatory to agonistic play (Gregory XVI, *Mirari Vos*; Pius IX, *Quanta Cura* and *Syllabus of Errors*). Yet those modern doctrines and the papal condemnations alike had venerable pedigrees in traditions of heresy, schism, and antinomianism. The harvest was gathered by civilization at play in the mutual repellence and attraction of religion and art in their roles as moral teachers and critics.

To speak of this harvest, which came from the exchange between suffering and art, is to open the door to a range of unexplored treasure rooms. Nor, given its devotional objectives, can art in this case be considered flight from the pain of existence. But just as not all suffering led beyond pain to martyrdom, so, in the idioms of Western art, not all suffering was permitted to disclose universal truths. The repertoire of pain that reverberated throughout the chambers of the imagination was large; the idioms of cult that transformed pain into purity of heart were limited.

Summary

I have now explored ideas about conscience, the agent of moral choice, disclosing a few more facets and consequences of the proportionality of faith. Part of the substratum of thought on which the idea of supernatural conversion was built has come to light. The doctrines that purity of conscience was necessary to salvation and that, even in saints, the conscience was always subject to trial by ordeal elucidate the picture of empathetic conversion as a gradual process of formation or education (see chaps. 2, 3). Given the combination of autonomy and dependence displayed by the idea of conscience, it is easy to understand how conversion could be regarded as a process that, idealizing purity, made vigilant and self-sacrificing doubt its price. Given the separateness of moral decision (in the conscience) and enforceable legal sanctions, it is also easy to see how, flowing from conscience, conversion could be subversive of political institutions in Church or civil government. The relentless, doubting scrutiny of conscience also made empathetic conversion an exercise in subversion of the self. Insofar as the life of the spirit was thought to duplicate in miniature that of the body politic, it was telling that the subversion of the old self was recognized as the cost of spiritual regeneration.

Later (see chaps. 5, 6), I shall consider how the mind was educated to subversion by various components in the pedagogical arsenal of conversion, including social myth and art. For the moment, it is enough to recall that ideas about the formation of conscience were of a piece with the ascetic educational program of monasticism, with its austere disciplines of mind and body.

A world of difference separated Catullus's portrayal of remorse from Peter Damian's of penance. An imponderable vastness, including the duty of resistance, was contained in the shift of a single word when John of Salisbury recast Terence's famous sentence to say that charity kept him from accounting anything human foreign to himself. It was for charity, John wrote, that one took up arms and fought with all one's powers—uncompromisingly, as he said— against the infringement of any article of the divine law, since charity was the fulfillment of the Law. The symbol of charity was fire.[87] A sea change in ideas of empathetic education divided Catullus and Terence from Peter Damian and John of Salisbury.

Likewise, the discussion of conscience brings us to a point at which there is little similarity to moral education in Buddhism. The third pledge of the bodhisattvas (see chap. 2 at n. 74)—"However immeasurable the dharmas, I vow to master them all"—establishes the distance. To be sure, the Stoic doctrine, taken up into scholastic philosophy, that the conscience was quickened by a *scintilla animae,* a divine spark, establishes an analogy with the doctrine that the Buddha-mind was present in each being. However, the doctrine of conscience to which the West was educated was essentially a juridical one demanding penitence and remorse. Lacking a theology of crime and punishment, Buddhism had no equivalent to it. There is a parallel between some doctrines of conscience and the Buddhist teaching that the morality of an act depends on intent, and not on legalistic or ritual correctness. However, the movement of moral action was not toward the legal goal of righteousness nor even toward the virtue of goodness, but rather toward a state of wisdom in which all things, being empty, were also the same. By this wisdom, not by righteousness, the dharmas (distinguishing categories of individual being) were overcome. By it, the bodhisattvas performed their task of saving all sentient beings, not in establishing the rule of justice but in the nonactivity of their silence.

Further, I hope that it will by now be impossible to confuse what was known as conscience in the period under review with what is known by the same name in a contemporary secular context. In discourse in which the right of resistance figured, the defining terms were not *right* and *wrong,* and certainly not *legal* and *illegal.* Obligations came in the second or third line of reasoning, after the right direction of the affects, which is to say, purity of heart, rather than certitude. Like articles of faith, the form of knowledge called conscience belonged to esthetics, the study of empathy, or feeling. Consequently, like articles of faith (and unlike legal sanctions), arguments from conscience depended upon methods of association that, though learned, were incapable of logical demonstration.

The supreme good was "charity"; the supreme evil, "blasphemy." Charity consisted primarily in loving God with a pure heart and a good and unfeigned conscience; blasphemy, in hating God out of impurity of heart and a bad conscience grounded in feigned belief. The filial fear that informed love of God had its counterpart in the servile fear that inspired the hatred that blasphemy was, either in the perfidy of disbelief in God or in despair of escaping the abyss of damnation.[88] Indeed, the right direction of conscience was inseparable from the dark mystery of Christian vocation, and so from that of predestination. Christ called both Peter and Judas. Both denied their Master. Love's remorse brought Peter, through bitter tears, to eternal life. Blasphemy's brought Judas, through bleak despair, to undying death.[89] It was ironic that the dominant orders in Western society, considering themselves God's chosen people and patterning their institutions on scriptural antecedents, should establish blasphemy as a capital crime and thus condemn themselves to replay endlessly in the role of judges, Judas's corruptors, the scenario of the trial of Christ.

In the little village of our world, these associative ideas, with the limits and degrees that they assign to empathy, continue to perpetuate and shape conflict, and not only in the ritualized play of personal devotion, such as the self-crucifixions that occur each Passiontide on opposite sides of the globe, in Italy and in the Philippines. I do not need to emphasize that in our own day these ideas, and the educational programs by which they are conveyed, do coexist in some minds with post-Kantian ones and that those minds may play separate parts of the repertoire of conscience at different moments in their lives. Living tradition combines ancient ideas with new ones, ill-matched though they may be, and gives them the same youthful vigor, the same fighting spirit. A veteran of religious conflict, John Dryden (1631–1700) repeated suspicions with which I began when he referred to conscience as chameleon-hued, a Proteus changing its form at will, a harlot equating interest with good.[90]

Let us try, finally, to visualize this gossamer, enduring artifact of an earlier world. In the period that I have considered, a lens of thought called "conscience" was made and polished in the workshop of learning. It was a glass made of many elements denied by post-Kantian discourse. They included God—a God who smites to heal and kills to make alive—and Satan, who received from God the power to tempt and harm us and even to infuse himself into our minds for the punishment of sin. They included miracle (not least the miracles of creation, atonement, and judgment), the duality of body and soul existing under the shadow of death, and eternal vengeance and reward. To purify the glass, its components were purged and its surface was polished with passionate, calculated disciplines of mortification and contrition, by imitating Christ in ritual play so as to experience in one's own mind and flesh the glorifying agonies of the Crucified.

External obedience belonged to another order of discourse, an order of logical demonstration and cogency, one distinct from penitential suffering. The lens of conscience broke through parallel beams of all forces in spirituality and art, bending them to a common axis and to one incandescent point. The varied rays faith beat through the glass upon each individual heart at that burning point, enkindling each with separate love and shame, each alone. I have only partly stated the facts. For conscience was both the scrutinizer and the scrutinized. Detached in self-judgment, as long as the transforming process of empathetic conversion ran on, every conscience was both flame and glass. Yet, in its brief shining, each was a witness both false and true to the single black light, playing yet unmoving, silent, beyond the glass.

CHAPTER 5

A *True* Myth

For the question of how some people can believe what others reject, theologians had a ready and proven answer: such things, they taught, lay beyond human understanding. But theological deference to imponderables does not exhaust motives for belief that are capable of historical inquiry, or explain what wider context may sanction deliberate fictions as truth and nurture tormenting dilemmas of conscience.

In this chapter, I shall address the question by stages. After a review of conclusions indicated thus far, I shall underscore the paradox of myth in Christianity: the paradox, namely, that, although Christian writers declared relentless warfare against the fables of unbelievers and misbelievers—of Jews, heretics, and schismatics as well as of pagans—they also openly recognized a penumbra of myth that imparted truth to their fictive teachings.

Next, I shall ask what made it possible for Christian writers to receive myth as an envelope conveying truth, while non-Christians rejected it as sheer fabrication. The answer proposed lies in habits inculcated by society, habits of empathy through which professed believers were expected to learn by doing: that is, to enact myth in daily life. Thus, a key to the distinction between those who could and those who could not believe is given by play, and in the ritualizations of play supplied by the arts.

From this point, it is only natural to ask what kinds of ritualized play were considered most apt to train the mind and heart to act in harmony with myth. In the age and culture with which I am most concerned, these appear to have been chiefly the occupations and diversions of warriors.

Finally, the conclusion appears inescapable that empathetic conversion was a social as well as a personal process. So far as my project—understanding conversion—is concerned, the characteristics of what was called conversion were prescribed by the classes that governed its social consequences. The familiar contours of a hermeneutic circle appear. For what a particular society called conversion was what, by learning, ritualizing, and enforcing mythic roles, its dominant members had been trained to recognize as such and to call by that name.

Thus far, I have found that empathetic conversion was regarded as a way of life. Rather than a single, transforming event, it was a continuous process of transition and, in fact, of education. It may have begun in a single moment—"the hour I first believed"—but it must advance and be perfected. The transformation by grace became permanent, if ever, after death, when the changefulness of earthly life was over. In this world conversion was not a dramatic peripety but a predicament moving toward resolution, and it was beset with risk of failure at every stage. In large part, the educational program advancing what was called conversion was ritualized play (or enactment). It was epitomized in monasticism; it showed its effects, not least, in the development of the idea of conscience.

I have maintained that, like that of conscience, the idea of conversion as a process of formation was built up through the ages. The eleventh and twelfth centuries marked a decisive moment in its history. Despite the reformulations that it then received, it remained an ensemble or repertory of ill-matched paradigms from different eras and cultures. However, experience in the early Church emphasized strands that represented conversion as the realization and unfolding of a predicament.

A definition of empathetic conversion was a solution for a problem. I have now examined two lines of reasoning that lay behind the solution. First, I considered penitential love and methods of educating body, intellect, and emotions through lifelong disciplines of pain. Next, I analyzed methods of association employed to verify the judgments of conscience—judgments of the sort that impelled people to embrace austere, formative disciplines. Here, the predicamental character of conversion was exposed in the proposition that the enlightened conscience was both autonomous and beside itself (or God-intoxicated). Further, because the sense of being inspired could come about by demonic illusion or wishful thinking, the enlightened conscience was also relentlessly self-doubting.

From the beginning I recognized that something was behind the lines of reasoning that lay behind the solution to the problem. Basic needs made the problem thinkable in the first place. In earlier chapters I found that empathetic conversion addressed common human needs, including those of life, love, and purity. However, I have not, until now, considered except by implication one of the greatest among them: the need for truth. The yearning for authentic knowledge pervades religion. In Christianity, early infused with gnosticism, that yearning and ways of answering it formed part of a tradition going back through the long centuries both of Hebrew doctrine and of Greek philosophy.

For this need is at the heart of questions called eternal. Thus, Augustine of Hippo anticipated that the blessed, living without death and loving without parting, would also know without error.[1] And, nearer the period under review, Caesarius of Heisterbach counted among the joys of Paradise that the saved would know the secrets of God and that they would "praise 'what the eye hath not seen' because such things are invisible and 'what the ear hath not heard' because they are in the most silent peace and, moreover, praise what has 'not arisen in the heart of man' because they are incomprehensible." Caesarius's other beatitudes, and thus needs satisfied, were life without end, love of God and neighbor, ineffable joy, quickness of spirit unhampered by the inert heaviness of matter, and freedom from care.[2] The mysteries of conversion centered on the need for truth.

At each stage in my discussion, vocabulary has opened windows on various aspects of understanding empathetic conversion. Yet, given the composite nature of the idea of conversion, the vernaculars used to speak of the need for truth were unusually complex and deeply marked with the idea of faith as proportionate. Indeed, they included much more than words. For by turning to the subject of truth, I also turn to myth and the opulence of arts employed to ritualize, proclaim, glorify, and teach myth.

Let me explain. Myth is the bridge between what is felt (empathy) and what is made (poetics). It is the context into which inmost and inexpressible feelings of one person are translated so that they can be intelligible to others—so that, adapting the Apostle Paul's words, what God has made known to one heart can be revealed "from faith to faith" (cf. Rom. 1:17).

The repertory of conversion paradigms taken up into Christian theology was also a repertory of myths. Neoplatonism supplied that of eternal egress and return, both for the cosmos (or macrocosm) and for the human soul (or microcosm). Stoicism framed its doctrines within the mythic contours of universal recurrence. The Old Testament made the myth of sacred history—from Creation on through Covenant to the messianic kingdom—the basis of communication from faith to faith. In the New Testament elements of the Old Testament mythology were given fresh emphasis. The motifs of sin and atonement were woven into a narrative in which the messianic prophecies had been fulfilled by Christ and the remaining promises of God to his chosen people were being fulfilled as the world moved toward apocalyptic consummation in the Messiah's second coming.

Each of these mythologies explained conflicts, injustices, and suffering in life as necessary way stations along the hard journey to enduring blessedness. Each proclaimed a truth manifest and triumphant in conflict. Each set a context in which conversion made sense.

It is important to emphasize that by *myth* I do not mean a story or romance concocted by an individual author. Instead, I am using the word in a newer sense, analytic rather than descriptive, given it by anthropology and other disciplines: "the sense of 'sacred tradition, primordial revelation, exemplary model.'" In this meaning, empathies ingrained by myth provide the moral cohesion of society. Initiation into its knowledge signals entrance into the network of obligations that binds individuals into community. As a bond of collective unity, the myth must be continually recalled; even more, it must be continually reenacted. Enacting, or living out, the myth ratifies personal as well as collective identity, often by using rituals to link daily existence and the cycle of life to powers ruling time and cosmos.[3]

As it spins out such contexts, myth is always true and false. Such was the "royal lie" that Plato envisioned the founders of his Republic inventing to explain for citizens then and yet to be the origins and nature of their community.[4] A canonical authority in Christian tradition, Augustine of Hippo, acknowledged that, tied to vagueness of language and limits of human minds, all human knowledge was governed by reasoning that was partly true and partly false. In Paradise, Augustine concluded, the blessed would see truth directly and have no need of such mediation, no need even of the gospel.[5] Christian interpreters generally found such ironic mingling of true and fictive elements in the parables, enigmas, and other puzzlements of which the Holy Spirit composed Scripture itself. And, moreover, they acknowledged that in this world they saw through a glass darkly, perceiving indirectly by faith, through cryptic signs, types, and symbols, what they hoped to see "face to face" after death.

As the poetics of conversion illustrated (see chap. 2), writers in the twelfth century recognized the fictive character of their doctrines about conversion and, indeed, of theology as a whole. They treasured what was true but fictive; they despised and dreaded the false. Thus, the vocabulary of myth was dominated by the polar opposites of *religion* and *superstition*. In sifting poetic truth from deceptive illusion, writers were dominated by the ancient equivalence of truth with beauty. Consequently, they added a third key word to the vocabulary of mythic expression. As they moved between the antonyms of religion and superstition, they spoke of *beauty* as a synonym of *truth*.

These words—*religion, superstition,* and *beauty*—give us an entrée into the vernaculars of myth. Thereby, they also open new aspects of the cognitive processes packed into the portmanteau word *conversion*. Using beauty as a cognitive norm indicated a powerful strand of irony in those processes. For it brought into play the ironies of pictorial art (which makes things appear to be what they are not), of symbolic language (such as metaphor, synedoche, antiphrasis, and other devices for saying one thing while meaning another), and of process itself (in which subjects both are and are not what they are coming to be). Indeed, because it is both false and true, myth itself is a study in irony, and doubly so when its narrative centers on the ironic distance between exemplars and images, as Christian doctrine does in presenting Christ as the model of life for all believers. Fictions of conversion were set into such a frame.

The contextual vocabulary bearing on the need for truth is therefore shot through with ironies, especially when one speaks of empathetic conversion, and particularly by imitating Christ, as an initiation into and exercise of mythic knowledge. For almost from its beginnings Christian doctrine was characterized above all by a revulsion from myth: that is, from what were called the lies of pagan poets.

In recent times the theological impulse of "demythologizing" Christianity —of framing a Christianity without Christ—has denied the historical authenticity of precisely those doctrines most germane to the theological myths of the twelfth century: the lordship and creative function of Christ as Logos, the Incarnation of the Word and, consequently, the sacrificial Passion of Christ, and, finally, the eschatological drama of Christ's ascension and second coming. To use the language of play, these denials, associated with the name of Rudolf Bultmann, define a game entirely different from the one keyed to imitation of Christ. Indeed, it differs from the imitation of Christ permitted by demythologizers of the eighteenth century who, like Thomas Jefferson (1743–1826), acknowledged Christ as a preeminent moral reformer while, advocating a natural religion, they rejected divine revelation in Scripture, the divinity of Christ, Trinitarian theology, miracle, and the organized Church with its orthodoxy and sacraments.[6] The gulf between that game and the one that I am attempting to reconstruct is also indicated by the rarity with which modern theologians attend to conceptions central to empathetic doctrines in earlier centuries: to God as beauty itself or to the beauty and sweetness of God, as stimuli of unifying love.

Modern scholars work within contextualizing myths of their own, and in some degree the demythologization of Christianity can only be the interpretation of one mythology in terms of another. Likewise, Christian rejections of other systems of thought present a double image. From their own perspective the Christian centuries, including the twelfth, were "an age hostile to myths."[7] From perspectives of those hostile to its doctrines, Christianity constituted a tyranny of myths, enforced by "priestcraft and superstition."[8] I have returned to the difference in perspectives taken by modern historians and twelfth-century theological writers. Because myths must be learned, I have also returned to the relation between conversion and education.

And, at that point, I find, open and resolute, the fact that ideas of conversion and the social myths that were their contexts were in the custody of an identifiable class, which adapted them in its own image. For guardianship of the tradition with which I am concerned was part of governing the Church. It had fallen to men professed to ascetic disciplines, educated in the literary arts, bred to the ethos of a warrior aristocracy. I shall need to consider whether the ways in which this class understood conversion and enacted its rituals were applicable to those outside it or on its borders, locating unspoken reasons behind the proposition, so often encountered in earlier chapters, that empathy must be trained to keep within set limits and to observe degrees.

Conditions for the Reception of Myth

How did it happen that myths were compelling truth for some, whom it bound into communities by revelations "from faith to faith," but repellent lies for others? Paul's doctrine of proportionality—that each thinks according to the measure of faith bestowed by God—must once more be the point of departure.

Writers of the eleventh and twelfth centuries were second to none in their understanding of the human power to evoke imaginary worlds. Although the spheres of myth (or *fabula*) and history were distinct, their functions as edifying amusements tended to elide. Encountering the fragments of Greek and Roman myths available to them, scholars explained them as embellishments of historical narrative; stripping them of their halos, they incorporated those shards of a lost culture into their chronicles of the distant past. Some remythologized characters of pagan Antiquity, particularly divinities of love—Cupid and Venus—and gave them places in the romantic allegories of troubadours. Still others cast their own imaginative conceptions of cosmos and soul in mythic form, purely as works of artistic virtuosity.[9]

Yet experience of these achievements sharpened awareness of the danger most at issue in the debate between Christians and unbelievers, notably Jews: idolatrously setting the heart's desires on one's own inventions. Here, too, writers acknowledged and condemned the regularity with which human beings set up idols in their hearts, not least that of Diana the huntress, symbolizing avarice and rapacity.[10] Whatever else it may have achieved, debate underscored for controversialists on each side the degree to which those on the other were captive to limits that their own myths set to empathy. As to the discrepancy between belief and action, it was true that while mercy was the Lord's path for all perfect Christians, few indeed kept that way of life.[11] Perhaps for these reasons Herman-Judah, after his conversion from Judaism to Christianity, abstained from invoking the mythic paradigm of the imitation of Christ except to rebuke Christians for their want of charity toward the Jews.[12]

When Pope Innocent II, then expelled from Rome by a rival for the papal throne, was welcomed at the abbey of St. Denis (1131), the Jews of Paris joined the great concourse of those greeting him "most honorably." They offered him a veiled Torah scroll. The veil and the theological commonplace that the synagogue was spiritually blind induced the pope to pray, using words of St. Paul (2 Cor. 3:13-14), that God would remove the veil of ignorance from the Jews' hearts.[13] When he prayed for the Jews of Paris, Innocent II may well have had his antipope, Anacletus II, in mind. For although Anacletus's family had long been Christian, his enemies derided him as the offspring of Jews and on that ground denounced what they called his "invasion" of the see of Peter as an affront to Christ.[14] And yet the irony was that Christians themselves recognized how dim and enigmatic their own knowledge of sacred things was and that few events revealed the indeterminacy of doctrine more plainly than the papal schism of 1130.

Christian attitudes toward Jews differed in intensity and ambiguity from those toward other unbelievers. We may discount the story that Richard the Lionhearted had the teeth of Jews extracted "by a lingering process . . . as an excellent jest," but we have it on impeccable authority that St. Louis (1214–1270) considered a sword through the belly the only defense a layman could give Christian law against a Jew.[15] The evidence of hostility is abundant, varied, and pervasive. Texts represent Jews as blasphemers perishing in deaths of exemplary pain, as moneylenders weakening saints by inconveniently drawing off their resources, as adepts in the forbidden arts of sorcery (although in this regard, as in moneylending, they could be usefully employed by Christians against each other).[16] Their malice, cunning, envy, cruelty, and lust were proverbial.[17] Christians judged that even as potential converts their notorious materialism made them both attractive targets and unsteady newcomers to the household of faith.[18] As objects of fear, they also became subjects of satire.[19]

Yet, unlike opprobrium cast on other unbelievers, the satire against Jews displayed the ambivalence of Christian attitudes toward themselves as well as toward Jews, and therefore the problematic character that empathy had for them. The experience of empathetic conversion itself underscored the fact that what one ardently embraced as true religion could later be unmasked as superstition. Christian writers amply professed the darkness of their own spiritual vision and, consequently, their fears of ignorance and error. It was essential for their own ideas about the legitimacy and goals of the Church that Christians affirm the Jews as God's elect and faithful people before the Incarnation and as his chosen agents in the eschatological drama being played out as history moved toward its appointed and terrible end. Thus, while satirists ridiculed Jews, they also praised them for the sake of throwing Christian wickedness into darker shadows.[20] Christians carefully noted correspondences between their own holy days and those kept by the Jews, as prescribed in the Old Testament.[21] Some made themselves "most beloved" to Jews by seeking them out, studying their books, and learning "the Hebraic truth."[22] Jews were thought to witness to authentic holiness, not least by joining in public lamentations at the funerals of saints.[23] Their conversions, even when produced in the course of legal or mercantile business, were acclaimed as great miracles, notably when they unmasked Christian fraud.[24] Their witness to truth, as adversaries or as advocates, was taken as an indispensable corroboration of Christian honesty and a powerful corrective of Christian failure.

Consequently, public and private disputations between Jews and Christians occurred with some frequency. To what purpose, apart from exchanging invective and ritually demarking the limits of empathy? Intransigence on each side left no room for compromise. The Jewish charge of exclusivism was wellplaced. For from Old Testament examples of Israel's own backsliding, Christians saw plainly the fatal danger of assimilation. The incident of the Golden Calf was followed by others down to the days of the Maccabees in which members of the chosen people had embraced Gentile practices and sacrificed to idols, only to incur the punishment due covenant breakers.[25] Myths were not for those who could not know and feel "in Christ."

The rigor of ill will consisted not only in the antagonism of doctrinal mythologies but also in social mythologies such as those on the Christian side that portrayed Jews as desecrators of sacred images and ritual murderers of Christians. Laws prescribing segregation of believers from infidels—forbidding Christians to break bread with Jews, Christian children to play with pagan, and Jewish children to "be sung to sleep to the sound of Christian melodies"—would have seemed more to the point than disputations.[26] Indeed, the same author who recorded the vision of a Jew being dragged to hell in chains of fire also recorded a solemn warning against disputations with Jews on pain of eternal torment.[27]

In the event, the twelfth century marked the beginning of a new ferocity in disputes between Jews and Christians, but, as the combatants came to know their enemies, "the increase of mutual knowledge was accompanied by a growing awareness of, and stress upon," what divided them. There was no wish, in "establishing fellowship with one another, [to open] a door of inner healing."[28] But that conclusion does not minimize the importance of ritualized adversarial play to the process of understanding and particularly to understanding empathetic conversion. Debates with Jews in Latin Europe did not end as did a debate between a Saracen and Crusaders at the siege of Jerusalem (1099). The Saracen, refusing to convert, was beheaded.[29] What did the debates indicate about the revelation of what may be known of God from faith to faith within the permitted bounds of empathy? Their theatrical character is a clue.

The Need for Play

The beginning of empathetic conversion, as I have shown, became only the first stage in the reception as true context of what earlier seemed a fable. The progress of empathetic conversion was the enactment or fulfillment of events that made sense in the contexts of mythic scenarios or dramas. Thus, a life of ascetic self-denial made sense when understood in the context of a Passion play, although, as the case of Herman-Judah demonstrated, it seemed absurd to those outside the context of Christian myth. Abbot Guerric of Igny, a disciple of Bernard of Clairvaux, provided a diagram of what reception demanded after one passed from disbelief to faith, and where it led. What we believe through faith, he wrote, we practice through works of justice. By doing those works, we come to knowledge of what had been believed. By the act of knowing, we come finally to contemplate wisdom.[30] Here is an application of the same doctrine—learn by doing—that entered into teachings about the sacraments of conversion, baptism, and the Eucharist. For regarding those sacraments, too, writers insisted that the form of conversion be lived out, that through ritualized action believers should become the exemplar that they emulated and loved. By empathetic participation, the "I" of the believer should become the "you" of Christ. Fiction (or fable) needed the ratifying penumbra of myth.

Enactment was the turning mechanism that moved the reception of myth from objective knowledge to inward faith. In the twelfth century Herman-Judah neatly bracketed the inquiries, meditations, debates, and misadventures that made up his conversion. At the outset he considered Judaism the authentic *religio* and Christianity a *superstitio,* driving its devotees mad with love of it. Through his *practicum* in belief, he came by dint of trial and error to repudiate the "most filthy and shameful sect of Jewish superstition" and to embrace ardent "love of the catholic faith and religion."[31] The roles of fable and myth had been reversed. Once the drama of fable (*superstitio*) was embraced as mythic truth (*religio*), it had to be performed; the actor had to enter into the dramatic context of myth. My discussion of the pathology of conversion locates the center of ritual enactment—and of the whole weight of symbolic interpretation—in the doctrine of Christ's incarnation, mission, and impending return. Perfecting empathetic conversion hinged on the ritualized imitation of Christ, especially in the conflict of his Passion.

My task in exploring the mystery of conversion leads me to play, and not only to play with words. For the dramatic structure of myth is all-embracing. From within the mythic world, there is one art that takes many forms—some verbal, others visual—and all require that believers perform the myth, that they project themselves in the works of art before them. At the center of any verbal description, there is a silence; at the core of any visual one, a blankness. Believers find themselves swept up into those spaces, swept up into a timeless performance of sacred drama by the force of their dramatic imagination. There they experienced the incommunicable enactment of the mysteries.

The Cistercian order was conspicuous by its rejection of the visual arts. Yet even it cultivated the visual imagination. In sermons for the Christmas season, Guerric of Igny exemplified the importance of theater performed before the eyes of the mind. "Although 'faith comes from hearing,'" he preached, "it comes more easily and quickly by sight, as we are taught by the example of him to whom was said: 'Because you have seen me you have believed.' . . . Incomparably more is now given to sight than was ever given to hearing; for now the Word which is God may be seen." With his own words, Guerric said, he was "wrapping Christ in lowly, mean swaddling clothes," giving Christ to his brethren in his sermons. "With all piety, therefore, let us think on Christ in the swaddling clothes with which his mother wrapped him, so that with eternal happiness we may see the glory and beauty with which his Father has clothed him."

Guerric had another role in mind for the men around him. To them he said: "You are mothers of the boy who is born to you and in you, by whom, indeed, in the fear of the Lord, you have conceived and given birth to the spirit of salvation." Guerric was evoking for the visual imagination the dramatic performance that Francis of Assisi (1181/82–1226) later provided for the eye of the body in his invention of the crèche.[32] Similar exercises to inflame religious ardor were practiced in meditations on other incidents in Christ's life, including notably the Passion.

To ask what purpose the ritualized public debates and private conversations between Jews and Christians had is to open very slightly the discrepancy between actual circumstances and the play that enacted contextual myth, not least the play of hide-and-seek. For, as we know, those encounters did result in cultural borrowing. The assimilation that myth forbade did occur, and its results are apparent in methods and propositions of scriptural interpretation by Christians that gained currency in the twelfth century. However staunchly plundering the enemy's intellectual wealth was defended, there remained a fear of assimilation's contagious effects, a suspicion that introducing the candles, icons, and choirs of pagan liturgies would profane the sacred, that appropriating Jewish interpretive devices would darken with Jewish literalism the light irradiating the Gospel. Imagination was prone to be captivated by illusion and fantasy. Thus, the rules of the mythic game required that assimilation cover its traces, just as it demanded that conversions of Christians to Judaism be buried in silence.[33] Myth demanded enactment, not modification.

In that enactment private disputations were engaged in for the pleasure of matching mind against mind; public debates, like those of more recent times, were sporting events, exhibitions of skill, spectacles of combat. Insofar as they could be regarded as instruments of conversion, they belonged to a repertory of play that included theatrical performances, the spectacle of liturgy, and the visual arts.[34] The power of such ritual devices is still to be felt, as, for example, in the enduring polemics over the Oberammergau Passion play. It is abundantly clear that the repertory enacted the ideals of those who were attacking the old ways, rather than of those whose conversion they sought. The Christian belief that human events followed a divine plan for human salvation, a scenario that ran from Creation to Last Judgment, meant that the repertory and those who invented and deployed it had parts to play in a cosmic drama which was still unfolding, a drama of suffering whose sense and direction were known only to the faithful and imperfectly known even to them. Behind it all was love, infused with the cathartic emotions of pity and fear.

Thus, for the sake of manifesting the things of God from faith to faith, imagination transformed suffering into art. Beauty (*pulchritudo*) was a synonym for truth, as it had been for Plato and varieties of Platonists after him, and also, as for them, a cause of love.

The quest for a beauty equivalent with truth, a beauty that did not deceive as did earthly loveliness, characterized most of the paradigms of conversion received into Christian doctrine. Further, mythic narratives that enshrined these paradigms also agreed that to perceive truthful beauty, a person must be like it. The need for purity belonged to this common doctrine of similitude and, moreover, of mimesis conforming the perceiver's empathies to the beauty that was the object of contemplation.

Of course, the mythic narratives varied widely, each contributing its own esthetic vocabulary. Eventually, unlikely combinations occurred. Abstraction was grafted to anthropomorphism. The esthetic vernacular of Neoplatonisms taught the eternal egress from and return of the macrocosm (and with it microcosmic human souls) to an abstract, impersonal, and self-absorbed divinity. From that origin and goal, all beings derived the natures that were their beauties. This mythic plot was melded with the Old Testamental doctrine that an entirely unabstract and personal God chose to create human beings in his own image and likeness and that he also, by grace, conveyed the beauty of holiness proper to himself to those of his own choosing.

Finally, the doctrines of Christ were drawn into this contextual amalgam of nature and grace. Supreme beauty was expressed in the Crucifixion, the atoning sacrifice by which Christ was believed to have redeemed the world, and which each Christian recapitulated in baptism and penitential discipline. The open, agonizing wounds of Christ and his dead and mutilated body were revered for their glorious beauty and, in their splendor, as spurs of love. Herman-Judah saw a painting that graphically expressed the irony of this beauty. Before his conversion he found in the cathedral of Münster a double representation of Christ which seemed to his still unenlightened mind a "lying picture," a "monstrous idol." The lower register depicted Christ crucified; the upper, Christ, enthroned and most beautiful, as one deified. And so Christ appeared "abased and exalted, despised and extolled, shamed and glorified."[35]

This rich composite of beauties and esthetic vocabularies received a particularly complex stamp from monasticism, the institutionalized form of conversion par excellence. In monasteries the beauty that was equivalent with truth and that acted both as a cognitive principle and as a stimulus of love was the antithesis of classical serenity; for, in its disciplines, it ritualized a truthful beauty intensified by self-hatred and contempt for the world. I have come to what Rupert of Deutz called "the great and delightful beauty of mystery."[36]

The contrast between ancient and medieval ideals was apparent in attitudes toward the most basic aspects of art: that is, in attitudes toward manual labor. Contempt for servile labor in Antiquity divided practicing artists from patrons and connoisseurs of art. However, the ascetic obligation of manual labor in monastic discipline created a social order in which patrons and connoisseurs were also artisans.[37] The example of Francis of Assisi, who rebuilt the churches of San Damiano and the Portiuncula with his own hands, is only one of the most celebrated instances in which ascetics exercised spiritual discipline by making works of art. Bishops and monks were expert structural engineers, builders, painters, sculptors, and metalworkers. They were able to admire the ingenuity of the craftsman in a work more than the work itself, for they knew that dazzling effects were produced by pedestrian techniques.[38] When they described the environments of cult that they had constructed for themselves and supervised for others, they praised elegance and beauty not only as critics but also with craftsmen's eyes.

Yet ascetic discipline ingrained a powerful contradiction that made the same person artist and iconoclast. Self-denial was paired with skill. Aristotle observed that artisans (and poets) loved their works because in them the workers made real what they had the potentiality for being,[39] but this avenue of pride was closed to Christian ascetics. According to a story from the earliest days of monasticism, "A brother asked an old man, 'What shall I do, for I am troubled about manual work? I love making ropes and I cannot make them.' The old man said that Abbot Sisoes used to say, 'One should not do work which gives you satisfaction.'"[40] Correspondingly, the *Rule* of Benedict forbade artisans who entered the monastery to practice their crafts unless permitted by the abbot. If any were found to pride themselves on knowledge of their art, they were to be denied every opportunity to apply it until they returned to humbleness of spirit.[41]

While *pulchritudo* was a cognitive norm, it was, for the spiritual imagination, also detached from material objects that could express it. The world gave all too many proofs of how souls starved while the senses were replete. The same objectives of moral formation that through love inspired the making of art also inspired, through hatred, pity, and fear, numerous modes of iconoclasm, including the continual demolition of buildings in styles that with time came to be regarded as crude, destruction of precious objects for reasons of gain, and exclusion of representational arts from the disciplines of some who praised others for their cultivation of those arts, as the Cistercian, Bernard of Clairvaux, praised the Benedictine, Suger of St. Denis.[42] Destruction of pagan art was obligatory, as when Bishop Otto of Bamberg demolished temples in Pomerania the artistry, opulence, and grandeur of whose paintings and sculpture—images of human beings, birds, and animals so true to life that they seemed to live and breathe—struck even their wreckers with awe.[43]

Pulchritudo was therefore detached from individual works of art and, indeed, from any particular art; it was a characteristic of truth, which could be known by reference to mythic context provided by artful representations. It was sought in scriptural interpretation and in the divine pattern unfolding in human events. As he looked back upon his spiritual journey, Herman-Judah realized the "most beautiful reasoning" by which Bishop Egbert of Münster explicated the allegorical meanings of Scripture, the "honey-sweetness of spiritual allegories" that he himself, in time, repeated to the Jews.[44] The anticlassical nature of *pulchritudo* marked these contextual inquiries as surely as it did the attitude toward manual labor and the pairing of art and iconoclasm. Like music, the visual arts were roads that prepared the Lord's way to the heart so that the mysteries of prophecy could be opened to the expectant mind or the grace of compunction bestowed.[45] The call to the imitation of Christ—to turn life into a Passion play—emphasizes that the imagination was trained to play a role in the theater of this world.[46] The formation of the mind and heart was an education in drama, one that followed its own esthetic ironies. For as Jewish outrage at crucifixes indicated, the spiritual imagination was trained to find beauty by placing subjects of visual repellency and moral horror in context and also to see sweetness in scenes of martyrdom and of the Crucifixion that were used to excite emotions of love and hatred.

Nor did the spiritual imagination fully formed in these ironies require art to be faithful to nature. Society was profoundly hostile to androgyny, and members of male religious orders were disciplined to avoid the sight of women as they avoided vipers. Yet writers found beauty in imagining, among the members of the body of Christ, the martyrs as his beard, showing in their torments the fortitude represented by the beard; the confessors as his breasts, nourishing the weak by word and example; and virgins and the continent as his womb (*venter*), choosing love of chastity over the fruit of the flesh.[47] To the dramatic imagination of the spirit, beauty was in the rightness of an act. It was beautiful to see Bishop Otto of Bamberg, associating like with like, abruptly separate pagan children from their Christian playmates. Baptism, he said, barred communion between believers and infidels; and the pagans huddled together at a distance, confused and terrified in their infidelity while the others gloried in the profession of their Christian name and abominated them. The "beautiful spectacle" was completed soon after when these taunts "out of the mouths of babes" were fulfilled in the destruction of the "enemy faction."[48]

To the imagination educated in its ironies, beauty was displayed in the drama of historical events that, by their correspondence with Scripture's hidden code, gave evidence of the divine order. Otto of Freising found such beauty of designed coincidence in the fact that the Crusaders entered Jerusalem on the eighth day of the siege (1099), their horses wading knee-deep in the blood of the conquered, for Christ's resurrection, too, had occurred on the eighth day to demonstrate that the Jewish Law, commanding Sabbath observance, had been abolished.[49]

In the esthetic ironies of ascetic discipline, self-denial combined with conspicuous consumption, ugliness with elegance, and violence with beauty. Adam of Bremen (d. 1081/85) records that when a goldsmith was breaking up particularly splendid crosses and a chalice for the melting pot, he heard amid the sound of his mallet a voice as though that of a weeping child.[50] There are many analogues in accounts of Christian desecrations of pagan idols in which demons fled from the images with cries of lamentation. The Christian doctrine of representation indicates how misleading those analogues could be. For the workman could not have considered the images beneath his mallet to have been haunted by good or evil spirits any more than he could have been greatly troubled by obeying his archbishop's command to destroy works of artistic merit. However, he could very well have borne in mind the mythic *pulchritudo* of reward and punishment in which those who revered the Cross were blessed and those who, in their malice, despised it were brought to ruin.

Thus, the cognitive principle of beauty, pervaded with ironies, ordered the emotions and governed the ritualized play of arts that supported monastic conversion; and the esthetic conscience that I have described contributed to the mutual repellency of Jewish and Christian beliefs. The conclusion is evident that play was not a means to truth so much as performance of truth in its ironic context, or rather that play was the performance of love, arousing the purifying emotions of pity and fear. Intoxicated with love and compassion of Christ, Francis of Assisi sometimes broke into song, using the courtly language of France, taking branches up from the ground and sawing the air as though he were playing a viol or some other stringed instrument. "But all this playing ended in tears, and this joy dissolved in compassion for the Passion of Christ. In these times, he would draw sighs continually; and, with deep-drawn groans, forgetful of those things which he held in his hands, he was raised to heaven."[51] Indeed, truth existed in dramatic participation in mythic ironies, in the direct experience of those mixed emotions, rather than in speculative thought and remembrance. Given the meshing of violence and beauty, it is important to remember that one effect of drama, and of art generally, is to define limits in the struggle for existence.

What have we thus far discovered? We have found that Christian writers were aware that the way to truth led through myth, through learned ignorance and fear of error. We have also found that the process by which myth was received was itself the subject of an elaborate contextual mythology. The reception of myth was thought to consist in two acts: in dissemination and in enactment. Human agency (as in preaching) was secondary in the act of dissemination, which came primarily through the Holy Spirit spread abroad in human hearts. However, revelation was always partial in this world, and this incompleteness intruded threatening uncertainties as to the enactment of myth. Because it was ritualized enactment or performance, this second aspect of reception depended above all on the dramatic imagination. It sought to engage the cathartic emotions of pity and fear. It applied the esthetic rule of beauty (*pulchritudo*), with all its ironies. The essential fact was that the performance enacted a mythic scenario given in the career of Christ. The essential danger was that through the ambivalence of irony, human imagination would insinuate errors into the performance and that an adulterated or perverse imitation of text and context would ensue. *Religio* was good imitation (or mimesis); *superstitio* was perverse, or more exactly idolatrous, because what was imitated was shifting fabrications of the human minds and desires, rather than the one, changeless archetype. By imitation, one participated empathetically by ironic likeness in one's model, whether Christ or idol.

It was necessary for its own purity that *religio* constantly be proven and that it purge itself of human inventions in conflict against perverse mimesis. Thereby, it continually redrew the line between those who had been initiated into the context of myth and outsiders, and it continually vindicated both its powers in the struggle for existence and the contours of that struggle. For evidently the rules of playing out the ironies of myth that were disclosed to Christians by no means corresponded with the contexts of games played by their adversaries. In this sense Christianity was both subject to the tyranny of myth and hostile to myth.

Two Illustrations

Two accounts will help us grasp what limits the theatrical imagination found in ritualized enactments of conversion and, therefore, how, it was thought, the contextual myths of Christian society could be convincing to some and repellent to others. Both illustrate the crucial role of empathy, its limits and degrees dramatized in myth. The first portrays the martyrdom of Archbishop Tiemo of Salzburg (c. 1040–1101/2), a member of a crusading expedition that fell into Saracen hands (1101). One of those who was with him, Otto of Freising wrote, prepared the history of the pitiable and grievous outcome "in the fashion of a tragedy."[52] The anonymous author began by recounting Tiemo's noble ancestry, virtuous character, and excellent education. He particularly noted that Tiemo had been educated both in the liberal and in the "mechanical" arts of painting, metal casting, carpentry, "and all other things of this sort" and that he had made objects of such ingenuity and usefulness that even after his death no artisan could claim to be his equal.[53]

Step by step the author traced Tiemo's troubled ecclesiastical career to the climactic moment of his capture. After the archbishop had been cast into chains with the other Christians, his eminent standing was soon disclosed to the Saracen ruler, who fetched him up for an interrogation. The ruler's first object was to discover what arts Tiemo was skilled in. After an elaborate play of point and counterpoint, in which he emphasized his charge of spiritual teaching, the archbishop at length admitted that he knew how to restore old things very well and that he was proficient in the crafts that the ruler had mentioned, including goldsmithing. As it happened, one of the ruler's idols had lost a hand, and giving thanks to his gods, the ruler commanded the archbishop either to make a new idol or to replace the missing hand.

With mocking pity Tiemo asked to be shown the idol. Casting out the unclean spirit that inhabited it, he raised the hammer that had been given him and smashed the huge statue into shards. The boundless evil of his captor exceeded itself in the circumstances under which the archbishop was brought to the noxious place of execution and subjected to a last interrogation. Tiemo was firm in his prayers to Christ and in his contempt for the gods of the pagans and their legendary acts—Saturn, Jove, Priapus, and all the rest—all worthy of ridicule. The parable of the sower came to his mind.

He realized that there was no reason to waste the seed of the gospel on that ruler, casting it where the Devil would snatch it away to prevent its germination, no possibility of empathetic participation. He was silent. Enraged by what he considered the archbishop's "mad effrontery," the ruler commanded that he be cut apart, joint by joint, from the feet up. Even then, Tiemo admonished his fellow Christians to stand fast and to rejoice with him in Christ, giving thanks to God, who had seen fit to choose him as a sacrifice of sweetness and a pattern for their blessed strife. The infidels set about their work with insane minds, fired with joyful impiety, bloodlust, and suave cruelty. Yet the triumph that Tiemo had foreseen came about, for they were unable to disperse the fragments of his body. The faithful collected and buried them in a church, where many wonders of healing were performed at the tomb of Christ's athlete; and all efforts of the idolatrous Saracens to profane the tomb were punished either by demonic possession or instant death.[54]

There is no need to seek historical accuracy in the account of Tiemo's martyrdom. The attribution of polytheism and idolatry to Muslims certifies ignorance of Islam, and the characterization of the Saracen ruler as totally depraved conforms with stereotypes in atrocity propaganda of many eras. Unbelievers were expected to deal cruelly with Christians whether they were Jews or Saracens or the Eastern peoples who were reported to tear out the viscera of Christians and to roast and eat their hearts so as to be strong against them.[55] For my purposes, those stereotypes of impenitent cruelty form part of a wider pattern.

They demonstrate the degree to which empathetic conversion presented a dramatic context in which unbelievers were included for the sake of perfecting the conversion of the faithful. Where there was no conflict, there could be no cathartic pity and fear nor any increase of love, no need for the love that casts out fear. It was essential to fear in order to know the consolation of that love; it was essential to be buffeted and in danger so that God's strength could be perfected in human weakness (2 Cor. 12:9). The more invincible the unbelief of the enemy, the more relentless his cruelty, and the more incapable he was of catharsis by pity and fear, the more perfectly was proven the fortitude, the hope, and the charity of the saints, the more surely they moved, by reliving the pattern of martyrdom, toward the beauty of holiness in which their faith could not falter or fail, and the more incontrovertibly was demonstrated the power of God in them. The context of a dramatic scenario, the ritualized imitation of Christ, through which the human "I" became one with the divine "you," was indispensable to this enactment.

The second account, which provides a kindlier view of Islam, also illustrates the dramatic paradigms of empathy, as prescribed by myth. This account, which can be traced to about 1270, purports to record the circumstances under which Thomas Becket's parents met and married. Departing far from historical fact, it narrates how Gilbert Becket, a young man from London, was captured by Saracens as he was returning from a pilgrimage to Jerusalem. During his captivity he attracted the attention of the young, beautiful, and only daughter of the emir who held him prisoner. She was fascinated by what he told her concerning his homeland, the beliefs and ways of life that Christians followed, and the hope of believers for rewards in a future life. To her consternation, Gilbert escaped from chains and prison and made his way back to London.

Giving up glory, wealth, security, and noble estate for love, she set out to follow him. Isolated by her ignorance of Western languages, she was able to indicate her wishes only by repeating the word "London." In time she arrived there, alone and trailed through the streets like some exotic animal by gangs of mocking youths. Through a series of circumstances, she found Gilbert, who sought advice from the bishop of London and six other bishops with whom he happened to be conferring. It was clear to the seven prelates that a divine vocation had gone forth, one that would produce a child destined for some glorious work. According to their judgment, the emir's daughter was baptized and married to Gilbert. On their first night of marital concord, Thomas à Becket was conceived. Without tarrying, Gilbert undertook another penitential voyage to Jerusalem. When he returned, three and a half years later, he found his son Thomas handsome in form and well-pleasing in the eyes of all.[56]

One particular interest of this story is its legendary character. Its origins have been traced to the Greek Sophists. From the twelfth century onwards, the romantic quest of a Western knight by a Saracen princess was woven into numbers of historical and quasi-historical accounts.[57] Indeed, the legendary character is underscored by the partial repetition of the motif in a story of a Jewish girl who was converted to Christianity by overhearing debates between a priest and her father and who, after receiving secret religious instruction from the priest, abandoned her home to be baptized.[58] Repetition of the dramatic scenario clearly enhanced the credit of the story by demonstrating that empathetic conversions from among peoples considered to be invincible in their malice toward Christ and bestial in their enmity toward Christians happened not once but in various times and circumstances.

The distinctive feature of this account is that the principal actors are not Gilbert and the emir's daughter but their son. For by contrast with Tiemo's decision not to waste the seed of the gospel by casting it on the Saracen ruler's stony heart, the issue of this encounter was a conversion and, in the life and career of Thomas, one that yielded a harvest of thirty, sixty, or a hundred fold. Here, as so often, fecundity is the sign of authentic conversion, in the conception of Thomas à Becket and in his glory as prelate and martyr.

The two stories also provide contrasting examples of how the ironies of beauty shaped empathy by the dramatic imagination. The *Passion* of Tiemo sets the destructive beauty of this world, represented by the visual arts, over against the authentic beauty of holiness, expressed in the horrific circumstances of Tiemo's death, in the therapeutic miracles performed at his tomb, and in the acts of divine vengeance visited upon his enemies and detractors. The analogue is clear with the Crucifixion which Herman-Judah saw represented as the glorification of Christ. As a master craftsman, Tiemo himself enacted the ironic distinction between material and spiritual beauty, and precipitated his death, when he refused to lend his talents as a craftsman to idolatry.

The romance of Gilbert and the emir's daughter portrays beauty on a grander scale, as the working out, through the already/not yet ironies of process, of a divinely predestined event through which Christ's own spouse, the Church, would be triumphantly exalted and beautified throughout the earth.[59]

The eroticism of the earthly romance is taken up as an instrument of the love between Christ and his bride. In this regard, the story reproduces the subordination of the Blessed Virgin to her Son and Spouse and that of Monica to her son, Augustine of Hippo.

To say this much is to confront one aspect of the mythic scenario shared by both accounts. The cast of characters in Tiemo's *Passion* is entirely male.

Despite the prominence of her conversion, the emir's daughter and her beauty serve the divine mission of her son. But they also address the erotic fantasies of men who dream of young noblewomen abandoning all to follow them to the ends of the earth, of momentous conjugal union, and of leaving the women to repine, perhaps in an alien land and certainly in marital fidelity, long awaiting their husbands' return. Both accounts represent "the maleness of the esthetic consciousness"[60] or, rather, a ritualized esthetic conscience that is exclusively male.

A late variation on the theme, which illustrates a further development of the ritualized male esthetic, occurs in Torquato Tasso's (1544–1595) *Jerusalem Delivered*, an epic of the First Crusade. There, love across religious lines also demanded a crossing of gender roles. Tancred, the Christian knight in Tasso's version, fell deeply in love with Clorinda, a Saracen princess. But Clorinda, like the Amazons of old, took the field of battle against the soldiers of the cross. Disguised by their armor, the lovers paired off in combat. Fatally wounded, Clorinda pardoned her slayer and asked him to wash away her sins with baptism. Lifting her helmet, Tancred recognized his beloved as his victim, and as he had slain her with the sword, so by baptism he buried her with Christ into death so that she might be raised with him to newness of life (Rom. 6:4–9).[61]

I have recovered some outlines of the ironic play which was thought to underlie conversion by forming the spiritual imagination, parts of the "deeply hidden structures of thought" in any mythology "which are independent of whether the stories of the gods are believed or not."[62] Although they were the condition of revelation from faith to faith, they were also contexts of struggle, of pervasive esthetic values (which is also to say values of feeling or emotion), and of gender.

In the second chapter, I compared the spiritual journey of Herman-Judah with Christina of Markyate's. Some of the chief differences appeared to be related to gender. These included the contrast between Herman-Judah's search for truth through active study of Scripture and frequent debates on scriptural interpretation and Christina's passive repetition of test passages and pastiches from Holy Writ. It is now clear that like the novelesque accounts of Tiemo and Becket's mother, those purportedly historical characterizations were shaped by the mythic context in which they were written and intended to be read. Their narratives purported to set forth instances in which life imitated the arts of ritual. It is also plain that that context was the touchstone of their authenticity and that they had to conform with what it taught about the nature and limits of empathy to be accepted as credible portrayals. Ritual stylization according to the templates of myth was essential to recognition and belief.

Forming Lines of Communication

How were the stylized templates of myth ingrained in the empathies? For they must have seemed both true and natural for the imagination—individual and collective—to achieve this enigmatic revelation from faith to faith. I have spoken of mental and physical discipline in monastic life in chapter 3. Expectations concerning spiritual enlightenment were shaped and ritualized by practices of reading, meditation, prayer, and contemplation. Each of these taught powerful habits of criticism that were basic to the penitential impulse of conversion. But gender distinctions now indicate a wider field.

In considering how the mythic context became ritualized in the spiritual imagination—how it was formed in society generally, and not exclusively in the cloister—it is helpful to remember the account of London with which one of Thomas Becket's closest associates, William Fitzstephen (fl. 1170), began his biography of Becket. Fitzstephen was convinced that the environment of London had contributed to the formation of great figures, famous and magnificent rulers, and above all Becket, "than whom earth has carried none who shone with brighter radiance, none who attracted to himself greater devotion."[63] In William's view the character of London itself, and therefore of the shape that it gave individual character, was largely defined by the games its citizens played. He inventoried theatrical spectacles, secular representations (*ludi scenici*), mystery plays, and portrayals of martyrs' passions. His list expands with one form of competition after another, whether in the disputations of scholars or schoolboy competitions aimed at wounding their fellows, in equestrian contests at great horse fairs, in the matches of fighting cocks with which boys began their sporting careers or in the more advanced fights of boars, bulls, bears, or dogs, in athletic contests, in the sports of summer and of winter simulating war and taking their casualties, all before the eyes of spectators ready to mock them. The dramatic scenario of remorseless, savage conflict crowned with glory and triumph figured not only in the games that William inventoried but also in the secular and religious dramas that he mentioned and, therefore, in the ideals in his audiences' minds that compelled them to perform myth in daily life. I return to the subject of devotion paid to self-image: that is, to the *cultus sui*.

Women are almost entirely absent from William's account. At the new moon, he wrote, girls form a chorus and dance; but they are assigned no part in the youthful eagerness for glory and lust for victory through battle, real or simulated, that impelled the world of sport.[64] The primal force of male bonding was at work in the deep structures by which rituals of play conformed the imagination to mythic contexts. In the destruction of indigenous cultures by missions and again in theological disputations with the Jews, the importance of the act was not in what was done to the adversary but rather in what aggressors demonstrated to themselves about their empathies. The eroticism of religious commitment in those remote centuries has a unexpected but recognizable parallel in our own day in incidents of gang rape. Significantly, it was an anthropologist who observed that in such incidents "the common denominator . . . was that the victim was almost irrelevant. The motivation, she said, was internal—the shared sense of brotherhood and risk among those committing the act."[65] At a more exalted and systemic level, recognizable similarities appear in social orders keyed to the ritualized establishment and vaunting of male identity through dominance over women and through the repeated demonstration of worth in contests of strength, courage, endurance, and cunning against other men, contests that moved through alliances established and changed on the scales of mutual esteem. Inevitably, the weaker strove, by demonstrating their valor, to earn honor, or "worship," from the stronger and to join forces with them.[66]

Understanding empathetic conversion as the reception of myth in the twelfth century strongly resembles attitudes toward the reception of the liberal arts in the patristic age. In both ages thought circled around the same predicament: the assimilation of knowledge that had formerly been considered alien, dangerous, and, indeed, malign.[67] As they considered incentives for appropriating the liberal arts, glittering with the fables of pagan poets, the Church Fathers, particularly Jerome and Augustine, employed the same tactics of disguise that I have noted in the reception of Jewish methods of scriptural interpretation and, indeed, in injunctions regarding conversion set forth in the parables of the sower and the hidden treasure. In both circumstances the strategy of assimilation excluded women assimilators and prescribed male incentives of friendship and dominance, tested, vindicated, ritualized, and sealed in conflict.

It is possible to identify one further similarity. For the values directing assimilation were, in both instances, those of males in dominant social orders seeking alliances. The conditions under which the imagination could be imprinted with Christian myth were set by life before conversion. Indeed, the framers of ascetic ideology in the patristic age specifically employed the language of Roman government and warfare drawn from their preconversion lives in defining their postconversion spiritual endeavors and thus their role as the *militia Christi*. In the eleventh and twelfth centuries, converts likewise carried their preconversion empathies with them as they moved from world to monastery, translating secular terms into spiritual contexts but retaining the emotional compulsions for mutual esteem represented by strength, wealth, fame, and honor, retaining, too, the need of the weaker to gain the esteem, or "worship," of the stronger.

Thus, Bernard of Clairvaux (and later Francis of Assisi) translated the warrior ethos into which they had been born into the monastic ethos into which they converted. In his Lenten sermons Bernard urged his brethren to rend their hearts with compassion for the Crucified, to mortify their bodies with fasting, and still not to despair because of human weakness. For even at this moment, he said, the Savior had called them, rude and simple as they were, to arms. Summoning warriors together from the ends of the earth, he was leading them against the enemy into a battle without quarter. From it, a great victory would lead him, their King, to glory and them to salvation.[68] If it were truly to be bonded to Christ, Francis believed, the life of the friar required gravity and modesty as "a wall and very strong shield against the shafts of the Devil. . . . The soul without the protection of this wall and shield was like a naked knight amongst very strong and well-furnished enemies, continually intent on his death."[69]

In Normandy the well-born monk Ordericus Vitalis (1075–1142) delighted in listening to the tales and songs of warriors who visited his monastery; he remembered and digested them into his history. From his vantage point at Westminster, Gilbert Crispin (fl. 1092) rejoiced to see a flood of men, once busy in affairs of the world, proud and powerful men, excellently trained in weaponry and eager for battle, aflame with desire for rapine, giving up all the pomp of their former lives, setting forth on pilgrimages to holy places, throwing themselves on the prayers of saints, and embracing disciplines of extreme self-denial as they sought to demonstrate their worth to celestial warriors.[70] As they reflected on their own experiences and on the pursuit of salvation in general, they also assimilated the play of the battlefield to that of conversion. The language of the footrace, the wrestling match, and deadly battle were commonly used to elucidate the way to Heaven not as a venture of solitaries but as the pilgrimage of a noble army.

Women could be seen as peripheral to the empathetic esteem that sealed this bonding, or even as endangering it. Prohibiting the marriage of clergy, the Gregorian Reform identified association with women as an impediment to clerical status and a threat to personal salvation of those in holy orders. The reformed papacy denied the sanction of reverence, or "worship," to men who defied this prohibition. Likewise, marriage led to a loss of worship when it entailed withdrawal from the field of battle. Chrétien de Troyes and Hartmann von Aue took up this theme in the story of Erec, who gave himself over entirely to the service of his wife, Enite, abandoning tourneys and chivalric obligations. As a result, he suffered shame, terrible losses, and mortal danger, from which he escaped only by an arduous rehabilitation in heroic knightly practices.[71]

If this ethos were visualized as an organism, its basic, irreducible cell would be found to be an institution that still flourishes in many societies of the world. That cell would be a band of men who cement and celebrate their friendship with conviviality that consists of distinctive and surprisingly universal acts: eating and drinking ("clubbing") together, bantering in risqué language, and vying to play jokes ("meaningless," "empty," "all in fun") on one another. The risks of this institution are clear. In atmospheres rarefied by drunkenness, raw familiarity and preposterous jokes engender fights; fights lead to homicides; homicides may break the companionage apart if its members reorganize to inflict or to evade revenge. This nursery bred Henry V's parricidal treason.[72]

The need for comrades and the dangers of their companionage pervaded the whole career of such a cell. What is striking is how these features of play were taken up and ritualized into the idea of conversion, with its fear of apostasy, most treacherous in the self-deceptions of the conscience. The common traits of commensality, collective intoxication, unfettered language, and joking relationships (*lusibusque atque iocis*) were also taken up into the vision of the blessed, each displaying wounds of valor, feasting together on Christ, the Lamb (or fatted Calf), uncontrollably inebriated by the Holy Spirit, uttering the wildnesses of ululation, and sporting with jocund merriment (*iocunditate*) in the play of love.

Ritualized into processes of conversion, this male esthetic was not without ambivalence, for the imagination does not need to be taught that gender has its complementarities. The counterweights of strength and weakness evoked another pattern of play, one that was recognized but not developed: namely, that indicated by Caesarius's androgynous Christ and Guerric of Igny's idea that he and his fellow monks were mothers of Christ. For those who considered most deeply the "form of conversion" acknowledged a femininity in their play.

They portrayed the soul as, like the Blessed Virgin, the spouse and mother of Christ. As spouses, male writers reenacted a scenario of ardent self-surrender, burning with love, melting in the Bridegroom's arms, impregnated by his power. As mothers, they gave birth to the fertile Word sown in them, swaddled the infant in words and works of art, tenderly nurtured and delighted in his sweetness, and presented him in countless epiphanies to the peoples of the earth. And yet, even though the Mother of Christ had experienced the deepest mysteries, she did not presume to write them. Rather, as a woman, she declined to teach men, confiding in the Apostles and Evangelists, who wrote down what had been singularly revealed to her.[73] Men referred to themselves as women to identify characteristics of weakness, irrationality (as lust), and pollution (through menstruation).[74]

They believed that in its redeemed femininity the soul strove to revere and serve in purity, humility, and obedience, thus to bind fast the love of its divine Spouse. I am not able to inquire into the possible effects of what could pass for an Oedipal complex in this network of associations.[75]

To a remarkable degree writings by and about women assumed the metaphors of conflict, athletic and military, rather than developing feminine alternatives. The greatness of a woman was proven by the virility of her mind and virtue.[76] While the reversal of gender roles for men brought powerlessness, that reversal for women brought attributes of power and rationality; terms of androgyny may, therefore, have come more readily to women writers and to male biographers of women than to men.[77]

However, it is also true that some male writers believed that women were more powerful than men, as in Ireland female hawks excelled male in power and violence. Etymologists supported this idea. The Latin word meaning woman (*mulier*), they argued, came from the verb (*moliri*) meaning "to undermine, to soften." Hence, "woman" was so called because she weakened a man and made him like herself, effeminate. A woman, Abbess Herrad of Hohenburg (fl. 1180), used the story of Ulysses and the Sirens to illustrate her argument that nothing drew men away from God and so destroyed them more than love of women. From this point of view, sensing their gender vulnerability, men could only comfort themselves with the thought that God had chosen the weak of this world to confound the strong.[78] But here, ambivalence also carried with it the sense that women turned their weakness into manipulative power over men, a sense expressed in more than one interpretation of God's declaration to the Apostle Paul: "My strength is made perfect in weakness" (2 Cor. 12:19).

Whether through the complementarities of gender or through a primal sense that the female of the species was more deadly than the male, and deadly to him and his virility, the empathetic needs of life, love, purity, and truth lead, finally, to the need for power through dependence. We have found the need for power through dependence veining ideas set forth by men of a certain class and age. We have also found a complex desire and fear of powerlessness. Awareness of the complementarities of gender worked together with the child's desire for nurturing dependence and the warrior's and athlete's fear of inevitable failure of strength. Consider the violet, the flower of humility, an author wrote. Growing so tenaciously close to the ground, it is hard to move, a symbol of security of conscience; its color is contemptible, as Christ crucified, the violet, was in the eyes of Jews and Gentiles. But its odor is sweet, signifying the praise of humility; it has a single flower, as Christ was a single flower from the root of Jesse; its vile color conceals the power within it. Let us be humbled, the author concluded, offering to the Lord Jesus the violet of his humility, so that, recognizing his flower in us, he may exalt us with him in the day of his coming.[79]

Some context of this sort composed what Rupert of Deutz found beautiful in mystery and what enabled him to delight in it.[80]

Conclusions

How was it possible for some to venerate as sacred mystery what others despised as fable? The answer pertains to the credibility of myth. In the first chapter I referred to the inconceivable and incommunicable "magic," "genius," or "miracle" at the core of conversion. With "the shared sense of brotherhood and risk," we have not apprehended that mysterious center; but we have come near to seeing where empathies found it and enabled revelation to occur from faith to faith. Conversion was not the destination but the journey, nor was the journey solitary. For by empathetic conversion, "the Lord Jesus is conceived and born in us. Likewise, he continually is nourished and grows in us 'until we all come together into a perfect man, into the measure of Christ full-grown.' "[81] By considering myth and ritualizing devices by which myths were ingrained into the mind, I have underscored the relation between supernatural conversion and education. In fact, I have identified a social context where fictions about conversion moved in a hermeneutic circle. For the empathies of those who dominated discourse about conversion had been trained, by ritually enacting conversion myths, in what was to be recognized as such, called by that name, and paid due consequences in the actual conduct of social relationships.

Let me try, as in earlier chapters, to indicate some landmarks by which those unfamiliar with eleventh- and twelfth-century Europe can orient themselves. Emphasizing common human needs, I have attempted to indicate, in broad strokes, points at which Christian quests for spiritual enlightenment ran parallel with those in some strands of Buddhism (particularly Zen) and where, by reason of theology and education, they diverged. The fourfold vow of the bodhisattva in late Buddhism (see chap. 2, n. 74) has guided me in addresses to the needs for life, love, and purity. I now come to the fourth, and last, vow: "However incomparable the truth of the Buddha, I vow to attain it."

Both Christians and Buddhists acknowledged that truth and the experience of truth were incommunicable. Thus, communications about truth took place through the indirect language of symbols, correctly understood by the enlightened but darkly enigmatic to others. The act of communication took place in the perception of beauty, the gesture that the symbol embodied. The inexpressibility of truth promoted an anti-intellectual spirituality, for truth could only be venerated in silence. But the need to disseminate truth produced a great flowering of music, architecture, the visual arts, and literature in which beauty of style was indeed both medium and message. Buddhist scholar-ascetics, like Christian, cultivated the arts; they also mistrusted them as possible impediments to spiritual advance. To evade the enticements of sensual beauty they were capable of destroying books, pictures, and other works of art that they or other practitioners of their spiritual discipline had made and revered.

Like the Christian, the Buddhist—particularly the Zen—esthetic of enlightenment combined violence with beauty in ideas drawn from male bonding through adversarial risk in athletic contests, for example, and military campaigns. It was a male esthetic informed by analogues to wrestling with deadly enemies, to swordplay, and to feats of physical power and endurance; and the esthetic of the warrior-monk was pervaded with fear of weakness.

However, the fourth vow of the bodhisattva contains a self-confident note foreign to Christian spirituality, one that highlights the culturally finite character of moral education. For Buddhism taught an esthetic transformation to which individual effort was primary and by no means dependent upon divine intervention, a change that achieved the death of passion together with the cessation of individual consciousness and existence. The experience of transformation in Christianity was, in the literal sense, passive or passionate. Divine intervention was the indispensable precondition.

Thus, at the outset of these inquiries, the words *myth, genius,* and *miracle* were used to explain how some could believe what others rejected. In the mythic contextualizations of Christianity, *magic* and even *genius* are less appropriate than *miracle;* for, as writers continually explained, the character of miracle was exactly that it lay beyond human manipulation. The transforming process of conversion was always a mystery, always wrapped in a concealment of types and symbols, always invisible, inconceivable, and inconceivable. How can a human mind, using human arts, penetrate the changing of a larva into a butterfly, a metaphor that Dante used to elucidate salvation?[82]

One author indicated the limits that empathetic education set to any search for a common morphology of conversion outside the supernaturalism of Christianity and its branches. Appropriately enough, he used a reference to the ritual commensality of the saved (see above at n. 72). Apparently dismissing abundant references to thanksgiving in the Old Testament, he wrote that none of the saints before Christ had given thanks to God because they knew that they were insufficient to the task. The parents of the human race had not given thanks to their creator and benefactor. On the contrary, poisoned by their gratitude to his enemy, they engendered children of wrath who, laboring under the congenital weight of ungrateful sin, were unworthy to give thanks to God. In the tabernacles of the righteous, Old Testament patriarchs and prophets were able to raise their voices in praise, witness, exultation, and salvation. But they were not yet in the eternal Temple, Christ's body. Thus, in his incarnation, Christ was the first to give thanks to God the Father on behalf of all his people when with a few loaves of bread he satisfied the hunger of a great multitude, and again later when he raised Lazarus from the dead, and, finally, when taking bread he gave thanks and broke it and gave it to his disciples, saying, "This is my body." "But what was his whole career [*conversatio*] in the world," the author added, "except a most worthy action of thanks?"—a continuous act that was perfected when he gave satisfaction to the Father through the saving sacrifice of his body and blood, consumed by his disciples. Sacramentally one with them, he acted in and through his disciples, as they did in and through him, to continue this sacrifice. On earth, they had only set out on the journey, persevering and fed by him until they should pass from the forecourts into the ineffable goods of his house, being filled by him who was their head.[83]

The empathetic limits defined here are those prescribed by mythic context. Four are perfectly evident: dependence on divine intervention; the idea that conversion was a universal historical process in which individual conversions were elements; the doctrine that the Incarnation of God was the unique medium in which conversion occurred; and, finally, the importance of the *imitatio Christi* as the pattern of empathetic conversion, begun, advanced, and perfected in the antechamber of this world but made permanent only in the inner temple of the Heavenly Jerusalem.[84] The parable of the treasure hidden in the field intersects with the doctrines that the treasures of wisdom and knowledge are hidden in Christ (Col. 2:3) and that through the exchanges of love between Christ and believers, each is in the other.

In the content and methods by which empathies of whole peoples were educated to the mythic contexts of their societies and cultures, the hermeneutic circle that I have described sets basic limits to a universal morphology of conversion. For the empathies allowed were limited and arranged by degree; and the ritualized stylizations provided by myth that define what is called conversion are socially (that is, historically) finite. The mutually exclusive attitudes that discussing the reception of myth has drawn out remind us "that a game is meaningful within itself but that it must appear useless and purposeless from an outside point of view." Mythic context is the equivalent of a game. My conclusions indicate the great importance that modes of play valued by a particular society can have on ways in which, through the ironic form and language of ritualized play, religion manifests itself empathetically from faith to faith in that society in the context of the game of myth.[85]

From Augustine's portrayal of his spiritual crisis in the garden at Milan—in which a codex of Paul's letters resting on a gaming table is the central element in an elaborate variety of kinds of play[86]—to John Bunyan's account of the divine call he heard one Sunday in the midst of a game of cat,[87] and beyond, the collective venture of play as a sign and tool of revelation through irony entered not only into descriptions of conversion but also into ways of understanding conversion. I have contended, especially, that it entered into the deep structures of thought and feeling and need that prepared the mind for, and impelled it toward, empathetic conversion. These mysterious and hidden structures were represented in myth by the play of God.

Quite naturally, ironic play in various forms became both the means by which the imagination was shaped to receive myth and that by which the mystery of revelation from faith to faith was explained. In play, especially but not only in drama, the actor imaginatively changes into another persona. In competitive play there is often something quite inexplicable in winning and losing. I have noted the use of ridicule and mockery as a standard motif in judgments by adherents of one religion on those of another, in the sporting events inventoried by William Fitzstephen, and in the commensality, shared inebriation, and joking relationships of companionage. This recurrence is a sign that by entering the game, a person risked losing or impairing the old identity if the outcome of the contest did not leave it vindicated and enlarged. In either case, through the power of dramatic imagination, play inflamed and shaped the emotions in challenge, conflict, and, finally, degradation or triumph. As a scenario of transformation, the imitation of Christ set a dramatic pattern in which the sting of degradation, not least through mockery, was a necessary prologue to the intoxication of victory.

People of the period under review touched a deep and universal truth when they spoke with awe of the revelatory power in the ironies of play as ritual and as ritualization. To be sure, acts that displeased or embarrassed were dismissed as "just play" or "child's play." But, as I have shown, the taunts of children could also be taken as prophetic, fulfilling the scriptural oracle "out of the mouths of babes and sucklings hast thou ordained strength" (Ps. 8:2; Matt.

21:16, "hast thou perfected praise").[88] A mock procession of boys and girls mimicking authentic litanies with their pranks coincided with monstrous apparitions that foretold death and desolation.[89] Even in the sixteenth century, Sir Thomas More noted instances in which children, "playing, making as it were corpses carried to church and sing[ing] after the childish fasshion the tewne of the dirige, there hath greate deth there shortly folowed after . . . [and having] made as it were parties and batayles and after their batayls in sport wherin some children have yet taken grete hurt, there hath fallen very batayle and dedely warr in dede."[90] Embattled and denounced as perverters of the Gospel, the followers of Thomas à Becket after his martyrdom took it to their comfort that "children, playing together in the streets, told his Passion, sang his glory and 'perfected his praise.'"[91] There was an uncanny power—"some secret mocion or instinct" More said—in play.

In games of empathetic bonding, play is social, not solitary. Could the pedagogic revelations of play, by empathy, from faith to faith be trusted? The ironic gap between the primordial need for truth and available strategies of verification created great doubts, which restless Christians and enemies of Christianity alike were quick to grasp. Assertions that Christianity was a superstition rather than a religion were raised from the beginning of the Church; their persistence through the centuries formed a long prologue to the development of a Christianity without Christ by demythologizers of the twentieth century.

I have noted some such doubts among the learned elite of western Europe, and it is only right to note something similar, in a later age, besetting the faith of a workingman. John Bunyan found himself assailed by questions "as whether there were in truth a God or Christ, and whether the holy Scriptures were not rather a fable and cunning story, than the holy and pure word of God." Did not the Muslims have written evidence proving that Mohammed was the savior every bit as good as the evidence Christians had for Jesus? And how was it possible that "so many ten thousands in so many countries and kingdoms should be without the knowledge of the right way to heaven, if there were indeed a heaven, and that we only, who live in a corner of the earth, should alone be blessed therewith? Everyone doth think his own religion rightest, Jews and Moors and Pagans; and how if all our faith and Christ and Scriptures should be but a think-so too?"[92]

Here, Bunyan touched the heart of one of the oldest disputes in philosophy, not to say in religious education, a dispute stirred up by the Eleatic philosopher Xenophanes when he attacked the anthropomorphic mythologies of the Greeks. Was it not a matter of direct observation, he asked, that every people portrayed its gods in its own likeness? If they had temples, would not oxen and lions also represent gods in their own forms? The word of God, Bunyan wrote, was a most excellent mirror. "It would present a man, one way, with his own features exactly; and turn it but another way, and it would show one the very face and similitude of the Prince of pilgrims himself."[93]

Long centuries before Bunyan, Augustine of Hippo wrote that the Holy Spirit descended upon the Apostles, enabling them to speak all tongues. Now, he wrote, "the whole body of Christ speaks in the tongues of all peoples. . . . I dare to say to you: I speak in the tongues of all. I am in the body of Christ. . . . If the body of Christ now speaks in the tongues of all . . ., Greek is mine, Syriac is mine, Hebrew is mine, and my language is that of all nations because I am in the unity of all nations."[94]

Yet, catholicity did not drive Augustine to a dilemma like Bunyan's. The bishop of Hippo did not mistrust the limits of his empathy. He denied catholicity to those whom he considered heretics, and by enlisting imperial repression of the Donatists, he framed the earliest programmatic justification of religious persecution, a justification that invoked obligations of brotherly love toward the persecuted. In what context, indeed, was the spiritual imagination to be educated to offer and receive authentic revelations through irony from faith to faith?

Some years ago a celebrated writer on mysticism, Dean William Inge (1860–1954), surveyed the large number of biographies of Christ that had been written since the middle of the nineteenth century. It was remarkable how accurately the lives mirrored the thinking of the writers. Renan's "very French romance" was "deficient in moral seriousness." "An Englishman of Jewish descent" produced a life with abundant references to Jewish customs. "The German Protestant *Lives*, with their emphasis on the 'frank manliness and power' of Christ's character, present us with a half-Teutonised portrait of their hero." Albert Schweitzer's quest for the historical Jesus, with "an irritatingly superior tone," portrayed a man of a particular time and place, "an apocalyptic prophet." Dean Inge's limited perception that "many people have lost faith in the Churches, but only the most violent enemies of society have lost faith in Christ" prevented him from exploring other bands on the spectrum of belief.[95] He could have enlarged his repertoire by including portrayals by those who had never believed in Christ, including some venerable portraits in the Jewish polemical tradition. He might, indeed, have recognized the ethnic and national empathies ritualized in his own mind that his judgments revealed.

Earlier in this chapter, I quoted Guerric of Igny's statement that reception of Christian doctrine required that one learn by doing—that faith be internalized by practice through works of justice and that through knowledge gained by reflecting on practice, one might come to contemplative wisdom. "Often," Guerric confessed, "faith shines out and justice glitters while the understanding is still in darkness and has no inkling how to unwrap the mystery of faith which it venerates, even while it holds it [in its own hands] wrapped," as was the infant Jesus, in swaddling clothes.[96] Thus, at the deepest point reached by human understanding, the possibility of breaking out of the hermeneutic circle prescribed by one's own social habits depends on a single act: a risk.

Pascal wrote, after reviewing the Scriptures (Were they fables? he asked), the history and doctrines of the Jews, and the new science of comparative religions, not to mention his mathematician's knowledge of nature: "The eternal silence of these infinite spaces terrifies me." This passage has scandalized Pascal's admirers and given some professional embarrassment to philosophers and theologians. Did God exist in those icy, incomprehensible abysses of the infinitely small and infinitely large? You can't see the other side of the cards in Nature's game. "Take a bet that he exists. . . . If you win, you win everything; if you lose, you lose nothing." The gain, if any, was life, love, joy, and certitude.[97] Kierkegaard's similar calculations pressed him to the leap of faith.

Yet no one could say that Guerric's swaddling clothes and Pascal's wager were metaphors to the same effect. The wager is a metaphor of probability. But Guerric's figure belongs to the interlace of ideas that has brought me through the mimetic powers of cult, words, and art, an interlace that always leads back to the Apostle Paul's teaching that believers must think according to the measure of faith dealt to each by God (Rom. 12:3). In its mythic context, Guerric's is a metaphor of proportion, not of probability. His mythic context prescribed a cast of actors performing a drama; Pascal's a game of solitaire.

So vast a panorama of hiddenness, ambiguity, and risk witnesses both to the predicamental character of conversion and to its origin in urgent, unfathomable need.

As one reflects on the doctrines of what was called conversion in the eleventh and twelfth centuries, and their limitations, it is worth recalling its mythic teaching about history, that human advancement was a movement of trial and error in which, without the later generations, the earlier "should not be made perfect" (Heb. 11:40). Insofar as we can say something general about human empathy in reflecting on the ironic gulf between ideals and actions, we can only speak metaphorically of ourselves. For, to modify Dean Inge's observations about the life of Christ, myths "of universal significance [have] a special message to each age in turn. We judge [them] from our own standpoint," and in time we shall be judged by them.[98]

CHAPTER 6

A Noble Humility

Nobility and Irony

The word *conversion* was and is a historical artifact. It was not, like a statue, carved whole at one time. I think of it as a nest of puzzles—a Chinese puzzle—to which a succession of contributors, in distant times and alien vernaculars, added casings, one over another. However, it might be more appropriate to recall a scriptural metaphor dear to the hearts of medieval commentators: Ezekiel's vision of a wheel inside a wheel, spinning and advancing.[1] In these chapters, the outer wheel has been the idea of empathetic conversion as an event of human nature in institutions and practices readily accessible to sociologists, anthropologists, and historians; the inner one, with which I have been chiefly concerned, the assumptions and ways of understanding (the hermeneutics) that made the supernatural phenomenon that was called conversion thinkable to writers of an earlier age.

Common human needs were at the hub of this confection, and my project of understanding has had to approach those needs through the words used to describe them. For language may not only "control the articulation of our thinking"[2] but also shape the very possibilities of what can be thought.

The trail of needs began with the most basic one, for life, and at the end reached the need for power and glory. Each step has been predicamental, even as conversion itself is predicamental. Throughout, irony has been a means of revelation. It is not surprising that the need for power and glory, like the others, had its kerygmatic irony in Christ's "noble humility."[3]

Attention to vocabulary has gradually brought me to the issue of power in another way as well. For in discussing the need for truth, I concluded that the vocabulary was bent to serve a male esthetic. The hermeneutic circle within the outward event of conversion itself conformed with, and was driven by, a social circle at the hub. The question thus arises whether or in what degree what was written about empathetic conversion could apply to persons outside the circle of those who composed the texts or at different points within it, closer to or more distant from the center. The experience of conversion (a thing felt) belonged to an order quite different from texts about conversion (things made). One consequence is that understanding conversion becomes a matter for historical, literary, or textual study.

The idea of empathetic conversion as a process of change established a relationship between it and education. The penitential life of monasticism was conceived as a kind of pedagogy; conscience was considered susceptible to moral formation; and education of empathies into the ritualized context of social myth had an important part in defining what was called conversion.

Thus far, it appears clear that empathetic conversion, so defined, is shaped by those who control education and therefore discourse and its ritualizations. Education set limits and degrees of empathy. An exclusivism in the male esthetic shut out Jews, Muslims, and other unbelievers who could read Scripture without detecting its meaning and at least ritually marginalized Christian women, whose existence and assigned activities in the Church were frequently consigned to silence.[4]

The mystical writer Mechthild of Magdeburg (c. 1207–c. 1294) lamented that if she had been a wise man, rather than a woman, her writings would have brought God eternal glory. Who could believe that the Lord had actually built his glorious house upon such a dung heap as she? Mechthild represented God as answering that she must not doubt herself or her divine inspiration. Even in this reassurance, the point of reference is still the relative weight of men and women in human discourse. And, in the vision of her spiritual nuptials, Mechthild saw herself, female, naked, and vulnerable, "conatured" with God, male, richly appareled, and all-supplying.[5]

That is not to say that women were incapable of ennoblement. But nobility is a matter of proportion, of degrees. The sacramental center of Christianity—in baptism and Eucharist—commemorated and reenacted by ritual the violence of men toward a man. Women were admitted to that center as witnesses and beneficiaries, but never as ministrants of sacrificial death with all its moral horror. Throughout, I have found ideas of empathetic conversion to be studies in proportion, hinging on the Apostle Paul's teaching that each believer must think according to the measure of faith granted that person by God. The idea of conversion was dominated by the rule of likeness, not least through the imitation of Christ. To what extent, or in what proportion, was similitude to Christ's "noble humility," and thus empathetic participation in Christ, considered to be open for those who were outside the hermeneutic circle that has now been identified or, indeed, to those toward its ritual periphery rather than at the center, admitted to discourse about conversion on sufferance, in borrowed vernaculars, and without authorization to sacrifice or to teach? The transforming dislocations of conversion commonly were made intelligible by a return to social normalcy, which, in the culture with which I am concerned, required that such women as were in the hermeneutic circle be marginalized.[6]

The vocabulary appropriate to the need for power and glory, or nobility, is familiar. It expresses the normalcies, including empathetic ones, of a world organized in hierarchic ranks, a world of proportionate degree and precedence, in short, of social ritual. One segment of that vocabulary is in the little glossary of terms, an amalgam drawn from late Antiquity and embellished with chivalric analogues, employed to speak of conscience. Purity of conscience was defined by *fama, honor* (or *honestas*), and *gloria;* impurity, by their opposites, *infamia, dedecus,* and *ignominia*. Another segment appeared when beauty (*pulchritudo*) was discussed as a cognitive principle, for an equation existed between the phrases "beauty of conduct" (*pulchritudo morum*) and "nobility of conduct" (*nobilitas morum*). This subject also figured in the review of visual aids used in the formation of conscience (see chap. 4 at n. 81).

However, even in those earlier discussions, application of relevant glossaries was intricately nuanced. The proportions were somehow irregular. One source of complexity was the theological inversion of worldly values, in which life was found in death, riches in poverty, and fecundity in continence. The controllers of ritualized discourse set forth a further level of paradox when they prescribed for themselves a form of *cultus sui* demanded by chivalric codes of honor, with the form of deference called worship. For they also portrayed their empathetic conversions as processes by which the soul, loathsome in the filth and deformity of sin, began to be beautiful and progressed from beauty to beauty as it was made worthy of its heavenly Bridegroom's embraces, that nuptial union in which two became one. The aggressively assertive worship demanded by the *cultus sui* was from this perspective subsumed in the submissively dependent worship of God. This movement through degrees of beauty was also a study in proportion.

Apart from drawing together implied, but still detached, lines of our own thinking, there are several reasons in the materials themselves for accenting the place that ideas of nobility had in understanding empathetic conversion as part of the *cultus sui,* chivalric and therefore cast in the ritualisms of aristocratic male discourse. These tend to emphasize the distinctiveness of education (and therefore of understanding) in particular cultures and epochs, rather than the general motives for conversion that appear independent of time and place.

Four such reasons are obvious. With its proportional gradations, the theme of nobility opens for inquiry the central ideal of similitude through the imitation of Christ, not only as the Man of Sorrows but also as the Lord of Courtesy.[7] Among the acts of Christ that expressed nobility of soul, the supreme was condescension (*dignatio*), that act of love by which the Word became flesh and offered himself a perfect and sufficient sacrifice for human sins. The most intricate paradoxes of language were framed to express the lowliness and sublimity with which the Lord of all broke through the categories of natural order and become the servant of all, exercising both the highest freedom and the deepest humility—"thys marvelous curtesy and homelynesse" of God in Christ, as Julian of Norwich (1342–c. 1416/23) said.[8]

This great condescension formed the pattern for the imitation of Christ, for it established the order of exchange between lovers, who in love's *cultus* honored each other and were honored in return. Christ's service of love imposed a debt that demanded not only obedience but also gratitude.[9] The rebellion of Lucifer and his minions was the great exemplar of the disordering madness of ingratitude; their expulsion from heaven, the pattern of vengeance for which it called as its own, destructive fulfillment. To respond in gratitude to Christ's love was to be bound with him in the condescension of necessity and freedom, to seek to experience with him the sweetness of affliction, participating in his agony, and in this way to be subsumed into his splendor, beauty, and glory.

For social historians the theme of condescending nobility provides yet another demonstration of how, in their search for likeness to Christ, converts carried over preconversion empathies into lives of conversion. The place of nobility of conduct in the literature of conversion owes much to the examples of those who turned from lives in the secular nobility to lives of ascetic spirituality. Thus, Thomas à Becket, Ailred of Rievaulx, and Otto of Bamberg were cherished in part because, as ascetics, they returned to normalcy after their spiritual disorientation by translating into another idiom the values that they had mastered as courtiers.[10] Further, the connection between beauty and nobility, together with the understanding of sanctification as ennoblement, is most obvious in the themes and structure of Dante's (1265–1321) *Divine Comedy*, above all in his image of Paradise as a mystic rose organized by proportional degrees from center to periphery, and in the characteristic combination of extremes of asceticism and elegance in the spiritual lives of many. The gracious condescension of man to men in violence is familiar in fabliaux and romances, where it is fatal for knights to lose the power of discourse, but it is also necessary for the noble to surrender discursive control and to win it back from other knights in order to use it authoritatively.

There is yet another, more complex reason. The relation that Boethius nonchalantly drew between beauty and worth[11] points to a fundamental matter of ethics. For on purely philosophical grounds, without any reference to Christian theology, Boethius was invoking an aristocratic scale of worth that scorned the moral values of the many. For him the values of birth and education, power and wealth, honor and, above all, pleasure tied the majority to acquired, transient, and sensory goods and drew them away from intrinsic, enduring, and intellectual (or spiritual) truth and beauty. Again, similitude—here between human practices and the norms that validated them—was the test for judgment.

This ancient philosophical contrast between worth and value entered into Christian estrangement from the world. As a key to an assumed esthetic unity of the arts, the idea of nobility highlights the importance of ironic likeness as a dominant trope in understanding conversion. Teasing, ironic likenesses have burgeoned forth at every turn: in the origin of the word *conversion* as a metaphor drawn from the manual arts, in the recurrent theme of play with its motif of God playing in (or with) human beings, in the vehement and ruthless criticism that ceaselessly held up the distance between ideal and earthly realities, in the irreconcilability between duty to conscience and the coercive obligations of the Church, and finally in the teaching of a beauty that, to the physical eyes, was distorted and terrible. Throughout, the ritualized imitation of Christ as a spiritual discipline intruded the ironic distance, common in all art, between the exemplar and the image.

Nobility captured the trope of irony in its gestures. The Buddha-like half smile was a signature of late Romanesque and Gothic art, a gesture that recovered the classical ideal of the golden mean, expressing neither extreme of laughter or despair. At what moments did writers represent smiles on the faces of those who exemplified the ennoblement of conversion? Bernard of Clairvaux recalled Archbishop Malachy of Armagh's (1094?–1148) smile as modest and joyful but not light-headed; it was rare and expressed or encouraged love.[12] Otto of Bamberg, "a serious man" (*homo gravis*), calculated all his actions, perhaps including the gesture of the smile. He is represented as smiling for the hospitality of a man who recognized his future greatness and laid upon him an obligation of gratitude to be repaid. He smiled when he argued in favor of missionaries going to certain death among the heathen and when he (wrongly) anticipated his own martyrdom.[13] Edmund Rich (or Edmund of Abingdon,

c. 1170–1240, reigned 1233–40), archbishop of Canterbury, displayed joy with becoming gravity. He smiled when about to perform a miraculous cure and when reproved for not sparing himself in his ceaseless labors. When he preached, he held a crucifix in his hands and looked at it constantly, smiling with reverence and gratitude for the blessings that had come to the whole world through the Cross and weeping with love because there were so many hearers, and so few doers, of the Word.[14] Indeed, the smile that expressed Edmund's "subtle and joyful graciousness" was inseparable from "his continual flow of tears." It expressed the same mentality that caused him to put Jewish obduracy to shame, confound the falsehood of heretics, and silence the ignorance of pagans.[15] With his "charming, sweet smile," Archbishop Arnold of Mainz expressed the character that strengthened him as he was slaughtered by his own people, a martyr and sacrificial victim.[16] As a signature of "beauty of conduct," and hence of moral order, the noble smile therefore disclosed the ironic similitudes ritualized in conversion, a happiness that was already and not yet present, a spiritual pilgrimage that was still in progress and at risk.

Significantly, these exemplars of ennoblement are all men, most of whom were of aristocratic birth. Edmund of Abingdon's parents were townsfolk of modest estate, but his education enabled him, as he advanced, to perfect the manners, and the empathies, cherished by higher social orders, to alter, as it were, the proportions.

Art and Religion

How does this quest for authentic, ennobling beauty through likeness help one grasp ways of understanding conversion? What new features can it add to outlining empathetic education? In these regards, as so often, the visual arts as tools of education cast light on conditions, methods, and objectives. Ideas about the pedagogical function of art in empathetic conversion also elucidate how the conscience became a subversive agent (see chap. 4). Works of art educated and exalted the spirit because they struck the mind with amazement. Writers praised them for their "incredible beauty" (*pulchritudo incredibilis*), their "amazing scale" (*mira magnitudo*), "amazing variety (or diversity)" (*mira varietas* [or *diversitas*])," "astonishing workmanship" (*mirum* [or *operosum*] *artificium*). Stupefied with "amazement and wonder" (*stupor et admiratio*), they marveled at the scale, costliness, and ingenuity of workmanship and materials. Their fascination with material aspects of art was matched by that with the intricate obscurities of symbolic meaning. Their minds sought bafflement and epiphany in exploring the coincidence or harmony of opposites, similitudes in dissimilar things, and dissimilar likenesses. The order of beauty intersected with that of irony in these unlike symmetries. Richard of St. Victor's (d. 1173) elaborate description of stages of contemplation establishes a connection with esthetics. For he charted the movement of the mind, in its conversion, from wonder to wonder, beginning with the wonder at things that sprang from thought about matter and form and, ever rising to higher things, culminating in wonder at divine precepts.[17]

The objective of amazement returns me to the importance of play both as a ritualized way of training the imagination and, even more, as a means of understanding—indeed, as understanding in action. Art, an educational tool of religion, was essential to forming habits of empathy according to the rules of religion's mythic game. It observed and taught rules governing qualification of players, game strategies, penalties, and gains and losses. As usual in art, and not only in ritual arts, the game existed in the act, and at the moment, of play; and participants inevitably subordinated to the action became creatures of the game prescribed by myth. They were played by it. They learned by doing.

Art created a designed and controlled practice field for the game of religion. But it was intended that, through ritualized play, the imagination move from the simulator of external things to the real playing field of the soul, as was thought to happen in the devotional use of images. A long tradition of synesthesia prevailed; highly developed strategies of transfer among the senses, especially sight and hearing, were practiced. Monastic communities, "schools" of Christ according to the Benedictine *Rule*, were training camps for the senses. On the principle that one learned through the body, kinesthetic discipline was built into all the daily observances of monastic *conversio*. The object was so to form the imagination that it could translate sensory perceptions into sacred theater with itself as actor and spectator.

The ironic similitudes of art were one means of marking the borders on the field of play. They were essential to the play of understanding as a quest not for clarification but for epiphany through bafflement.

Renaissance and Baroque artists were ruthlessly hostile to works made between the eleventh and thirteenth centuries. Their scorn demonstrates that what caused amazement was in the minds of the original artists and audiences, rather than in the works of art. This is to say that the rules of play had changed, not that an entirely new sport had been invented. Like their followers in the age of Leonardo, Romanesque and Gothic artists made works that answered an expectation derived from classical Antiquity. In their quest for wonder, the ancient link between art and religion survived—the use of art as a ritual means to experience the sublime. As in Antiquity, the stupefying power of art was not that of convincing but that of raising viewers outside themselves, confounding their judgment, and eclipsing all that was reasonable, pleasant, or familiar. The experience of the sublime disoriented the mind with a chiaroscuro of delight and terror, and thereby it also freed the mind from the normal circumstances of existence. Renaissance artists could no longer detect how Romanesque and Gothic art produced these effects.

The mystical writings attributed to Dionysius the Areopagite contained the theology of beauty essential to this way of thinking. Dionysian ideas were expounded by Hugh of St. Victor and given visible expression by Suger (c. 1081–1151) in his reconstruction of the abbey church of St. Denis; they pervaded twelfth-century spirituality.[18]

Dionysian theology left no doubt that the disorienting perception of the sublime changed the soul in another way as well, for the soul received the imprint of what it beheld. In fact, the likeness established in that searing, revelatory experience became the means by which the soul was actually assimilated to the sublime and was transformed—ennobled—by participating in its nature. At this point, the ritualized *cultus sui* became identical with the cult of God. Through the process of empathetic conversion, a relationship of balanced asymmetry had come about, uniting the soul with the divine.

Miracles performed through images testify in a special way to this same transforming power in ironic likeness. The voice that spoke from a crucifix commanding Francis of Assisi to rebuild the Church provides one example, completed in the later vision by which the stigmata were imprinted on Francis's body, leaving him the image of the Crucified. Similarly, Edmund of Abingdon's betrothal to the Virgin by placing on the finger of her statue a ring that no one could later remove was considered evidence of how the virginity of the one was assimilated to that of the other, Edmund pledging himself in chastity to the Virgin and she promising to be united with him. (This account is a variation of a story that, according to William of Malmesbury, Roman mothers commonly told their children about a young man who insouciantly placed his wedding ring on the finger of a bronze statue of Venus and found himself wedded to a demon.)[19] In such instances the amazement of art propelled the ennoblement of conversion.

The ennobling and disorienting power of beauty, as a principle of order, separated the few who were changed by it and divided them from the many. It also established degrees of excellence among the chosen, ordering them in serried ranks of greater and lesser lights. Eventually, New Testament doctrines, especially those of St. Paul, combined with this pre-Christian concept. Classical writers had described the exaltation of soul possessed, it might be, by an onrush of divinity or divine madness, sudden and brilliant as a lightning flash; Paul set forth a corresponding infusion of the Holy Spirit. He described a sequence by which this illumination occurred, beginning in the foreknowledge of God; brought about through predestination, vocation, and the conformity of the soul with the image of the Son (by which likeness the righteousness of the Son was imputed to the soul and the sinfulness of the soul, to the Son); and finally consummated in glorification (Rom. 8:29–30). Through the participation of likeness, the redeemed were in the Spirit, even as the Spirit of Christ dwelled in them. The glory that was revealed was that of God, or Christ, in them (Rom. 8:9, 21). Finally, having become by adoption children of God and having passed from the bondage of corruption into glorious liberty, they were free from sin, from death, and from all human beings (Rom. 6:18, 22, 8:2, 21; 1 Cor. 9:19). Few were the chosen, and they were hierarchically ranked according to the proportion of faith dealt by God to each. One encounters here, from another angle, the idea of the morally educated conscience as potentially subversive.

The hiddenness of election, the fewness of the chosen, and the invisible hierarchic rankings of the elect belonged to a wider pattern. They were encompassed in an idea of ennoblement that could subvert and destroy existing social norms and orders. Ennoblement through conversion brought about a subversive mentality according to which an enlightened few withstood the benighted many; the elect were in, but not of, the world. In this regard, doctrines of empathetic conversion were true to their hybrid character. For in their exclusivism they combined the aristocratic values of classical Antiquity with Paul's teachings on election. To these, they added the distinctions prized by Romanized elites in Germanic Europe: nobility of birth, education, mental sharpness, and feelings, or perception (*nobilitas sensus*).[20] At their separate origins, these ideas about order expressed the fragile eminence of an aristocracy that felt itself hated and menaced, whether the danger was seen to come from the plebeian orders (as in Antiquity) or from the unredeemed world (as in New Testament Christianity). Ennoblement through conversion retained this manner of self-definition through danger in the period under review.

What emerged was an aristocratic scale of worth potentially opposed to that of worldly values. For when they reflected on the court of God, their King, Christian writers knew that it contained no image and that its palaces were made up of living stones—of patriarchs and prophets, a vast army of martyrs, apostles, virgins, and legions of confessors, all of whom had withstood prevailing social values.[21] Their reflections on beauty and redeeming similitudes opened up the discrepancy between worth and values. They discovered that worth existed independently of human perception. In its manifestation as beauty that was also truth, it was an intrinsic good, whether or not anyone perceived it. By contrast, values, in the market or elsewhere, were created by perception. Thus, they were not intrinsic but acquired, and the goods that they served were transitory. Those contingent goods were instrumental (enabling one to perform a task); they gave pleasure; their utility produced other goods, just as medical operations, which are not good, produce health. Worth was apprehended by the mind or spirit; value, by the senses. The object of worth was happiness; that of value, welfare. Like pagan philosophers before them, Christian writers taught that the truth and beauty in which worth consisted were universal but that they could be found only by the few. By contrast, the goods valued by the world were particular—limited by time, place, and other contingencies—but they could be seen by all.

Art and metaphors drawn from art were central to this exclusivism. Some texts pose the encounter between the *cultus* of minds that were ordered by similitudes of beauty and rejection of those that were disordered by sin as a confrontation between superior and inferior cultures.[22]

Empathetic conversion advanced by stages of likeness between the soul and its exemplars; but as it advanced, it widened the affective distance—the area of unlikeness—from others. Bonding and aversion were two sides of the same coin. Since New Testament doctrines made authentic faith the keystone of glorified humanity, the most evident connection with the disorienting principle of beauty as an aristocratic order came in ways of thinking about unbelievers. As my comments on attitudes toward Jews indicate, the character of the non-Christian was framed as a counterfoil to that of the Christian. Interestingly, although Christians acknowledged objective standards of nobility among unbelievers—birth, education, mental sharpness, and feelings—they did not think that in themselves these qualities could confer true nobility. The orders of non-Christian societies displayed their noble classes and, among them, persons of undeniable ability. Unbelievers were able to create "most noble" cities and to construct buildings adorned with works of consummate skill and beauty.[23] And yet, in terms of order, "a believer has nothing in common with an unbeliever."[24] Pagans were "detestable to God and men," and pagans who destroyed churches could be killed with impunity. Indeed, those who killed them were worthy of all praise, honor, and veneration, for the guilt of paganism far exceeded that of homicide.[25] When Pomeranians seeking to accommodate the "German god" offered Otto of Bamberg a great treasure to preserve their temple "of amazing size and beauty," even by rededicating it as a church, he repelled their petition. It was unworthy, he said, for a building constructed in honor of demons and profaned with impure rites to be transferred to sacred uses. The "execrable building" must be destroyed.[26]

Like Jews, pagans wandered in what Augustine of Hippo (following Plato) had called "the region of dissimilitude."[27] Ignorant of God, the source of human dignity, they lacked the inner beauty of soul, or likeness to God, that characterized humanity. The *cultus sui* of conversion demanded the contrast between knowledge and ignorance of God. In their spiritual blindness pagans remained enslaved to their bodily senses and could not rise above brute animality. Worse still, the void of ignorance had been filled with demonic possession; their temples were inhabited by demons, and their hearts, inspired with demonic rage and malice. Superstition reigned in place of religion. Were unbelievers human?[28] The noble order conferred upon the mind by Christian faith confronted the barbarism of the pagans, a barbarism characterized by ignorance, stupidity, lawlessness, and cruelty, a disordered mentality fertile in atrocities against practitioners of "Christian meekness."[29] The "sanity" of Christian wisdom was contrasted with the "madness" of heretics, Jews, and unbelievers.

The same reasoning, applied according to hierarchic assumptions of proportion, had subversive consequences for Christian society. There, too, idealization of nobility imposed sanctions against dissimilitude. Although the terms were easily confused, nobility was more than courtliness. Long after the period with which I am chiefly concerned, Teresa of Avila observed the categorical confusion in the minds of those who argued that "convents should be courts and schools of good breeding . . . to teach those who want to be courtiers of Heaven."[30] If it is true that the courtly life was a strategy for advancing civilization, developed by aristocratic clerics and disseminated by them to repress "coarse and harsh behavior,"[31] it is also true that the aspiration for the sublime, combining ecstasy with terror, subverted ideals of courtliness. For where courtliness taught "the peace and tolerance necessary for civilized interaction," nobility ruthlessly advanced the ideal of honor and vengeance as its medium. Where courtliness required refinement of manners and grandeur of display, nobility taught the virtue of spiritual poverty. Where courtliness permitted the assimilation of enervating delicacies, nobility scorned effeminacy and required manly struggle against all that excited the flesh to war against the spirit.[32]

Thus, in the literature of empathetic conversion, the *cultus* of spiritual beauty, or sanity, called ennoblement turned against "madness," not only in unbelieving societies but also among agents of degradation within the Christian world. These included clerics, even great prelates, who ravaged their churches like wolves and in their impious rapacity kept open the wounds of

Christ.³³ Such abusers existed even in the papal court. With cruelty and disbelief they polluted with blood the hands that had been consecrated to make the body of Christ in the Eucharist. All their nobility of descent, their learning, the exquisite beauty with which they adorned their churches and liturgies were of no spiritual value, for they were rebuilding Babylon within the walls of Jerusalem. They were repaganizing the Church.³⁴

Likewise, the *cultus* of beauty contrasted nobility with spiritual disorder and degradation in two enterprises characteristic of emerging European society: commerce and law. Edmund of Abingdon's career exemplifies this attitude. Although as archbishop of Canterbury he was forced to borrow from moneylenders to give to the poor, he considered money beneath contempt. Even earlier, while master of arts at Paris, he had put the fees that he received from students on his windowsill and covered them with dust, burying them with the funereal words "earth to earth, dust to dust," "and they would be taken away secretly, either in jest by his companions or by thieves with evil intent." A disciple recalled, "He did not deign, I will not say to touch, but even to look at money, save that which with his own hands he distributed to the poor."³⁵

Edmund despised money, but he was not indifferent to its uses. Likewise, he bridled the concupiscence of the eyes "so strictly that he hardly knew by sight a brother who had waited on him at table for more than a year,"³⁶ but he displayed all the beauty of virtue that God bestowed upon him by building and adorning churches, by prodigal expenditures on hospitality for "courtiers and men of the world" as well as for the poor, and by accumulating precious books and works of art made from the most costly materials.³⁷ Yet just as the threat of litigation drove him to resign the cure of a church which he had restored in order to avoid distraction from his studies, so, eventually, he was driven into exile by the nit-picking machinations of lawyers retained by the king and insubordinate monks of Canterbury, calculatingly reinforced by public indignities that brought upon him universal contempt. In happier days Edmund had received papal dispensation from attending and presiding over legal proceedings. But, combining litigation with indignity, his enemies prepared cruelty for him exceeding even that of those who crucified Christ.³⁸

As the sciences of law and theology developed in later centuries, writers were able to distinguish three kinds of nobility: political, natural, and supernatural.³⁹ A prince could bestow political nobility by decree; natural nobility inhered in nature, even in brute animals, for some (such as the lion) were noble while others (such as the wolf) were ignoble. Supernatural nobility, with respect to integrity and virtue, was evident to, and conferred by, God alone; it inhered in the mind, which, by grace, was the image of God. Writers who equated nobility with gentility were able to give a materialist cast to the nobility of virtue, as Aristotle had done when he argued that modest wealth was essential to education in wisdom and habituation to independent moral choice. Such writers were able to parody Scripture ("Faith without works is dead," James 2:20) with the maxim: "Nobility without riches is dead."[40] But such a proposition was far from the ascetic writers as they reflected on the beauty in the image-likeness of the human mind to God.

The nobility of the well-ordered mind, conformed in beauty of virtue, was not seated in descent, education, esthetic sensibility, lordship, or wealth. Nor was it defined by gender. Christ was glorified both in women and in men.[41] Writers between the eleventh and thirteenth centuries remained true to the traditions of the early Church when they invoked the social eminence of exemplary Christians to extol Christianity. Writers about women employed this device as freely as those about men, and they likewise adhered to the rule that nobility of mind was of greater moment than nobility of lineage, although in this regard excellence of education and acuity of judgment do not, on the whole, figure in accounts of women.[42]

Generally written by men, ruled by norms of male dominance, and expressed in discourse controlled by men, the extant texts portray women in their virtues as the nurturers and enablers of men. The *cultus sui* subsumed a male esthetic, applied proportionately to women as well as to men but by a different scale. Since man was considered morally as well as physically stronger than woman,[43] moral excellence in individual women was explained as virility. Long before, Aristotle wrote: "A man would be thought a coward if he had no more courage than a courageous woman," for "the courage of a man is shown in commanding, of a woman in obeying" (*Politics*, 1.13, 3.4.1260a, 1277b). Portrayals of nobility in women during the period under review tend to follow this double standard of proportionality, even when they affirm that women of exceptional virtue united "a woman's way of thinking with a male spirit [*animum*]."[44] So great a ruler as the Countess Matilda of Tuscany (1046–1115), placing her armies, wealth, and if need be her life at the defense of the papacy, was represented as fighting "with the spirit [*animo*] of a man," yet also in subordination as "the daughter of St. Peter."[45]

Theological tradition conveyed a pervasive scorn for effeminacy, reinforced by the Gregorian Reformers' attacks on the "most wretched women, abominable to God," with whom clerics "prostituted" and dishonored their sacred ministries;[46] and it thereby circumscribed the independence with which women could be seen to exercise their moral nobility on the great stage of ecclesiastical life. Thus, Mabel, the mother of Edmund of Abingdon, displayed the manliness of her virtue within a narrow domestic scope, in the spiritual and physical asceticism that she waged to subdue herself and in the considered and persistent methods that she employed to educate her sons in the ways of holiness. It is notable how little emphasis is given the effects of her teaching on her daughters, whom Edmund eventually enrolled in the convent at Catesby. Amazement at women's spiritual nobility arose from its proportionate affinity to men's; that at men's, from its similarity to Christ's.

Even so, the disorienting amazement of perceiving God in his beauty proved its subversive powers among women in disrupting patterns of converts' lives and in the acts to which conversion led: rejection of patriarchal order, of marital roles prescribed for women by class or family,[47] and of the moral authority of those anointed rulers of the Church who corrupted and despoiled it.

Finally, the demands of beauty were subversive even of art. My whole discussion has been guided by the ineffability and incommunicability of the experience of empathetic conversion, as a thing felt. All theological writers, and none more consistently and powerfully than Augustine of Hippo, stressed the disparity between things and words and the inadequacy of language to convey even human emotions or sensory impressions, much less joys confided to the heart by God.

Gradually, ancient teachings on art's cultic power to ennoble human nature by calming and refining its animal savagery—that is, imposing due order in the faculties of mind and the passions—were received and assimilated. However, even when authors proclaimed the nobility of the artist, they observed that divine condescension was essential to such reform and that it led to the ultimate subversion: the transformation of human nature itself. Thus, Dante declared that the art of poetry conferred fame and immortality on its most accomplished practitioners, awaking in its audience the sweetness and love of virtue. However, human nature was ennobled and restored to beauty by Christ's incarnation, not by art. Although Dante honored great poets of pre-Christian Antiquity, he judged language and art were inadequate to represent the sublimity in which truth was both manifested and revealed. For Dante, even the words of Scripture and paintings in a church accommodated the limits of human understanding and expression. What later ages recognized as supernatural ennoblement demanded not the reform of human nature but its subverting through divinization (or "transhumanization"), a change analogous with the transformation of a larva into a butterfly.[48] And this was accomplished through grace, responded to in faith. For him, even Virgil, who practiced every virtue except the theological ones of faith, hope, and charity, fell short of heaven because he lacked faith in Christ. Human nature, the image-likeness of the mind to God, was only the precondition of supernatural nobility; the grace of election had to be added to it if supernatural nobility were to be attained. Noble as were Virgil's mind and verse, he was barred from the all-forgetting rapture, eclipsing thought and language, in which the human soul was raised to participation in the beauty that was God, reordered in the likeness of Christ, and thus brought to perfect freedom and nobility.

In politics, the rituals of empathetic conversion often became rituals of rebellion. In the visual arts the subversive character of supernatural nobility could be expressed by iconoclasm. The argument that art was superstitious and the tool of superstition against true religion was by no means limited to Jewish critics of Christianity. I shall now turn to a particular incident in which two conceptions of art as a tool for ennobling the understanding conflicted.

Art and Understanding

The amazement of art, as the bafflement of anticipated order, coincided with the amazement of condescension by Christ in his incarnation and in the lives of those who manifested him to the world. This bafflement of the understanding is part of the hermeneutic strategy of play that I am recovering. Wonder, as Plato said, was the beginning of wisdom; but it was also the beginning of *cultus,* or worship. The combination of asceticism and opulence that I have described indicates a very complex idea of how the order of art contributed to the ritualized order of understanding conversion.

The dispute over Edmund of Abingdon's tomb, a major cultic monument, provides some clarification; it also illustrates difficulties posed in a single community by the moral contrast of worth with value. Rendered a politically impotent laughingstock in England, Edmund found refuge and was buried at the Cistercian monastery of Pontigny (1240). From its very beginnings the Cistercian discipline had austerely rejected all but the most restrained ornamentation. The antagonism between Hellenic delight in images and Hebraic iconoclasm had been a constant in the Christian tradition. Seven years after Edmund's death, it erupted in the cloisters of Pontigny.

Shortly after Pope Innocent IV had proclaimed Edmund's canonization (11 January 1247), a great host of people converged on the abbey for the translation of his relics. The mighty of the earth came to revere the new saint—King Louis IX of France, his mother Queen Blanche of Castile, two cardinals, and many other secular and ecclesiastical princes. A numberless throng of peasants from the countryside joined them. The body was raised from the grave, found to be incorrupt, and, after being ceremoniously laid on the high altar, moved to a secret place to safeguard it against being roughly handled by acquisitive, pious hands.

Night fell. The monastery seemed to resume its accustomed calm. But "civil war" abruptly broke out. The chronicler of these events took comfort in remembering that even Christ's disciples had indiscreetly argued over who was greatest among themselves. Now, he said, the same question tore the brethren at Pontigny apart.

Surprisingly, given the nature and celebrity of the event, the community appears not to have decided what to do with Edmund's body after exhuming it. Recognizing the archbishop's sanctity, the abbot and prior suggested that his body should be deposited "in a stone chest, decorated with some emblems in sculpture and painting." Such plainness accorded with the Cistercian obligation to humility, not to mention with the example of Christ himself who, though Lord of all, "had chosen a lowly burial place." It had been followed in the burials of Malachy, the saintly archbishop of Armagh and primate of all Ireland, who died at Clairvaux, and of "the blessed Abbot Bernard, the great father of the Cistercian order." A plain or slightly ornamented marble sarcophagus such as theirs, without gold or jewels, would strike the middle course, approved by all. It would be neither shoddy nor extravagant, and it would not invite the charge of hypocrisy from the order's critics.

The invisibility of worth did not appeal to other brothers, who were prepared to embrace the transient goods of earthly values. They argued, in devotion rather than in malice, that an ordinary tomb, only a bit more exalted than what bishops were generally accorded, was inappropriate to so great a saint. Edmund, "the noblest among the foundation stones in Sion," buried in Pontigny by express permission of the Apostolic See, was owed "gold and every precious stone." His resting place should be adorned with the rarest and most costly materials, wrought by the most accomplished artists. The precedents of Malachy and Bernard did not count, since their burials, as well as their lives, were governed by the rules of the order. Edmund's circumstances were comparable with those of his predecessor, Thomas à Becket, whose tomb none other in all the world equaled in costliness and beauty.

The controversy became so bitter that some brethren threatened to secede from the community, until, on seeking Edmund's own views from his companions, the advocates of simplicity prevailed. But the matter was not ended. Even as the advocates of splendor assented, they regarded the burial in a plain stone sarcophagus a temporary measure and gathered their strength for better days. In this charged atmosphere the ceremony of translation went to its solemn conclusion.

Not much later the cause of splendor was revived. A visitation by the abbots of Cîteaux and other Cistercian houses deposed the prior and appointed as his successor a man who had heavy debts to pay in Rome. The abbot was persuaded to abdicate. Cardinal John of Albano, the protector of the Cistercian order in Rome, intervened. Splendor was appropriate, he argued, for the stated reasons but also because a shrine in gold and precious stones would gratify "the devotion of the faithful when they offered their gifts," assuring them of the fulfillment of their hopes. Armed with the cardinal's mandate, the new prior constructed a tomb of marvelous workmanship that dazzled the eyes of those who saw it and surpassed the power of language to express. Edmund's body was translated to its new shrine in 1249. In time, even Edmund's enemy, the king of England, presented costly ornaments to the noble tomb, as did his queen and many other great princes. Eminent bishops, too, presented "images representing pontiffs in a lifelike style, as can be seen on the slabs surrounding the sarcophagus."[49]

The importance of extrinsic circumstances—of values rather than worth—to these arguments is striking. For the abbot and prior who argued for simplicity, the defense of their order from malicious critics was a cogent matter. For the cardinal of Albano and the new abbot and prior, the riches that satisfied pilgrims would deposit at Pontigny dictated splendor. My concern is with the insistence in both camps that art furthered conversion: in other words, that it manifested worth from faith to faith.

The judgment that the figures of bishops on Edmund's tomb were lifelike provides a clue to a strategy of ritualized play that encompassed the opponents in the same cultic game. The sanctity attributed to Edmund, already believed to have been demonstrated in miracles, was considered a manifestation of Christ in him and of his passage from death into life, which is also to say from ignorance into truth, from corruption into purity, and from enmity with God into love. Like the altar above which it stood, his tomb was both a monument to life's triumph over death and a repository of life under the appearance of death. It was a pledge of the peace into which the blessed entered, reconciled with God. Thus, the advocates of simplicity called for forms of art that evoked the self-emptying of noble humility, the death to self that led to eternal life beyond the limits of imagery. The advocates of magnificence demanded forms of art that represented in ways accessible to the eye the invisible glory, honor, and power of heavenly life imparted to Edmund in this world. In simplicity or in splendor, art was to engage the visual imagination and through it the cathartic emotions of love, compassion, and fear, and finally the peace that passes all understanding.

Both factions laid upon art the burden of verisimilitude; their mutual repugnance illustrates how independent the impression of lifelikeness was from style and even from subject. The long history of art in the period under review underscores the fact that the effect of verisimilitude depended upon the imagination of the viewer, rather than the objective characteristics of the work: that is, on the willing suspension of disbelief, rather than on objective analysis. A ninth-century writer observed that those who knew how to paint well could represent faces so expressively that they seemed to speak.[50] One of his contemporaries argued against venerators of sacred images that one had to view a painting as something that lacked life, feeling, and reason. But even he recognized that one could "feed" the eyes on seeing a portrait. The Greek word for "picture," he wrote, was *"zoegraphé,"* "that is, 'live writing,'" and pictures and carvings that represented scriptural events should be "live writing," living histories, before the eyes of all, and not only of the illiterate.[51]

Perhaps recalling work by Arnolfo di Cambrio, Dante portrayed, on the ascent through Purgatory, three relief sculptures that in their dramatic effect also appeared to be not likenesses but the actual subjects speaking.[52] Between these brackets there are many witnesses to the lifelike vividness of paintings and sculpture, figures that, in the words of one author, seemed to stand out from the walls and walk.[53] To the Christian wreckers, the beauty of pagan art consisted not only in its exquisite workmanship and materials but in the impression it gave them of human beings, birds, and animals that lived and breathed. Its cultic dangers consisted in the demons that inhabited the figures, though it was possible for Otto of Bamberg to send one such image as a trophy to the papal court.[54] The constant through these centuries is not the outward order of style but the demand for empathetic participation in an unseen order of verisimilitude made manifest in ritual. That this demand of *cultus* was gratified by an extreme variety of styles, including the austere and the gorgeous that conflicted in the debate at Pontigny, indicates that art exerted its lifelike effects through the fictive order imposed by the visual imagination.

The degree to which the imagination could achieve those effects through the labyrinth of dissimilarity is indicated by the original housing of the Hereford world map (the *Mappa mundi,* executed between 1280 and 1289). Detached from the composition for which it was made, the map consists of a large sheet of vellum. Generally circular, but with a gabled top, the manuscript displays in pictures and words an encyclopedic representation of the world, its cities, peoples, plants, and animals. In its original setting the map was the centerpiece of a triptych that represented the Annunciation. The angel of the Annunciation appeared on the left wing; the Virgin on the right. Through the rule of dissimilar similarity, the map between them portrayed the body of Christ, very much in the spirit of the now-lost Ebstorf world map (executed c. 1235).

> What master of the graver or the pen
> Such lines as these, such shading could contrive
> For subtle minds to find amazement in?[55]

As the original conception of the Hereford *Mappa mundi,* the Christological centerpiece of a triptych, indicates, art produced its effect of astonishment through a game of hiddenness and disclosure.[56] It was essential that the work of art not be self-contained or explanatory and that what it was, as well as what it meant, be hidden and only revealed in parts, and then only to those discerning enough to penetrate its code, only to those capable of being amazed by its cunning. Thus, the symbolic obscurity by which the Hereford map represented the body of Christ was matched by the physical arrangement of the wings of the triptych, which concealed the entire composition.

In a more elaborate fashion, Edmund of Abingdon's tomb exemplified the same ritualized game of hide-and-seek. Even though it stood at the high altar of Pontigny, still it had to be approached in that inner sanctum from a distance, through the various screens of monastic architecture. The elaborate structure of the shrine concealed the body of the saint; its artistry was also an exercise in concealment. This consisted partly in the symbolism of the materials used, the numbers of particular elements in the structure, the figures represented, and, of course, the position of the shrine itself. It came about, too, because the figures adorning the tomb were too small and too far from the viewer, not to mention too poorly lit, to be readily apparent. Further, whatever the original design, independent offerings from great and powerful donors soon made the shrine a pastiche of separate works of art. The effect can only have been to bring together a concatenation of separate scenes, allegories, and motifs, an architectural album of unrelated episodes, and a montage of works in different materials and styles. Finally, it would have been quite usual to find, in an inventory of ornaments, palls in costly fabrics for covering the shrine. Multiple concealment was essential to the amazement of revelation.

The ritual substitution of image for reality is a familiar experience, and not only in historically remote societies. When Friedrich Wetter, archbishop of Munich and Freising, first returned to Munich from Rome as cardinal (2 June 1985), he celebrated a solemn Eucharist in his cathedral. The Frauenkirche is a long, narrow building, with a nave and two side aisles from which it is very hard to see what is going on at the high altar. Closed-circuit television screens were installed along the exterior walls for the benefit of those in the side aisles, and I was astonished to see, at the elevation of the Host, that worshipers there knelt outward toward the nearest television screen, rather than inward toward the altar. Like pilgrims at the shrine in Pontigny, the devout venerated the veiling images that they could see, rather than the realities ambiguously concealed and manifested at the altar.

The points that I am making are that in the period under review, the visual imagination was an essential part of understanding empathetic conversion as the intersection of the *cultus sui* and the worship of God and that through ritually playing out the ironic concealment and revelation of art, the visual imagination was educated by the institutions and methods that interpreted, taught, and enforced an identifiable hermeneutic circle to be a powerful instrument for the ennoblement of the soul. It was trained to see elements that were invisible in the visible, just as the aural imagination was educated to hear the unsaid in the said. When Dante first conceived the *Divine Comedy*, he was "drawing an angel on some wooden boards."[57] Disorienting ennoblement came about through wonder at the unseen and invisible likenesses that could be, as at Edmund's tomb, exquisitely presented to the informed imagination. It could also be disruptive of community.

I have now traced out a general program of education underlying ideas about what was called conversion within a hermeneutic circle that issued from and served an identifiable social circle. I began with the general notion that empathetic conversion was not one cataclysmic event but a long process of change, not a dramatic peripety so much as a continuing transformation full of risk. I then examined ways in which the mind was educated to a life of penitence through ritualized disciplines of spirit and body: that is, educated to practice relentless criticism. A review of mythic context brought me to social norms and institutions from which monasticism transposed its rituals of aggressiveness and vigilance. That context inculcated an ethos of male dominance, a warrior's ethos that prescribed a testing of the soul in conflict and a bonding of those who proved in battle a dependence that secured even the most valiant warrior against his own weakness. Now, by considering art as a means of education, I have added another piece to the puzzle. I have found that art expressed the ambivalences with which the ideas about empathetic conversion were veined; for even while it proclaimed the opulence and conspicuous waste of chivalric society, it also displayed the perishability of mortal things, and even as it glorified dominant social orders, it ritualized lessons of subversion.

Contrasts in Nobility

My discussion of art has also confirmed the proposition that conversion was considered a supernatural work of God, a reordering of the soul, performed in individuals for the edification of the community, not least by means of subversion of an existing order for the establishment of another.

Thus far it is evident that the idea of empathetic conversion as the sanctifying, proportional transit from the sensual contingencies of value to spiritual and enduring worth—ennoblement—belonged to the mimetic tradition of reform.[58] Affinity by likeness and estrangement by unlikeness, visualized as degrees of nearness to, or remoteness from, the center of a circle, were the keys. A certain nobility of virtue was possible to the unconverted (such as Virgil) because their minds were made in the image of God. However, attainment of supernatural nobility required the grace of election, which led to justification from sin through spiritual and sacramental likeness to Christ and, finally, to glorification in him. Through ennoblement, grace perfected human nature and thereby subverted it. However, the complex modes of understanding that I have identified were by no means general throughout that tradition. Despite many resemblances the ordering principle of nobility, and with it the hermeneutic circle and its *cultus sui*, reviewed here was markedly different from those set forth at other moments in the history of the mimetic tradition, notably in classical Antiquity and during the Romantic epoch and its aftermath. At those moments, empathy might have little or no part to play.

Throughout, while concentrating on materials from Romanesque and Gothic Europe, I have attempted to suggest landmarks in other areas, coordinates for persons not generally familiar of those materials. Here, such an orientation can well begin with Aristotle.

Aristotle gave classic expression to the moral discrepancy between universal worth, accessible to the few, and contingent (or particular) value, sought by the many. He was the source of the equation between nobility and happiness and of the doctrine that happiness was the goal of human life. But where the ideas that I have reviewed derived both from God, through grace, Aristotle located them in nature: that is, in the perfection of life according to reason. Doctrines of conversion posited dependence on God and interdependence within the community; humility was the primary virtue.

Happiness, Aristotle taught, derived from self-sufficiency in material existence as well as in intellectual resources; pride was, for him, the primary virtue, being honor on the grand scale. Thus, in Aristotle's version of the *cultus sui*, the noble and truly pleasant lay beyond the ken of the many, and certainly beyond that of mechanics and laborers, for no one engaged in manual toil could practice the virtues. Barbarians were by nature slaves. Even among Greeks, only exceptional men could attain the happiness of the virtuous life, although, to be sure, women could attain some proportional virtue appropriate to their weaker nature. Death was the ultimate test of nobility: that is, of the power to withstand dread. For death was the most terrible of all things. Since the greatest and noblest dangers occurred in battle, the noblest death came in battle.

Accordingly, the noble man preferred a short period of intense pleasure to a long one of genial contentment, one great and noble action to many ordinary ones. He will sacrifice to his friend because, giving the benefit and gaining nobility, he claims the greater benefit for himself. Yet friendship between men of different social positions could endure only if each loved the other according to the proportion of their dignities (or status), the greater being loved more than he loved in return.[59]

Empathy and the esthetics of play have no role in Aristotle's doctrines of nobility, and this exclusion of the visual imagination marks a profound difference both from the doctrines of Plato and the Neoplatonists and from those which I have examined. It is all the more notable, because Aristotle was the source, par excellence, of Western theories about the empathetic effects of drama.

Aristotle's counterpart of spiritual peace was serene self-approval. His doctrines of nobility and happiness presupposed the social structure of Hellenic society in his day; they were by no means subversive, except in the idiosyncratic choice of a noble death. Immortality through fame was an unstable beacon; so it proved when Herostratus destroyed the temple of Diana at Ephesus for the glory of the deed. The contrast with Samson's self-immolation in the destruction of the temple of Dagon is evident, for, as Milton observed, Samson's act heroically avenged himself on his enemies, demonstrated that God had not abandoned him despite his degradation, brought honor and freedom to his people, and left the memory of a noble death to inflame the hearts of long posterity.[60] However, Christ exhibited yet another exemplar of nobility in his prophecy "Destroy this temple, and in three days I will raise it up," speaking of the temple of his body (John 2:19–20). Herostratus sought fame; Samson invoked God's power in avenging himself on the Philistines for his blindness (Judg. 17:28). Christ's death was a sin offering, and in it grace perfected nature. According to the doctrines that I have reviewed, it was performed so that others could, and must, pass from enmity to peace through this atoning death, so that the beauty and sweetness hidden in Christ was transfused from his heart to those joined to him, as from vine to branches.

Doctrines of empathetic conversion encapsulated the imitation of Christ, with its particular ideal of nobility. Herostratus and Samson laid claim to nobility by single, defiant actions. Aristotle, too, idealized the heroic gesture.

But Christ set forth an exemplar of nobility by his entire life. Taken up into doctrines of conversion as a ritualized process or way of life, this conception of nobility revealed, tested, and glorified through tribulation inspired many works of literary and historical imagination. In them life was portrayed as education through rituals of journey, pilgrimage, or knightly quest. The lasting effects are readily apparent in such different works as Spenser's *Faerie Queene* and Bunyan's *Pilgrim's Progress*. Later, in the Romantic era, they found new adaptations in philosophical speculations, not least in those of Hegel, and in a host of literary works.[61]

To illustrate the difference between the static pose of the great peripety and the idea of ennoblement by empathetic conversion as an unfolding predicament, I shall offer two Romantic ideals for comparison with previous examples: the muscular Romanticism of *Moby-Dick* (published in 1851) and the esthetic Romanticism of James Joyce's (1882–1941) *A Portrait of the Artist as a Young Man* (published in 1916). These texts illustrate both the continuity of a narrative line provided by the hermeneutics of conversion and departures from theological patterns: in other words, reworkings of the idea of conversion according to the circumstances of nineteenth-century society comparable in some ways with the reconstructions of the twelfth. Yet, empathy is by no means prominent in either work. Notably, both books portray characters from social classes in which, according to Aristotle's standards, nobility was unthinkable. Melville (1819–1891) particularly emphasized that his subjects, whalers, were socially despised as butchers, despite the utility of their work.

The *cultus sui* for both authors was of an order entirely different from Aristotle's, for both are enduring quests for ennoblement through suffering. Of the two books, Joyce's *Portrait* falls the closer to my theme. This is patently so because Joyce deliberately assimilated the vocabulary of empathetic conversion in Roman Catholicism, which he imbibed as a child, to his narrative of how a writer passed from inspiration to utterance and, by a double conversion, first to the Church and then to art. The vocabulary passed to Joyce, despite many variations, with an uninterrupted continuity from the twelfth century. However, Melville wrote within a Protestant tradition. As he received the vocabulary of conversion, it had been sifted through the filter of the Reformation and, from the Enlightenment on, had been subjected to the reinterpretations of historical criticism and philosophical relativism.

Tacitly modeling the artist's voyage of self-discovery on the conversion of John Henry Newman, Joyce carefully built his account as a sequence in which he was first called to conversion by the Church and later, rejecting that call, converted to art and became a priest "of the eternal imagination." For Dante, the ennoblement of the poet required the intervention of divine grace, responded to by faith; freedom came in purification from sin, transcendence of death, and assimilation to God in his manifestations of truth and beauty.

For Joyce, the ennobling of the artist came through defiance of the Church's God, indeed, through relegating him to the status of hypothetical possibilities. Freed from the Church, "he felt that the spirit of beauty had folded him round like a mantle and that in revery at least he had been acquainted with nobility."[62] Traces of empathy survive in his portrayal of inspiration. Ennoblement through the experience of beauty occurred gradually within the artist's own mind. Beauty as a principle of order was a private matter. What remains of the sublime, "the mystery of esthetic," is accomplished when the artist's personality is entirely poured into the work, "refines itself out of existence, impersonalizes itself, so to speak" (p. 194), and is subsumed in the text. Deftly employing terms and analogues of the discarded theology, Joyce portrays art as religion, but one without the promise of peace.

The idea of condescension, crucial to the doctrines that I have considered, is lost together with the possibility of empathy toward other human beings. Joyce not only banished the heavy apparatus of divine condescension in itself and as an order for human action. He also replaced the key virtue of condescension, humility, with pride; its characteristic impulse, the desire to serve, with the refusal to serve; and its driving passion, love, with a "cold and cruel and loveless lust" (p. 88). Ambiguous in his sexuality, he was disdainful of women. Even in the erotic montages that constituted his moments of spiritual enlightenment, he withdrew from them. The humanizing power of art was for him a continual flight from the robust masculinity of his companions, a flight attended also by a sense of rejection. Therefore, where the ideas of nobility in conversion required an exchange of deference and honor in community, Joyce's conversion to art produced isolation. Even though he withdrew into his own transcendental Ego in order, by art, to form "the uncreated conscience of his race," he found his tools in "silence, exile, and cunning" (p. 222). All benevolence in the religion of his art is veined with malice, and this marks one essential point of similarity with his perception of Christian doctrine.

The subversive effects of conversion remain, for Joyce, in the soul's lusting for its own exultant destruction. This Romantic counterpart of the noble death characterizes Ahab's pursuit of Moby Dick. Insofar as, within the Protestant vernacular, Melville's novel is a "sacred text" and the great white whale a metaphor for God,[63] the entire voyage of the *Pequod* is an allegory of conversion, a turning of Ahab's heart to his God in all-consuming vengeance. It is strikingly in contrast with the grand gestures of Herostratus and Samson but, in

Ahab's quest for what proved untransforming and unredemptive death, a dark counterpoise also to Christ's career and *via crucis*.

As in Joyce's account, pride is the virtue that ennobles as it destroys, although Melville portrays its destructive effects as operating within the dynamics of a malign Christianity. The word *noble* came readily to Melville's pen: customs, whales, coins, robust male physiques, acts, aspirations, and many other things are called noble. The concept of the nobility as a particular ordering of the soul was, for Melville, profoundly colored by the myth of the noble savage. Filtered through doctrines of cultural relativism, this ideal, invented as a norm of self-criticism in Western culture, profoundly colors Melville's satirical equation between Christianity and civilization (e.g., chaps. 57, 110, 126). It found a dramatic representation early in the novel when Ishmael, "a good Christian, born and bred in the bosom of the infallible Presbyterian Church," was brought by his feelings of kinship with Queequeg to "turn idolator," bowing before and serving Queequeg's "innocent little idol" (chap. 10). The "poor pagan," the "noble savage," expressed "whatever is truly wondrous and fearful in man, [yet] never put into words or books" (chaps. 34, 110). Several generations of historical criticism applied to Scripture showed their effects in Melville's portrayal. Queequeg's extraordinary strength and beauty, his unflinching and selfless endurance, modesty, delicate regard for the feelings of his companions, and generosity cast into dark relief the "civilized hypocrisies and bland deceits" that had rendered "Christian kindness" nothing more than "hollow courtesy," capable of degrading and defiling the innocent and satisfying the dark axiom that "all mortal greatness is but disease" (e.g., chaps. 12, 16).

Nobility, as an ordering principle that established worth and discounted value, lay in "immaculate manliness" (chap. 26), "the royal mantle of humanity," exemplified by Queequeg in its benign form and by Ahab in its tragic one. It had no powers of disorientation, but only those of fulfillment. The feminine is omitted from Melville's diagram of life's progress from boyhood through adolescence to manhood and negatively included in his description of human souls as orphans of unknown paternity born to unwed mothers (chap. 114). Nobility required "real strength" which bestowed beauty and harmony, as in the paintings of Michelangelo. It had nothing in common with representations of "the divine love in the Son, the soft, curled, hermaphroditical Italian pictures, in which his idea has been most successfully embodied. These pictures, so destitute as they are of all brawniness, hint nothing of any power, but the mere negative, feminine one of submission and endurance, which on all hands, it is conceded, form the peculiar practical virtues of his teachings" (chap. 86).

Even the broad conception of nobility through manhood, with God, in a characteristically Protestant vernacular, as "the center and circumference of all democracy" (chap. 25), did not exhaust Melville's quest for sublimity. For "there is an aesthetics in all things" (chap. 60). No heart beats, no brain thinks "unless God does that beating, does that thinking, does that living" (chap. 132). All lives, everywhere and in all ages, were ordered parts of one great whole; the personal was absorbed into a universal impersonality, the historical into a vast and indeterminate series of repetitions (chaps. 45, 98, 107). Thus, in the global unity of manliness, the ignominy of any individual was covered by the "abounding dignity" of others (chap. 26). The benign nobility of the pagan and the tragic nobility of the apostate Captain belonged to the same living mass, each mirroring the same primal reality, each turned by Fate (chap. 132).

A further difference may turn on the fact that Joyce was interpreting a tradition of Catholicism, while Melville worked within revised versions of doctrines taught by the magisterial Reformers. Like Joyce, Melville excluded grace and located ennoblement within nature; but he placed it within a nature whose ultimate reality was untrammeled power in a relentlessly moving cycle of creation and destruction. Thus, while Joyce portrayed the quest for noble freedom as ending in "futile isolation" (p. 90), Melville cast it as tragedy. Tragedy dominates, even as Ahab draws Queequeg into his ruin. "That mortal man who hath more of joy than sorrow in him . . . cannot be true. . . . The truest of all men was the Man of Sorrows." But while the doctrines with which I have been preoccupied portrayed Christ's Passion as the means of glory, Melville returned to Calvin's Stoicism. The non-Christian Solomon was right: all was vanity. Human nature was marked for sadness (chap. 96).

There was no intersection of divine worship with the *cultus sui*. Ahab's noble melancholy pervades the narrative. Stubb, the coward, and Pip, vulnerable and despised, laugh; gallows humor provokes mirth while whales are slaughtered; the hospitable English ships, inept in whaling, and the lascivious crew of the *Bachelor*, carousing with abducted Polynesian women, provided lighthearted diversions. Ahab laughed once, when he explained the ominous howling of seals, and a second time, when he wrongly believed that he had escaped the prophetic signs of death (chaps. 126, 135).

For Melville, nobility is a principle of order inherent in the soul and gradually unfolded from it in quest. It is without empathy. Thus drawn forth and formed, nobility brings freedom to encounter the order of Fate boldly and to experience defiantly inevitable destruction by its impersonal power. Always testing itself and being tried, nobility allowed no peace. At the beginning of these chapters, I referred to Latimer's *Sermon on the Cards*, in which the bishop urged his listeners to throw their trump—that is, their heart—on Christ. He appealed to their freedom and to the greater freedom and nobility that they would win through love. The distance between beauty as the principle of order in conversion and the iron fatalism in Melville's portrayal of nobility—the distinctions between two *cultus sui*—is underscored by comparing Latimer's words with Ahab's comment on life. "Here some one thrusts these cards into these old hands of mine; swears that I must play them and no others." To which Starbuck, his mate, added: "And damn me, Ahab, but thou actest right; live in the game, and die it!" (chap. 118). Possibly, for Melville (as for Joyce), "the sublime [was] an egotistical event that operate[s] through the medium of language."[64]

There are many other expressions of the tragic isolation of the hero, of nobility achieved without empathy in questing for the greater self, defying the sad, futile transit of human existence, embracing death without transfiguration. Tennyson's *Ulysses*, another instance of muscular Romanticism, resembles Melville's ethic in idealizing constant struggle but lacks his transcendental theology. However, Whitman combined them in his profoundly moving verses:

> Sail forth, steer for the deep waters only,
> Reckless O Soul, exploring, I with thee, and thou with me,
> For we are bound where mariner has not yet dared to go,
> And we will risk the ship, ourselves and all.
>
> O my brave Soul!
> O farther, farther sail!
> O daring joy, but safe! are they not all the seas of God?
> O farther, farther, farther sail![65]

Evidently, Aristotle, Joyce, and Melville, no less than the framers of the hermeneutics of conversion, were fighting against their own weaknesses, the vulnerability of the human condition. Aristotle portrayed a static ideal of nobility; Joyce and Melville, dynamic ones, recognizably embodying remnants of their historical antecedents in Christian thought. What distinguishes the Romantic and post-Romantic *cultus sui*, those ideas of the transit to nobility, from others that I have considered?

Two differences are immediately obvious. The one is the absence of religious cult and its ritualizations of thought from Aristotle, Joyce, and Melville alike. The other is this: neither was human nature made for, nor did nobility bring, sanctification or happiness. The perfecting of nature did not require the grace of election by God to salvation. Correspondingly, the common empathetic needs that others had considered obstacles to happiness—those of life, love, purity, and truth—were discounted by Joyce and Melville. Only the need for power and glory remained. The accent that Joyce and Melville placed on pride as the sovereign virtue and their contempt for what Melville called the feminine power of "submission and endurance" drove them to ignore or to discount empathetic needs that required the strength of humility and compassion, needs that could be satisfied by the condescension of the strong to the weak. By their denial of self-giving, they departed even from Aristotle, who in his exaltation of pride as a virtue yet taught that nobility required receiving as well as giving and brought serenity to the mind. They were played by a game of art entirely different from the one that played Dante and his predecessors.

One sign of the difference is in the varieties of conversion that they deployed. In my discussion of penitential discipline, I found that Edith Stein and Simone Weil retained the paradigm of spiritual conversion epitomized in the imitation of Christ but discarded other paradigms, including cosmological ones, that explained change brought about within nature, rather than change produced by the intervention of divine grace. By contrast, among the paradigms available in the twelfth century and conveyed through tradition to the nineteenth century, only some of those explaining change within nature entered the portrayals of Joyce and Melville.

Hermeneutic paradigms of empathetic conversion by grace and models that taught the transformation of the soul into something entirely other than what it was had no place. Moral speculation, too, became a study in the human condition, no longer overshadowed by the theodical quandary of God's responsibility for evil. The depersonalization of esthetic life represented by Joyce and Melville, including the depersonalization of the artist, made it impossible for them to consider the moral world, as writers from the patristic age onward had done, a painting in which God added colors of good and evil for the beauty of the whole or history as his song being sung, in which human lives were individual notes. Perhaps, other generations had also thought, the moral world was like a mosaic over which individual human beings moved as would little worms, finding fault with the artist for the sharpness of a particular stone that hurt them and unable to see the variety and design with which he had composed the loveliness of the pattern as a whole.[66] The blind forces directing human affairs had no such informing benevolence as had made it possible in those earlier cultures to consider history the transit of Jesus, "Christ in us, moving to the Father."[67]

Even the paradigms that were retained appeared with a different cast. Conversion within the limits of nature explained how something changed into a higher form of what it already was. Thus, pre-Christian ideas of philosophical conversion brought about by a sage's ingenuity, intuition, or reason were applied together (as by Melville) with ideas of recurrent cycles in the world. The sense that individual conversions were part of a collective movement through transforming pain toward a glorious consummation of the ages had been discarded. Released from the theological framework given them by Christianity, paradigms of autonomy emphasized the loneliness of the sage, and those of cosmic cycles the icy meaninglessness of human striving, redeemed from absurdity, if at all, by the assertion of the individual will, both heroic and tragic.

No longer bound by formal beauty as an ordering principle in the world and human existence, they were likewise free to abandon the ironic similitudes of art as a way to ennoblement of soul. For them, nobility was not a study in gradations or proportion.

Consequently, while art served religion by its incompleteness—indeed, its self-denial in the face of the higher realities to which it was meant to lead the mind—art as religion declared its autonomy. The nobility of condescension had required humble self-emptying. The nobility of expression required self-fulfilling. The work of art became self-referential and explanatory, complete in itself. Isolated in alienating and possibly self-destructive genius, the artist did not speak for and to the community. Symbolic games of hide-and-seek were still possible, as in the works of Joyce and Melville; amazement, perhaps as shock, was still a goal. But love was no longer the goal of wonder, as it had been in the literature of conversion, nor was art intended, through wonder, to elevate the heart by opening to it the order of a world ruled by love. *Charity,* like *condescension,* became a term of reproach. Dante's exhortations to his audience to abandon base and ignoble ways, the unmitigated scorn that he cherished for such models of depravity as Florence and the papacy, all admonitions to spiritual reform, stand in sharp contrast with the effects that Joyce and Melville intended to stir in their readers. The hiddenness of their art could reveal no compelling vision of a noble, sane, and just world: that is, of peace. And still, in their paradigms of conversion as formative process, they were true to the aristocratic distinction between worth and value. To be sure, they are marked by the same shift from proportionality to probability that I detected in comparing Guerric of Igny's portrayal of the incarnate Word with Pascal's wager (see chap. 5, after n. 97).

The doctrine of empathetic conversion presupposed that human nature possessed a dignity, an honor, a glory that was hidden and that must be freed from its obscurity. That it presupposed beauty as an ordering principle synonymous with peace gave food for satire, not last or least to Voltaire. Often, the equation of Christianity with humanity (or civilization) was worked out with narrowness of mind and heart and with cruelty disguised as mercy. There is no need to mention wars and civil disabilities of religion. Who were the qualified players of the game? Here, there was some continuity, even though Dante's was quite a different sport from Melville's.

There is, in the works reviewed here, a reminiscence of the angry interview between Olav Tryggvessön and Sigrid the Strong-minded with which I began. Writing for a contentedly Christian audience, Snorre recalled how Olav rejected marriage to the "heathen bitch" and Sigrid, her paganism intact, resorted to another marriage in order to secure, covertly, a male avenger.

Even within the charmed circle of Christian culture, play was pervaded by an aristocratic male esthetic, which survived, though attenuated, in Romantic and post-Romantic ideas about the formation of the mind. Dante's idealization of Beatrice and of the feminine was quite self-consciously not a representation of Beatrice's words or actions but a fiction by a man "concerning her [of] what ha[d] never been written in rhyme of any woman." Indeed, this act of homage was meant to gain the favor not of Beatrice but of another man, "the Lord of Courtesy."[68] The tradition of this esthetic long remained constant, although it connoted different orders without proportion for men and women. "It really amazed me," Melville wrote to Sophia Hawthorne, "that you should find any satisfaction in [*Moby-Dick*]. It is true that some *men* have said they were pleased with it, but you are the only *woman*—for as a general thing, women have small taste for the sea."[69] Yet visions of the sublime are always partial. Much can be learned from doctrines, rooted in enduring institutions and in the arts, that set forth the fulfillment of human nature in benevolence and love of truth. Much can be gained by perfecting them.

The hermeneutic circle that I have considered is an artifact of a particular culture, in limited historical circumstances. By appealing to the works of Melville and Joyce, I do not mean to indicate that the immense splendors in those earlier teachings on beauty and peace, ritualized into life, have now departed from us. A scholar's hauteur, perhaps also a hierarch's, was advanced by John Henry Newman when he wrote that "the religion of the multitude is ever vulgar and abnormal; it ever will be tinctured with fanaticism and superstition. . . . A people's religion is ever a corrupt religion, in spite of the provisions of Holy Church."[70]

But the perennial distinction between the wise and the simple, common in philosophy from the beginning, inverted in Christianity and here asserted by Newman, has little to do with the concepts of empathetic education in the writings of Edith Stein and Simone Weil. What I have said about education to supernatural nobility or greatness of soul is also spread through the writings of a companion unknown to them, Dietrich Bonhoeffer (1906–1945), executed in the concentration camp at Flossenberg. Convinced that honor inhered in human nature, Bonhoeffer believed that Jesus found honor in becoming human; but he also taught that the Incarnation glorified humanity. The Christian's calling to union with the Word of God was therefore both aristocratic and empathetic. Its nobility consisted in sacrifice, courage, and the performance of spiritual duties toward all, whether friend or foe. This nobility of soul was by no means opposed to the leveling of social classes; it was intensely hostile to the idea that all moralities were equal and equivalent, a position that Bonhoeffer scorned as cheap and degrading. "The hall-mark of the Christian," he wrote, "is the 'extraordinary,'" epitomized in Christ's Passion and lived out by Christ's followers, subversively if need be, as they endured his suffering through their own acts of self-renunciation and love, even "unreserved love for our enemies," indeed, in "brotherly forgiveness" for them.[71]

Summary

Understanding conversion was a hermeneutic project in the twelfth century as it is in our own day. One purpose of this work has been to recover the broad outlines of that project as it was grasped in that distant era. I have regained part, at least, of what was read into St. Jerome's sentence "Christians are made, not born" (*ep. 107*, 1). From beginning to end the hermeneutic project was a task in metaphorical analysis. In the languages of philosophy and theology, "conversion" was a metaphor taken over from arts and crafts, especially from those employed in transforming raw materials into works of art or achieving some such alteration of metals as occurs in the production of bronze.

I found that those engaged in spiritual conversion employed a parable of Jesus to describe their task as recovering a treasure buried in another's field. The Apostle Paul provided an alternate metaphor when he wrote: "Now we see through a glass, darkly; but then face to face: now I know in part; but then shall I know even as also I am known" (1 Cor. 13:12). Paul added what was taken to be a crucial gloss on this text when he wrote that each person must think according to the measure of faith dealt out by God (Rom. 12:3). Thus, spiritual enlightenment depended upon grace, not on human traditions, laws, or actions. And inegalitarian grace, bestowed in arbitrary proportions by God's hidden judgment, established serried ranks of greater and lesser lights. In fact, Paul's metaphor, expanded with this gloss, epitomized the entire hermeneutic project.

What conclusions can be proposed? Three seem obvious. Perhaps too self-evident is that the word *conversion* is not a reliable tool of analysis. Far from being (so to speak) clinically sterile, it comes laden with connotations rooted in

Christian history that transmit their coloration on contact to materials under investigation. There is reason to assume that the word has no equivalent in major languages outside Europe. The question is certainly worth considering whether applying the word *conversion* can impose Western conceptions on non-Western experiences and ideas.

Further, what is called "conversion" is defined by contexts of time and place. Consequently, it is important to determine what is called conversion, by whom it is so called, and the language used to analyze it.

I have discovered that ideas about conversion in twelfth-century Europe had two senses. In the first, conversion was obvious. It occurred within the confines of human nature, expressed by the ideas and words and shaped by the capacities and institutions that grew out of human nature. Sociologists, anthropologists, and historians recognize this kind of conversion, as manifested, for example, in acceptance of Christianity and submission to the Church or in a change of affiliation or discipline within the ecclesiastical order. However, these inquiries have established that eleventh- and twelfth-century writers recognized this variety as conversion only in a formal sense.

For them, authentic conversion was not formal but supernatural and empathetic. The heart turned not to Christianity or Church but to Christ; by mystic union, it turned into Christ. Indeed, it was turned by grace, rather than by any logical deductions or emotional discoveries of its own. Indemonstrable and mysterious, this mystic turning of the heart into something else was not bound to formal, institutional obedience, nor could its outcome, hidden in God's foreknowledge, be predicted. To the contrary, reversing human expectations, it frequently proved subversive of formal obedience and customs.

Thus, a second outcome of the work at hand has been to define these twinned but entirely separable ideas of conversion and, moreover, to identify them as historical artifacts, souvenirs of the ascetic wing of a military, literary, and ascetic male aristocracy in western Europe.

The implications of insisting that the hermeneutics of conversion is a historical artifact are wide, but they are quite the same as some disclosed by the historical criticism of the Bible and the "quest for the historical Jesus." They can only entail asking whether the objects of faith, too, were historical fictions. This is my third conclusion.

Polemical experience with philosophical skepticism and the critical demands of Christianity itself prompted the Church Fathers to anticipate this query when they glorified in the great improbabilities: that God revealed the truth needed by all to an obscure and despised people in a remote corner of the world; that God became man and submitted to death; that God long withheld revealing the way of salvation, leaving whole nations to live and die in their sins; and that, condemned by lying witnesses and wicked priests and executed by a cowardly ruler and ignorant soldiers, the crucified God would bring about universal redemption through the crime of those who mocked and slew him. Given the first two conclusions, I should stress that the Fathers addressed such doubts not on the level of what could be demonstrated by natural logic but on the indemonstrable grounds of supernatural revelation and grace.

Let me recapitulate how this point was reached. I first distinguished the phenomenon (what was called "conversion"), the name ("conversion"), and the process by which the phenomenon came to be called by the name. What began in esthetics, the realm of inexpressible feeling and intuition, was transposed into that of poetics, the realm of representation. It has been important to realize that *conversion* is a metaphor-word and, as such, a historical artifact. Thus, whatever may be said about the experience of conversion, the word *conversion* and the vernaculars used to define and express its meanings were by no means universal. I assumed that like other works of art, the name "conversion" contained elements of the process by which it was made and that they could be unpacked by analyzing the artifact.

As a technical word in the language of manufacture, *conversion* denoted a variety of processes. Correspondingly, as a metaphor, it contained not one meaning but a large repertory of them, each with its own history and paradigm of change. The experience of the word in the world left its marks, especially during persecutions suffered by the early Church. One result of persecution was that for the survival of the institutional Church, devices were invented that enabled believers who succumbed to temptation, even to the point of denying their faith, to return to the fold and that in time permitted the cycle of confession, lapse, penitence, and reconciliation to be repeated throughout life. Monasticism was the great institutional form of conversion as a penitential way of life. Thus, in the repertory of paradigms, those became dominant that represented conversion as a process of transformation, full of perplexities and dangers, rather than a sudden, decisive peripety. However, they were supplemented and melded, in a highly eclectic way, with other patterns.

I have not argued that understanding the metaphor-word *conversion* was, or is, a matter of playing with words, or entirely a rhetorical exercise. Yet it seems inescapably true that access to that understanding comes through texts, which are written, historical documents, and that the ideas informing those texts are set forth in words and syntax that are likewise bound by time and place. I had to ask at the beginning whether Olav Tryggvessön's words to Sigrid the Strong-minded—"Why should I wed you, you heathen bitch?"—

and his sharp blow to her face were really part of the confrontation between Christianity and paganism in tenth-century Scandinavia or a reconstruction tailored to suit expectations in a thirteenth-century Christian society.

It seems indisputable, moreover, that the language in the text, and the thoughts in the language, and the perceptions in the thoughts are also creatures of time and place and, consequently, that they have antecedents, possibly also consequences, that, being historical, are not universal.

This emphasis has had one further effect. To speak of language as historical evidence is to ask whose language it was. By whom, for whom, with whom did it signify, especially in concealed, metaphorical senses? The vernaculars of conversion were used in discourse. I have found correlations between the ways in which they were used and the identities of those who controlled discourse and its rituals and who, as a result, received, interpreted, enacted, and conveyed tradition. Hermeneutic circles are made by social circles.

I have also been acutely aware that all of these qualifications apply to me, seeking to understand how others understood conversion and thus working within a two-tiered hermeneutic structure that from some perspectives of hermeneutic circularity may resemble a gallery of mirrors.

Another object of these investigations has been to recover guiding ideas. Here the real point of departure was the proposition, inherited in different forms from Hebraic and Hellenic traditions, that human nature was made for happiness but lived in misery. What was called conversion was a way to survive and escape the wretchedness of this world and achieve happiness. And yet "conversion" stood at the juncture of imperative and impossibility. Thus, understanding conversion was not susceptible to direct, logical demonstration; true to the nature of metaphors, it required poetic imagination—that is, fiction, built up by a strategy of criticism. Universal myths (including that of the noble origins of a people, its exile through catastrophe, and eventual return to a land of milk and honey) were brought to bear. Faith was accepted as a mode of knowledge, by no means opposed to reason. But among the varieties of faith—such as intellectual assent, common sense, and trust—only one was adequate to empathetic conversion. "Believing in" through love produced the union of believer with the object of belief and therefore the transcendence of the believer's self and circumstances. This was, specifically, the kind of faith granted by God according to measure. In its poetics empathetic conversion was of the heart, not the mind. Emotions were dominant; mind served heart, each according to its own measure of faith.

Because it was understood as a gradual process of formation, rather than as an instant, irreversible event, what was called conversion entailed pathology.

Fear of error and apostasy among professed believers demanded relentless, lifelong vigilance, for since carnal desires could not be plucked out by the roots, one could only repeatedly shave off the wicked deeds that kept growing out from them.

Institutionalizing conversion in monastic order had two effects on understanding. The first was to establish ritualized methods of spiritual discipline (such as reading and prayer), each of which hinged on kinesthetic pain. The second enlarged the sphere of ambivalence created by the mysterious and ungovernable proportionalities of faith. For, devoted to imitation of Christ crucified, monastic discipline focused understanding on ironies.

Overarching all the ironies that I have examined were those of theodicy. Empathetic conversion was an essay on the existence, power, and goodness of God. If there were a God, how could there be evil? If there were no God, how could there be good? Why were those who served and obeyed God in purity of heart afflicted with temptation and physical pain, while the manifestly evil, the hypocrite, and the unbeliever prospered? Why did virtuosos in ascetic disciplines and eminent theologians experience spiritual aridity and dejection? One key to these queries was the ironic distance between appearance accessible to human minds and divine reality, as in that between Christ the victim on the Cross and Christ the universal Ruler and Judge. Not far behind came the ironic distance between Christ, as perfect archetype, and the human soul as his flawed image. Thus, understanding the metaphor-word *conversion* presupposed the inversion of values that the Apostle Paul had constructed in his theology of the Cross: what was to the world pain was to believers pleasure; the world's ignorance was God's wisdom; its degradation, his honor; its servitude, his freedom; its weakness, his power; its death, his life. Irony became the dominant trope for understanding conversion and its subversive effects.

Reflections on conscience underscored this irony. For, given the hiddenness and incommunicability of conscience, the spiritual condition of the soul was hidden even to the soul itself. The soul's capacity for self-deception meant that the great need of conscience was for purity, which could only be proportionate, and not for certitude, which could at least pretend to be absolute. And yet, meditations on conscience produced a method of association by likeness, contiguity, and contrast that was intended to guide the soul in its venture of self-knowledge but that also lacked the power to convince others.

The mystery of empathetic conversion demanded conflict in the enactment of myth. As always, myth made sense of history. Myth was the context that gave meaning to what was known as conversion, the game in which what might have been random events became recognizable as ritualized play. Authentic "believing in" was put to the test and certified by endurance and scorn for hardship. Rather than demanding clarity and simplicity, scholars accepted the mythic character of their doctrines, types, and shadows of reality. They delighted in fictive paradox and enigma, such as they found by unlocking the spiritual meaning hidden in the words of Scripture. They contended that there was great profit in exercising the mind with difficulty and obscurity; much could be discovered, and the ardor of love was stirred up by adversities that delayed achieving its object. Understanding conversion was itself a form of play: conflict. But this paradigm of perfection through struggle embraced beauty (*pulchritudo*) as a cognitive principle. Directed and ritualized by a male esthetic, enacting the mystery of conversion demanded valor and beauty, a *cultus sui* veined, to be sure, with acknowledgment and fear of one's own weakness.

I began with the idea of conversion as a transit to happiness. All lines of inquiry led to the mythic context of a *cultus sui* crowned by an ideal of nobility infused in its spiritual as well as in its secular form by hierarchic ideas of proportion, degree, and precedence. Roman imperial imagery, preserved in that great living remnant of late Antiquity, the Church, was combined with language and symbolism from the world of chivalry. "Conversion" was a metaphor for a process of sanctification, represented as ennoblement, for each according to a rank assigned by grace. Irony was the fundamental mode of understanding, but the keystone of that structure was the irony of noble humility in the divine condescension by which the Word became flesh.

At this point, opposites coincided: the opposites of necessity and freedom. The condescension of Christ, mingling the imperative of atonement with divine freedom, pervaded and explained that other basic contradiction: the imperative of conversion for salvation and the impossibility of achieving salvation by human effort. The irony of Christ's voluntary sacrifice so resolved that of the terrifying human predicament as to enjoin continual criticism.

For understanding this mystery, correspondence was fundamental between the ironies that shaped understanding and the ironies of art, including those of appearance and reality and the similarity of dissimilars. Thus, in its obscure proportionalities (including that between subject and image), art not only supplied the central metaphor of empathetic conversion but also became one area in which understanding ritualized itself in play, in which the mind re-created, represented, and explained to itself the metaphorical ironies of conversion. And this was appropriate. For while nobility and beauty are principles of order, what fascinated the culture with which I have been concerned was their power, in sublime manifestations, to bring about shattering disorientation and renewal of the feelings. The fulcrum of this disorientation was the discrepancy between the moral orders of worth and value.

Summary 191

It was significant that the hermeneutic project began in and was described in metaphors of art. For the core of understanding could not be grasped directly, and those who sought to reach it knew that they could generally define only the space where it was, rather than what it was. Like paintings, metaphors were studies in the proportionate, fictive likeness of things that were essentially dissimilar. Thus, reasoning through metaphor, the art of discerning similarities in dissimilars, they accepted approximation and creative misunderstanding as both the cost and the means of their search. They recognized their doctrines as fictions, their broadest conceptions as myth; and they incorporated the elusive ironies of art into their analytical methods. They knew that interpretation always falsifies.

However, they also knew that their creative misunderstanding had limits given them by tradition. Just as spiritual gifts, charismata, including those of understanding, were given individuals for the edification of the community, so, correspondingly, were boundaries of imagination set by collective wisdom. Comparing the ideal of the Lord of Courtesy that they constructed with the scriptural bases of their reasoning shows how luxuriantly free the imagination was from literalism. Yet the magnitude of the freedom with which materials provided by tradition were reworked was as hidden from those who recast it as it was from the Thais, in this century, who venerated a statue of Queen Victoria as a fertility goddess, making offerings of flowers and incense to it, and even insisting that the protective casing erected in time of war be opened so that the eyes of the image could still fall upon its devotees.[1] How community was understood and by whom it was authoritatively understood went far toward determining the social function of understanding itself.

In the era under review, community was determined by need. Thus, Wido of Ferrara pointed out that no individual person could know all things but that all knowledge was possessed by the human race as a whole. A person could be a skilled craftsman without being able to read or knowing how to use figures of speech. Likewise, some gifted readers had no idea of how to use a die and mallet. Those who sang well could be ignorant of what was being sung. One could read without understanding or understand without the ability to read. Cicero was right, Wido concluded, in teaching that nature knit human lives together by distributing reciprocal needs and strengths so that each needed what others provided.[2] The idea of conversion raised this principle to a higher level. Employing the metaphor of organic unity in the body of Christ, it taught that each member depended upon the others in such fashion that, as Augustine concluded, what one possessed belonged to all.[3]

Discussion of conversion as a transition of ennoblement demonstrates that satisfaction of the empathetic needs for life, love, purity, and truth required something further. There were aspirations for exaltation of spirit—for power as ennoblement—that would break through the barriers of need and the finitudes of all that could satisfy need. Hunger for the sublime led to a quest for amazement of the imagination as well as for dazzlement of the reason, such that one could enter into the dark, sanctifying abyss of celestial light.

Fictive understanding—or creative misunderstanding—of the metaphor "conversion" moved on two levels, both characterized by ritualizations of communal play. The easier to grasp is certainly the latter, which came after the moment of enlightenment. Then, as Dante's comments on his memory of heavenly visions indicate, the fresh vigor of direct perception failed and became increasingly distant and elusive. What had been experienced as a whole was dissected into parts. Certitude dissolved into indeterminacy. One entered into the play of reconstituting in fiction what had happened in fact. The ritualized use of metaphor and myth belonged to the poetics of conversion, enacted in the *cultus sui*, conceived as a process by which the soul was progressively made more beautiful, more worthy of its Bridegroom.

For this reason, empathetic conversion is linked with the methods and objectives of education and, from some formal perspectives, is indistinguishable from them. In fact, all that I have said resolves into a diagram of a vast educational program, including the concept of conversion as a ritualized, formative process, the physical and mental disciplines of monasticism, techniques for the moral formation of conscience, assimilation of social myth, and the pedagogical functions of art. But the ambivalences of natural and supernatural that I have found in every facet of this schema, menacing as they may be in their paradoxes of subversive renewal, are not readily transferable to other cultures.

The more difficult level of creative misunderstanding was the moment of enlightenment itself, when all its aspects were perceived directly as a whole. Augustine identified the instant of understanding as a tossing back and forth, like the ball games that engaged his boyhood ardor no more enduring than a flash of lightening.[4] Rilke (1875–1926), too, on different grounds, represented our conscious existence as a ball game of the gods, a play of lights flashing from mirror to mirror. This, of course, is the true moment of apprehension, and thus of understanding; all that follows is fictive remembrance. Understanding is the playing in the play. Dante captured this as he contrasted the effaced memory of enlightenment that he retained with the ecstatic self-forgetting in "the flash of understanding" when, encompassed by the "smile of all creation," he, too, was turned in joy by "the love that moves the sun and the other stars."[6]

Referring to linguistic meter, ancient grammarians called accent "the soul of words." Meanings, too, ensouled words, sometimes in ways that are hard to recover after the lapse of centuries. For us, texts and the visual arts provide access to the hermeneutic "soul" of the word *conversion*. We cannot hear the music of the twelfth century with equal immediacy. And yet, for men and women in the era with which I have been preoccupied, music was at least as sure an access as words. True to pre-Christian philosophy, they believed that the individual heart moved to the same rhythms as the spheres of heaven, since all had been framed to one harmony by the Creator's will. The wise were so because they apprehended and participated in that divine wisdom.

For numerous reasons, music became an essential part of Christian worship, not least because it was thought to provide a stepping-stone from the material beauties and transient nobility of this world to the archetypal beauty of God's everlasting courts. With the intensity of prayer, its ritualization of play lifted the mind from sensory to heavenly things. As a contemplative discipline, music was developed to train the soul, refreshing it with sweet delights that savored of heaven, and purifying it for the charismata of the Holy Spirit. Music could be ecstatic spirituality in action, as numerous biographies of saints witness when they represent angelic singers preceding or attending divine visitations.

In general, music was performed collectively, in community. In convents and monasteries, ascetics spent their lives in psalmody, a kind of song which made the cult of God a most inward part of the *cultus sui* that assisted empathetic conversion and advanced it toward its final consummation. Yet, in this ritualized choral play of beauty, some distinctions that I observed regarding the visual and verbal arts also appeared. Although a practiced psalmodist, Christina of Markyate did not sing with the monks of St. Albans but watched their choir at a distance. Hildegard of Bingen asserted that while she chanted and wrote plainsong for her community, she had not been taught by human means. Some, ignorant of music, sang out of greed; such were street entertainers, mimes, actors, and others who were poor. Following nature rather than art (which had to be learned), these illiterates—in fact, any mere vocalists—were like a drunkard groping through the night, having not the slightest idea which lane led home. The dominance of a literate, male, military aristocracy also showed its hand in music as a tool and analogue of conversion. (As Edmund of Abingdon's career has illustrated, some members of lower social orders learned the arts of aristocratic culture by leaving the class into which they were born and entering the clergy or submitting to monastic discipline. I recall a modern analogue of class privilege: untouchables in India had access to formal musical education only through the schools of Christian missionaries.)[7]

It was characteristic of these ideas that for the community of those who converted to truth, the veils of understanding through likenesses, including those of metaphoric dissimilar similitudes, would eventually fall away, and there would be no lapse from the beauties of direct vision, no such failure of memory as Dante reported following his spiritual exaltation, no decline from harmony into silence. The paradigms of conversion in nature and by supernatural grace were drawn to this point where the metaphor of conversion was exhausted. The disparity between esthetics and poetics ceased. Restored and redeemed, souls were snatched up "above similitude" into God. Theodical perplexities would then be swept away, for the converted had won the ritualized game of love and been subsumed into the everlasting harmony of love's inmost play. There they joined Christ, crucified and glorified, the leader of the dance of the blessed, the cantor and precentor of heaven, singing "with his glorious sweet voice an endless canticle of the praise and honor of his heavenly Father." Where were the afflictions of the good and the rejoicings of the evil then? For the art and science of Christ's singing was the Holy Spirit. The song was faithfulness, humility, and eternal love. The serried chorus with him were those who, loving God and neighbor, imitated him in noble humility and, "according to the greatness and multiplicity of [their] toils, torments, and sufferings," were converted into one with the Being who was inexhaustible life, love, truth, and goodness.[8]

ABBREVIATIONS

NOTES

INDEX

Abbreviations

Migne	J. P. Migne, *Patrologiae Cursus Completus*
PG	*series graeca*
PL	*series latina*
MGH	*Monumenta Germaniae Historica*
Conc.	*Concilia Aevi Karolini*
Conc. Suppl.	*Concilia, Supplementum*
Ldl	*Libelli de Lite*
MGHSSrrG	*Scriptores Rerum Germanicarum in Usum Scholarum*
SS	*Scriptores*

Notes

Preface

1. Rosalie Green et al., eds., *Herrad of Hohenbourg: Hortus Deliciarum*, 2 vols., Studies of the Warburg Institute, 36 (London: Warburg Institute, 1979), 1:187, 2:316 (illus. no. 248).

2. The six acts are foreknowledge, predestination, conformation with the image of the Son, vocation, justification, and glorification. The illumination is called the "conversion of Apostle Paul" in the edition cited above, n. 1, and the "conversion de Saint Paul" in A. Straub and G. Keller, eds., *Herrade de Landsberg: Hortus Deliciarum* (Strasbourg: Schlesier & Schweikhardt, 1901), second supplement, 6. On the exegetical tradition (from Augustine of Hippo to the ninth century) figuralizing Paul's change of heart as the transformation of a wolf into a lamb, see Herbert L. Kessler, "An Apostle in Armor and the Mission of Carolingian Art," *Arte medievale*, 2d ser., 4 (1990): 30. The representation of Saul transformed from wolf into lamb occurs in Hermannus quondam Judaeus, *Opusculum de Conversione Sua*, chap. 2 (*MGH, Quellen zur Geistesgeschichte des Mittelalters* 4:75).

3. Athanasius of Alexandria, *On the Incarnation of the Word of God and His Manifestation to Us through the Body*, chap. 14 (trans. Robert W. Thomson [Oxford: Clarendon, 1971], 167–69 [adapted]).

4. Bernard of Clairvaux, *Sermo in Conversione Sancti Pauli*, chap. 2 (Jean Leclercq and Henri Rochais, eds., *Sermones*, S. Bernardi Opera, 6, 1 [Rome: Editiones Cistercienses, 1970], 3:29). But see also Bernard's caution against the empty "form of conversion" followed by hypocrites who kept bodily disciplines without an authentic change of heart (*Sermo in Quadragesima*, 2.2 [Jean Leclercq and Henri Rochais, eds., *Sermones*, S. Bernardi Opera, 4 (Rome: Editiones Cistercienses, 1966), 1:360]).

5. Martin Luther, "Predigt von der Bekehrung S. Pauli wider die Mönchen (26. Januar, 1546)," *Luthers Werke* 51 (Weimar: Böhlaus Nachfolger, 1914): 135–48. For

comparative purposes, see also John Henry Newman, "Sermon 15: Sudden Conversions," *Parochial and Plain Sermons* 8 (London: Longmans, Green, 1908): 224–29.

6. Dorothy L. Sayers, *The Lost Tools of Learning* (London: Methuen, 1948).

Chapter 1. *Posing the Question: Perspectives from a Historian's Desk*

1. Snorre Sturlason, *Heimskringla, or The Lives of the Norse Kings*, chaps. 61, 91, 108 (ed. and trans. Erling Monsen and A. H. Smith [New York: Dover, 1990], 165, 184, 204). Snorre provides a subplot. Tyri, daughter of the Christian king Harald of Denmark, was betrothed to Borislav, king of the Wends. She found the prospect of marriage to "a heathen old man" repugnant. But eventually the union was consummated by force, and so much against Tyri's will that she refused to accept food and drink from the pagans whose queen she had become. Soon she escaped to King Olav Tryggvessön's court. Their marriage followed. However, by abandoning her pagan husband, Tyri had lost control of her dower lands, which Olav died attempting to regain (ibid., chap. 92 [p. 184]).

2. For a definition of conversion as "un changement d'ordre mental" that can produce either a change of opinion or a complete alteration of personality, see Pierre Hadot, "Conversion," in Hadot, *Exercises spirituels et philosophie antique* (Paris: Etudes Augustiniennes, 1981), 175. Hadot also provides schematic discussions of the idea of conversion in ancient philosophy, in Old Testamental Judaism and early Christianity (Clement of Alexandria), and in modern psychophysiological, sociological, religious, and philosophical thought. I am obliged to Professor Peter Brown for referring me to Hadot's studies.

3. *Jesu, dulcis memoria*, trans. J. M. Neale (modified), in Percy Dearmer, Ralph Vaughan Williams, and Martin Shaw, eds., *Songs of Praise*, enlarged ed. (London: Oxford Univ. Press, 1931), nr 548, p. 659. The text is printed in André Wilmart, *Le "Jubilus" dit de Saint Bernard (Etude avec textes)* (Rome: Storia e Letteratura, 1944), 183–84: "Iesu dulcis memoria/Dans vera cordi gaudia . . . / Nec lingua ualet dicere, / Nec littera exprimere, / Expertus potest credere, / Quid Iesum diligere." On the incommunicability of conversion in a wide historiographical context, see Gavin I. Langmuir, *History, Religion, and Antisemitism* (Berkeley: Univ. of California Press, 1990), 194–95. However, Langmuir here considers the conversions of the Apostle Paul and Augustine of Hippo as instantaneous events, rather than as gradual processes.

4. Arthur Darby Nock, *Conversion: The Old and the New in Religion from Alexander the Great to Augustine of Hippo* (New York: Oxford Univ. Press, 1933).

5. G. A. Oddie, ed., *Religion in South Asia: Religious Conversion and Revival Movements in South Asia in Medieval and Modern Times* (London: Curzon, 1977), introduction, p. 5.

6. Brock Kilbourne and James T. Richardson, "Paradigm Conflict, Types of Conversion, and Conversion Theories," *Sociological Analysis* 50 (1988): 1–21. Professor Richard Ring kindly brought this study to my attention.

7. E.g., S. A. A. Rizvi, "Islamic Proselytisation (Seventh to Sixteenth Centuries)," in Oddie, *Religion in South Asia*, 14.

8. Richard W. Bulliet, *Conversion to Islam in the Medieval Period: An Essay in Quantitative History* (Cambridge: Harvard Univ. Press, 1979), 1, 4, 39, 59, 138.

9. Ibid., 128–29.

10. Bernard of Clairvaux, *Sermo ad Clericos de Conversione*, 19.32–33, 20.34, 36 (Jean Leclercq and Henri Rochais, eds., *Sermones*, S. Bernardi Opera, 4 [Rome: Editiones Cistercienses, 1966], 1:109–13; Guerric of Igny, *The Fourth Sermon for the Epiphany*, chap. 2 (John Morson and Hilary Costello, eds., *Sermones*, Sources chrétiennes, 166 [Paris: Cerf, 1970], 1:288–92). See my essay, "The Church as Play: Gerhoch of Reichersberg's Call for Reform," James Ross Sweeney and Stanley Chodorow, eds., *Popes, Teachers, and Canon Law in the Middle Ages: Essays in Honor of Brian Tierney* (Ithaca, N.Y.: Cornell Univ. Press, 1989), 114–44.

11. See Augustine, *De Baptismo*, 4.25.32 (Migne *PL* 43:176): "Neque enim ullo modo dicenda est conversio cordis ad Deum, cum Dei sacramentum contemnitur." Caesarius of Heisterbach, *Dialogus Miraculorum*, 1.2, wrote that the heart's conversion was "to God" (*ad Deum*) (Joseph Strange, ed., *Caesarii Heisterbacensis Monachi Ordinis Cisterciensis Dialogus Miraculorum* 1 [Cologne: Heberle, 1851]: 8). Peter the Venerable, abbot of Cluny, ridiculed the Jews for retaining the stony hearts that prevented conversion "to Christ" (*ad Christum*) and full humanity. *Petri Venerabilis adversus Iudeorum Inveteratam Duritiem*, chap. 3 [*Corpus Christianorum, continuatio medievalis* 58:58]: "Nescio, inquam, utrum [Iudaeus] homo sit, de cuius carne nondum cor lapideum ablatum est, cui nondum datum est cor carneum in cuius medio nondum positus est divinus spiritus, sine quo ad Christum nunquam potest converti Iudaeus." On Abelard, see below, chapter 4, n. 42. See also Anon., *The Life of Christina of Markyate, a Twelfth Century Recluse*, chap. 17 (ed. and trans. C. H. Talbot [Oxford: Clarendon, 1959], 62). Cf. Bernhard Citron, *New Birth: A Study of the Evangelical Doctrine of Conversion in the Protestant Fathers* (Edinburgh: Univ. Press, 1951), 30: "There is no such thing as conversion to Christianity, but only conversion to Christ."

12. For example, Langmuir, *History, Religion, and Antisemitism*, 3–17, 51–57. Langmuir judges that "what historians produce as history is a selective series of related verbal associations about some aspects of some past actions," all determined by the historians' own preoccupations and vocabularies.

13. Jaroslav Pelikan, *The Growth of Medieval Theology (600–1300)*, vol. 3 of *The Christian Tradition: A History of the Development of Doctrine* (Chicago: Univ. of Chicago Press, 1978), 246; Valerie I. J. Flint, "Anti-Jewish Literature and Attitudes in the Twelfth-Century," *Journal of Jewish Studies* 37 (1986): 187; Jeremy Cohen, "The Mentality of the Medieval Jewish Apostate: Peter Alfonsi, Hermann of Cologne, and Pablo Christiani," in Todd M. Endelman, ed., *Jewish Apostasy in the Modern World* (New York: Homes and Meier, 1987), 32 (Professor Robert Lerner kindly drew my attention to Cohen's article); David Berger, "Christian Heresy and Jewish Polemic in the Twelfth and Thirteenth Centuries," *Harvard Theological Review* 68 (1975): 298. See also the ex-

change of articles by Berger and Cohen in *American Historical Review* 91 (1986): David Berger, "Mission to the Jews and Jewish-Christian Contacts in the Polemical Literature of the High Middle Ages," 576–91; Jeremy Cohen, "Scholarship and Intolerance in the Medieval Academy: The Study and Evaluation of Judaism in European Christendom," 592–613, with a judicious commentary by Gavin I. Langmuir, 614–24.

14. Caroline Walker Bynum, "Did the Twelfth Century Discover the Individual?" *Journal of Ecclesiastical History* 31 (1980): 3, 5, 16–17.

15. M.-D. Chenu, *L'Eveil de la conscience dans la civilisation médiévale*, Conférance Albert-le-Grand, 1969 (Montreal: Institut des Etudes Médiévales, 1969), 13. See also Gerhart B. Ladner, "Aspects of Patristic Anti-Judaism," *Viator* 2 (1971): 362: "Even Saint Augustine did not for a moment consider that the Jews might be justified by their subjective conscience in denying what to him was objective truth. Nor did he doubt that the Jews were collectively guilty for the death of Christ. This question of conscience began to be perceived in its whole magnitude only much later, perhaps from the age [of] Abelard onward."

16. These are Chenu's reasons in *L'Eveil de la conscience dans la civilisation médiévale*, 15, 24–25, 33, 42–45, 79.

17. Cf. Gerhoch of Reichersberg, *Tractatus in Psalmum 64*, chap. 145 (Migne PL 194:98).

18. Otto von Simson, *The Gothic Cathedral: Origins of Gothic Architecture and the Medieval Concept of Order*, Bollingen Series, 48 (New York: Pantheon, 1965), 105; Edgar de Bruyne, *Etudes d'esthétique médiévale* 2 (Bruges: De Tempel, 1946): 203. For an argument that Hugh of St. Victor's theology was predominately Augustinian, not Dionysian, see Conrad Rudolph, *Artistic Change at Saint-Denis: Abbot Suger's Program and the Early Twelfth-Century Controversy over Art* (Princeton, N.J.: Princeton Univ. Press, 1990), 50 (referring specifically to Hugh's *De Sacramentis*). Rudolph acknowledges that Augustinian and Dionysian systems of thought were compatible because of their common Neoplatonism and that they were sometimes inextricably mingled in twelfth-century thinking (ibid., 48). Grover A. Zinn presents an argument for Hugh's Dionysianism in "Suger, Theology, and the Pseudo-Dionysian Tradition," in Paula Lieber Gerson, ed., *Abbot Suger and Saint-Denis: A Symposium* (New York: Metropolitan Museum of Art, 1986), 33–40, reinforcing earlier conclusions of Erwin Panofsky and Otto von Simson.

19. Augustine, *City of God*, 22.7 (*Corpus Christianorum, series latina* 48:815).

20. On this very complex period in Church history, see Allan Fitzgerald, *Conversion through Penance in the Italian Church of the Fourth and Fifth Centuries: New Approaches to the Experience of Conversion from Sin*, Studies in the Bible and Early Christianity, 15 (Lewiston, N.Y.: Edwin Mellen, 1988).

21. For one monk's contented impression that the proud and mighty of the world were giving up their pomp and martial ways and surrendering to lives of monastic humility and withdrawal, see Gilbert Crispin, *Disputatio Iudei et Christiani*, chap. 60 (Anna Sapir Abulafia and G. R. Evans, eds., *The Works of Gilbert Crispin, Abbot of Westminster*, Auctores Britannici Medii Aevi, 8 [London: Oxford Univ. Press, 1986], 22).

22. See James Thayer Addison, *The Medieval Missionary: A Study of the Conversion of Northern Europe, A.D. 500–1300*, Studies in the World Mission of Christianity, 2 (New York: International Missionary Council, 1936), esp. pp. 75–105.

23. My typology of conversions is drawn chiefly from the fundamental study by Gerhart B. Ladner, *The Idea of Reform: Its Impact on Christian Thought and Action in the Age of the Fathers*, rev. ed. (New York: Harper, 1967). However, in gathering the types into a repertory which composed an ensemble *imitatio Christi*, I cannot claim to follow Ladner.

24. On the Stoic assignment of new meanings to Aristotelian terms in its key doctrine of assent, see Harry Austryn Wolfson, *The Philosophy of the Church Fathers*, vol. 1, 3d ed. (Cambridge: Harvard Univ. Press, 1970): 117–18. See also Marcia L. Colish, *The Stoic Tradition from Antiquity to the Early Middle Ages*, Studies in the History of Christian Thought, 34 (Leiden: Brill, 1985), 1:139–40.

25. M. H. Abrams, *Natural Supernaturalism: Tradition and Revolution in Romantic Literature* (New York: Norton, 1971), 96, 113–14.

26. Ibid., 136.

27. See below, chapter 2, after n. 16.

28. See chapter 1 ("Augustine of Hippo's *Confessions*") in Karl F. Morrison, *Conversion and Text: The Cases of Augustine of Hippo, Herman-Judah, and Constantine Tsatsos* (Charlottesville: Univ. Press of Virginia, forthcoming).

29. See ibid., preface at n. 1.

30. Abrams, *Natural Supernaturalism*, 168.

31. Wilfrid Ward, *Last Lectures by Wilfrid Ward* (London: Longmans, 1918), 22; see also 4–5.

32. John Dryden, "The Hind and the Panther," pt. 1, ll. 122–27 (John Sargeaunt, ed., *The Poems of John Dryden* [London: Oxford Univ. Press, 1959], 119).

Chapter 2.   *Posing the Problem: Perspectives from a Lector's Ambo*

1. Baldassare Castiglione, *The Book of the Courtier*, bk. 1 (trans. Thomas Hoby [London: Dent, 1928], 51).

2. Guerric of Igny, *First Sermon for the Epiphany*, chap. 2 (John Morson and Hilary Costello, eds., *Sermones*, Sources chrétiennes, 166 [Paris: Cerf, 1970], 1:242). See also Hugh of St. Victor, *De Arha Noe Morali*, 3.6 (Migne PL 176:651–54).

3. Bernard of Clairvaux, *Sermo ad Clericos de Conversione*, 1.1 (Jean Leclercq and Henri Rochais, eds., *Sermones*, S. Bernardi Opera, 4 [Rome: Editiones Cistercienses, 1966], 1:70).

4. See Anon., *Treatise on the Spirit and the Soul*, prologue (Bernard McGinn, ed., *Three Treatises on Man: A Cistercian Anthropology*, Cistercian Fathers Series, 24 [Kalamazoo, Mich.: Cistercian Publications, 1977], 181); Richard of St. Victor, *The Twelve Patriarchs*, chaps. 71, 75 (Grover A. Zinn, trans., *Richard of St. Victor: The Twelve Patriarchs, The Mystical Ark, Book Three of the Trinity* [New York: Paulist Press, 1979], 129,

133). The history of the Delphic command "Know thyself" in Western culture has still to be written. On classical Antiquity and the era of the early Church, see Eliza Gregory Wilkins, *"Know Thyself" in Greek and Latin Literature*, Dissertation, Department of Greek (Chicago: Univ. of Chicago Libraries, 1917). On the ancient and medieval periods, with especially full consideration of twelfth-century texts, see Pierre Courcelle, *Connais-toi toi-même de Socrate à saint Bernard*, 3 vols. (Paris: Etudes Augustiniennes, 1974–75).

5. Gilbert Crispin, *Disputatio Iudaei et Christiani*, chaps. 37, 76 (Anna Sapir Abulafia and G. R. Evans, eds., *The Works of Gilbert Crispin, Abbot of Westminster*, Auctores Britannici Medii Aevi, 8 [London: Oxford Univ. Press, 1986], 16, 26), the explanation by a Jew why he could not "believe in" Christ.

6. Hugh of St. Victor, *Quaestiones in Epistolas Pauli: In Epist. ad Rom.*, quaest. 32 (Migne PL 175:438–39); Peter Lombard, *Collectanea in Epist. D. Pauli: In Epist. ad Rom.* (Migne PL 191:1324). For the striking and, I judge, correct translation of *credere in* as "believe into," or "enter into," see Edith Stein, *The Science of the Cross: A Study of St. John of the Cross*, trans. Hilda Graef (London: Burns & Oates, 1960), 180. Cf. William of St. Thierry, *Speculum Fidei*, chap. 43 (M.-M. Davy, ed., *Deux Traités sur la Foi: Le mirroir de la foi; L'énigme de la foi* [Paris: Vrin, 1959], 60): "Credere enim in eum, amando in eum ire est."

7. William of St. Thierry, *Expositio in Epist. ad Rom.*, 1.17 (Migne PL 180:557).

8. Caesarius of Heisterbach, *Dialogus Miraculorum*, 1.2 (Joseph Strange, ed., *Caesarii Heisterbacensis Monachi Ordinis Cisterciensis Dialogus Miraculorum* [Cologne: Heberle, 1851], 1:8).

9. See above, chapter 1, n. 11.

10. Paschasius Radbertus, as cited in Karl F. Morrison, *The Mimetic Tradition of Reform in the West* (Princeton, N.J.: Princeton Univ. Press, 1982), 123.

11. See Karl F. Morrison, *Conversion and Text: The Cases of Augustine of Hippo, Herman-Judah, and Constantine Tsatsos* (Univ. Press of Virginia, forthcoming).

12. Hugh of St. Victor, *Soliloquium de Arha Animae* (Migne PL 176:970) and *De Arca Noe Morali* 4.4 (Migne PL 176:670).

13. On Thomas Aquinas's doctrines concerning the necessity of grace for conversion (disposing the will to conversion), see Henri Bouillard, *Conversion et grace chez S. Thomas d'Aquin: Etude historique* (Paris: Aubier, 1944), esp. pp. 41, 46–47.

14. Thomas Shepard, *The Sincere Convert* (London: T. P. and M. S., 1643), 266. I am obliged to Ms. Renée S. House for the observation on the parable of the wise and foolish virgins.

15. Teresa of Avila, *The Life of Teresa of Jesus*, chap. 11 (E. Allison Peers, trans., *The Autobiography of St. Teresa of Avila* [Garden City, N.Y.: Image Books, 1960], 130).

16. Guerric of Igny, *Second Sermon for Lent*, 1–2, 4 (John Morson and Hilary Costello, eds., *Sermones*, Sources chrétiennes, 202 [Paris: Cerf, 1973], 2:26–30, 34–36).

17. C. N. L. Brooke, in W. J. Millor, H. E. Butler, and C. N. L. Brooke, eds., *The Letters of John of Salisbury* 1 (London: Nelson, 1955): 98 n. 5. Brooke notes that, while

the age excelled in forgery, it also developed methods of sifting false documents from genuine.

18. See Giles Constable, "Forged Letters in the Middle Ages," *MGH, Schriften*, vol. 33, pt. 5, pp. 22–23; František Graus, "Fälschungen im Gewand der Frömmigkeit," ibid., 265–66. I am grateful to Professor Charles Wood for the following information about Glastonbury.

19. Georg Scheibelreiter, "Die Verfälschung der Wirklichkeit: Hagiographie und Historizität," ibid., 286–87, 290.

20. Graus, "Fälschungen im Gewand der Frömmigkeit," 262.

21. Wolfgang Speyer, "Religiöse Betrüger: Fälsche göttliche Menschen und Heilige in Antike und Christentum," *MGH, Schriften*, vol. 22, pt. 5, p. 342.

22. J. M. Wallace-Hadrill, *Bede's Ecclesiastical History of the English People: A Historical Commentary* (Oxford: Clarendon, 1988), 72, on Coifi's speech in the *Ecclesiastical History*, 2.13 (Bertram Colgrave and R. A. B. Mynors, eds., *Bede's Ecclesiastical History of the English People* [Oxford: Clarendon, 1969], 182–84).

23. Bede, *Ecclesiastical History*, 1.30 (ed. Colgrave and Mynors, 106–8). See Wallace-Hadrill, *Bede's Ecclesiastical History of the English People*, 44–45. On pagan survivals in Rome, see Leo I, *Sermo 27 (In Nativitate Domini, 7)*, chap. 4 (Migne *PL* 54:218–19), and Boniface, *Letters 50, 51* (*MGH, Epistolae* 3, *Karolini Aevi* 1:301, 304–5).

24. Bede, *Ecclesiastical History*, 2.13 (ed. Colgrave and Mynors, 184). For a similar but geographically distant practice with Anglo-Saxon connections, see below, n. 27.

25. Herbord, *Dialogus de Vita S. Ottonis Episcopi Babenbergensis*, 3.16. (ed. Jan Wikarjak, Monumenta Poloniae Historica, n.s., vol. 7, fasc. 3 [Warsaw: Państwowe Wydawnictwo Naukowe, 1974], 176–77). See below, n. 28.

26. Bede, *Ecclesiastical History*, 2.15, 4.27 (ed. Colgrave and Mynors, 190, 432). In its regulations against what were considered aberrant local practices (including witchcraft), Burchard of Worm's (d. 1025) *Decretum* provides a notable example of how Germanic and Christian beliefs comfortably fused in the minds of some of his contemporaries.

27. Snorre Sturlason, *Heimskringla, or The Lives of the Norse Kings*, chap. 67 (ed. and trans. Erling Monsen and A. H. Smith [New York: Dover, 1990], 169). Olav recalled that "King Hacon, the foster-son of Athelstan" had, though a Christian, joined his chief men in sacrificing. In this context, he made his proposal of human sacrifice.

28. Hans Kuhn, "Das Fortleben des germanischen Heidentums nach der Christianisierung," in *La conversione al cristianesimo nell'Europa dell'alto medioevo* (Settimane di Studio del Centro Italiano di Studi sull'alto Medioevo) 14 (1966, published 1967): 754.

29. Bruno of Merseburg, *Liber de Bello Saxonico*, chap. 36 (*MGH, Deutsches Mittelalter* 2:38).

30. *New York Times*, 26 June 1986.

31. Ibid., 1 May and 15 Aug. 1989.

32. Anon., *The Life of Christina of Markyate, a Twelfth Century Recluse*, chap. 23

(ed. and trans. C. H. Talbot [Oxford: Clarendon, 1959], 74); Adam of Bremen, *Gesta Hammaburgensis Ecclesiae Pontificum*, 3.39 (38), 47 (46), 55 (54), 64 (63) (*MGHSSrrG*, 182, 191, 200, 210).

33. Honorius Augustodunensis, *Gemma Animae*, 1.139 (Migne *PL* 172:587–88).

34. Tertullian, *De Carne Christi*, chap. 5.

35. Hugh of St. Victor, *Quaestiones in Epistolas Pauli: In Epist. ad Rom.*, quaest. 229 (Migne *PL* 175:488).

36. *Petri Venerabilis adversus Iudeorum Inveteratam Duritiem*, prol., and chaps. 2, 3, 5 (*Corpus Christianorum, continuatio medievalis* 58:1, 33, 43, 57–58, 134, 175).

37. Ibid., chap. 4 (pp. 111–14).

38. Geoffrey Chaucer, *Canterbury Tales*, "The Miller's Tale," ll. 194–95.

39. On the ninth-century prohibition, see Agobard of Lyons, *ep.* 6 (*MGH, Epistolae* 5, *Karolini Aevi* 3:180). No friend to Jews, especially those of his own diocese, Agobard wrote that he could scarcely believe that a judgment "so contrary to ecclesiastical rule" could have gone forth from the face of the "most Christian and most pious emperor." Benjamin Z. Kedar, *Crusade and Mission: European Approaches toward the Muslims* (Princeton, N.J.: Princeton Univ. Press, 1984), 24–25, 35, 48, 51, 53, 77, 82–85; Eadmer, *The Life of St. Anselm, Archbishop of Canterbury*, chap. 33 (ed. R. W. Southern [Oxford: Clarendon, 1972], 111–12): James Thayer Addison, *The Medieval Missionary: A Study of the Conversion of Northern Europe, A.D. 500–1300*, Studies in the World Mission of Christianity, 2 (New York: International Missionary Council, 1936), 137. The established proposition that infidels were, in some sense, brute animals suggests an analogy with the attitude of Shah Wali Allah (1703–1762), in India, "whom many scholars consider to have been the pioneer of Islamic modernism, [but who] regarded the infidel [Hindu] cultivators as animals who were allowed to survive in order to produce food and pay *jizya* (poll tax)" (S. A. A. Rizvi, "Islamic Proselytisation (Seventh to Sixteenth Centuries)," in G. A. Oddie, ed., *Religion in South Asia: Religious Conversion and Revival Movements in South Asia in Medieval and Modern Times* [London: Curzon, 1977], 20).

40. Thomas Aquinas, *Summa Theologiae*, Ia.q.1.a.9.r.2 (Robert Busa, ed., *S. Thomae Aquinatis Opera Omnia* 2 [Stuttgart: Fromman-Holzbog, 1980]: 186).

41. Kedar, *Crusade and Mission*, 17, 126; Hincmar of Rheims, *LV Capitula*, chap. 55 (Migne *PL* 126:499).

42. Athanasius of Alexandria, *Vita Antonii*, chap. 10 (Migne *PG* 26:860); *The Sayings of the Desert Fathers: The Alphabetical Collection*, Anthony the Great, nr 5 (trans. Benedicta Ward, Cistercian Studies, 59 [Kalamazoo: Cistercian Publications, 1975], 2).

43. Cf. Bernard of Clairvaux, *Sermo in Quadragesima* 3, 1, 4 (Leclercq and Rochais, *Sermones* 1:364–65, 367).

44. Guigo II, *The Ladder of Monks*, chaps. 10–12 (Edmund Colledge and James Walsh, eds., *Lettre sur la vie contemplative*, Sources chrétiennes, 163 [Paris: Cerf, 1970], 102–6).

45. Guerric of Igny, *The First Sermon for the Epiphany*, 2–3 (ed. Morson and Costello, *Sermones* 1:240–46).

46. Hermannus quondam Judaeus, *Opusculum de Conversione Sua*, chap. 21 (*MGH, Quellen zur Geistesgeschichte des Mittelalters* 4:126); Gerhoch of Reichersberg, *Tractatus in Ps. 118*, 63, Heth (Migne *PL* 194:773). Both authors allude to Ecclesiastes 9:1.

47. E.g., Guerric of Igny, *The Second Sermon for Advent*, chap. 4 (Morson and Costello, *Sermones* 1:114).

48. Guigo II, *The Ladder of Monks*, chap. 8 (Colledge and Walsh, *Lettre sur la vie contemplative*, 96–100).

49. Bernard of Clairvaux, *Sermo ad Clericos de Conversione*, 1.2 (Leclercq and Rochais, *Sermones* 1:71).

50. Rupert of Deutz, *Commentum in Apocalypsim*, 1.1 (Migne *PL* 169:851).

51. Guerric of Igny, *The Second Sermon for Lent*, chap. 3 (Morson and Costello, *Sermones* 2:32).

52. Professor Avrom Saltman has argued that though composed in the twelfth century, this text was not written by a Jewish convert ("Hermann's *Opusculum de Conversione Sua*: Truth or Fiction?" *Revue des Etudes juives* 147 [1988]: 31–56). From a different viewpoint, I, too, am arguing for the fictional character of the text, and indeed of all conversion accounts. My reasons for accepting the usual attribution to Herman-Judah are stated in the companion work to this volume, *Conversion and Text*; an English translation of Herman-Judah's *Account* appears among the case studies. Professor William C. Jordan kindly directed me to Professor Saltman's article. On occupations open to Jews that permitted social transactions with Christians, see William Chester Jordan, *The French Monarchy and the Jews: From Philip Augustus to the Last Capetians* (Philadelphia: Univ. of Pennsylvania Press, 1989), 23–30; on Jewish aversion to Latin as the language of hostile ruling classes, ibid., 15; on the extreme difficulty of determining actual circumstances of Jewish life from one feudal domain to another, ibid., 4–37. Mr. David Nirenberg brought to my attention the argument by Professor Sander L. Gilman that the *Opusculum* could only have been written by a person in whom Jewish patterns of thought had been deeply ingrained. See Sander L. Gilman, *Jewish Self-Hatred: Anti-Semitism and the Hidden Language of the Jews* (Baltimore: Johns Hopkins Univ. Press, 1986), 29–32. The entire second chapter in Gilman's book is entitled "The Drive for Conversion" (pp. 22–67) and covers the period from the thirteenth to the sixteenth century.

53. Anon., *The Life of Christina of Markyate*, chaps. 1, 13 (ed. Talbot, 34, 56).

54. Caroline Walker Bynum, "Women's Stories, Women's Symbols: A Critique of Victor Turner's Theory of Liminality," in Frank E. Reynolds and Robert L. Moore, eds., *Anthropology and the Study of Religion* (Chicago: Center for the Scientific Study of Religion, 1984), 105–25; Bynum, "'. . . And Woman His Humanity': Female Imagery in the Religious Writing of the Later Middle Ages," in Bynum, Stevan Harrel, and Paula Richman, eds., *Gender and Religion: On the Complexity of Symbols* (Boston: Beacon, 1986), 277–78.

55. On this expectation, see Scheibelreiter, "Die Verfälschung der Wirklichkeit: Hagiographie und Historizität," 282–319.

56. See below, chapter 3, n. 7.

57. Anon., *The Life of Christina of Markyate*, chaps. 16–17, 34, 37, 82 (ed. Talbot, 60–62, 92, 98, 188).

58. See the *Chronicle of Solomon bar Simson*, in Shlomo Eidelberg, trans. and ed., *The Jews and the Crusaders: The Hebrew Chronicles of the First and Second Crusades* (Madison: Univ. of Wisconsin Press, 1977), 46–53.

59. Anon., *The Life of Christina of Markyate*, chaps. 3, 4 (ed. Talbot, 36, 38).

60. Ibid., chaps. 4, 13 (pp. 40, 56).

61. Ibid., chap. 4 (p. 40).

62. Ibid., chaps. 45, 73 (pp. 118, 168).

63. Ibid., chaps. 54, 78 (pp. 132, 178).

64. E.g., ibid., chaps. 3, 46–47, 48–50, 55, 59, 61, 77 (pp. 38, 120–24, 126, 134, 142, 144, 174).

65. Mary Stroll, *The Jewish Pope: Ideology and Politics in the Papal Schism of 1130*, Brill's Studies in Intellectual History, 8 (Leiden: Brill, 1987), 98, 166.

66. Herbord, *Dialogus de Vita S. Ottonis Episcopi Babenbergensis*, 2.26 (ed. Wikarjak, 112).

67. Anon., *The Sayings of the Desert Fathers*, Omicron, Olympios nr 1, (trans. Ward, 135).

68. The argument "that Christianity grew out of the former pagan creeds and is in its general outlook and origins continuous and of one piece with them" has often been made. See Edward Carpenter, *Pagan and Christian Creeds: Their Origin and Meaning* (New York: Harcourt, Brace, 1921), 163. For arguments to the contrary, which I find cogent, see Paul Aubin, *Le problème de la "conversion,"* Théologie historique, n.s., 1 (Paris: Beauchesne et ses fils, 1963), 5 (Jean Daniélou's summary), 187, 195 (among Christians, God labors for human conversion); Gustave Bardy, *La conversion au christianisme durant les premier siècles* (Paris: Aubier, 1949), 9, 26, 40–45 (Apuleius's conversion compared with Christian experiences), 182, 202 (Christian sense of the distinctiveness of their doctrine of conversion in the Age of the Fathers). See also Arthur Darby Nock, *Conversion: The Old and the New in Religion from Alexander the Great to Augustine of Hippo* (New York: Oxford Univ. Press, 1933), 14; Walter Burkert, *Ancient Mystery Cults* (Cambridge: Harvard Univ. Press, 1987), 2–4, 31, 51, 53, 101, 109; and Jean-Pierre Belche, "Die Bekehrung zum Christentum nach Augustins Büchlein *De Catechizandis Rudibus*," *Augustiniana* 27 (1977): 348–50.

69. Aristotle, *Nicomachean Ethics*, 9.2.1165a, 9.8.1169a.

70. H. S. Versnel, "Religious Mentality in Ancient Prayer," in Versnel, ed., *Faith, Hope, and Worship: Aspects of Religious Mentality in the Ancient World*, Studies in Greek and Roman Religion, 2 (Leiden: Brill, 1981), esp. p. 27.

71. Aristotle, *Nicomachean Ethics*, 8.3.1156b, 8.7.1158b–1159a, 9.4.1166a, 9.8.1168b, and *Magna Moralia*, 1208b; Walter Burkert, *Greek Religion: Archaic and*

Classical, trans. John Raffan (Cambridge: Harvard Univ. Press, 1985), 268–75. On the Christian idea of conversion in the patristic era, see Elisabeth Fink-Dendorfer, *Conversio: Motive und Motivierung zur Bekehrung in der Alten Kirche*, Regensburger Studien zur Theologie, 33 (Frankfurt a. M.: Lang, 1986), and Ramsay MacMullen, "Conversion: A Historian's View," *The Second Century* 5 (1985–86): 67–81, with commentaries by William S. Babcock and Mark D. Jordan, 82–90. A much fuller development of MacMullen's argument occurs in his book, *Christianizing the Roman Empire (A.D. 100–400)* (New Haven: Yale Univ. Press, 1984).

72. E. Louis Backman, *Religious Dances in the Christian Church and in Popular Medicine*, trans. E. Classen (London: George Allen & Unwin, 1952), 40–41; Hermannus quondam Judaeus, *Opusculum de Conversione Sua*, chap. 16 (*MGH, Quellen zur Geistesgeschichte des Mittelalters* 4:112).

73. See Alfred Clair Underwood, *Conversion: Christian and Non-Christian. A Comparative and Psychological Study* (London: Allen & Unwin, 1925), 143–52, 258–77.

74. Heinrich Dumoulin, *Zen Buddhism: A History*, trans. James W. Heisig and Paul Knitter, 1 (New York: Macmillan, 1988): 32. This vow was also part of a ceremony devised by the leader of the First Zen Institute of America for persons accepting the discipline of Zen Buddhism (Victor Solomon, *A Handbook on Conversions to the Religions of the World* [New York: Stravon Educational Press, 1965], 305). Cf. the translation in George Appleton, ed., *The Oxford Book of Prayer* (Oxford: Oxford Univ. Press, 1985), nr 936, p. 307: "Living beings are without number: I vow to row them to the other shore. Defilements are without number: I vow to remove them from myself. The teachings are immeasurable: I vow to study and practice them. The way is very long: I vow to arrive at the end."

75. W. Y. Evans-Wentz, *The Tibetan Book of the Great Liberation* (New York: Oxford Univ. Press, 1954), xxxvii.

76. Bernard of Clairvaux, *Sermo in Psalmum "Qui Habitat," 17*, chap. 3 (Leclercq and Rochais, *Sermones* 1:488–89).

77. Plato, *Laws*, 1.644.

78. Bernard of Clairvaux, *Sermo in Psalmum "Qui Habitat," 3*, chaps. 1, 5 (Leclercq and Rochais, *Sermones* 1:392–93, 396–97).

79. Honorius Augustodunensis, *Elucidarium*, 3.79–109, 114–21, quoted by Herrad of Hohenburg, *Hortus Deliciarum*, text nr 887 (Rosalie Green et al., eds., *Herrad of Hohenbourg: Hortus Deliciarum*, 2 vols., Studies of the Warburg Institute, 36 [London: Warburg Institute, 1979], 2:452.

80. Thérèse of Lisieux, *The Autobiography of St. Thérèse of Lisieux: The Story of a Soul*, trans. John Beevers (New York: Image Books, 1957), 85; William Roper, *Life of Sir Thomas More*, ed. E. E. Reynolds (London: Dent, 1963), 37–38.

81. Latimer, *Sermons on the Cards, First Sermon*, in Hugh Latimer, *Sermons* (London: Dent, 1906), 6, 10, 13.

82. S. J. Newman, *Dickens at Play* (New York: St. Martin's Press, 1981), 2.

Chapter 3. *Love and Penitence*

1. See below, n. 55. An early form of this chapter was tried out as a lecture in a symposium at Princeton University on marginality and authority (1989). I am grateful to Professor William C. Jordan and Mr. Jonathan M. Elukin, the organizers of the conference, for the opportunity to begin drawing my thoughts together.

2. Augustine, *Enarrationes in Psalmum 147*, 18–22 (*Corpus Christianorum, series latina* 40:2155–58).

3. See below, n. 73.

4. Walter Burkert, *Ancient Mystery Cults* (Cambridge: Harvard Univ. Press, 1987), 102.

5. John Bunyan, *Grace Abounding*, chap. 10, in Bunyan, *The Pilgrim's Progress*, special tercentenary ed. (New York: American Tract Society, n.d.), 117.

6. See chapter 4, n. 77.

7. Rupert of Deutz, *Commentum in Apocalypsim*, 4.5 (Migne *PL* 169:925). Rupert's list, more exactly, is: incarnation, Passion, resurrection, ascension, gift of the Holy Spirit, calling of the Gentiles, and Second Coming to judge the world. For Thomas Aquinas's statement (following Augustine of Hippo) that all figurative passages of Scripture must refer to Christ, see Karl F. Morrison, *The Mimetic Tradition of Reform in the West* (Princeton, N.J.: Princeton Univ. Press, 1982), 122. See above, chapter 2, at n. 9.

8. John of the Cross, *The Living Flame of Love*, 2.2–8 (E. Allison Peers, trans., *The Complete Works of Saint John of the Cross* 3 [London: Burns, Oates & Washbourne, 1935]: 40–44).

9. Hildegard of Bingen, *Liber Divinorum Operum Simplicis Hominis*, 10.34 (Migne *PL* 197:1034–35).

10. See Lawrence L. Besserman, *The Legend of Job in the Middle Ages* (Cambridge: Harvard Univ. Press, 1979).

11. Cosmas of Prague, *Chronica Boemorum*, 3.62 (*MGHSSrrG*, 241), citing Gregory the Great, *Dialogues*, 2.2.

12. Donald Weinstein and Rudolph M. Bell, *Saints and Society: The Two Worlds of Western Christendom, 1000–1700* (Chicago: Univ. of Chicago Press, 1982), 81.

13. On the dream of castration, see Caesarius of Heisterbach, *Dialogus Miraculorum*, 4.97 (Joseph Strange, ed., *Caesarii Heisterbacensis Monachi Ordinis Cisterciensis Dialogus Miraculorum* 1 [Cologne: Heberle, 1851]: 265–66). On the dream of unction, see Gerhoch of Reichersberg, *De Investigatione Antichristi*, 1.pref. (*MGH, Ldl* 3:305). See also Karl F. Morrison, *"I Am You": The Hermeneutics of Empathy in Western Literature, Theology, and Art* (Princeton, N.J.: Princeton Univ. Press, 1988), 223–24. On the gift of chastity to Thomas Aquinas, see Weinstein and Bell, *Saints and Society*, 82. On Christina of Markyate, see Anon., *The Life of Christina of Markyate, a Twelfth Century Recluse*, chaps. 45, 73 (ed. and trans. C. H. Talbot [Oxford: Clarendon, 1959], 118, 168).

14. Bernhard Citron, *New Birth: A Study of the Evangelical Doctrine of Conversion in the Protestant Fathers* (Edinburgh: Univ. Press, 1951), 166.

15. For conversion to paganism as a hypothetical possibility, see Wido of Ferrara, *De Scismate Hildebrandi* (*MGH, Ldl* 1:540).

16. See Amos Funkenstein, "Basic Types of Christian Anti-Jewish Polemics in the Later Middle Ages," *Viator* 2 (1971): 375: "Judah Halevi developed the biological criterion of Jewish self-understanding almost *ad absurdum* in determining that the superhuman sense of the divine and its succession among men was dependent upon, and guaranteed by, the biological succession only—even converts are excluded from it."

17. Herbord, *Dialogus de Vita S. Ottonis Episcopi Babenbergensis*, 2.26 (ed. Jan Wikarjak, Monumenta Poloniae Historica, n.s., vol. 7, fasc. 3 [Warsaw: Państwowe Wydawnictwo Naukowe, 1974], 112).

18. Bertrand Russell, *Why I Am Not a Christian and Other Essays on Religion and Related Subjects* (London: George Allen & Unwin, 1957), 14–16.

19. Caesarius of Heisterbach, *Dialogus Miraculorum*, 1.15 (ed. Strange, 1:22).

20. Edward Shils, "Centre and Periphery," in *Selected Essays by Edward Shils* (Chicago: Univ. of Chicago, Department of Sociology, 1970), 11–12.

21. See Leo C. Ferrari, *The Conversions of Saint Augustine*, Saint Augustine Lecture Series, 1982 (Villanova, Pa.: Villanova Univ. Press, 1984), 68–69, 80. On the Donatists' suspicion that Augustine never lost his Manicheanism, see Morrison, *"I Am You,"* 187–88.

Early in the twentieth century, Christian proselytes among Jews likewise noted that "the ex-Jews had lost their 'at-home-ness' with the Jewish people and had not attained such a feeling with the Gentile Christians" and, furthermore, that "a Jew who became a Christian was snubbed by Gentile Christians and treated as a 'stranger in the Church' " (Max Eisen, "Christian Missions to the Jews in North America and Great Britain," *Jewish Social Studies* 10 [1948]: 44, 49).

22. Roger of Hoveden, *Chronicle* (a. 1189) (William Stubbs, ed., *Chronica Magistri Rogeri de Houedene*, Rolls Series, 51, pt. 3 [London: Longman, 1870], 3:12). On inhibitions concerning, and limiting, Jewish-Christian dialogues, see William Chester Jordan, *The French Monarchy and the Jews: From Philip Augustus to the Last Capetians* (Philadelphia: Univ. of Pennsylvania Press, 1989), 11, 17–20, 31–32. Although degrees of apostasy were identified in the Talmud, allowing apostates to lose certain privileges and yet continue to be Jews, in practice apostates to Christianity were expelled from their communities. See Yosef Hayim Yerushalmi, "The Inquisition and the Jews of France in the Time of Bernard Gui," *Harvard Theological Review* 63 (1970): 365–66.

The repatriation of Hindu prisoners of war by their Muslim captors in India elicited similar hostility from the Hindu communities. On capture, the prisoners had been forced to convert to Islam. Although, when repatriated, some escaped the rigor of the Brahman priests, others were allowed to return to their communities as untouchables. Occasionally, purification rituals were demanded in which the repatriated were buried in dung heaps for some days, then dug out and compelled to eat the fermenting materials in which they had been embedded. See S. A. A. Rizvi, "Islamic Proselytisation (Seventh to Sixteenth Centuries)," in G. A. Oddie, ed., *Religion in South Asia: Religious Conversion and Revival Movements in South Asia in Medieval and Modern Times* (London: Curzon, 1977), 21. On one Hindu who chose death over conversion, see ibid., 24.

23. See Mary Stroll, *The Jewish Pope: Ideology and Politics in the Papal Schism of 1130* (Leiden: Brill, 1987), 156–68; Kenneth R. Stow, *The "1007 Anonymous" and Papal Sovereignty: Jewish Perceptions of the Papacy and Papal Policy in the High Middle Ages*, Hebrew Union College Annual Supplements, 4 (Cincinnati: Hebrew Union College, 1984), 14. On Christian suspicions against Muslim converts to Christianity, see Benjamin Z. Kedar, *Crusade and Mission: European Approaches toward the Muslims* (Princeton, N.J.: Princeton Univ. Press, 1984), 51–52, 76. On Muslim suspicions against converts to Islam, see Richard W. Bulliet, *Conversion to Islam in the Medieval Period: An Essay in Quantitative History* (Cambridge: Harvard Univ. Press, 1979), 42, 47.

24. Kedar, *Crusade and Mission*, 62, 75, 83, 121. On comparable lapses of Hindus from Islam, see Rizvi, "Islamic Proselytisation (Seventh to Sixteenth Centuries)," 15, 17, 19.

25. Juan de Torquemada, *Tractatus contra Madianitas et Ismaelitas (Defensa de los Judios Conversos)*, ed. Nicolas Lopez Martinez and Vicente Proano Gil, Publicaciones del Seminario metropolitano de Burgos, ser. B, vol. 2 (Burgos: n.p., 1957), 54, 93, 95–96.

26. Stroll, *The Jewish Pope*, 164, citing Bernard of Clairvaux, *ep. 363*.

27. See Gavin I. Langmuir, *History, Religion, and Antisemitism*, (Berkeley: Univ. of California Press, 1990), viii, 275–305. On the persistence into twentieth-century evangelism of anti-Jewish stereotypes—"that Jewish morality is lower than Christian, that Jews are selfish, love money, lie habitually, use sharp business practices, have no sense of sin, and are drunken and impure"—see Eisen, "Christian Missions to the Jews in North America and Great Britain," 43.

28. Ian Ker, *John Henry Newman: A Biography* (New York: Oxford Univ. Press, 1990), 473.

29. Othloh of St. Emmeram, *Libellus de Suis Tentationibus*, and *Liber Visionum*, chap. 3 (Migne *PL* 146:29–30, 347).

30. Hermannus quondam Judaeus, *Opusculum de Conversione Sua*, chaps. 12–17 (*MGH, Quellen zur Geistesgeschichte des Mittelalters* 4:106–16).

31. Othloh of St. Emmeram, *Liber Visionum*, chap. 3 (Migne *PL* 146:350–51).

32. Gerhoch of Reichersberg, *Tractatus in Ps.* 64, chaps. 101–3 (Migne *PL* 194:68–70); Othloh of St. Emmeram, *Libellus de Suis Tentationibus* (Migne *PL* 146:31); Rupert of Deutz, *Commentum in Apocalypsim*, 2.3 (Migne *PL* 169:897).

33. Othloh of St. Emmeram, *Libellus de Suis Tentationibus* (Migne *PL* 146:41). Cf. *agnitio nominis tui* in Othloh's *Paraphrasis Latina in Precationem Theodiscam* (Migne *PL* 146:432). On *cognitio Dei et cultus*, see John of Salisbury, *Vita Sancti Anselmi*, prol. (Migne *PL* 199:1009).

34. Othloh of St. Emmeram, *Libellus de Suis Tentationibus* (Migne *PL* 146:33) (part of temptation), and *Liber Visionum*, prol. (Migne *PL* 146:341) (part of Othloh's hermeneutic method).

35. For the term *voluntas conversionis,* see Othloh of St. Emmeram, *Libellus de Suis Tentationibus* (Migne *PL* 146:29).

36. Pierre Hadot, "Exercises spirituels antiques et 'philosophie chrétienne,'" in Hadot, *Exercises spirituels et philosophie antique* (Paris: Etudes Augustiniennes, 1981), 59–74. Professor Peter Brown kindly directed me to this article.

37. Othloh of St. Emmeram, *Libellus de Suis Tentationibus* (Migne *PL* 146:34).

38. Othloh of St. Emmeram, *Liber Visionum*, chap. 3 (Migne *PL* 146:348). See Irven M. Resnick, "*Literati, Spirituales,* and Lay Christians according to Otloh [*sic*] of Saint Emmeram," *Church History* 55 (1986): 174: "The simple ability to read the Scriptures does not guarantee a proper understanding of the first two types of *additamenta*. Nor does literacy alone guarantee a proper understanding of scripture. A spiritual understanding is a precondition for a fuller appreciation of all that God has revealed both in the book of nature and in the scriptures."

39. Othloh of St. Emmeram, *Libellus de Suis Tentationibus* (Migne *PL* 146:38 (on his retentive learning of *lectiones et cantica*), 56–57 (on his learning calligraphy); Hermannus quondam Judaeus, *Opusculum de Conversione Sua*, chaps. 2, 20 (on gaining facility in Latin) (*MGH, Quellen zur Geistesgeschichte des Mittelalters* 4:76, 122). See also Gilbert Crispin's account of St. Herluin's rapid mastery of the elements of literacy when he was more than forty years old as a gift of heavenly grace (*Vita Herluini*, chap. 28 [Anna Sapir Abulafia and G. R. Evans, eds., *The Works of Gilbert Crispin, Abbot of Westminster*, Auctores Britannici Medii Aevi, 8 (London: Oxford Univ. Press, 1986), 190]).

40. Guigo II, *The Ladder of Monks*, chaps. 5, 8 (Edmund Colledge and James Walsh, eds., *Lettre sur la vie contemplative*, Sources chrétiennes, 163 [Paris: Cerf, 1970], 90–92, 100).

41. Othloh of St. Emmeram, *Libellus de Suis Tentationibus* (Migne *PL* 146:52).

42. Guigo II, *The Ladder of Monks*, chap. 3 (Colledge and Walsh, *Lettre sur la vie contemplative*, 84–86). Othloh of St. Emmeram embellished the section of the *Libellus de Suis Tentationibus* that describes his own writings with a grand array of metaphors drawn from cooking, feasting, and digesting (Migne *PL* 146:51–58).

43. Othloh of St. Emmeram, *Libellus de Suis Tentationibus*, and *Liber Visionum*, chap. 3 (Migne *PL* 146:51, 349).

44. Othloh of St. Emmeram, *Libellus de Suis Tentationibus*, and *Liber Visionum*, chap. 10 (Migne *PL* 146:32, 41, 379); Helga Elisabeth Schauwecker, *Otloh von St. Emmeram: Ein Beitrag zur Bildungs- und Frömmigkeitsgeschichte des 11. Jahrhunderts*, Geschichte des Benediktinerordens und seiner Zweige, 74, Sonderausgabe (Munich: Abtei St. Bonifaz, n.d.), 65.

45. Othloh of St. Emmeram, *Liber Visionum*, chap. 3 (Migne *PL* 146:348–49).

46. Guigo II, *The Ladder of Monks*, chap. 3 (Colledge and Walsh, *Lettre sur la vie contemplative*, 84–86).

47. Othloh of St. Emmeram, *Libellus de Suis Tentationibus*, and *Liber Visionum*, prol. (Migne *PL* 146:40, 342); Gerhoch of Reichersberg, *Epistola ad Innocentium Papam Quid Distet inter Seculares et Regulares (MGH, Ldl* 3:203).

48. E.g., Rupert of Deutz's view as rendered by Herman-Judah (Hermannus quondam Judaeus, *Opusculum de Conversione Sua*, chap. 4 [*MGH, Quellen zur Geistesgeschichte des Mittelalters* 4:80]).

49. Anon., *S. Ottonis Episcopi Babenbergensis Vita Prieflingensis*, 3.3 (ed. Jan Wikarjak, Monumenta Poloniae Historica, n.s., vol. 7, fasc. 1 [Warsaw: Państwowe Wydawnictwo Naukowe, 1966], 58).

50. Othloh of St. Emmeram, *Liber Visionum*, chap. 4 (Migne *PL* 146:354).

51. Gerhoch of Reichersberg, *Tractatus in Ps. 1*, Gloria, *Tractatus in Ps. 41*, 6, *Tractatus in Ps. 54*, 20, *Tractatus in Ps. 136*, 8, *Tractatus in Ps. 37*, 7 (Migne *PL* 193:656–57, 1505–6, 1657, Migne *PL* 194:908; Damian van den Eynde and Odulph van den Eynde, eds., *Gerhohi Praepositi Reichersbergensis Opera Inedita*, vol. 2, pt. 2, Spicilegium Pontificii Anthenaei Antoniani, 10 [Rome: Pontificium Athenaeum Antonianum, 1956], 628–29). On Gerhoch's experience, parallel with Augustine's, of being distracted from the words of the Psalms by the beauty of the music, see Morrison, *"I Am You,"* 200.

52. Othloh of St. Emmeram, *Libellus de Suis Tentationibus* (Migne *PL* 146:31).

53. Ibid. (Migne *PL* 146:33); Othloh of St. Emmeram, *De Cursu Spirituali*, chap. 21 (Migne *PL* 146:218); Hermannus quondam Judaeus, *Opusculum de Conversione Sua*, chap. 12 (*MGH, Quellen zur Geistesgeschichte des Mittelalters* 4:108). Though evident, Othloh's unacknowledged allusion to Augustine's account is interesting in view of the exceptional fact that he appears never to have referred to Augustine's writings elsewhere. He relied (apart from Scripture) chiefly on texts by Benedict of Nursia, Gregory the Great, John Cassian, and Jerome (Schauwecker, *Othloh von St. Emmeram*, 67–69). On the rarity with which the *Confessions* were cited in the Middle Ages, see E. Ann Matter, "Conversion(s) in the *Confessiones*," in Joseph C. Schnaubelt and Frederick Van Fleteren, eds., *Collectanea Augustiniana: Augustine, "Second Founder of the Faith"* (New York: Peter Lang, 1990), 25–26.

54. Othloh of St. Emmeram, *Liber Visionum*, prol. (Migne *PL* 146:342).

55. Augustine, *Confessions*, 1.9.14, 3.10.18, 6.6.9, 6.14.24 (*Corpus Christianorum, series latina* 27:8, 37, 79–80, 89–90).

56. Othloh of St. Emmeram, *Libellus de Suis Tentationibus* (Migne *PL* 146:41).

57. Caesarius of Heisterbach, *Dialogus Miraculorum*, 1.2 (ed. Strange, 1:8).

58. Concerning Thomas Aquinas's doctrines on the duty of Christians to seek the conversion of others in brotherly love and on acts of coercion that might be required, see Morrison, *The Mimetic Tradition of Reform in the West*, 182–86. Thomas judged that killing a sinner could be a better preventive of evil than killing a wild beast. For Manegold of Lautenbach's conclusion that it was laudable to kill pagans who destroyed churches, since their crime was far worse than the Christians' homicide would be, see chapter 6, n. 24.

59. For a recent statement of this position, see the interview with Mother Theresa of Calcutta in *Time*, 4 Dec. 1989, p. 31.

60. See Adam of Bremen, *Gesta Hammaburgensis Ecclesiae Pontificum*, 3.21 (22) (*MGHSSrrG*, 164), for Archbishop Adalbert of Hamburg-Bremen's admonition to Prince Gottschalk of the Winuli, a Slavic tribe. See ibid., 3.70 (71) (p. 218), concerning Adalbert's own wish to die while preaching to the heathen. On proselytism of Muslims, see Kedar, *Crusade and Mission*, 14: "But for the few individuals who overcame the barrier of fear, the quest of a martyr's death at the hands of the Muslims was far more important than the wish to actually convert them, and the superiority of Christianity was mainly proclaimed by publicly vilifying Islam." See ibid., 66, concerning motives of the leaders of the Second Crusade. On conversion of monks through the ministry of others (especially by teaching (*sermone*), prayer (*oratione*), and exemplary observance (*exemplo religionis*), see Caesarius of Heisterbach, *Dialogus Miraculorum*, 1.15 (ed. Strange, 1:22).

61. Adam of Bremen, *Gesta Hammaburgensis Ecclesiae Pontificum*, 3.56 (55) (*MGHSSrrG*, 202).

62. Third Annual Report of the Ambala Mission Station (undated), Archives of the United Presbyterian Church, Philadelphia. Mrs. Annie Fredericks kindly brought this report to my attention.

63. Ebo, *Vita S. Ottonis Episcopi Babenbergensis*, 3.10 (ed. Jan Wikarjak, Monumenta Poloniae Historica, n.s., vol. 7, fasc. 2 [Warsaw: Państwowe Wydawnictwo Naukowe, 1969], 111); Herbord, *Dialogus de Vita S. Ottonis Episcopi Babenbergensis*, 2.17, 33 (ed. Wikarjak, 91, 126). See also Kedar, *Crusade and Mission*, 81, on Innocent III's decree, concerning Muslim converts, that the new Christians could not retain polygamous marriages, despite Old Testament precedents.

64. Ebo, *Vita S. Ottonis Episcopi Babenbergensis*, 1.9, 16 (ed. Wikarjak, 21, 30); Herbord, *Dialogus de Vita S. Ottonis Episcopi Babenbergensis*, 1.28, 29 (ed. Wikarjak, 30–31).

65. Bonizo of Sutri, *Liber ad Amicum*, 1 (*MGH, Ldl* 1:572).

66. Kedar, *Crusade and Mission*, 72–73. On the doctrine, deduced from Innocent III's decree, that unless the baptisand declared unwillingness to be baptized, the sacrament was valid and irrevocable and that Jews baptized under coercion who returned to Judaism could be punished as heretics, see Yerushalmi, "The Inquisition and the Jews of France in the Time of Bernard Gui," 329–30, 340–41.

67. Anon., *S. Ottonis Episcopi Babenbergensis Vita Prieflingensis*, 3.5 (ed. Wikarjak, 62): "ad feces pristinas devoluti."

68. Peter Damian, *Vita beati Romualdi*, chap. 13 (ed. Giovanni Tabacco, Fonti per la storia d'Italia, 94 [Rome: Istituto storico italiano per il medio evo, 1957], 35–36).

69. Walter Daniel, *The Life of Ailred of Rievaulx*, chaps. 15, 22, 28 (ed. and trans. F. M. Powicke [London: Nelson, 1950], 24–25, 30–32, 35–36).

70. Caesarius of Heisterbach, *Dialogus Miraculorum*, 1.14 (ed. Strange, 1:20–21).

71. Resnik, "*Literati, Spirituales,* and Lay Christians according to Otloh of Saint Emmeram," 174: "But it remains true for Otloh that the layperson may live rightly and merit God's reward even when there is no good model in the Church to serve as guide."

72. The fear of "judaizing" interpretations generally refers to the Arian, or Arianizing, doctrine of the Incarnation. See Gerhoch of Reichersberg, *Tractatus in Ps.* 64,

chaps. 119–20 (Migne *PL* 194:79); Rupert of Deutz, *Commentum in Apocalypsim*, 7.12 (Migne *PL* 169:1059–60). Cf. ibid., 1.1 (Migne *PL* 169:852), referring to interpretations of prophecies of the millenial reign of the saints as anticipating material delights in this world. Otto of Freising likewise considered this interpretation characteristic of the Jews (*Chronicon*, 8.26 [*MGHSSrrG*, 431–32]). See the virulent tirade by Manegold of Lautenbach against introducing "Jewish superstition" and thereby voiding the Cross of Christ, in *Liber ad Gebehardum*, chap. 42 (*MGH, Ldl* 1:384).

73. Caesarius of Heisterbach, *Dialogus Miraculorum*, 8.18 (ed. Strange, 2:96).

74. Othloh of St. Emmeram, *Libellus de Suis Tentationibus* (Migne *PL* 146:45).

75. Rupert of Deutz, *Commentum in Apocalypsim*, 5.9, 8.13, 9.15, 10.17 (Migne *PL* 169:999, 1002, 1063–64, 1105, 1119, 1133, 1135–36).

76. Ibid., 1.1, 4.6, 5.9, 9.15 (Migne *PL* 169:854, 954–55, 993–98, 1001, 1113).

77. On the liturgical poem "Put Them to Shame," composed after the pogroms of the First Crusade and recited on the Day of Atonement as curses against Christians and Muslims, see Yerushalmi, "The Inquisition and the Jews of France in the Time of Bernard Gui," 360–61.

78. Anon., *Gesta Treverorum*, chap. 21 (*MGH, SS* 8:195).

79. Heinrich Dumoulin, *Zen Buddhism: A History*, trans. James W. Heisig and Paul Knitter, 1 (New York: Macmillan, 1988): 196.

80. William Theodore de Bary, ed., *Sources of Japanese Tradition* (New York: Columbia Univ. Press, 1958), 254.

81. Hugh of St. Victor, *De Sacramentis Christianae Fidei*, 1.4.13, 23 (Migne *PL* 176:239–40, 243–44). See also Hugh of St. Victor, *Quaestiones in Epistolas Pauli, In Ep. ad Rom.*, quaest. 43, 44 (Migne *PL* 175:442–44).

82. Rupert of Deutz, *Commentum in Apocalypsim*, 10.17 (Migne *PL* 169:1146).

83. Thomas Shepard, *The Sincere Convert* (London: T. P. and M. S., 1643), 144–48.

84. Peter Henry Lemcke, *Life and Work of Prince Demetrius Augustine Gallitzin*, trans. Joseph C. Plumpe (New York: Longmans, 1941), 82–83.

85. James Bryce, "The Beginnings of Virginia" and "Missions Past and Present," in Bryce, *University and Historical Addresses* (New York: Macmillan, 1913), 9–10, 139, 142, 146–50.

86. Besserman, *The Legend of Job in the Middle Ages*, 2, 27.

87. Simone Weil, "The Love of God and Affliction," in Weil, *Waiting for God*, trans. Emma Craufurd (New York: Harper & Row, 1973), 120, 126.

88. Ibid., 124.

89. Simone Weil, "Concerning the Our Father," ibid., 219.

90. Simone Weil, "Forms of the Implicit Love of God," ibid., 163–64.

91. Edith Stein, *The Science of the Cross: A Study of St. John of the Cross*, trans. Hilda Graef (London: Burns & Oates, 1960), 180.

92. G. W. F. Hegel, *Vorlesungen über die Philosophie der Geschichte*, in *Sämtliche Werke*, Jubiläumsausgabe, 16 (Stuttgart: Fromann, 1928): 77, 81–85; Augustine, *Confessions*, 1.13.21, 10.35.55 (*Corpus Christianorum, series latina* 27:11, 185).

93. Stein, *The Science of the Cross*, 175, 179.

94. Cf. two passages by Augustine concerning the resurrection of the flesh: *Enchiridion*, 23 (89), and *City of God*, 22.19 (*Corpus Christianorum, series latina* 46:97, 48:838).

Chapter 4. The Ordeal of Conscience: Purity and Doubt

1. Josef van Ess, "Sunnites and Shi'ites: The State, Law, and Religion," in Hans Küng et al., *Christianity and the World Religions: Paths of Dialogue with Islam, Hinduism, and Buddhism* (Garden City, N.Y.: Doubleday, 1986), 46. The original version of this lectture was delivered at the Casassa Conference, at Loyola Marymount University, in 1987. I am grateful to Professor David C. Blake and his colleagues for the opportunity to take part in the conference.

2. See *Thesaurus Linguae Latinae*, s.v. "*Conscientia.*"

3. Timothy C. Potts, *Conscience in Medieval Philosophy* (Cambridge: Cambridge Univ. Press, 1981), 12, and "Conscience," in Norman Kretzmann et al., *The Cambridge History of Later Medieval Philosophy* (Cambridge: Cambridge Univ. Press, 1982), 690. For a discussion of *synderesis*, chiefly in thirteenth-century theology and philosophy, see Odon Lottin, *Psychologie et moral aux XIIe et XIIIe siècles* 2 (Louvain: Abbay du Mont César, 1948): 103–305, and the further discussion of doubts and obligations of conscience as considered by Franciscan and Dominican teachers, ibid., 353–417.

4. See above, n. 3 and chapter 1, n. 15.

5. Otto of Freising, *Chronicon*, 8.16, 19 (*MGHSSrrG*, 414, 418).

6. Walter Daniel, *The Life of Ailred of Rievaulx*, chap. 4 (ed. F. M. Powicke [London: Nelson, 1950], 9).

7. Hermannus quondam Judaeus, *Opusculum de Conversione Sua*, chap. 11 (*MGH, Quellen zur Geistesgeschichte des Mittelalters* 4:105–6).

8. William of St. Thierry, *The Enigma of Faith*, chaps. 11, 12, 21, 89 (trans. John D. Anderson, Cistercian Fathers Series, 9 [Washington, D.C.: Cistercian Publications, 1974], 44, 46, 52, 116).

9. Emil Brunner, *The Divine Imperative: A Study in Christian Ethics*, trans. Olive Wyon (New York: Macmillan, 1942), 156.

10. Augustine, *Confessions*, 10.2.2 (*Corpus Christianorum, series latina* 27:155). Cf. Sigebert of Gembloux, *Gesta Abbatum Gemblacensium*, chap. 13 (*MGH, SS* 8:530): the conscience of the heart is a cavern.

11. Anon., *Tractatus de Conscientia*, chap. 1 (Migne *PL* 184:553, 554); Anon., *Tractatus de Ordine Vitae*, chap. 8 (Migne *PL* 184:576); Anselm of Havelberg, *Antikeimenon*, 1.10, 13 (Migne *PL* 188:1154, 1160).

12. Bruno of Magdeburg, *De Bello Saxonico*, chap. 5 (*MGH, Deutsches Mittelalter* 2:16).

13. Anon., *Vitis Mystica*, chap. 176 (Migne *PL* 184:740); Rupert of Deutz, *Commentum in Apocalypsim*, 4.6 (Migne *PL* 169:958). See Gerhart B. Ladner, "Aspects of Patristic Anti-Judaism," *Viator* 2 (1971): 362.

14. Thomas Shepard, *The Sincere Convert* (London: T. P. and M. S., 1643), 137–38.

15. John of Salisbury, *ep. 177* (W. J. Millor and C. N. L. Brooke, eds., *The Letters of John of Salisbury* 2 [Oxford: Clarendon, 1972]: 184). Cf. Gerhoch of Reichersberg's comparison of the sinful Church, polluted in conscience and repute, with the woman in Luke 7:41–50, "quae neque bonam conscientiam neque bonam haberet famam" (*Tractatus in Ps.* 6, 1 [Migne *PL* 193:714]).

16. Thomas Aquinas, *Quaestiones Disputatae de Virtutibus, quest. de correctione fraterna*, a.2, resp. (Raymundo Spiazzi, ed., *Quaestiones disputatae* [Turin: Marietti, 1964], 2:799).

17. Thomas Aquinas, *Quodlibeta*, 10.6.2 (*Opera Omnia*, 25 vols. [Parma: Fiaccadori, 1852–73], 9:609).

18. Thomas Aquinas, *Super Ev. Matt.*, 18.2 (Parma ed., 10:170), *Super Ev. Johann.*, 12.1 (Parma ed., 10:507), *Super Ep. ad Rom.*, 10.3 (Parma ed., 13:107), and *Summa Theologiae*, IIa–IIae.33.7, 74.2 (Parma ed., 3:139–40, 271–72).

19. Thomas Aquinas, *Summa Theologiae*, IIa–IIae.73.2 (Parma ed., 3:268–69), and *Quodlibeta*, 10.6.2 (Parma ed., 9:609). See the story, told by William of Canterbury, that when St. Denis met Thomas à Becket, newly arrived in Paradise, he delegated the performance of a miracle to Thomas so that he might become famous (Beryl Smalley, *The Becket Conflict and the Schools: A Study of Intellectuals in Politics* [Oxford: Blackwell, 1973], 191).

20. Thomas Aquinas, *In IV. Sent.*, dist. 1, q. 2, art. 1 (Parma ed., 7, pt. 2:816–17).

21. Nicholas Harpsfield, *Life of Sir Thomas More*, in E. E. Reynolds, ed., *Lives of Saint Thomas More* (New York: Dutton, 1978), 136.

22. On the *honor* of Henry II, see John of Salisbury, *epp. 139, 150;* on his *honestas, ep. 181*. For Becket's struggle against Henry II to save the king's honor, *ep. 157*. For the phrases "honor Dei," *ep. 217*, "honorem Dei et honestatem ecclesiae," *ep. 305*. The phrase "honor ecclesiae" is common in texts of the period. See the interesting text, *ep. 288*, that describes Becket putting himself in God's hands and Henry's "ad honorem Dei et vestrum," only to stir up wrangling among all parties as to whether the term "God's honor" concealed some sophistical evasion (Millor and Brooke, *Letters* 2:22, 48, 66, 200, 367, 638, 640, 726). The association of love, honor, and dedication (*cultus*) is suggested by John's statement: "Porro si philosophie professores persequuntur philosophantium amatorem, plane iniuriosi sunt, et meam male remunerant caritatem. Eos enim, etsi nequam imitari, certe amare, honorare, et colere propositum est" (*Metalogicon*, prol. [Clement C. J. Webb, ed., *Ioannis Saresberiensis Episcopi Carnotensis Metalogicon Libri IIII* (Oxford: Clarendon, 1929), 2]).

23. See, for example, Henry II's allegation that the clergy was nowhere held in greater honor than in his lands, although they were for the most part grossly impure and wicked men, sacrilegious, adulterers, robbers, thieves, rapers of virgins, arsonists, and murderers. The king produced clerical and lay witnesses to sustain each of his assertions, but this was part of a performance that convinced the French that he was a bit uncouth (*inurbanus*) (John of Salisbury, *ep. 288* [Millor and Brooke, *Letters* 2:642]). The phrase *cultus sui* has an ambiguous tone in John's account of Henry II and a distinctly negative one in Bruno of Magdeburg's comment on a pompous lordling (Bruno

of Magdeburg, *De Bello Saxonico*, chap. 16 [*MGH, Deutsches Mittelalter* 2:23]: "Willehalmum quoque, qui propter nimium cultum sui rex de Lotheslovo appellabatur, tanta crudelitate persequitur"). My point is that the idea of conversion, and reflections on purity of conscience, required a *cultus sui* in the quest for holiness. See also John's use of Aristotelian categories (place, time, mode, person, and cause) to determine whether an action were *utilis et honesta* (*Policraticus*, 1.4.8.12 [Clement C. J. Webb, ed., *Ioannis Saresberiensis Episcopi Carnotensis Policratici . . . Libri VIII* (Oxford: Clarendon, 1909), 1:31–35, 2:316]).

24. Cf. John of Salisbury, *Policraticus*, 8.2, 5.15 (Webb, *Ioannis Saveberiensis . . . Policratici . . . Libri VIII* 2:233, 244–45 [quoting liberally from Augustine, *City of God*, 5.11.12 (*Corpus Christianorum, series latina* 47:143–46)], 335–36). The preceding paragraphs on internal-external relationships arose from discussions with Professors Jeffrey Burton Russell and Robert L. Benson. I am obliged to both colleagues for their advice.

25. Peter Damian, *Opusculum 7* (= Reindel 31): *Liber Gomorrhianus*, chaps. 5, 20, 22, 24 (Kurt Reindel, ed., *Die Briefe des Petrus Damiani*, pt. 1, *Die Briefe der deutschen Kaiserzeit*, 4.1 [Munich: Monumenta Germaniae Historica, 1983], 292, 318, 320, 324). Cf. 3 Kings 2:31–33.

26. Peter Damian, *Liber Gomorrhianus*, chap. 6 (Reindel, *Die Briefe*, pt. 1, 294–97).

27. Ibid., chaps. 3, 13 (pp. 290, 306).

28. Ibid., chaps. 5, 11 (pp. 294, 302).

29. Ibid., chaps. 5, 6 (pp. 292–97).

30. Ibid., chap. 25 (p. 326).

31. Ibid., chaps. 5, 25, 26 (pp. 292, 325–26, 329).

32. Peter Damian, *Opusculum 30* (= Reindel 146): *De Sacramentis per Improbos Administratis*, chap. 3 (Migne *PL* 145:528).

33. See my essay, "Peter Damian on King and Pope: An Exercise in Association by Contrast," *ACTA* 11 (1986, for 1984): 89–112.

34. Peter Damian, *Opusculum 32* (= Reindel 160): *De Quadragesima*, chap. 9 (Migne *PL* 145:560).

35. Peter Damian, *ep.* 1.12 to Desiderius (= Reindel 164) (ibid., 145:278–82).

36. E.g., Adam of Bremen, *Gesta Hammaburgensis Ecclesiae Pontificum*, 3.47 (46) (*MGHSSrrG*, 191): "Cuius delicti conscientia cum fere omnes episcopi et principes regni tangerentur, unanimi odio conspirabant, ut ille [solus] periret, ne ceteri periclitentur," and Rahewin, *Gesta Friderici*, 4.22 (19) (*MGHSSrrG*, 261). See also the words that Rahewin attributed to Count Guido of Biandrate in his exhortation to the Milanese: "Nisi forte bonae conscientiae, bonae voluntatis obsequium aliquod mihi aput vos meritum pepererit" (*Gesta Friderici I. Imperatoris*, 3.46 [*MGHSSrrG*, 219]).

37. Gregory VII, *Reg.* 2.10 (*MGH, Epistolae Selectae* 2:140–42).

38. Ibid., 2.11, 8.18, 19 (pp. 142–43, 540–41). See also ibid., 5.23 (p. 387): "remordente eum conscientia sua."

39. Ibid., 2.5, 5.13, 7.23 (pp. 133, 366, 500).

40. *Peter Abelard's Ethics*, ed. D. E. Luscombe (Oxford: Clarendon, 1972), 23, 97.

41. Ibid., 98–100.

42. Ibid., 18. See above, chapter 1, n. 11.
43. Ibid., 20, 36.
44. Ibid., 28.
45. Ibid., 28, 54, 56, 62.
46. Ibid., 104–26.
47. John of Salisbury, *ep. 225* (Millor and Brooke, *Letters* 2:393).
48. On the ease with which the monks of Canterbury, who had dishonored Becket in his lifetime, promoted his cult after his death, see R. W. Southern, *The Monks of Canterbury and the Murder of Archbishop Becket*, William Urry Memorial Lecture, 1 (Canterbury: Friends of Canterbury Cathedral, 1985).
49. John of Salisbury, *Policraticus*, 3.15, 8.17–18 (Webb, *Ioannis Saresberiensis . . . Policratici . . . Libri VIII* 1:232, 2:345, 358, 376–77).
50. John of Salisbury, *ep. 144* (Millor and Brooke, *Letters* 2:32–34). On John, see the general discussion by Smalley, *The Becket Conflict*, 87–108.
51. Alan of Tewkesbury, *Vita S. Thomae*, in James Craigie Robertson, ed., *Materials for the History of Thomas Becket Archbishop of Canterbury*, 7 vols., Rolls Series, 67, (London: Longmans, 1875–85), 2:324. For various associations of *fama, honestas,* and *gloria,* see John of Salisbury, *epp. 167, 191, 207, 229, 257* (Millor and Brooke, *Letters* 2:96, 260, 262, 404, 521). For the ideal counsel, *salubre ad conscientiam et honestum ad famam,* see *ep. 191* (p. 262). Association with a man excommunicated by Becket injures both *conscientia* and *fama;* see *ep. 297* (p. 686). For a further identification of conscience as pertaining to God and *fama,* to one's neighbor, see *ep. 186* (p. 228).
52. Thomas à Becket, *ep. 73* (Robertson, *Materials for the History of Thomas Becket* 5:137).
53. Herbert of Bosham, *Vita S. Thomae*, 3.37 (ibid., 3:305).
54. Karl F. Morrison, *"I Am You": The Hermeneutics of Empathy in Western Literature, Theology, and Art* (Princeton, N.J.: Princeton Univ. Press, 1988).
55. Frank Barlow, *Thomas Becket* (Berkeley: Univ. of California Press, 1986), 4, 238, 245.
56. John of Salisbury, *ep. 305* (Millor and Brooke, *Letters* 2:728).
57. Ibid., *ep. 305* (pp. 728, 730).
58. Ibid., *ep. 305* (pp. 728, 732, 734).
59. Ibid., *epp. 176, 278* (pp. 166–68, 598).
60. Ibid., *ep. 187* (pp. 238–42).
61. Ibid., *ep. 307* (pp. 746–48).
62. Ibid., *ep. 176* (pp. 166–68). Instructively, John used similar phrasing when he described how holy kings could actually pass from the delights of this world to those of the next (*Policraticus*, 4.11 [Webb, *Ioannis Saresberiensis . . . Policratici . . . Libri VIII* 1:268]): "Atqui et reges florere possunt et mundialium florum dulcissimos et utilissimos in eternum carpere fructus. Quid autem beatius est quam si de divitiis ad divitias, de deliciis ad delicias, de gloria ad gloriam principes transferantur, de temporalibus ad eterna?"

63. E.g., John of Salisbury to Becket, *ep. 176* (Millor and Brooke, *Letters* 2:170).

64. Ibid., *ep. 301* (p. 708). See also John of Salisbury, *Historia Pontificalis*, chap. 11 (Marjorie Chibnall, ed., *John of Salisbury's Memoirs of the Papal Court* [London: Nelson, 1956], 11): "Hoc tamen ad humanum non spectat examen, quia nemo novit penitus quid sit in homine, nisi spiritus qui in ipso est, et conscientiarum iudex, solus novit abscondita cordis."

65. E.g., Thomas à Becket, *ep. 155* (Robertson, *Materials for the History of Thomas Becket* 5:283).

66. John of Salisbury, *ep. 176* (Millor and Brooke, *Letters* 2:168).

67. Ibid., *ep. 300* (p. 700).

68. Cf. ibid., *epp. 136, 168, 181, 182, 217* (pp. 102, 202, 206, 364). See also Otto of Freising's discussion of books of conscience opened at the Last Judgment, cited above, n. 5.

69. John of Salisbury, *ep. 174* (Millor and Brooke, *Letters* 2:138).

70. E.g., Herbert of Bosham, *Vita S. Thomae*, 4.8, 4.26 (Robertson, *Materials for the History of Thomas Becket* 3:335–36, 428).

71. Thomas à Becket, *ep. 162*, and Henry II, *ep. 185* (ibid., 5:302, 362).

72. John of Salisbury, *ep. 150* (Millor and Brooke, *Letters* 2:48).

73. Arnulf of Lisieux, *ep. 42* (Frank Barlow, ed., *The Letters of Arnulf of Lisieux*, Camden Society, 3d ser., 61 [London: Royal Historical Society, 1930], 69–70).

74. Henry II, *ep. 71*, and English clergy, *ep. 205* (Robertson, *Materials for the History of Thomas Becket* 5:134, 411).

75. John of Salisbury, *ep. 480* (Millor and Brooke, *Letters* 2:480, 668).

76. Ibid., *ep. 260* (p. 526). Variants of this phrasing occur in *Policraticus*, 8.12, 14 (Webb, *Ioannis Saresberiensis . . . Policratici . . . Libri VIII* 2:309, 328). See also *ep. 196* (Millor and Brooke, *Letters* 2:278–80), against an autocratic prelate who emptied the purses of Christ's poor to give aid and comfort to "the enemies of the Crucified, actors, mimes, and other plagues of that kind."

77. Gilbert Foliot, *ep. Multiplicem* (1166) (Z. N. Brooke, Adrian Morey, and C. N. L. Brooke, eds., *The Letters and Charters of Gilbert Foliot* [Cambridge: Cambridge Univ. Press, 1967], nr 170, pp. 239–40): "At martirem non pena facit, sed causa." On Gilbert's embarrassingly abrupt recuperation from a serious illness after he allowed his friends to ask the intercession of Becket as a martyr, see Adrian Morey and C. N. L. Brooke, *Gilbert Foliot and His Letters* (Cambridge: Cambridge Univ. Press, 1965), 166–167, esp. p. 172. For the encomium on Gilbert, see ibid., 3. John of Salisbury turned to the same Augustinian maxim in *ep. 305* (Millor and Brooke, *Letters* 2:726): "et si causa martirem facit."

78. John of Salisbury, *epp. 152, 249* Millor and Brooke, *Letters* 2:54–56, 502). On Foliot, see Smalley, *The Becket Conflict and the Schools*, chap. 7, esp. pp. 167–86.

79. Gerhoch of Reichersberg, *Tractatus in Ps. 22*, 5, and *Tractatus in Ps. 67*, 14 (Migne *PL* 193:1051, 194:185).

80. Augustine, *Confessions*, 2.6.13–14 (*Corpus Christianorum*, series latina 27:23–

24). Cf. ibid., 10.42.67 (ibid., 191–92), and John of Salisbury, *Policraticus*, 8.23 (Webb, *Ioannis Saresberiensis . . . Policratici . . . Libri VIII* 2:410): "Omnis enim persona Deo servit et dispensatrix est clementiae vel iustitiae suae. Servit angelus, servit homo, serviunt boni, serviunt mali, et ipse princeps mundi diabolus servit."

81. Alan of Tewkesbury, *Vita S. Thomae*, pref. (Robertson, *Materials for the History of Thomas Becket* 2:299–301).

82. Thomas More, *A Dialogue of Comfort against Tribulation*, 2.16 (Louis L. Martz and Frank Manley, eds., *The Complete Works of St. Thomas More* 1 [New Haven: Yale Univ. Press, 1976]: 164). The decisive moment in Teresa of Avila's conversion occurred when, contemplating a picture of the Man of Sorrows, she entered into the subject of the painting with all vividness (*The Life of Teresa of Jesus*, chap. 9 [E. Allison Peers, trans., *The Autobiography of St. Teresa of Avila* (Garden City, N.Y.: Image Books, 1960), 115]).

83. *Peter Abelard's Ethics*, 48–50. I am obliged to Professor Marcia Colish for drawing my attention to this passage.

84. Third Session, interrogation of 24 Feb.

85. Michael Wilks, *The Problem of Sovereignty in the Later Middle Ages* (Cambridge: Cambridge Univ. Press), 371–72 (on the canonist Zabarella); Arthur Stephen McGrade, *The Political Thought of William of Ockham* (Cambridge: Cambridge Univ. Press, 1979), 64–66.

86. P. Doncoeur and Y. Lanhers, *La réhabilitation de Jeanne la Pucelle*, Documents et recherches relatifs à Jeanne la Pucelle, 3 (Paris: Argences, 1956), 95.

87. John of Salisbury, *epp. 187, 195* (saying that Terence himself stated that charity accounted nothing human foreign to it), 250 (Millor and Brooke, *Letters* 2:234, 274, 504); John of Salisbury, *Vita S. Anselmi*, chap. 4 (Migne PL 199:1014).

88. Herbord, *Dialogus de Vita S. Ottonis Episcopi Babenbergensis* 2.35 (ed. Jan Wikarjak, Monumenta Poloniae Historica, n.s., vol. 7, fasc. 3 [Warsaw: Państwowe Wydawnictwo Naukowe, 1974], 129).

89. Cf. Gerhoch of Reichersberg, *Tractatus in Ps. 64*, chaps. 101–2 (Migne PL 194:68–69). Judas followed the example of Achitophel, who hanged himself "gravi conscientia tortus." See the similar phrasing in John of Salisbury, *ep. 298* (Millor and Brooke, *Letters* 2:690): "Pacem universalis ecclesiae sperant omnes, et eam ferre universi desiderant, nec alios excipiendos esse crediderim, nisi quos scelerum conscientia torquet, convincens eos propriae damnationis meruisse sententiam." Otto of Freising wrote that the damned would be tortured in body by the flames of hell and in mind by the *vermis ad cruciatum conscientiae* (*Chronicon*, 8.21 [*MGHSSrrG*, 424]; see also ibid., 8.18, 22, 28 [pp. 418, 426, 439]).

90. John Dryden, "The Hind and the Panther," pt. 3, ll. 786–859 (John Sargeaunt, ed., *The Poems of John Dryden* [London: Oxford Univ. Press, 1959], 143–44).

Chapter 5. A True Myth

1. See Augustine, *City of God,* 22.24, 30 (*Corpus Christianorum, series latina* 48:852, 866), *De Trinitate,* 13.7.10, 13.8.11, 15.25.45 (*Corpus Christianorum, series latina* 50A: 394–95, 396–98, 524), and *Enchiridion,* 8.23 (*Corpus Christianorum, series latina* 46:63): "vita sine morte, sine errore veritas, sine perturbatione felicitas."

2. Caesarius of Heisterbach, *Dialogus Miraculorum,* 12.59 (Joseph Strange, ed., *Caesarii Heisterbacensis Monachi Ordinis Cisterciensis Dialogus Miraculorum* 2 [Cologne: Heberle, 1851]: 363).

3. See Mircea Eliade, "The Structure of Myths," in Eliade, *Myth and Reality,* trans. Willard R. Trask (New York: Harper and Row, 1988), 1–20. See also Leszek Kolakowski, *The Presence of Myth,* trans. Adam Czerniawski (Chicago: Univ. of Chicago Press, 1989), 9–18, 110–29.

4. Plato, *Republic,* 3.414–15.

5. See Augustine, *Soliloquiorum libri duo,* 2.10.18 (Migne PL 32:893). Cf. *De Ordine,* 2.11.33–34 (*Corpus Christianorum, series latina* 29:126–27), and *Tractatus in Evangelium Johannis, 124,* 5 (*Corpus Christianorum, series latina* 36:683–86). On no need for the Gospels in Paradise, see *Tractatus in Evangelium Iohannis, 35,* 9 (*Corpus Christianorum, series latina* 36:322–23).

6. See Dickinson W. Adams, ed., *Jefferson's Extracts from the Gospels: "The Philosophy of Jesus" and "The Life and Morals of Jesus"* (Princeton, N.J.: Princeton Univ. Press, 1983), esp. 6–7, 42.

7. Hans Robert Jauss, discussion in Manfred Fuhrmann, ed., *Terror und Spiel: Probleme der Mythenrezeption,* Poetik und Hermeneutik: Arbeitsergebnisse einer Forschungsgruppe, 4 (Munich: Fink, 1971), 618.

8. Jaroslav Pelikan, *Christian Doctrine and Modern Culture (since 1700),* vol. 5 of *The Christian Tradition: A History of the Development of Doctrine* (Chicago: Univ. of Chicago Press, 1989), 77. On the distinction between *religio* and *superstitio,* see Dieter Harmening, *Superstitio: Überlieferungs- und theoriegeschichtliche Untersuchungen zur kirchlich-theologischen Aberglaubensliteratur des Mittelalters* (Berlin: Erich Schmidt, 1979), 17, 62–67, 270–92.

9. Hans Robert Jauss, "Allegorese, Remythisierung und neuer Mythos: Bemerkungen zur christlichen Gefangenschaft der Mythologie im Mittelalter," in Fuhrmann, *Terror und Spiel,* 188; also discussion, ibid., 619; Jan De Vries, *Forschungsgeschichte der Mythologie,* Orbis Academicus, 1.7 (Munich: Alber, 1961), 59–60; Brian Stock, *Myth and Science in the Twelfth Century: A Study of Bernard Silvester* (Princeton, N.J.: Princeton Univ. Press, 1972), 54–55 (on William of Conches), 277, 280–81. See Karl F. Morrison, *History as a Visual Art in the Twelfth-Century Renaissance* (Princeton, N.J.: Princeton Univ. Press, 1990), 203, 208–10.

10. Gerhoch of Reichersberg, *Tractatus in Ps.* 29, 5 (Migne PL 193:1254–55), against the clerics of his day, who, he said, had set up idols of pride and avarice in their hearts. Burchard of Worms's *Decretum* (c. 1008–12) suggests that Gerhoch intended

more than a learned allusion by referring to Diana. Burchard prescribed that two years' penance be invoked against those who believed some evil women, ensnared by demons, who posed as "devotees of the pagan goddess, Diana," and alleged that they could ride through the night sky (Migne *PL* 140:963–964). See Augustine of Hippo, *Tractatus in Evangelium Iohannis* 40, 4 and *Tractatus* 74, 1 (*Corpus Christianorum, series latina* 36:351, 513), on the making of idols in the heart.

11. Gilbert Crispin, *Disputatio Iudei et Christiani*, chap. 66 (Anna Sapir Abulafia and G. R. Evans, eds., *The Works of Gilbert Crispin, Abbot of Westminster*, Auctores Britannici Medii Aevi, 8 [London: Oxford Univ. Press, 1986], 23). For a survey of Christian-Jewish polemics in this period and a definition of the militance that followed, see David Berger, "Mission to the Jews and Jewish-Christian Contacts in the Polemical Literature of the High Middle Ages," *American Historical Review* 91 (1986): 576–91, with a comment by Gavin I. Langmuir, 614–24.

12. Hermannus quondam Judaeus, *Opusculum de Conversione Sua*, chap. 5 (*MGH, Quellen zur Geistesgeschichte des Mittelalters* 4:85–86).

13. Suger, *Vita Ludovici Grossi Regis*, chap. 32 (ed. Henri Waquet, Les classiques de l'histoire de France au Moyen Age [Paris: Les belles lettres, 1964], 264). On the dramatic contrast between Innocent II's reception into the opulence of St. Denis and into the austerity of Cîteaux, see Conrad Rudolph, *Artistic Change at Saint-Denis: Abbot Suger's Program and the Early Twelfth-Century Controversy over Art* (Princeton, N.J.: Princeton Univ. Press, 1990), 3–4.

14. See above, chapter 2, n. 65.

15. On Richard I, see James F. Dimock, introduction to *Giraldi Cambrensis Opera*, Rolls Series, 21, pt. 1 (London: Longmans, 1861): 1:lxiii. On St. Louis, see Gerhart B. Ladner, "Aspects of Patristic Anti-Judaism," *Viator* 2 (1971): 355, citing Joinville's *Histoire de Saint Louis*, chap. 53.

16. For an exemplary death, with gnashing of teeth and foaming of mouth, see Giraldus Cambrensis, *Gemma Ecclesiastica*, dist. 1, chap. 51 (James S. Brewer, ed., *Giraldi Cambrensis Opera*, Rolls Series, 21, pt. 2 [London: Longmans, 1862] 2:153). For a saintly victim of creditors (not all of whom were Jews), see Anon., *Martyrium Arnoldi Archiepiscopi Magontini*, in Johann Friedrich Böhner, ed., *Fontes Rerum Germanicarum* 3 (Stuttgart: Cotta, 1858): 325. For a Jewess sorceress, employed by a Christian mother against her saintly daughter, see Anon., *The Life of Christina of Markyate, a Twelfth Century Recluse*, chap. 23 (ed. and trans., C. H. Talbot [Oxford: Clarendon, 1959], 74).

17. For documentation, see the prefatory chapter to my translation of Herman-Judah's *Account* in Karl F. Morrison, *Conversion and Text: The Cases of Augustine of Hippo, Herman-Judah, and Constantine Tsatsos* (Charlottesville: Univ. Press of Virginia, forthcoming).

18. Cf. Anon., *Gesta Treverorum*, chap. 21 (*MGH, SS* 8:194–95).

19. Robert Levine, "Why Praise Jews: Satire and History in the Middle Ages," *Journal of Medieval History* 12 (1986): 291–96.

20. Ibid., 295.

21. Anon., *Vita Adalberonis Episcopi Wirziburgensis*, chap. 13 (*MGH, SS* 12:135).

22. Anon., *Gesta Abbatum Gemblacensium*, chap. 72 (de Liethardo Abbate) (*MGH, SS* 8:550).

23. Anon., *Vita Bardonis Archiepiscopi Mogontini Prolixior*, chap. 28 (Böhner, *Fontes Rerum Germanicarum* 3:245).

24. Giraldus Cambrensis, *Gemma Ecclesiastica*, 1.52 (Brewer, *Giraldi Cambrensis Opera* 2:156-57). Giraldus added with satisfaction that the Jew through whom the miracle was performed converted to Christianity.

25. E.g., Rupert of Deutz, *Commentum in Apocalypsim*, 5.9 (Migne *PL* 169:999, 1002).

26. Herbord, *Dialogus de Vita S. Ottonis Episcopi Babenbergensis*, 3.19 (ed. Jan Wikarjak, Monumenta Poloniae Historica, n.s., vol. 7, fasc. 3 [Warsaw: Państwowe Wydawnictwo Naukowe, 1974], 181-82); Anna Sapir Abulafia, "Invectives against Christianity in the Hebrew Chronicles of the First Crusade," in Peter W. Edbury, ed., *Crusade and Settlement* (Cardiff: Univ. College Cardiff Press, 1985), 70.

27. Othloh of St. Emmeram, *Liber Visionum*, chaps. 10, 13 (Migne *PL* 146:364, 368).

28. Amos Funkenstein, "Basic Types of Christian Anti-Jewish Polemics in the Later Middle Ages," *Viator* 2 (1971): 373, 382. See also Berger, "Mission to the Jews," esp. pp. 579-84; Gavin Langmuir, "Anti-Judaism as the Necessary Preparation for Anti-Semitism," *Viator* 2 (1971): 385-88; and Jeremy Cohen, "Scholarship and Intolerance in the Medieval Academy: The Study and Evaluation of Judaism in European Christendom," *American Historical Review* 91 (1986): 592-613, with Langmuir's comment on the articles by Berger and Cohen, 614-24; David K. O'Rourke, *A Process Called Conversion* (Garden City, N.Y.: Doubleday, 1985), 29.

29. Benjamin Z. Kedar, *Crusade and Mission: European Approaches toward the Muslims* (Princeton, N.J.: Princeton Univ. Press, 1984), 63.

30. Guerric of Igny, *The Third Sermon for the Epiphany*, chap. 4 (John Morson and Hilary Costello, eds., *Sermones*, Sources chrétiennes, 166 [Paris: Cerf, 1970], 1:278).

31. Hermannus quondam Judaeus, *Opusculum de Conversione Sua*, chaps. 3, 9, 10, 16, 21 (*MGH, Quellen zur Geistesgeschichte des Mittelalters* 4:79, 96, 101, 105, 112, 126).

32. Guerric of Igny, *The Third Sermon for the Nativity*, chap. 5, *The Fifth Sermon for the Nativity*, chaps. 1, 4, 5, and *The Third Sermon for the Epiphany*, chaps. 1, 4 (Morson and Costello, *Sermones* 1:198, 222-24, 230-32, 234, 270-74, 276-80). For an ancient affirmation of the superiority of sight over hearing, see Polybius, *Histories*, 12.27.1-2. I am obliged to Mr. Thomas Freeman for this citation of Polybius. On Guerric's representation of Christ as a lactating mother, see Caroline Walker Bynum, "'. . . And Woman His Humanity': Female Imagery in the Religious Writing of the Later Middle Ages," in Bynum, Stevan Harrel, and Paula Richman, eds., *Gender and Religion: On the Complexity of Symbols* (Boston: Beacon, 1986), 264-65.

33. On a Christian proselyte who ritually slaughtered himself during the pogroms of 1096, see the *Chronicle of Solomon bar Simson*, in Shlomo Eidelberg, ed. and trans.,

The Jews and the Crusaders: The Hebrew Chronicles of the First and Second Crusades (Madison: Univ. of Wisconsin Press, 1977), 58. Ladner refers to the fear in John Chrysostom's day that Antiochene Christians would convert to Judaism ("Aspects of Patristic Anti-Judaism," 358). For literature on Christian converts to Judaism, see Morrison, *Conversion and Text*, introduction to Herman-Judah's *Account of His Own Conversion*, nn. 82, 83.

34. The thirteenth-century writer Henry of Livonia records the performance of a play on the story of Gideon designed to convert the people of Riga in *Chronicon Lyvoniae*, 9.14 (*MGH, SS* 23:252). However, given the survival of dramatic performances "ex gentili ritu" among the converted peoples (Cosmas of Prague, *Chronicon Boemiae*, 3.1 [*MGHSSrrG*, 161]: "scenas quas ex gentili ritu faciebant") and the proliferation of secular and religious drama among the converters (for London, see William Fitzstephen, *Vita S. Thomae Cantuariensis Archiepiscopi*, prol. [Migne *PL* 190:108]), it is hard to think that this educational device was not widely employed.

35. Herman-Judah, *Opusculum de Conversione Sua*, chap. 2 (*MGH, Quellen zur Geistesgeschichte des Mittelalters* 4:75).

36. Rupert of Deutz, *Commentum in Apocalypsim*, 1.1 (Migne *PL* 169:846–47).

37. See Joseph Neubner, *Die heiligen Handwerker in der Darstellung der Acta Sanctorum: Ein Beitrag zur christlichen Sozialgeschichte aus hagiographischen Quellen*, Münsterische Beiträge zur Theologie, 4 (Münster: Aschendorf, 1929), 168–69, on Bernward of Hildesheim.

38. Gerhoch of Reichersberg, *Tractatus in Ps. 27*, 2 and *Tractatus in Ps. 144*, 4 (Migne *PL* 193:1224, 194:964); Anon., *The Life of Christina of Markyate*, chap. 52 (ed. Talbot, 128). The Ovidian tag "materiam superabat opus" (*Metamorphoses*, 2.5) is common and indicates a knowing eye for craftsmanship. See also, for example, Anon., *Vita Arnoldi Archiepiscopi Magontini*, in Philipp Jaffé, ed., *Monumenta Mogontina*, Bibliotheca Rerum Germanicarum, 3 (Aalan: Scientia Verlag, 1964), 620–21; Suger, *De Administratione*, chap. 33 (197) (Erwin Panofsky, ed. and trans., *Abbot Suger on the Abbey Church of St-Denis and Its Art Treasures*, 2d ed. [Princeton, N.J.: Princeton Univ. Press, 1979], 60–62). With others, R. W. Swartwout severely discounted the characterization of monks as artists, artisans, and architects. See Swartout, *The Monastic Craftsman: An Inquiry into the Services of Monks to Art in Britain and in Europe North of the Alps during the Middle Ages* (Cambridge: Heffer, 1932).

39. Aristotle, *Nicomachean Ethics*, 9.7.1167b–1168a.

40. *The Sayings of the Desert Fathers: The Alphabetical Collection*, Sisoes, nr 39 (trans. Benedicta Ward, Cistercian Studies, 59 [Kalamazoo: Cistercian Publications, 1975], 184).

41. *Rule of St. Benedict*, chap. 57.

42. See the "modalities of iconoclasm" (notably bowdlerism) discussed by Leo Steinberg, *The Sexuality of Christ in Renaissance Art and in Modern Oblivion* (New York: Pantheon, 1983), 174–83.

43. Herbord, *Dialogus de Vita S. Ottonis Episcopi Babenbergensis* 2.32 (ed. Wikarjak,

122–23). See also Ebo's comment on the destruction of idols "of astounding size, carved with incredible beauty by the sculptor's art," in *Vita S. Ottonis Episcopi Babenbergensis*, 3.10 (ed. Jan Wikarjak, Monumenta Poloniae Historica, n.s., vol. 7, fasc. 2 [Warsaw: Państwowe Wydawnictwo Naukowe, 1969], 111).

44. Hermannus quondam Judaeus, *Opusculum de Conversione Sua*, chaps. 2, 16 (*MGH, Quellen zur Geistesgeschichte des Mittelalters* 4:74, 113).

45. Anon., *S. Ottonis Episcopi Babenbergensis Vita Prieflingensis*, 3.3 (ed. Jan Wikarjak, Monumenta Poloniae Historica, n.s., vol. 7, fasc. 1 [Warsaw: Państwowe Wydawnictwo Naukowe, 1966], 58).

46. See Morrison, *History as a Visual Art in the Twelfth-Century Renaissance*, 146–47, 180–81, 204 n. 23.

47. Caesarius of Heisterbach, *Dialogus Miraculorum*, 8.40 (ed. Strange, 2:113).

48. Herbord, *Dialogus de Vita S. Ottonis Episcopi Babenbergensis* 3.19 (ed. Wikarjak, 181–82); *S. Ottonis Episcopi Babenbergensis Vita Prieflingensis* 3.9 (ed. Wikarjak, 68).

49. Otto of Freising, *Chronicon*, 7.4 (*MGHSSrrG*, 314).

50. Adam of Bremen, *Gesta Hammaburgensis Ecclesiae Pontificum*, 3.46 (45) (*MGHSSrrG*, 190).

51. Francis of Assisi, *The Mirror of Perfection*, sect. 7, chap. 93 (trans. Robert Steele, ed. T. Okey [New York: Dutton, 1944], 267).

52. Otto of Freising, *Chronicon*, 7.7 (*MGHSSrrG*, 317).

53. Anon., *Passio Thiemonis Archiepiscopi Iuvavensis*, chap. 1 (*MGH, SS* 11:53). See Neubner, *Helige Handwerker*, 167–68.

54. Anon., *Passio Thiemonis Archiepiscopi Iuvavensis*, chaps. 11–15 (*MGH, SS* 11:58–62).

55. Henry of Livonia, *Chronicon Lyvoniae*, 26.6 (*MGH, SS* 23:317).

56. *Vita et Passio Sancti Thomae Cantuariensis Archiepiscopi et Martyris*, chap. 2 (Migne *PL* 190:346–49).

57. F. M. Warren, "The Enamoured Moslem Princess in Orderic Vital and the French Epic," *Publications of the Modern Language Association of America* 29 (1914): 341–58; Kedar, *Crusade and Mission*, 69. Although the story was by then recognized as a fabrication, it still appears as historical in Charles François Chevé, *Dictionnaire des conversions*, in J. P. Migne, *Encyclopédie théologique*, 2d ser., vol. 33 (Paris: J. P. Migne, 1866), 914. See *Dictionary of National Biography*, s.v. "Becket."

58. Caesarius of Heisterbach, *Dialogus Miraculorum*, 2.25 (ed. Strange, 1:95–98).

59. Anon., *Vita et Passio Sancti Thomae Cantuariensis Archiepiscopi et Martyris*, chap. 2 (Migne *PL* 190:346).

60. Robert and Janice A. Keefe, *Walter Pater and the Gods of Disorder* (Athens: Ohio Univ. Press, 1988), 106.

61. Torquatto Tasso, *Jerusalem Delivered*, 12.66–67.

62. Ferdinand Fellmann, discussion in Fuhrmann, *Terror und Spiel*, 637.

63. William Fitzstephen, *Vita S. Thomae Cantuariensis Archiepiscopi*, prol., chap. 19 (James Craigie Robertson, ed., *Materials for the History of Thomas Becket, Archbishop of*

Canterbury, Rolls Series, 67 [London: Stationery Office, 1877], 3:12–13). On William Fitzstephen's alternations between Becket's entourage and Henry II's, see Frank Barlow, *Thomas Becket* (Berkeley: Univ. of California Press, 1986), 6, 126, 131, 140, 243, 245.

64. William Fitzstephen, *Vita S. Thomae Cantuariensis archiepiscopi*, chaps. 13–18 (Robertson, *Materials for the History of Thomas Becket* 3:8–13). See also M. Stanesco, *Jeux d'errance du chevalier médiéval: Aspects ludique de la fonction guerrière dans la littérature du Moyen Age flamboyant* (Leiden: Brill, 1988).

65. *New York Times*, 27 Aug. 1989, quoting Professor Peggy R. Sanday.

66. See, for example, Michael Herzfeld, *The Poetics of Manhood: Contest and Identity in a Cretan Mountain Village* (Princeton, N.J.: Princeton Univ. Press, 1985). See also William A. Christian, Jr., *Person and God in a Spanish Valley*, 2d ed. (Princeton, N.J.: Princeton Univ. Press, 1989), 171–72, noting the "isolation of the man from the family unit": "His attention is elsewhere, in the male society." Christian made this observation while he was in a village in northern Spain (1968). Twenty years later, he wondered whether it reflected his own preoccupations and commitments (ibid., 189). But there is no need to question an aspect of social order so commonly observed by anthropologists.

67. See Karl F. Morrison, "Incentives for Studying the Liberal Arts," in David Wagner, ed., *The Seven Liberal Arts in the Middle Ages* (Bloomington: Univ. of Indiana Press, 1983), 32–57.

68. Bernard of Clairvaux, *Sermo in Quadragesima* 6, chap. 4 (Jean Leclercq and Henri Rochais, eds., *Sermones*, S. Bernardi Opera, 4 (Rome: Editiones Cistercienses, 1966), 1:380.

69. Francis of Assisi, *The Mirror of Perfection*, sect. 8, chap. 96 (trans. Steele, ed. Okey, 270).

70. Gilbert Crispin, *Disputatio Iudei et Christiani*, chap. 60 (Abulafia and Evans, *Works*, 22). The persistence of preconversion ways of thinking in men after they entered monasteries is specifically acknowledged in Paschasius Radbertus, *Epitaphium Arsenii*, 1.7.8 (ed. Ernst Dümmler, in *Abhandlungen der kgl. Akademie der Wissenschaften zu Berlin*, phil.-hist. Kl., 2 [1900]: 31): "Idcirco quidam, ut comperimus, e seculo recedentes, adhuc versantur in fluctibus, quia non satis mente exisse probantur. At vero nonnulli, quos tyrocinia virtutum enutrirunt in militaribus rebus, postmodum ad Christi militiam puriores ac perspicatiores veniunt, quam si essent inexperti."

71. See Henry Osborn Taylor, *The Mediaeval Mind: A History of the Development of Thought and Emotion in the Middle Ages*, 4th ed., 1 (London: Macmillan, 1925): 602. Penny Shine Gold comments similarly, regarding twelfth-century romances: "The pursuit of the love of a woman invariably interferes with the hero's pursuit of honor and valor in the sphere of men, and this conflict in turn causes anxiety, tension, and sometimes death for the hero" (*The Lady and the Virgin: Image, Attitude, and Experience in Twelfth-Century France* [Chicago: Univ. of Chicago Press, 1985], 146). Professor Jo Ann McNamara kindly reminded me of the story of Erec and Enite, and the parallel incident of Roland and Aude in *The Song of Roland*. One may note parenthetically the

refusal to admit women to the Virginia Military Institute because so doing "would destroy a system [of discipline] that fosters an intense bonding" among men (*New York Times*, 5 Feb. 1990).

72. For the terms "commessatio, ebrietas, turpia verba, et ioca in conviviis celebrata," all of which lead to fights and homicides, see two fragmentary texts by the ninth-century writer Hrabanus Maurus in *MGH, Epistolae* 5, *Karolini Aevi* 3:524–25. For "ebrietates et commessationes," see also *MGH, Epistolae* 5, *Karolini Aevi* 3:540. For one drinking party, engaging a priest and his brother-in-law, that ended in the death of the first and the mutilation of the second, see Hincmar of Rheims, letter to Pope Hadrian II (Migne *PL* 126:646–47). Women could be present at such events (Hincmar of Rheims, *Capitula Presbyteris Data Anno 852*, chap. 16 [Migne *PL* 125:778]). But it is not clear whether their functions on such occasion were limited to serving, as in *Beowulf*, or in the tasks alloted to Christina of Markyate (Anon., *The Life of Christina of Markyate*, chap. 9 [ed. Talbot, 49]). The wife of the Emperor Louis the Pious is represented on her knees at one feast (D. A. Bullough, *Friends, Neighbours, and Fellow-drinkers: Aspects of Community and Conflict in the Early Medieval West*, H. M. Chadwick Memorial Lectures, 1 [Cambridge: Department of Anglo-Saxon, Norse, and Celtic, 1991], 14). See the critical application of Deuteronomy 44:18–21 to Louis the Pious's son, Lothar, in Thegan, *Vita Ludovici Imperatoris*, chap. 53 (*MGH, SS* 2:601–2). For comparative purposes, see François Lissarrague, *The Aesthetics of the Greek Banquet: Images of Wine and Ritual*, trans. Andrew Szegedy-Maszak (Princeton, N.J.: Princeton Univ. Press, 1990). See *Vita Heinrici IV*, chap. 9 (*MGHSSrrG*, 29).

73. On Gerhoch of Reichersberg's development of this argument, see Morrison, *"I Am You,"* 220.

74. Bynum, "'. . . And Woman His Humanity,'" 268–69, 273, 279.

75. See Ladner, "Aspects of Patristic Anti-Judaism," 359–60, referring to a suggestion by Norman Cohn regarding Christian dealings with Jews.

76. See Morrison, *History as a Visual Art in the Twelfth-Century Renaissance*, 169.

77. Bynum, "'. . . And Woman His Humanity,'" 270, 273, 277.

78. See Morrison, *History as a Visual Art in the Twelfth-Century Renaissance*, 32, 160–62.

79. Anon., *Vitis Mystica*, chap. 17 (Migne *PL* 184:667–72).

80. See above, n. 36.

81. Ailred of Rievaulx, *Tractatus de Jesu Puero Duodenni*, chap. 4 (Migne *PL* 184:852), paraphrasing Ephesians 4:13. The first phrases of the verse, which Ailred knew and presupposed in the minds of his hearers, is "till we all come in the unity of the faith, and of the knowledge of the Son of God."

82. Dante, *Divine Comedy, Purgatorio*, 10.124–29.

83. Gerhoch of Reichersberg, *Tractatus in Ps. 64*, chaps. 81–87 (Migne *PL* 194:59–60).

84. On the importance of Christological kerygma to any quest for a universal morphology of religion, see Hans Waldenfels, "Offenbarung als Selbstmitteilung Gottes

im Sinne des spezifisch Christlichen," in Walter Strolz and Shizuteru Ueda, eds., *Offenbarung als Heilserfahrung im Christentum, Hinduismus, und Buddhismus*, Veröffentlichungen der Stiftung Oratio Dominica, 8 (Vienna: Herder, 1982), 13–32.

85. Jürgen Moltmann, *Theology of Play*, trans. Reinhard Ulrich (New York: Harper & Row, 1972), 5–6.

86. Morrison, "I Am You," 72–81.

87. John Bunyan, *Grace Abounding*, chap. 2, in *The Pilgrim's Progress*, special tercentenary ed. (New York: American Tract Society, n.d.), 15.

88. See above, n. 48.

89. Rahewin, *Gesta Friderici*, 4.16 (*MGHSSrrG*, 255), relates prodigies anticipating the death of Otto of Freising and incineration of his see.

90. Thomas More, *A Dialogue of Comfort*, bk. 3, pref. (Louis L. Martz and Frank Manley, eds., *The Complete Works of St. Thomas More*, 12 [New Haven: Yale Univ. Press, 1976]: 192–93).

91. William Fitzstephen, *Vita S. Thomae Archiepiscopi Cantuariensis*, chap. 157 (Robertson, *Materials for the Life of Thomas Becket* 3:153); Beryl Smalley, *The Becket Conflict and the Schools: A Study of Intellectuals in Politics* (Oxford: Blackwell, 1973), 190.

92. Bunyan, *Grace Abounding*, chap. 5, in *The Pilgrim's Progress*, special tercentenary ed., pp. 40–41.

93. Bunyan, *Pilgrim's Progress*, pt. 2:609.

94. Augustine, *Enarrationes in Psalmum* 147, 19 (*Corpus Christianorum*, series latina 40:2155–56).

95. "Lives of Christ," in William Ralph Inge, *Lay Thoughts of a Dean* (New York: G. P. Putnam's Sons, 1926), 360–66.

96. Guerric of Igny, *The Third Sermon for the Epiphany*, chap. 5 (Morson and Costello, *Sermones* 1:280).

97. Blaise Pascal, *Pensées*, nrs 343, 392 (*Paschal's Pensées*, trans. Martin Turnell [New York: Harper & Brothers, 1962], 202–3, 221); Nicholas Rescher, *Pascal's Wager: A Study of Practical Reasoning in Philosophical Theology* (Notre Dame: Univ. of Notre Dame Press, 1985), 1–2, 43 (the parallel of Hans Küng), 117–33 (on the rationality of faith as understood by Pascal in the wager text).

98. Inge, "Lives of Christ," 366.

Chapter 6. *A Noble Humility*

1. Karl F. Morrison, *History as a Visual Art in the Twelfth-Century Renaissance* (Princeton, N.J.: Princeton Univ. Press, 1990), 69–70.

2. M. H. Abrams, *Natural Supernaturalism: Tradition and Revolution in Romantic Literature* (New York: Norton, 1973), 66.

3. Jan van Ruysbroeck, *The Seven Steps of the Ladder of Spiritual Love*, fifth step (trans. F. Sherwood Taylor [Westminster: Dacre, 1944], 31).

4. On portrayals of women in twelfth-century historical writings, see Morrison,

History as a Visual Art in the Twelfth-Century Renaissance, 154–96. See also Janet Nelson, "Women and the Word in the Earlier Middle Ages," in W. J. Sheils and Diana Wood, eds., *Women and the Church* (Oxford: Blackwell, 1990), 63–78.

5. Emilie Zum Brunn and Georgette Epiney-Burgard, *Women Mystics in Medieval Europe*, trans. Sheila Hughes (New York: Paragon, 1989), 54–60.

6. See above, chapter 2, after n. 21.

7. Dante, *La Vita Nuova*, chap. 42 (Dante Alighieri, *La Vita Nuova (Poems of Youth)*, trans. Barbara Reynolds [Baltimore: Penguin, 1969], 99). In 42.3, Dante refers to Christ as "sire de la cortesia"; in 12.2, to Beatrice as "la donna de la cortesia." See also 12.4, where Christ is called the "segnore de la nobiltade."

8. Julian of Norwich, *Revelations*, chap. 7, rev. 1 (*A Book of Showings to the Anchoress Julian of Norwich*, ed. Edmund Colledge and James Walsh, pt. 2 [Toronto: Pontifical Institute of Medieval Studies, 1978], 314–15).

9. See chapter 5, at n. 83.

10. C. Stephen Jaeger, *The Origins of Courtliness: Civilizing Trends and the Formation of Courtly Ideals, 939–1210* (Philadelphia: Univ. of Pennsylvania Press, 1985), 19–53.

11. Boethius, *Consolation of Philosophy*, 3.pros. 4: "dignitas propria virtuti," "propria dignitatis pulchritudo."

12. Bernard of Clairvaux, *Vita Sancti Malachiae Episcopi*, 19.43 (Jean Leclercq and Henri Rochais, eds., *Tractatus et Opuscula*, S. Bernardi Opera, 3 [Rome: Editiones Cistercienses, 1963], 348), and *Sermo de Sancto Malachia*, chap. 4 (Jean Leclercq and Henri Rochais, eds., *Sermones*, S. Bernardi Opera, 6, 1 [Rome: Editiones Cistercienses, 1970] 3: 53). See Jaeger, *The Origins of Courtliness*, 171, on the monastic rejection of "excessive *hilaritas* and *iocunditas*." However, one must also bear in mind the monastic desire for the inexpressible joys of spiritual intoxication. Extreme spiritual joys were licit.

13. Ebo, *Vita S. Ottonis Episcopi Babenbergensis*, 1.5, 3.14 (ed. Jan Wikarjak, Monumenta Poloniae Historica, n.s., vol. 7, fasc. 2 [Warsaw: Państwowe Wydawnictwo Naukowe, 1969], 15, 119); Herbord, *Dialogus de Vita S. Ottonis Episcopi Babenbergensis*, 1.7, 2.24 (ed. Jan Wikarjak, Monumenta Poloniae Historica, n.s., vol. 7, fasc. 3 [Warsaw: Państwowe Wydawnictwo Naukowe, 1974], 10, 107).

14. Bernard Ward, *St. Edmund, Archbishop of Canterbury: His Life, as Told by Old English Writers* (London: Sands, 1903), 45, 56, 96. A similar alternation of tears and smiles appears in Walter Daniel's description of Ailred of Rievaulx on his deathbed, listening to the Passion of Christ. At some points in the narrative, Walter wrote, Ailred's lips gained the "likeness of a certain spiritual smile." At others, he wept with grief. "Inter hec videres gaudia omnium et dolores concurrere simul, risus et lacrime, vox exultacionis et suspiria uno ex ore, uno in tempore, eadem in omnibus et omnia in singulis in rem quamdam publicam progredi" (Walter Daniel, *The Life of Ailred of Rievaulx*, chap. 56 [ed. F. M. Powick (London: Nelson, 1950), 61]). When Ailred prayed, he was profuse with tears (ibid., chaps. 11, 42 [pp. 20–21, 50]). But, mastering a crisis with a miracle, he was capable of smiling with virile gravity (Walter Daniel, *Epistola ad Mauricium*, chap. 3 [ibid., 73]).

15. Ward, *St. Edmund, Archbishop of Canterbury*, 46–47, and see above, n. 14; Decree of Pope Innocent IV canonizing Edmund of Abingdon, in Edmond Martène and Ursine Durand, eds., *Thesaurus Novus Anecdotorum* 3 (Paris: Delaulne, 1717): cols. 1856–57.

16. Anon., *Vita Arnoldi Archiepiscopi Magontini*, in Philipp Jaffé, ed., *Monumenta Mogontina*, Bibliotheca Rerum Germanicarum (Aalen: Scientia Verlag, 1964), 621 ("risus blandus et suavis"), 667–68.

17. Richard of St. Victor, *The Mystical Ark*, 2.6 (Grover A. Zinn, trans., *Richard of St. Victor: The Twelve Patriarchs, The Mystical Ark, Book Three of the Trinity* [New York: Paulist Press, 1979], 182–83).

18. As noted above (chapter 1, n. 18), Conrad Rudolph has concluded that Hugh of St. Victor's theology was predominately Augustinian, rather than Dionysian. However, the easy and habitual interpenetration of the Augustinian with the Dionysian system seems to me a caution against classifying Hugh as an Augustinian, particularly in view of his profound study of *The Celestial Hierarchies*. Rudolph described Suger's reception of Hugh's theology and translation of it into artistic and architectural programs at St. Denis as a "synthesis." Plainly, the Dionysian ideas could be assimilated because they appeared to explain and expand existing patterns of belief. Assimilation was by synthesis for Hugh as well as for Suger. But the changes that Dionysian expansions introduced into Augustinian patterns, and their esthetic possibilities, were considerable.

19. G. Huet, "La Légende de la statue de Vénus," *Revue de l'histoire des religions* 68 (1913): 193–217, esp. pp. 202–3. The reference is to William of Malmesbury, *De Gestis Regum Angliorum*, 2.13 (ed. William Stubbs, Rolls Series, 90, pt. 1 [London: Stationery Office, 1887], 1:256–58).

20. Paschasius Radbertus, *Epitaphium Arsenii*, 2.15.2 (ed. Ernst Dümmler, in *Abhandlungen der kgl. Akademie der Wissenschaften zu Berlin*, phil.-hist. Kl., 2 [1900]: 82): "quia pro genere, pro vitae merito, pro institutione, quam percoeperat pene ab ineunte aetate infra senatum et sapientes regni, pro mentis efficacia et nobilitate sensus plurimum ab omnibus audiebatur et venerabatur a singulis." The stereotypal character and the long survival of these characteristics are indicated by Jaeger's profile of the courtier-bishop in *The Origins of Courtliness*, 28–29.

21. Anon., *Libri Carolini*, 2.3 (*MGH, Conc.* 2, *Suppl.*, 65).

22. Herbord, *Dialogus de Vita S. Ottonis Episcopi Babenbergensis*, 3.30 (ed. Wikarjak, 193).

23. Ebo, *Vita S. Ottonis Episcopi Babenbergensis*, 3.1, 9–10 (ed. Wikarjak, 91, 109–11); Herbord, *Dialogus de Vita S. Ottonis Episcopi Babenbergensis*, 2.32, 3.6–7 (ed. Wikarjak, 122–25, 160, 162).

24. Manegold of Lautenbach, *Liber ad Gebehardum*, chap. 77 (*MGH, Ldl* 1:429).

25. Ibid., chap. 40 (p. 381). For Thomas Aquinas's doctrine that killing sinners could be even better a work than killing wild beasts, see above, chapter 3, n. 58.

26. Herbord, *Dialogus de Vita S. Ottonis Episcopi Babenbergensis*, 3.7 (ed. Wikarjak, 162). The term "teutonicus Deus" appears in Ebo, *Vita S. Ottonis Episcopi Babenbergensis*, 3.1 (ed. Wikarjak, 94).

27. Augustine, *Confessions*, 7.10.16 (*Corpus Christianorum, series latina* 27:103–4). On the history of this term, see Pierre Courcelle, *Connais-toi toi-même de Socrate à Bernard* 2 (Paris: Etudes Augustiniennes, 1975): 241 n. 36, 285 n. 99.

28. See above, chapter 2, at n. 36.

29. Bernard of Clairvaux, *Vita Sancti Malachiae Episcopi*, 1.1, 3.6, 8.16–17, 10.19 (Leclercq and Rochais, *Tractatus et Opuscula*, 309–10, 315, 325–26, 330); Ebo, *Vita S. Ottonis Episcopi Babenbergensis*, 2.2, 4, 5, 11, 14, 3.8, 11, 14, 23 (ed. Wikarjak, 55, 63, 65, 72, 78, 108–9, 111–12, 119–20, 134).

30. Teresa of Avila, *The Life of Teresa of Jesus*, chap. 37 (E. Allison Peers, trans., *The Autobiography of St. Teresa of Avila* (Garden City, N.Y.: Image Books, 1960), 360).

31. Jaeger, *The Origins of Courtliness*, x, 101, 157, 211.

32. See ibid., 37, 38, 149 (on the courtly ethics's disapproval of revenge), 70 (on Adalbert of Bremen), 178. The idea that by its ideals of mercy and affability, courtliness opposed revenge seems to be very much qualified by instances in which the courtly executed revenge upon one another and sought their objects with manifold "acts of inhumanity and violence" (ibid., 77–78, 106, 163 [an exhortation to slaughter is an example of *urbanitas*], 248).

33. Hildegard of Bingen, *ep.* 52 (to Werner of Kirchheim) (Migne *PL* 197:270), and *Scivias*, visio 11.13 (*Corpus Christianorum, continuatio medievalis* 43A:583).

34. Karl F. Morrison, *"I Am You": The Hermeneutics of Empathy in Western Literature, Theology and Art* (Princeton, N.J.: Princeton Univ. Press, 1988), 230–31, on Gerhoch of Reichersberg.

35. Ward, *St. Edmund, Archbishop of Canterbury*, 30, 54, 93.

36. Ibid., 36.

37. Ibid., 30, 35, 36, 48, 52, 53–54, 162, 165.

38. Ibid., 54, 120, 122, 137, 141, 145.

39. William Segar, *Honor, Military and Civill, Contained in Foure Bookes*, 4.15 (London: Robert Barker, 1602), 225, citing Bartolus. Segar also drew on Scripture, Aristotle, Lucas de Penna, and Boethius.

40. Ibid., 228, citing Bono da Cortile.

41. Anon., *The Life of Christina of Markyate, a Twelfth Century Recluse*, chap. 64 (ed. and trans. C. H. Talbot [Oxford: Clarendon, 1959], 150).

42. E.g., ibid., chap. 1 (p. 34); Bernard of Clairvaux, *Vita Sancti Malachiae Episcopi*, 1.1, 23.52 (Leclercq and Rochais, *Tractatus et Opuscula*, 310, 356).

43. Cf. Anon., *The Life of Christina of Markyate*, chap. 43, 73 (ed. Talbot, 114, 168). On moral strength, see below, n. 44.

44. Anon., *Vita Beati Edmundi Cantuariensis Archiepiscopi et Confessoris*, in Martène and Durand, *Thesaurus Novus Anecdotorum* 3: col. 1775: "cogitatione femineae masculum animum inseruit"; Ward, *St. Edmund, Archbishop of Canterbury*, 3.

45. Bonizo of Sutri, *Liber ad Amicum*, chap. 8 (*MGH, Ldl* 1:620).

46. Manegold of Lautenbach, *Liber ad Gebehardum*, chap. 23 (ibid., 353).

47. See Anon., *The Life of Christina of Markyate*, chap. 15 (ed. Talbot, 58): "Quocirca vos obsecro rogate [eam] ut misereatur nostri et in Domino nubens [aver]tat a

nobis notam imminentis ob[pro]brii. Ut quid degeneret? Ut quid parentes dishonoret? Mendacitas illius universe nobilitati erit notabile dedecus."

48. Dante, *Divine Comedy, Purgatorio*, 10:112–29, and *Paradiso*, 1.64–84 (Dorothy L. Sayers, trans., *The Comedy of Dante Alighieri the Florentine* [Harmondsworth: Penguin, 1955], 2:160; unless otherwise indicated, all citations of the *Divine Comedy* will be from Sayers's translation).

49. *Historia Translationis B. Edmundi* and *Causa Quare Brachium Sancti Edmundi extra Capsulam Collocatur*, in Martène and Durand, *Thesaurus Novus Anecdotorum* 3: cols. 1866–71; Wilfrid Wallace, *Life of St. Edmund of Canterbury from Original Sources* (London: Kegan Paul, Trench, Trübner, 1893), 402–9, 414–15; Ward, *St. Edmund, Archbishop of Canterbury*, 200–202, 204, 208. Wallace placed the dispute after the 1247 translation. The documents, papal and Cistercian, allowing lavish ornamentation of Edmund's tomb are catalogued in C. H. Lawrence, *St. Edmund of Abingdon: A Study in Hagiography and History* (Oxford: Clarendon Press, 1960), 322 (no. 36), 324 (no. 64). See the quite rapid survey of Cistercian attitudes toward art in Helmut Feld, *Der Ikonoklasmus des Westens* (Leiden: Brill, 1990), 46–55.

50. Paschasius Radbertus, *Epitaphium Arsenii*, 1.1.9 (ed. Dümmler, 39): "Idcirco etsi adumbratur titulus, lineamenta tamen gestorum produnt, uti pictorum mos est, qui bene pingere norunt, qui sepe ita vultus exprimunt, ut sine litteris et voce loquantur."

51. Agobard of Lyon, *Liber de imaginibus sanctorum*, chaps. 21, 31 (Migne *PL* 104:216, 225). Agobard's reference to "feeding" on pictures is an allusion to Virgil, *Aeneid*, 1.446–93, where Aeneas is represented "feeding" his mind on "empty" pictures.

52. Dante, *Divine Comedy, Purgatorio*, 10.37–45, 94–96. Dante may have seen, and had in mind, the *Annunciation* by Arnolfo di Cambrio, formerly in Santa Croce at Florence, now in the Victoria and Albert Museum (Inv. 7563-1861), or the one still in situ. See also *Purgatorio*, 12.64–60.

53. Rupert of Deutz, *Anulus*, bk. 3 (Migne *PL* 170:607–8), quoting 3 Kings 6:29.

54. Herbord, *Dialogus de Vita S. Ottonis Babenbergensis Episcopi*, 2.32 (ed. Wikarjak, 124).

55. Dante, *Divine Comedy, Purgatorio* 12.64–66.

56. I have developed this argument in the section entitled "The Invisibility of Art" in *"I Am You,"* 269–345. My interpretation of the "album" or "fascicle" method of composition is set forth in *History as a Visual Art in the Twelfth-Century Renaissance* (Princeton, N.J.: Princeton Univ. Press, 1990), 25–28, 103–4, 128, 239–40.

57. Dante, *La Vita Nuova*, chap. 34 (trans. Reynolds, 87–88).

58. See Karl F. Morrison, *The Mimetic Tradition of Reform in the West* (Princeton, N.J.: Princeton Univ. Press, 1982).

59. Aristotle, *Nicomachean Ethics*, 1.7.1097a–b, 1.8.1099a, 3.6.1115a–b, 4.3.1123 a–b, 8.7.1158b, 9.8.1169a, 10.6.1176b, 10.7.1178a, 10.9.1179b, and *Politics*, 1.6.1255a, 1.13.1260a, 3.4.1277b, 3.5.1278a.

60. Milton, *Samson Agonistes*, ll. 1708–44.

61. Abrams, *Natural Supernaturalism*, 168, 175–76, 188, 220–21, 310–25.

62. James Joyce, *A Portrait of the Artist as Young Man* (New York: Granada, 1964), 160. See further the discussion in Morrison, *"I Am You,"* 99–114.

63. Lawrence Buell, "Moby-Dick as Sacred Text," in Richard H. Brodhead, ed., *New Essays on Moby-Dick* (Cambridge: Cambridge Univ. Press, 1986), 53–72.

64. Bryan Wolf, "When Is a Painting Most Like a Whale? Ishmael, *Moby-Dick*, and the Sublime," ibid., 164.

65. Walt Whitman, "Passage to India," in Louis Untermeyer, ed., *The Prose and Poetry of Walt Whitman* (New York: Simon and Schuster, 1946), 386.

66. Cf. Augustine, *City of God*, 11.18,23 (*Corpus Christianorum, series latina* 48:337, 341–343), *Confessions*, 11.26.33–28.38 (*Corpus Christianorum, series latina* 27:211–14), and *De Ordine*, 1.1.2 (*Corpus Christianorum, series latina* 29:90). For Ruysbroeck's use of song as a metaphor for the unity of the blessed with Christ, see below, Summary, n. 8.

67. The term is derived from Paschasius Radbertus. See Morrison, *The Mimetic Tradition of Reform in the West*, 123–28.

68. Dante, *La Vita Nuova*, chap. 42 (trans. Reynolds, 99).

69. Herman Melville, *Moby-Dick*, ed. Charles Child Walcutt (New York: Bantam, 1986), 537.

70. Cited in Ian Ker, *John Henry Newman: A Biography* (Oxford: Oxford Univ. Press, 1990), 585. Christianity's persistent absorption of indigenous customs gives some edge to Newman's observation. See above, chapter 2, at n. 23; chapter 5, at n. 21.

71. The quotation is from Dietrich Bonhoeffer, *The Cost of Discipleship*, rev. ed. (New York: Collier Books, 1963), 170–71, 323.

Summary

1. *New York Times*, 27 Jan. 1990.

2. Wido of Ferrara, *De Schismate Hildebrandi*, 2.praef. (*MGH, Ldl* 1:550).

3. Augustine, *De Trinitate*, 15.11.20 (*Corpus Christianorum, series latina* 50:499).

4. Karl F. Morrison, *"I Am You": The Hermeneutics of Empathy in Western Literature, Theology, and Art* (Princeton, N.J.: Princeton Univ. Press, 1988), 179–83.

5. Rainer Maria Rilke, "Da stehen wir mit Spiegeln," in *Späte Gedichte* (Leipzig: Inselverlag, 1935), 88.

6. Dante, *Divine Comedy, Paradiso*, 27.1–6, 33.133–45 (Dorothy L. Sayers and Barbara Reynolds, trans., *The Comedy of Dante Alighieri* [Harmondsworth: Penguin, 1962], 3:291, 347).

7. Anon., *The Life of Christina of Markyate, a Twelfth-Century Recluse*, chap. 80 (ed. and trans. C. H. Talbot [Oxford: Clarendon, 1959], 186); Barbara Newman, *Saint Hildegard of Bingen: Symphonia* (Ithaca, N.Y.: Cornell Univ. Press, 1988), 17–18; Edgar de Bruyne, *Etudes d'esthétique médiévale* 2 (Bruges: De Tempel, 1946): 119, citing John Cotton, *Musica*, chap. 2 (Migne *PL* 150:1394). Although cognate observations con-

cerning the comparison of the cantor with the master of music (*musicus*) occur in the Carolingian text by Aurelian of Réôme, the exact analogy with the drunken man is lacking (Aurelian of Réôme, *Musica Disciplina*, chap. 7 [Lawrence Gushee, ed., *Aureliani Reomensis Musica Disciplina*, Corpus Scriptorum de Musica, 21 (Rome: American Institute of Musicology, 1975), 77–78]). Cf. John Stevens, *Words and Music in the Middle Ages: Song, Narrative, Dance, and Drama, 1050–1350* [Cambridge: Cambridge Univ. Press, 1986], 376). I am obliged to Mrs. Jayarani Fedson for my Indian analogue.

8. Jan van Ruysbroeck, *The Seven Steps of the Ladder of Spiritual Love*, steps 4, 5 (ed. F. Sherwood Taylor [Westminster: Dacre, 1944], 28–55). For a similar idea in Augustine of Hippo's writings, see above, chapter 6, n. 66.

Index

I am very much obliged to Mr. Michael Cavey and Mrs. Anne C. Morrison for assistance in compiling this index.

Abelard, Peter, 104–5, 110, 116
Abraham, patriarch, 37
actors, 112, 118, 150, 193, 219 n. 76. *See also* theater
Adalbert, archbishop of Hamburg-Bremen, 80
Adam, protoplast, 34, 61, 82
Adam of Bremen, 135
adoption, x, xii, 162
adultery, 19
Agrippa, king, 37, 39
Ailred, abbot of Rievaulx, 81, 157, 229 n. 14
Alexander III, pope, 9
allegory, x, 10, 25, 39, 40, 41, 54, 134. *See also* Christology; symbolism
Ambrose, bishop of Milan, 72
Anacletus II, antipope, 56, 72, 81, 128
Ananias, x, xx
ancestors, worship of, 44
Andrew, apostle, 40
androgyny, 131, 135, 145, 146
angels, 69, 88, 113, 171
animals, 30, 45–46, 54, 75, 167, 204 n. 39, 212 n. 58, 230 n. 25
Annunciation, 171
Anselm, archbishop of Canterbury, 46, 91

Anthony of Egypt, 48
Antichrist, 84, 96
Antiquity, classical, 9, 10, 30, 58, 97, 127, 133, 156, 160, 162, 167, 174, 190. *See also* tradition
apatheia, 67
apocalypse, 6, 10, 34, 38, 71, 79–80, 94, 125
apocrypha, 40–41
Apollo, 17, 30
apostasy, xix, 14, 24, 37, 44, 70, 72, 81–82, 83, 84, 88, 90, 91, 145, 189
Apostles, 146, 152, 162. *See also individual apostles*
apostolate, xx, 38, 40, 43, 74, 79, 82, 85, 93
apostolic life, xix, 67
Apuleius, Lucius, 59, 71
Aquinas, Thomas. *See* Thomas Aquinas
Arabia, 11, 38
architecture, 17, 33, 63–64
Areopagus, 37
Arians, 14, 213 n. 72
Aristotelianism, 16
Aristotle, 2, 59, 134, 166, 174–75, 176, 180, 181
Arnold, archbishop of Mainz, 159
Arnolfo di Cambrio, 171

235

art, xiii, xv, xix, 10, 15, 17, 31, 33, 42, 67, 91, 100, 115, 117, 119, 122, 127, 134, 137, 158–59, 160, 163, 176, 190; amazement of, 159–61, 168, 182; liberal arts, 76, 83, 143; objects of, 80; visual arts, 131, 148, 193. *See also* music; painting; sculpture; theater
Arthur, king, 40
artisans, xix, 57, 133–34, 138, 191
artists, xiii, 31, 133, 167, 177, 181
asceticism, xvi, xvii, xviii, xix, xxi, 14, 24, 38, 50, 53, 61, 69, 78, 80, 85, 90, 112, 116, 127, 134, 157–58, 167, 168. *See also* pain; suffering
asexuality, 21
association, method of, 108–10, 189
astrology, 75, 90
Athanasius, bishop of Alexandria, xiii, 48
Athenians, 39
athletes, 82, 115, 138, 146
Attis, 100, 101
audience, 4, 23, 51
Augustine, bishop of Hippo, xii, xiv, xxiv, 10, 16, 23, 24, 25, 35, 66, 68, 72, 78, 79, 89, 112, 114, 124, 125, 140, 143, 150, 152, 164, 167, 191, 192, 200 n. 15
Augustinian order (canons), xix, xx, xxi, 50, 56; Norbertines, 9
Auschwitz, xxiv, 89

Babylon, 82, 165
bafflement, 159. *See also* reason
ball, 64, 192. *See also* game; play
banquet, 54, 62
baptism, x, xi, xx, 3, 7, 11, 14, 24, 54, 67, 69, 72, 81, 130, 133, 140, 141, 155; font for, 83; forced, 81, 213; rites of, 5
barbarism, 164, 174
Baroque, 160
Beatrice dei Portinari, 183
beauty, xviii, 10, 21, 33, 35, 78, 88, 125, 126, 131, 132, 133, 134–35, 136, 148, 156, 158, 159, 165, 177, 190, 193, 212 n. 51. *See also* esthetics
Becket, Thomas, 106–13, 115, 116, 118, 139–41, 142, 151, 157, 169, 216 n. 19
Bede, the Venerable, 6, 42, 43, 44

Benedict of Nursia, 14, 69, 134
Benedict of York, 72
Benedicta of the Cross. *See* Edith Stein
Benedictine order, 134; *Rule,* 70, 160
Bernard, abbot of Clairvaux, xiv, xv, 6, 15, 19, 30, 56, 59, 62, 63, 72, 73, 106, 130, 134, 144, 158, 169
Bethanites, 41, 52
bishop, office of, 25, 105, 108, 110, 111, 116, 133
blasphemy, 120, 128
blindness, viii, ix, xx, 12, 30, 46, 82, 83; spiritual, 82, 83, 101, 128
bodhisattvas, 62, 83, 84, 120, 147
body, 16, 22, 38, 49, 55, 61, 67, 100, 149, 151. *See also* carnality; flesh
Boethius, Anicius Manlius Severinus, 68, 158
Bonhoeffer, Dietrich, 184
Boniface, Apostle of the Germans, 43
bridegroom, 145, 192. *See also* marriage; spouse
Britain, 40, 42
Bryce, James, 86
Buddhas, 83, 147
Buddhism, 60, 61, 71, 83, 84, 119, 120, 147, 148. *See also* Zen
Bultmann, Rudolf, 126
Bunyan, John, 68, 70, 150, 151
butterfly, 148, 167

Caesarius of Heisterbach, 33, 79, 81, 82, 124, 145
Calvin, John, 70
cannibalism, 88, 114
cards, 65, 179–80
Carmelite order, xxiv, 87–89
carnality, 75, 82, 101, 102, 189. *See also* body; flesh
Carolingians, xx
Catullus, Gaius Valerius, 100–101, 102, 103, 119
certitude, 45, 95, 189, 192
charismata, 52
charity, 31, 38, 84, 98, 102, 106, 108, 110, 112, 113, 119, 120, 128, 167, 182. *See also* love
chastity, 56, 68, 69, 135
Chaucer, Geoffrey, 46
children, 30, 55, 67, 68, 85, 86, 105,

109, 116–17, 129, 135, 136, 149, 150–51, 153, 178
chivalry, xviii, xix, 20, 25, 91, 97, 145, 156, 173, 190
Chrétien de Troyes, 144
Christ, viii, ix, x, xi, xviii, 6, 7, 11, 15, 16, 19, 20, 22, 30, 33, 35, 36, 37, 40, 41, 45, 47, 48, 52, 55, 59, 64–65, 68, 69, 72, 74, 75, 76, 82–83, 87, 89, 91, 93, 105, 108–9, 124, 126, 144, 147, 151, 152, 170, 175, 180, 186; as image, xiii–xiv; as Man of Sorrows, 179, 220 n. 82; as master of heavenly music, 194; as spouse, 55, 94, 156; anatomy of, 135; biographies of, 152; body of, 38, 80, 149, 172, 191; likeness of, 168; passion of, 83; picture of, 133, 220 n. 82; wounds of, 69, 133, 164–65; false Christs, 82. *See also* Cross; crucifixion; image; imitation; Jesus; Passion
Christianity, 1, 7, 15, 33, 42–43, 50, 148–49, 186
Christians, false, 75, 96
Christina of Markyate, 50, 51, 54–57, 69, 141, 193
Christocentricity, 51
Christology, 41, 51, 68, 133, 149, 172
Church, 31, 33, 40, 67, 71, 81, 82, 94, 97, 100, 105, 108, 117, 151, 158, 161, 183, 190; repaganizing of, 165
Cicero, Marcus Tullius, 94, 191
Cistercian order, xix, 8–9, 30, 47, 131, 134, 168, 170, 232 n. 49
Cîteaux, 170
Clarendon, Constitutions of, 106–7
Claudia Procula, 40
Coifi, 43, 45
colonialism, 86
commensality, 145, 149, 150
condescension, 157, 168, 177, 181, 182, 190
conscience, xvii, 6, 9, 17, 67, 92–121, 156, 158, 177, 189
contemplation, 75, 77, 83, 88, 142, 160
conversions, false, 35, 37, 51; form of, xiv, xvi, xii, 6, 7, 56, 59, 69, 107, 114, 130; repertory of patterns of, xii, xv, 23
cosmos, 16, 25, 35, 124, 127, 132

courtesy, 178, 216 n. 19, 216 n. 23; Lord of, xviii, 157, 183, 191
Covenant, New, 37. *See also* Testament, New
Cowper, William, 3
craftsmanship, 33, 140
Creation, xv, 5, 29, 34, 132
Crispin, Gilbert, 144
criticism, 41, 70, 142, 159
Cross, 6, 15, 32, 68, 69, 81, 107–8, 136, 189. *See also* crucifixion
crown, of martyrdom, 112; of righteousness, 38
crucifixion, xviii, 67, 88, 98, 105, 109, 133, 135, 144, 147, 159, 161, 165, 187, 189, 194; recrucifixion of Christ, 83, 111, 113; self-crucifixions, 121
cruelty, 58, 71, 77, 86, 95, 98, 128, 138–39, 164, 165
crusades, 46, 47, 53, 54, 130, 135, 137–41, 214 n. 77
cults, 20, 77
cultus sui, 47, 48, 86, 97, 99, 109, 115, 142, 156, 161, 164, 166, 171, 173, 174, 176, 179, 196, 216 n. 23
Cupid, 127
Cybele, 100, 103

Damascus, viii, ix, x, xx, 11, 23, 38, 39
dances, 59, 100, 142, 194
Daniel, prophet, 52, 54, 94
Dante Alighieri, 148, 157, 166–67, 171, 173, 176, 181, 182, 183, 192
David, king, 106
deaf, the, 46, 102
death, 30, 32, 38, 64, 68, 100, 107, 109, 112, 124, 175, 178
deceit, 37, 129; self-deception, 66, 96, 98, 189. *See also* hypocrisy
Delphi, 30
demons, xxi, 42, 43, 44, 48, 71, 88, 98, 105, 115, 123, 136, 138, 161, 164, 171, 221 n. 10. *See also* Devil; Satan
demythologizing, 126, 151
Denmark, king of, 1
depression, postenlightenment, 48, 70, 74
Devil, 31, 44, 68, 72, 77, 82, 85, 95, 138. *See also* demons; Lucifer; Satan; Tempter

dharmas, 61, 62, 120
Diana, 128, 175, 221 n. 10
diet, 54, 104
Dionysius the Areopagite, 10, 17, 161
discipline, 83, 84, 142, 144, 158, 159
disease, 78, 178. *See also* medicine
Diotima, 21
disguise, 22, 143
dissimilarity, 2, 20, 164, 171. *See also* similitude
divinities, 21
divinization, 17
Dominican order, 9
doubt, xvii, 21, 32, 49, 54, 119
drama, 7, 24, 47, 48, 76, 142. *See also* theater
dreams, 54, 69. *See also* vision
Dryden, John, 121

Ebstorf world map, 172
ecstasy, 60
Eden, Garden of, 35, 54
Edmund of Abingdon (Edmund Rich), archbishop of Canterbury, 158, 159, 161, 165, 166, 168–71, 172, 173, 193
education, xvii, xix, 14, 25, 66, 68, 70, 75–79, 83, 84, 85–86, 88, 90, 92, 119, 123, 127, 135, 147, 155, 158, 159, 162, 166, 173, 192
effeminacy, xviii, 146, 164, 166, 178
Egbert, bishop of Münster, 56, 134
Egypt, 11
elect, 19, 82, 162
election, xii, 19
Elisha, prophet, 54
Elizabeth of Schönau, 42
emasculation, 100. *See also* eunuch
emperors, 14
Empire, 11. *See also* Rome
Enite, 145
enlightenment, era of, 8, 15, 85; experience of, 60, 61, 62, 70, 73, 78, 83, 84, 85, 147, 148, 177, 192
Epicureans, 71
Erec, 144–45
eroticism, 48, 49, 69, 114, 141, 143, 177. *See also* love
Esther, queen, 52
esthetics, xvii, 16, 18, 21–22, 120, 135,
160, 175, 177, 179; male, xvii, 141, 148, 155, 183, 190. *See also* masculinity; virility
Ethiopian, 47
Eucharist, 56, 69, 109, 130, 149, 155, 172
eunuchs, 39, 69. *See also* emasculation
evangelists, 82, 146
Eve, protoplast, 82
evil, 6, 29, 61, 78, 84, 88, 181, 194
exegesis, xvi, 32, 39–40, 46, 54, 82, 129, 132. *See also* hermeneutics, interpretation
eyes, mental, viii; spiritual, xx; concupiscence of, 165

fable, 39, 122, 127
faith, xx, 27, 28, 36, 37, 38, 43, 49, 55, 70, 90, 95, 119, 124, 130, 152, 153, 188; categories of, 31–32, 33, 59
fama, 97, 100, 101, 102, 104, 107, 109, 111, 113, 116, 156, 167, 175
Fathers, of the Church, 10, 20, 44, 79, 186
Faust, 114
fecundity, 30, 37, 38, 56, 140, 156. *See also* sower, parable of
female, 21, 50, 155
femininity, 145, 146, 178, 181. *See also* women
fiction, 34, 39, 41, 42, 45, 51, 52, 89, 125, 186, 192
Fitzstephen, William, 142, 150
flesh, xviii, 51, 53, 135, 164, 190. *See also* body, carnality
forgery, 40–42
fornication, physical, 98, 101, 103; spiritual, 55
Fragestellung, 7, 34, 35, 46, 58
Franciscan order, 9
Francis of Assisi, 131, 133, 136, 144, 161
Frauenkirche (Munich), 172
friendship, 55, 143, 175

Gallitzin, Demetrius Augustine, prince, 85
game, 27, 48–49, 63, 65, 142, 150, 151, 153, 160, 170, 181; of hide-and-seek, 49, 172, 182. *See also* ball; love; play

gender, 51, 141, 142, 145, 166; reversal of, 146
Genesis, 5
genius, 63, 147
gentiles, x, 38, 83
Geoffrey, abbot of St. Albans, 55, 56
Gerhoch, provost of Reichersberg, 106
Gilbert Foliot, bishop of London, 112
Glastonbury, 40
glory, 113, 117, 131, 142, 154, 156, 170, 179
God, xv, 15, 19, 20, 21, 22, 23, 29, 30, 31, 33, 37, 38, 43, 45, 48, 49, 52, 53, 59, 65, 66, 75, 77, 78, 82, 86, 92, 93, 102, 103, 106, 107, 121, 133, 139, 174, 181, 194; immanent, 19, 179; of Germans, 44, 163; cannibalism of, 88; possibility that there is none, 91; Word of, 36. *See also* image; king
gods, 63, 138, 146, 152, 191, 192
good, 6, 29, 84, 88, 194
gospel, 48, 83
grace, xx, 19, 24, 29, 30, 45, 46, 54, 59, 95, 174, 194; of election, 174
Grail, Holy, 40
gratitude, 157
Greeks, 16, 34, 59, 94, 127, 140, 151, 152
Gregorian Reform, 144, 166
Gregory I, pope, 43, 107
Gregory VII, pope, 103–4
Guerric, abbot of Igny, 30, 130, 131, 145, 152, 153, 182

Habakkuk, prophet, 32
hagiography, 40, 41, 51
Hartmann von Aue, 144–45
hearing, sense of, 160
heart, xx, 33, 36, 46, 49, 65, 79, 94, 96, 111, 113, 127, 186; cavern of, 30; idols in, 221 n. 10
heathen, 1, 183, 187. *See also* pagan
Heaven, Kingdom of, 10, 30, 37, 80, 151, 162, 164, 193–94; rapture of, 521; banquet in, 54
Hegel, Georg Wilhelm Friedrich, 89, 176
Hellenism, 42
Henry V, emperor, 145

Henry II, king of England, 106, 107, 110, 111, 112, 216 nn. 22, 23
Henry III, king of England, 170
Henry VIII, king of England, 98
Henry of Livonia, 224 n. 34
Hereford world map, 171, 172
heretics, 14, 61, 71, 72, 75, 81, 98, 102, 105, 117, 122, 159. *See also* unbelievers
Herman-Judah of Cologne, xii, 51, 52, 53–57, 73, 78, 83, 95, 128, 130, 133, 134, 140, 141
hermeneutics, of conversion, xiii, xix, xxii, 2; circle of, xviii, xxii, 113, 123, 147, 155, 173, 188; project, xxii, 19, 36, 113, 185; problems of, 39. *See also* exegesis; interpretation; misunderstanding; understanding
heroism, 170, 180
Herostratus, 175, 177
Herrad, abbess of Hohenburg, ix, xi, xii, xiii, xx, 146
hiddenness, 36, 48, 52, 76, 91, 111, 117, 149, 162, 172, 175, 189. *See also* obscurity; secret
hierarchy, 57, 77, 102, 105, 162
Hildegard, abbess of Bingen, 69, 193
history, 11, 19, 20, 34, 35, 40, 45, 61, 89, 108, 124, 127, 129, 171, 179, 181–82, 186
holiness, 21, 26, 34, 68, 133, 139, 167
Holy Land, 46
Holy Spirit, xi, 9, 68, 90, 108, 111, 136, 145, 152, 162, 194; gifts of, 193
homosexuality, 101–2, 110
honor, xviii, 57, 98–100, 107, 109, 111, 113, 115, 116, 117, 156, 164, 170, 174, 194
Hopkins, Gerard Manley, 26
Hortus Deliciarum, ix, xi, xx
Hosius, bishop of Cordova, 14
Hugh of St. Victor, 10, 36, 45, 84, 161
humility, 38, 146, 154–84, 190, 194
hunt, 63, 88. *See also* predator
Hypatia, 21
hypocrisy, 22, 71, 96, 169, 178, 197 n. 4. *See also* deceit

iconoclasm, 134, 135, 168

idolatry, 22, 31, 43, 58, 72, 127, 129, 133, 136, 137–38, 140, 178, 221 n. 10, 224 n. 43
ignorance, 35, 61
image, xi, xiii, 32, 58, 100, 118, 126, 127, 129, 133, 134, 158, 168–73; of Christ, 55, 115, 152, 189; of God, 30, 99, 165, 166, 167–68. See also likeness
imagination, xix, 39, 90, 131, 134, 135, 137, 140, 152, 160, 171, 173, 176, 192; visual, 171, 173, 175
imitation, xviii, 59, 114, 118; of Christ, 11, 15, 16, 19, 20, 59, 68, 74, 87, 88, 121, 126, 128, 131, 135, 139, 149, 150, 156, 157, 175, 181, 189. See also mimesis; mirror; Passion; similarity
impregnation, 45, 49
India, 80, 193, 204 n. 39, 209 n. 22
inebriation, 48, 94, 97, 123, 145, 150, 210 n. 27
Inge, William, 151–53
innocence, 32, 105, 110, 113, 116–17, 178. See also purity
Innocent II, pope, 72, 81, 128, 222 n. 13
Innocent III, pope, 81, 213 n. 63
Innocent IV, pope, 168
insanity, 45, 46, 84, 130, 138, 157, 164. See also madness
interpretation, xvi, xxi, 36, 41. See also exegesis; hermeneutics; misunderstanding; understanding
Investiture Conflict, 6, 103–4
Ireland, 146
irony, 25, 26, 29, 30, 31, 32, 33, 45, 57, 77, 78, 82, 125, 133, 135, 140, 154, 158, 159–60, 182, 189, 190
Isaiah, prophet, 36
Islam, 5, 6, 7. See also Muslims
Israel, xxiii, 21
Israelites, 19, 43. See also Jews

Jefferson, Thomas, 126
Jerome, 62, 68, 73, 143, 185
Jerusalem, 32, 53, 62, 82, 96, 130, 135, 139, 149, 165
Jesus, ix, 3, 36, 37, 58, 64, 81, 82, 147, 151, 152, 181, 184, 185. See also Christ

Jews, xxiv, 9, 20, 34, 37, 39, 44, 45, 46, 47, 51, 52, 53–54, 55, 56, 57, 58, 72–73, 75, 82, 83, 96, 104, 112, 122, 128–30, 134, 140, 151, 152, 153, 155, 163, 164, 222 n. 16; as critics of Christianity, 168; rebuked, 32; forced baptism of, 213 n. 66; guilt of, alleged, 200 n. 15; stereotypes of, 51, 210 n. 27; stony hearts of, alleged, 199 n. 11; physician, 83. See also Israel; Israelites; Judaism; persecution; slaughter; unbelievers
Joan of Arc, 117
Job, 86, 87
John of Albano, cardinal, 170
John of Salisbury, bishop of Chartres, 97, 106–13, 114, 118, 119
John of the Cross, 69, 88, 90
John Paul II, pope, xxvi
John the Evangelist, 41
Joseph of Aramathea, 40
Joyce, James, 25, 87, 176–78, 180
Juan Cirita, 69
Judaism, xvii, 50, 128, 130. See also Jews
Judas, 37, 74, 81, 112, 120, 121, 220 n. 89
Judgment, Last, 24, 34, 40, 61, 90, 94, 96, 132
Julian of Norwich, 157
Juvenal, Decimus Junius, 30

karma, 60
Kierkegaard, Søren, xxi
king, 102, 106, 111, 165, 218 n. 62; gentile, 54; heretical, 54; God as, 162
kingdoms, 46, 124
knowledge, 35, 36, 59

labor, manual, 133–34, 135, 174
lamb, ix, x
language, xiv, 93, 143, 152, 167, 180, 187, 188, 190, 192
Latimer, Hugh, bishop of Worcester, 65, 179
laughter, 179. See also smile
law, xx, 106, 109, 110, 117, 119, 135, 165, 185; canon, 24, 104–5, 106, 108, 117
Lazarus, of Bethany, 40

Leo I, pope, 43
Leo IX, pope, 102
Leonardo da Vinci, 160
leprosy, 32, 54
Liberia, 44
life, xxiv, 38, 50, 53, 68; penitential, 62
light, x, 10, 113–14, 116, 185, 192
likeness, 174, 191. *See also* image
Lin-chi, 83
literacy, 76
Logos, 16
London, 142
Longinus, 40, 41
Louis VII, king of France, 47
Louis IX, king of France, 128
love, xxix, 31, 32, 53, 55, 64, 66, 68, 74, 83, 88, 89, 90, 132, 133, 145, 158, 159, 170, 177, 182, 192; brotherly, 49, 79, 102; cruel (or savage), 78, 69, 95; divine, 45; righteous, 29; of Christ, xi, 55, 74, 157; of God, xi, 59, 102, 124; of neighbor, 102, 124; of women, 146; games of, 48–49, 63, 194; wounds of, 69. *See also* eroticism
lovers, 48, 63
Lucifer, 6, 157. *See also* Devil; Satan; Tempter
Luke, evangelist, 12
lust, 146, 177
Luther, Martin, xx–xxii, 98
Lydia, 39

macrocosm, 16, 124, 133
madness, xiii, 164. *See also* insanity
magic, 17, 26, 43, 44, 63, 75, 90, 128, 147, 148. *See also* witchcraft; wizards
Malachy, archbishop of Armagh, 158, 169
Manichaeism, 24
Mantua, 40
Mark, evangelist, 37
marriage, 1, 48–50, 53, 56, 57, 102, 139–41, 156, 183, 198 n. 1, 213 n. 63. *See also* bridegroom; spouse; wives
Marseilles, 40
Martha, of Bethany, 40, 52
martyrdom, 38, 40, 68, 80, 82, 135, 137, 138–39, 151, 158
martyrs, 19, 32, 43, 47, 56, 105, 108, 109, 110, 135, 159, 162
Mary, of Bethany, 40, 52
Mary, Virgin, 40, 52, 131, 140, 145
Mary Magdalene, 38, 39, 40, 41, 65
masculinity, 21, 50, 51, 52, 64, 79, 140–41, 166, 177, 178, 179, 183, 186; male bonding, 79, 142, 148, 159; male dominance, 166, 173. *See also* esthetics; men; virility
Mathilda, countess of Tuscany, 166
Matthew, evangelist, 37
meaning, stability of, 4. *See also* interpretation
Mechthild of Magdeburg, 155
medicine, 69, 81, 96, 102, 104, 163
meditation, 75, 77, 83, 88, 142
Mellitus, abbot, 43
Melville, Herman, 25, 87, 176, 177–80, 183
memory, 35, 76, 193, 194
men, xix, 1, 4, 17, 21, 34, 55, 112, 155, 164, 166, 178, 179, 183. *See also* esthetics; masculinity; virility
menstruation, 38, 146
metaphor, xiii, xiv, xvii, 2, 4, 7, 15, 16, 19, 20, 33, 34, 38, 39, 63, 64, 126, 148, 154, 163, 177, 184, 187, 190, 191; metaphor-word, xxv, 187, 189
metaphysics, xv, 10, 16, 24, 25
Michelangelo Buonarroti, 178
microcosm, 16, 124, 133
Milan, 23, 24
militia Christi, 143
Milton, John, 175
mimesis, xiv, 95, 118, 130, 132, 137, 173. *See also* Christ; imitation; mirror; similarity
mind, viii, xvii, 16, 35, 61
miracles, 55, 76, 147, 161
mirror, 29, 30, 33, 58, 89, 115, 152, 179, 185, 188, 192. *See also* imitation; mimesis; similarity
missionary, 47, 80, 85, 86, 193
misunderstanding, 38, 45, 191. *See also* exegesis; interpretation; understanding
mockery, xxi, 53, 58, 64, 66, 102, 128, 138, 150, 183, 187
monasticism, xvii, xix, xxi, 8, 14, 24, 53, 54, 61, 67, 70, 81, 101, 119, 123,

monasticism (*cont.*)
133, 142, 155, 160, 173, 187, 192;
monastic ethos, 144
monk, xx, xxi, 14, 133, 165
Mordecai, 54
More, Thomas, 64, 98, 115, 151
morphology, xv, xx, xxvi, 10, 57, 148
Mozart, Wolfgang Amadeus, xvi
music, 44, 90, 118, 129, 136, 148, 181, 191, 193–94, 212 n. 51. *See also* psalmody; songs
Muslims, 46, 47, 53, 92, 93, 94, 130, 137–41, 151, 155, 209 n. 22, 210 n. 23, 213 nn. 60, 63. *See also* Islam
mysteries, 39, 124, 131
mystery, 3, 17, 20, 21, 37, 58, 78, 103, 133, 147, 190
mysticism, xiv, xvii, 10, 15, 35, 70
myth, xvi, xviii, xix, xxii, 10, 11, 18, 57, 91, 116, 117, 119, 122–53, 155, 160, 178, 188, 189, 191, 192

Naaman, the Syrian, 54
nakedness, xi
nature, animal, 49; human, 6, 18, 28, 30, 39, 42, 67, 92, 99, 167, 174, 179, 186, 188, 191, 194; transhumanization of, 167
need, xvi, xxiv, 33; common, 22, 31–32, 53, 55, 66, 107, 148, 154, 180–81, 191–92
Neoplatonism, 16, 20, 21, 124, 133, 175, 200 n. 18
Nero, emperor, 40, 45
Newman, John Henry, cardinal, xxiv, 26, 63, 73, 176, 183, 197 n. 5
Nicodemism, 74
Nicodemus, 39, 74
nirvana, 62
nobility, xvii, xxiv, 11, 20, 33, 50, 57, 80, 154–84, 190, 191–92, 193–94

obedience, 19
obscurity, 2, 29, 31, 39, 42, 54, 67, 91, 111, 190. *See also* hiddenness; secret
Olav Tryggvessön, king of Norway, 1, 2, 4, 44, 57, 183, 187
Olympios, abba, 58
ordeal, 54, 91, 92, 119
Origen, 30, 62
Orpheus, 17

Othloh of St. Emmeram, 73, 74, 75, 76, 77, 78, 91
Otto, bishop of Bamberg, 46, 47, 58, 71, 80, 85, 86, 90, 134, 135, 157, 158, 163, 171
Otto, bishop of Freising, 94, 135

pagans, 11, 14, 17, 19, 30, 42, 43, 44, 58, 68, 71, 75, 76, 80, 81, 82, 99, 122, 127, 132, 134, 135, 138, 151, 159, 163, 164, 178, 183, 187–88, 198 n. 2. *See also* heathen; unbelievers
pain, 67, 68–91, 83, 87, 89, 91, 117, 189. *See also* asceticism; suffering
painting, 112, 115, 118, 133, 134, 137, 167, 171, 178, 181, 190, 220 n. 82. *See also* picture
papacy, xxi, 6, 44, 56, 81–82, 102, 107, 110, 111, 165, 166, 171, 182. *See also* popes
parables, 35, 36, 37, 39, 45, 52, 54, 63, 73, 143. *See also* listings of *individual parables*
Paradise, 11, 124, 125, 157
Pascal, Blaise, 153, 182
Passion, 20, 40, 41, 67, 69, 83, 89, 108, 109, 115, 126, 130, 131, 132, 136, 142, 179, 184, 229 n. 14. *See also* Christ; imitation; Jesus; similarity
Paul, apostle, viii, ix, x, xi, xvii, xx, xxi, 11, 12, 23, 24, 29, 37, 38, 39, 40, 45, 52, 71, 82, 91, 95, 106, 124, 127, 128, 146, 150, 153, 155, 161, 162, 185, 189
Paulinus, bishop of York, 43, 45
penitence, xix, 67, 76, 77, 80, 90, 96, 102, 104, 107, 108, 115, 133, 142, 181, 187
perception, 162
peripety, xii, xv, xxi, 3, 4, 26, 63, 66, 90, 123, 173; paradigm, 3, 4, 5, 7, 23
persecution, ix, x, xx, 9, 11, 20, 40, 47, 79, 82, 105, 112, 128, 152, 187. *See also* Jews; slaughter
Peter, apostle, 6, 37, 38, 55, 56, 72, 74, 82, 93, 105, 106, 107, 120, 128, 166
Peter Damian, cardinal, 100–105, 107, 116, 119

Peter the Chancellor, 93
Peter the Venerable, abbot of Cluny, 45, 46, 53, 199 n. 11
Philo of Alexandria, 20
philosophers, 19, 21, 22, 23, 163
philosophy, xix, 9, 16, 21, 35, 67, 75, 88, 99, 106, 120, 185, 193, 198 n. 2
physics, 18
picture, ix, xiii, 171. *See also* painting
Pierleoni, Pietro. *See* Anacletus II
pilgrimage, 25, 66, 139, 144, 159
plagiarism, 41
Plato, 16, 18, 20, 63, 125, 132, 164, 175
Platonism, 16, 20, 42, 132
play, 63–65, 66, 80, 88, 89, 118, 122, 130, 131, 150–51, 158, 160, 168, 170, 187, 189, 190, 192–94; children's, 135, 150–51; chivalric, xviii; of love, 145; mystery, 142; mythic, xvii; rules of, 160. *See also* ball; cards; game; puppets; race
poetics, xvi, xxiv, 4, 10, 23, 29, 31, 34, 35, 42, 45, 57, 90, 91, 125, 188, 192
polygamy, 44
Pomeranians, 44, 46, 47, 58, 71, 80, 134, 163
Pontigny, monastery of, 168–72
Pontius Pilate, 40, 41
popes, 6, 9, 56, 72, 102, 107, 117, 118. *See also* papacy
poverty, 38
power, 56, 90, 146, 192; stupefying, 160
powerlessness, 146
prayer, 54, 59, 75, 77, 78, 83, 88, 101, 104, 142
predator, x, 21. *See also* hunt
predestination, x, xii, 24, 120
predicament, 26, 143
priesthood, 5, 80, 101, 107, 176
prodigal son, 38, 52, 54
Prometheus, 114
prophecy, 78, 82
prophet, 19, 22, 48, 49; false, 44, 82
proportionality, xvii, xviii, xxii, 29, 32, 33, 36, 38, 39, 45, 58, 63, 66, 70, 91–97, 114, 119, 127, 153, 155, 157, 164, 185, 189, 190, 191
proselytism, 9, 30, 47, 61, 80
prostitution, 64, 120

Provence, 40
Prussia, 46
psalmody, 78, 101, 193. *See also* music
Psalms, 44
psychomachia, 75
puppets, 63
Purgatory, 171
purity, xxiv, 32, 54, 84, 95, 113, 132, 156, 170, 189

race, 38
Raedwal, king of Kent, 44
rank, xviii
Ranulf Flambard, bishop of Durham, 55
rape, 143
reading, 75, 77, 142, 191
reason, 18, 27, 30, 35, 105, 174, 192
Redemptoris Missio, xxvi
relics, 42, 43
Renaissance, 25, 160, 161
Rich, Edmund. *See* Edmund of Abingdon
Richard I, king of England, 72, 128
Richard of St. Victor, 160
Richenza, queen, 56
Ridley, Nicholas, bishop of Rochester, 65
Rilke, Rainer Maria, 192
Roger, count of Siciliy, 46
Roger Pont l'Evêque, archbishop of York, 110
Rome, 6, 9, 11, 18, 21, 34, 43, 44, 59, 60, 83, 94, 97, 99, 110, 127, 143, 190
Romuald, abbot of Camaldoli, 81
Rupert, abbot of Deutz, 56, 96, 133, 147
Russell, Bertrand, 71
Russia, xxiv

sacrament, 7, 149. *See also* baptism; Eucharist
sacrifice, 19, 32, 38, 43, 44, 54, 61, 64, 68, 69, 88, 100, 114, 119, 126, 133, 138, 149, 155, 156, 159, 175, 184, 190
saints, 20, 35, 40, 41, 42, 43, 68, 96, 100, 108, 114
St. Albans, monastery of, 50, 55, 56, 193
St. Denis, monastery of, 128, 161, 230 n. 18
St. Michel, monastery of, 2
Samaritan, Good, 77

244   Index

Samson, 175, 177
Satan, xxi, 22, 34, 36, 37, 40, 63, 73, 74, 75, 77, 81, 94, 107, 109, 112, 114; synagogue of, 82. *See also* Devil; Lucifer; Tempter
Saul. *See* Paul, apostle
Sayers, Dorothy, xxii
Scripture, xvi, 41, 49, 52, 76, 82, 125, 151; ignorance of, 52. *See also* Testament, New; Testament, Old
sculpture, 90, 134, 137–38, 154, 191, 224 n. 43
secret, 37, 124. *See also* hiddenness; obscurity
self-emptying, 38, 61, 84, 182
self-fulfillment, 38, 182
self-hatred, 133
self-knowledge, 30, 97, 111
semi-Christians, 53
Seneca, Lucius Annaeus, 40
senses, 35
serf, 46
sexuality, 69, 72, 78, 80, 100–103, 104–5, 177
shame, 32
signs, 32, 36, 78, 112, 125, 179
Sigrid the Strong-minded, queen of Sweden, 1, 4, 183, 187
similarity, 2, 20, 68, 108–10, 132, 152, 156, 157, 159, 160, 164, 172, 190, 193–94. *See also* imitation; likeness; mimesis; mirror; similitude; verisimilitude
similitude, 158, 162, 163, 182. *See also* dissimilarity
Simon Magus, 37
simony, 75, 103, 105
sin, 29, 53, 65, 68, 69, 70, 81, 85, 95, 98, 104, 105, 110, 156, 162, 187; wounds of, 77. *See also* temptation
slaughter, xi, 53, 54, 223 n. 33. *See also* Jews; persecution
slavery, 21, 46
smile, 64, 158, 192, 229 n. 14. *See also* laughter
socialism, 87
Socrates, 21
sodomy. *See* homosexuality
Solomon, king, 81

songs, 144. *See also* music
soul, 16, 22, 30, 71, 79, 90, 93, 100, 124, 127, 133, 161, 173, 184
sower, 36, 37, 38, 39, 73, 138, 143
Snorre Sturlason, 1, 2, 44, 183
Spain, 46, 86, 89, 226 n. 66
Spenser, Edmund, 176
spirituality, 48, 158
spouse, 48, 53, 55. *See also* bridegroom; marriage; wives
Stein, Edith, 87–89, 90, 181, 184
stereotypes, 41, 57, 210 n. 27, 230 n. 20
stigmata, 161
Stoicism, 17, 18, 20, 21, 71, 94, 95, 104, 124, 179
style, 171
subversion, xix, 6, 7, 51, 56, 62, 162, 164, 167, 173, 175, 177, 184, 186, 189, 192
suffering, 32, 37, 48, 78, 80, 81, 84, 96, 102, 110, 115–16, 121, 132, 157; gospel of, xxi. *See also* asceticism; pain; tribulation
Suger, abbot of St. Denis, 134, 161, 230 n. 18
supernatural, the, xv, 6, 24, 25, 26, 28, 39, 42, 56, 60, 63, 119, 174
superstition, 18, 22, 43, 80, 125, 127, 129, 130, 137, 151, 164, 183, 213 n. 72
survival, strategy of, 30, 64
sword, ix, x, xi, 15, 101–2, 113, 128
symbolism, x, 172. *See also* allegory
syncretism, 43, 74
synesthesia, 160

Tasso, Torquato, 141
television, 172–73
temple, 64, 80, 81, 114, 163, 175; eternal, 43
temptation, 37, 48, 51, 55, 74, 78, 95. *See also* sin
Tempter, 48, 57, 82. *See also* demons; Devil; Lucifer; Satan
Tennyson, Alfred, 180
Terence, Publius, 119
Teresa of Avila, 38, 70, 164, 220 n. 82
Tertullian, Quintus Septimius Florens, 45

Testament, New, 31, 48, 51, 60, 93, 163.
    See also Covenant, New; Scripture
Testament, Old, 11, 20, 21, 32, 34, 48,
    54, 101, 124, 129, 133, 149. See also
    Scripture
Thaddeus, apostle, 40
theater, xi, 76, 99, 112, 115, 117, 118,
    130, 131, 132, 135, 136, 137, 142,
    193, 224 n. 34. See also actors
Thecla, 40
theodicy, 29, 64, 66, 84, 85, 181, 186–
    87, 189, 194
Thérèse of Lisieux, 64
Thomas, apostle, 40
Thomas Aquinas, 47, 69, 97, 99, 202
    n. 13, 230 n. 25
Tiemo, archbishop of Salzburg, 137–38,
    140
Times, Last, 83
tomb, 40, 168–70, 172, 173
Torah, 128
Torquemada, Juan de, cardinal, 72
tradition, ix, 56, 57, 125, 185, 188;
    classical, xii, 2. See also Antiquity
tragedy, 89, 90
transformation, xii, 31, 35
treasure, buried, 30, 33, 49, 60, 62, 143
tribulation, 29, 82
Trier, 83
Trojans, 11
troubadours, 9, 70
truth, xxiv, 29, 32, 36, 170
Tsatsos, Constantine, xii, xxv
tyrannicide, 106

Ulysses, 146
unbelief, 37, 39, 45, 47, 129, 139
unbelievers, 36, 37, 47–48, 155, 163,
    164; wrong-believers, xvi–xvii. See
    also heretics, Jews; pagans
understanding, 38, 45, 70, 75, 191,
    192. See also exegesis; hermeneutics;
    interpretation; misunderstanding
Ursula, 42
usury, 72, 128, 165

values, 158, 162, 178, 182, 189, 190
vengeance, 46, 52, 53, 54, 103, 110, 113,
    115, 140, 157, 164, 177–80, 183

Venus, 127
verisimilitude, 171
Vézelay, monastery of St. Mary Magdalene, 41
vices, 75
Victoria, queen, 191
violet, 146–47
Virgil, Publius, 11, 59–60, 167, 232
    n. 51
Virginia, 86
virgins, 37, 52, 55–57, 58, 68, 98–99,
    135, 161, 162, 171, 216 n. 23. See
    also Mary, Virgin
virility, 146, 166. See also masculinity;
    men
virtue, xviii, 30, 75, 166, 174
vision, apparition, ix, xxii, 55, 62, 73,
    77, 95, 182, 192. See also dreams
vision, sense of, xix, 131, 160
visualization, 77
Vitalis, Ordericus, 144
vocation, xi, xx, xxi–xxii, 19, 38, 53, 56,
    71, 74, 103, 120, 176, 184
voluntas conversionis, 75, 76. See also will

wager, 63, 153, 182
warrior, xvii, xviii, xix, 57, 127, 144,
    146, 148, 173
Weil, Simone, 87–89, 181, 184
Wetter, Friedrich, archbishop of Munich-Freising, cardinal, 172
wheel, 34, 35, 154
Whitman, Walt, 180
Wido of Ferrara, 191
will, 35, 45, 88, 116, 121. See also *voluntas conversionis*
William of Malmesbury, 161
William of Ockham, 117
William the Conqueror, king of England, 106
William Rufus, king of England, 55
witchcraft, 44, 203 n. 26, 221 n. 10, 222
    n. 16. See also magic
wives, 66, 139–41. See also marriage;
    women
wizards, 44
wolf, x, 164
women, xviii, 1, 4, 17, 21, 26, 34, 44,
    54, 57, 65, 81, 104, 105, 116,

women (*cont.*)
    135, 139–41, 142, 143, 144, 145, 146, 155–56, 166–67, 177, 179, 183, 193, 216 n. 15, 216 n. 23, 221 n. 10, 226 n. 71. *See also* femininity; wives
world, 33, 34, 45, 59, 81, 89, 102, 114, 188
Worms, Diet of, xxi
worship, 58, 97, 143, 156, 168, 179, 193

worth, 158, 162, 169, 170, 174, 178, 182, 190

Yamoussoukro, Basilica of Our Lady of, xxiv

Zacharias, pope, 43
Zen, 62, 83–84, 147–48. *See also* Buddhism
Zeus, 59

DATE DUE

MAR 19 1996			
APR 17 1999			

HIGHSMITH 45-220